SHAKESPEARE, MEDICINE AND PSYCHIATRY

—Bettman Archive

1. William Shakespeare

SHAKESPEARE, MEDICINE AND PSYCHIATRY

An Historical Study in Criticism and Interpretation

by

Irving I. Edgar A.M., M.D.

PHILOSOPHICAL LIBRARY

New York

15 East 40 Street, New York, New York 10016

Library of Congress Catalog Card No. 76-118308
SBN 8022-2343-5

Manufactured in the United States of America

DEDICATED

to the

Memory of my wife,

Frieda

TABLE OF CONTENTS

PART II

The Psychopathology in Shakespeare's Dramas

List of Illustrations

PREFACE

This book is an outcome of literary, historical, and medical interests. To add merely another commentary to the ever-increasing deluge of Shakespearean criticism, however, is not its purpose. Undoubtedly, the spirit of Shakespeare must already laugh hilariously up his sleeve at the mountainous literature about the products that his brain conceived, possibly only in the hope of pure entertainment for rustics and groundlings, possibly only in the appropriation of pre-existing plots, characterizations and contemporary events, possibly only in conformity to the physical characteristics of the actors of his company, or possibly only for the mere satisfaction of a passing whim.

On the contrary, by demolishing the foundations of bardolatry in the fields of medicine and psychiatry, we fervently hope to diminish the possible future flow of commentary in this area of Shakespearean criticism.

There has been a great need for the clarification of the atmosphere, in regard to the true status of Shakespeare's medical and psychiatric knowledge, especially from the historical standpoint; for in spite of the fact that such scholars as E. K. Chambers, Tucker Brooke, J. M. Robertson, Levin L. Schucking, A. H. Thorndike, W. A. Neilson, E. E. Stoll, R. L. Anderson and others have brought back sanity into their respective fields of Shakespearean criticism, nevertheless, in the field of medical and psychiatric commentary, such sanity seems still to be lacking even today. It is my hope that this book will place Shakespeare's medical and Psychiatric knowledge in its true historical light, and thereby bring us closer to a correct understanding of the great poet's art.

Originally the core of this book represented a Master's thesis tendered to Wayne State University in 1933. Portions of the material appeared in *The Annals of Medical History, The Journal of Abnormal and Social Psychology, The Canadian Medical Association Journal, Medical Life and Medical Record, Journal of The Michigan State Medical Society, Canadian Psychiatric Association Journal, Psychiatric Quarterly,* and the *Psychiatric Quarterly Supplement,* all of which I wish to thank for permitting its use. However, most of the material is new particularly the portions dealing with the psychoanalytic approach to *Hamlet* and *King Lear.*

I want to express my thanks especially to the late Professor Robert W. Babcock of Wayne State University for his excellent guidance and encouragement. I want to express my gratitude to the late Professor Hilberry, for many years President of the University, and to the now retired Professor John Wilcox, for the inspiration that their lectures in English Literature had always been to me. I also want to thank Dr. William J. Stapleton, formerly Professor of Jurisprudence, Ethics and Economics at the University Medical School in whose Department I was special Lecturer in Medical History, who also encouraged and inspired me by his high devotion to the Art of Medicine.

I am sincerely grateful to Wayne State University in general for my education in its various departments.

I. I. E.

SHAKESPEARE, MEDICINE AND PSYCHIATRY

PART I

CHAPTER I

INTRODUCTION

The sixteenth century had little premonition of the true greatness it harbored in William Shakespeare. Absorbed in the pomp and intrigue of court life, and tuned to the madcap adventures of daring seamen, the century passed him by. His death was a matter of almost complete indifference. But the glory of England lay in that man. And he gilded the century into a veritable Golden Age of Literature. Today, Elizabeth is but a name and a memory, and the Spanish Armada recalls merely an historical incident. But this man Shakespeare continues to be the crowning achievement of his century.

Shakespeare wrote primarily in the fields of drama and of poetry. It is within these two spheres of art, and only within these two spheres of art, wherein he is the true supreme creative genius. The phenomenon of idolatry that arose in the eighteenth century[1] and flourished so luxuriantly in the nineteenth, made of Shakespeare an all-pervading, all-comprehensive, all-knowing God-man. Even our own twentieth century is not free from it. Again and again, the commentators have dipped their pens, taxed their ingenuity for superlatives, ransacked their brains for fitting eulogies and ended in a confusion of exclamatory rhetoric. They have named Shakespeare a great scientist in almost every field of knowledge. They have made of him a classic scholar and a linguist.[2] They have invested him with a lawyer's knowledge of law. Finally, the medical idolators have outdone all the others and made of him a great physician and psychiatrist, with conception far in advance of the age in which he lived. The task of scholarship in the last thirty years, however, has been to bring back Shakespeare within the realm of intelligent appreciation as a creative artist in the poetic drama where he belongs.

As a result, Shakespearean criticism has found its true center of gravity. No more is emphasis placed on the poet's classical learning. No more are treatises written to prove that he was a student of law. No more is he termed botanist, astronomer, horticulturist, etc. Only in the field of medical and psychopathological knowledge do commentators still praise Shakespeare as a physician. Possibly the reason for this is obvious. Literary critics have feared to tread on unfamiliar ground. There are few critics who are doctors, and fewer doctors who are literary critics. At any rate, the anomaly remains. Criticism of Shakespeare's medical and psychopathological knowledge, with few exceptions, has taken the form of exposition rather than that of adjudgment. Medical commentators have, for the most part, merely listed the references to medicine found in Shakespeare's plays and accepted them as evidence of the poet's medical learning. Very few have attempted to analyze these references or to evaluate them as true medical knowledge. It is the purpose of the following pages to make this evaluation. We shall trace as completely as possible and adjudge as completely as possible the attitude of critical opinion on Shakespeare's medical and psychopathological knowledge.

NOTES AND REFERENCES

CHAPTER I

1. See R. W. Babcock's, "The Genesis of Shakespeare Idolatry," Chapel Hill, Univ. No. Carolina, 1931, for an extensive study of the subject.
2. See Richard Farmer's, "An Essay on the Learning of Shakespeare," London, Rodd, 1821, for a complete refutation of this. This Essay was originally printed in 1767.

CHAPTER II

A PRELIMINARY SURVEY OF THE ATTITUDE OF THE MEDICAL IDOLATORS TOWARD SHAKESPEARE'S MEDICAL KNOWLEDGE

Generally speaking, practically all commentators concede to Shakespeare an extensive knowledge of the healing art. Thus as far back as 1859, A. O. Kellogg speaks of the "extent and accuracy of the medical physiological . . . knowledge"[1] of Shakespeare, holding also that "there is scarcely a department of scientific knowledge which he has not enriched,"[2] and concluding that "the knowledge (he) displayed was very far in advance of the age in which he lived, and was not possessed by any one in his time, however eminent in any special department of science. . ."[3] And as late as 1950 we find Dr. Walter E. Vest calling him "One of (The Race's) Greatest Masters of Medicine,"[4] and Dr. Herman Pomeranz (1934) calling "Shakespeare's knowledge of the general medical topics of his day . . . amazing," at the same time affirming that many of his medical ideas were considerably in advance of current education and teaching,[5] and Dr. V. B. Green-Armytage (1930) speaking of "Shakespeare's enormous wealth of medical lore" and remarking that ". . . it is astounding to discover the wonderful knowledge of physiology, pathology and psychology to which the plays bear witness."[6] Meanwhile, in the intervening years, voices of praise are hardly lacking. Thus, Gillespie (1875) writes of having "been struck, when reading Shakespeare, with the amount of medical knowledge he displayed. . ."[7] Donnellan (1902) speaks of the poet's ". . . extensive knowledge of the art of medicine . . . so exact and intimate is his familiarity with the healing art. . ."[8] Hagemann (1916) considers that he had a "profound knowledge of medical subjects" and that "his knowledge of medical themes was not only matchless but that in spots it was almost predictive."[9] Likewise, Knott (1903), Rogers (1914), Walter Lindley (1916), Sir St. Clair Thompson (1919), and others,—all attest to Shakespeare's intelligent "familiarity with every branch of medicine,[10] and to his "through mastery of the principles of the healing art," Knott going to the extent of holding that "Shakespeare's ideas were in advance of even the average medical knowledge of his time,"[11] Rogers adding that "from the twentieth century point of view, he was, and is a great physician. . . ," a "teacher of health" who "stands among the first,"[12] and Sir St. Clair Thompson concluding that ". . . Shakespeare is, and always must be, one of the greatest masters of medicine."[13] Indeed, when we consider that there are over seven hundred quotations containing references to medicine and psychiatry; when we consider that the plays show evidence of Shakespeare's familiarity with the most important medical theories then in vogue, we cannot help agree with the wonderment of the critics. However, carried away by the idolatry that Schlegel, Coleridge, Hazlitt and others infused into the century, most of these commentators have succumbed to the temptation of substituting, all too often, a blind adoration for clear-eyed logic. Thus, one of these critics, Robert Cartwright (1888), sees enough medical and pharmacological knowledge in Shakespeare's works to be actually deluded into the "conviction" that "Shakespeare must have been" not only "an Apothecaries' Apprentice,"[14] but also a "Licentiate of the Apothecaries' Company";[15] and not only a "medical student," who "must at some period or other have studied medicine"[16] and "dissected in a school of medicine,"[17] but also a practicing physician "and a member of the Royal College of Surgeons,"[18] "such a mastery over the theory and practice of physic"[19] does he show! Thus, also, Hackman (1888) concludes that Shakespeare "must . . . have had opportunities of learning the practice of medicine . . . ."[20] And thus too, Orville W. Owen (1892) has come to a similar conviction, for he definitely states that Shakespeare ". . . must have been (if not a doctor of Medicine) a close student of our learned art," "a Master of Medicine."[21] This same commentator continues as follows:

> Was he an anatomist? Every portion of the human body known to his day is mentioned. Was he a student of physiology? Physiological functions are given in detail. Had he knowledge of Materia Medica? He speaks of many medicines[22] . . . Was he a Neurologist? It might be called his speciality; . . . his wonderful descriptions and delineations in this great field of our science[23] [shows that he had] thoroughly mastered the subject in all its branches.[24]

In similar fashion, Wainwright (1904) comes to the conclusion that,

> We may with . . . certainty claim that he had been a student of medical science, for his works contain most marvelous references to this science which it has never been thought existed in his time, yet which reads today as if written by a twentieth century scientist.[25]

The trouble has been that these commentators have fallen into the error of regarding Shakespeare's medical knowledge not in the light of the medicine of the sixteenth century, but rather in the light of the medicine of modern times. They have brought to their tasks the preconceived premise that Shakespeare was endowed with a universality of knowledge not only of things in the past and present, but also of things in the future;[26] and they have attempted to draw out of his plays all manner of evidence to bolster this premise. Consequently these commentators have read into his works things which are not there at all. The tendency has been to give an all too liberal interpretation to the medical lore in the dramas. "The most careless and casual lines in his plays have been twisted and squeezed in the hope that they will yield some medicinal secret."[27] Matters of general medical knowledge, no doubt common to all people, have been considered as showing Shakespeare's unusual knowledge of the healing art. References to fever, fainting, diet, nausea, vomiting, puberty, the perverted appetite in pregnancy, seasickness, rheumatism, etc., are put down as showing Shakespeare's medical learning. Thus, Sir St. Clair Thompson, among other things, quotes the following lines from Shakespeare to prove his knowledge of medical science:

Stand from him, give him air; he'll straight be well.[28]

> So play the foolish throngs with one that swoons;
> Come all to help him, and so stop the air
> By which he should revive.[29]

Under the heading, "Open Air-Treatment" he says, "Three centuries before the profession had thought of open-air treatment, Shakespeare had advised:[30]

The most wholesome physic of the health-giving air.[31]
I pray you give her air, Gentlemen.[32]

So Shakespeare was a great physician because he knew enough to call for air in case of unconsciousness from syncope! Upon such evidence do his commentators raise him up to the pinnacle of physicianship; Similarly, V.B. Green-Armytage[33] quotes the following lines from Shakespeare to show that he knew about quickening and the longings of pregnancy, and that consequently, he had unusual obstetrical and gynecological knowledge:

> Faith, unless you play the honest Trojan, the poor wench is cast away, she's quick and the child brags in her belly already, she's yours.[34]

> Sir, she came in great with child; and longing (saving your honour's reverence) for stewed prunes; sir, we had but two in the house, which at that very distant time stood, at it were, in a fruit-dish, a dish of some three pence; your honours have seen such dishes; they are not China dishes, but very good dishes.[35]

Likewise, such lines from Shakespeare as follow have been put down as evidence of his great mastery in the field of Medicine:

> Many will swoon when they do look on blood.[36]

. . . a gaping wound
Issuing life blood . . .[37]

The Queen's in labour,
They say, in great extremity.[38]

What wound did ever heal but by degrees . . .[39]

Even the drugs mentioned in Shakespeare's plays, while not familiar to the average person today, were well known and even in common use in the days of Shakespeare. The fact that the grocers and apothecaries were united into one company certainly fostered such a knowledge of drugs, and particularly, of the plants from which they were derived. These grew on every roadside, and were recognized by every housewife. Thus foxglove or digitalis, mandrake or mandragora, hemlock or conium, the nightshade or belladonna, henbane or hyocyamus, monkshood or aconitum and many others, all entered into the daily lives of the people. Chaucer in his "Nonnes Preestes Tale" affords us interesting evidence in support of this:

A poure wydwe, somdel stape in age,
Was whilom dwellung in a narwe cotage
Beside a greve, standynge in a dale. . . .

Hir diete was accordant to hir cote;
Repleccioum ne made hire neer sike,
Attempree diete was all hire phisik,
And exercise, & hertes suffisaunce
The goute lette hre nothung for a daunce,
Nopolexie shente not hir heed;
No wyn ne drank she, neither whit nor reed; . . .

'Now, sire', quod she, whan we flee from the bemes,
For Goddes love, as taak som laxatyf,
Up peril of my soule, and of my lyf,
I conseille yow the beste, I wol not lye,
That bothe of colere, and of melencolye

Ye purge yow, and, for ye shal not tarie,
Though in this toun be noon apotecarie,
I shall myself two herbes techen yow,
That shul been for youre hele and for youre prow;
And in our yeerd, the herbes shal I fynde,
To purge yow bynethe, and eke above
Sire, forget not this, for Godes owene love;
Ye been ful coleryk of conpleccioun.
Ware the Sonne in his ascentioun.
No fynde yow nat repleet of humours hoote;
And if it do, I dar wel leye a grote
Or an agu, that may be youre bane,
A day or two ye shul have digestyves
Of lawriole, centaure, and fumetere,
Or elles of ellabor, that groweth there,
Of katapuce, or of gaitrys beryis,
Or herbe yve growyng in oure yeerd, thay mery is;
Pekke hem up right as they grow, and ete him yn.'[40]

Likewise, in Heywood's "The Plays called the Foure P.P." the "Poticary" mentions many drugs that must have been familiar to the common people in Shakespeare's day:

If ye wyll taste but thys crome that ye se,
If euer ye be hanged, neuer truste me!
Here haue I dispompholicus,–
A speciall oyntment as doctours discuse;
For a fistela or a canker
Thys oyntment is euen shot-anker,
For thys medecyn helpeth one and other,
Or bryngeth them in case that they nede no other.
Here is syrapus de Byzansis,–
A lyttel thynge is i-nough of this,
For even the weyght of one scruppull
Shall make you stronge as a cryppul,
Here be other, as diosfiallios,
Diagalanga, and sticados,
Blanka Manna, diosopliticon

Mercury, sudylyme, and metridaticon,
Pelitory, and arsefetita,
Cassy, and colloquintita.[41]

Thomas Tusser's poem, "Five Hundred Good Points of Husbandry," a popular poem of the period, also points to our contention:

Good housewives provide ere sickness do come
Of sundry goud things in her house to have some
Good aqua composita and vinegar tart
Rosewater and treacle to comfort the heart
Cold herbs in her garden for aques that burn
That over-strong heat to good temper may turn
White endive and succory, with spinach enow;
Ask medicus' counsel ere medicine you make
And honor that man for necessity's sake
Though thousands hate physic, because of the cost
Yet thousands it helpeth, that else should be lost. . .[42]

Nor is that all. Shakespeare has had foisted upon himself the weighty honor of discovering the circulation of the blood, one of the greatest discoveries in medical history. He has been considered as evincing a knowledge of the action of antitoxins.[43] He has been applauded as antedating Newton in the discovering of the laws of gravity.[44] There are other fantastic claims of like nature,[45] such as the astounding assertion by Dr. Walter E. Vest as late as 1950, that ". . . as to the curability of tuberculosis, his thinking was well in advance of . . . his physician contemporaries,"[46] basing his conclusion on a few lines in *Much Ado About Nothing,* (*V., iv*) in which the "consumption" is used with its then general meaning, but most certainly not the word 'Tuberculosis,' for this word and its definitive meaning of today did not then even exist. Suffice it to say, these claims have more roots in the minds of the critics than in the mind of Shakespeare.

NOTES AND REFERENCES

CHAPTER II

1. Shakespeare's Delineations of Insanity, Imbecility and Suicide, N.Y., 1868, p. 1. This quote first appeared in 1859, footnote #3.
2. Op. cit., p. 9.
3. "William Shakespeare as a physician and psychologist." Am. J. Insanity, 16: 130, 1859.
4. "William Shakespeare, Therapeutist," Canad. Doctor, Dec., 1946, p. 36.
5. "Medicine in the Shakespearean Plays and Era," Med. Life, 41: 477-532, p. 493.
6. Green-Armytage, V. B. "Gynecology and Obstetrics in Shakespeare," J. Obst. & Gynec., 36: 272, 1930.
7. "Medical Notes About Shakespeare and His Times," Edinb. M. J., 20: 1061, 1875.
8. "Medical Allusions in Shakespeare's Plays," American Med., 3: 278, 1902.
9. "Shakespearean Conceptions of Some Medical Topics." Med. Rec., 8: 780, 1916.
10. Lindley, W., "Dr. John Hall—Shakespeare's son in law." Med. Rec., 89: 911, 1916.
11. Knott, J. "The Medical Knowledge of Shakespeare." Westminster Rev., 159: 437, 1903.
12. "Shakespeare as a Health Teacher." Scient. Monthly, 2: 589, 1914.
13. "Shakespeare as a Guide in the Art and Practice of Medicine." Canadian M. A. J., 9: 901, 1919.
14. The Footsteps of Shakespeare. London, 1888, p. 24.
15. Ibid., p. 117.
16. Ibid., p. 14.
17. Ibid., p. 15.
18. Ibid., p. 117.
19. Ibid., p. 76.
20. Hackman, L. H. H., "Shakespeare and Harvey," Lancet, 2: 789, 1888.
21. "The Medicine in Shakespeare." Detroit Med. & Lib. Assoc. Trans. (1892-1893), p. 103.
22. Ibid., p. 105.
23. Op. cit., p. 103.

24. **Ibid.**, p. 104.
25. "A Few Quotations from Shakespeare." **Med. Rec., 56: 135, 1905.**
26. "It seems that Shakespeare's wonderful mind not only comprehended matters of the past,—imbibed the ideas of his present, but with prophetic grasp anticipated the most important events which were to transpire ages after he ceased to be." Chesney, J. P., **Shakespeare as a Physician.** Chicago, Chambers, 1884, p. 154.

    "But this man seemed to be a little ahead of his sphere, giving to succeeding generations much more than his environment could possibly give to him. . . . " Whitmire, C. L., "Psychoses of Shakespeare's characters." **Illinois M. J., 53: 64, 1928.**

    ". . . but he was a seer foretelling gravitation, the circulation and even the rapidity of modern communication. That the poet far antedated Newton in understanding the principle of gravity is evident . . . " Walter E. Vest, "William Shakespeare, Therapeutist," **Southern Med. J., 37: 457-464, Aug. 1944.**
27. Raleigh, Sir W., Shakespeare. London, Macmillan, 1928, p. 3.
28. **II Henry IV, IV, 4, 114-116.** All quotations from the plays in this work are based on the Student's Cambridge Edition of **Shakespeare's Complete Works, ed. by W. A. Neilson, N.Y.,** Houghton Mifflin, 1906.
29. **Measure for Measure, II, 4, 24-26.**
30. **Op. cit.,** 14 p. 903.
31. **Love's Labour's Lost,** I, 1, 235.
32. **Pericles,** III, 2, 91.
33. **Op. cit., p.** 274.
34. **Love's Labour's Lost,** V, 2.
35. **Measure for Measure,** II, 1.
36. **As You Like It,** IV, 3.
37. **A Merchant of Venice,** III, 2.
38. **Henry IV,** V, 1.
39. **Othello,** II, 3.
40. Pollard, A. W., **The Works of Chaucer, London, Macmillan, 1925,** pp. 132-134, II, 4011-4157.
41. Adams, J. Q., **Pre-Shakespearean Dramas. N.Y., 1924, p. 376.**
42. Quoted by Herman Pomeranz in "Medicine in the Elizabethan Plays and Era," **op. cit.,** p. 505.
43. "That Shakespeare was aware of the theory of the action of antitoxin is evident. . . . " Wainwright, J. W., "A Few Quotations from Shakespeare," **Med. Rec.,** 56: 94 (1904).

    "And here seems to be a foreshadowing of the bringing about of immunity. . . " Pomeranz, H., "Medicine in the Shakespearean Plays and Era," **Med. Life,** 41: 502.
44. "Could Shakespeare also have known the theory of gravitation

at this early date? . . . it seems that the great poet refers to it in Troilus and Cressida (Act IV, Sc. 2)." Epstein, H., William Shakespeare M.D. Newark, Lasky, 1932, p. 9.

"The reference is quite sufficient to convince one that Shakespeare had a correct theory of gravitation." 25

Citing the same lines as Dr. Epstein, Dr. Pomeranz remarks that ". . . it can be observed that quite an amazing fact about Shakespeare's scientific knowledge is that he seems to have foreshadowed Newton . . . " "Medicine in the Shakespearean Plays and Era," Med. Life, 41: 497.

45. "The action of this 'stuff' [some of the medicine prepared by Cornelius for the queen to cause one to appear dead for a time] of Shakespeare is most beautifully typical of chloroform and had we the slightest evidence that a drug of that character had ever existed as such, save in the fertile brain of the greatest writer of the world, we well might doubt the priority of discovery of anaesthesia by both Morton and Wells." Chesney, J. P., Shakepeare as a Physician. Chicago, Chambers, 1884, p. 122. So then Shakespeare might have discovered chloroform and anaesthesia.

46. "Shakespeare's Knowledge of Chest Diseases," Journ. Amer. Med. Assoc., Dec. 9, 1950.

CHAPTER III

THE ATTITUDE OF CRITICAL OPINION ON SHAKESPEARE'S MEDICAL KNOWLEDGE, CHRONOLOGICALLY CONSIDERED

Let us now go into greater detail on the subject, chronologically and historically. The sixteenth, seventeenth and eighteenth centuries are practically mute with regard to comment on Shakespeare's medical learning. Nor is this to be wondered at, for these centuries were generally more or less indifferent to Shakespeare's greatness.[1] It was not until the nineteenth century that the critics awoke to the all-sided, myriad-minded, universal genius evident in the plays of Shakespeare. But as is the way with human nature, these critics swung to the opposite extreme, and, as already mentioned, as a result of the leadership of Schlegel, Coleridge, Hazlitt and others of their school, the poet came to be idolized as an all-knowing, all-comprehensive "Oceanic" Mind. The attitude of criticism of his medical knowledge did not escape this spirit of idolatry. That Shakespeare was familiar with the medical lore of the times all critics agree. That he was acquainted with the principles and theories of the medical writers of the past and of his own time, few deny. But that he had any special or technical knowledge of medicine or that he made any scientific discoveries—here is where there are some differences of opinion. Nevertheless, as already stated, medical commentators, for the most part, seem to have been satisfied with exposition, and the mere listing of medical references, rather than with real criticism. And so there are few works on Shakespeare's medical knowledge that are worthy of the critics' art.

As early as 1815, we find Bell's "Principles of Surgery," Vol. II, noting Shakespeare in the capacity of a physician:

—Bettman Archive

2. Sir William Harvey (1578-1657).
From an engraving by John Hall
from a painting by Cornelius Jansens

EXERCITATIO
ANATOMICA DE
MOTV CORDIS ET SAN-
GVINIS IN ANIMALI-
BVS,
GVILIELMI HARVEI ANGLI,
Medici Regii, & Professoris Anatomiæ in Col-
legio Medicorum Londinensi.

FRANCOFVRTI,
Sumptibus GVILIELMI FITZERI.
ANNO M. DC. XXVIII.

—Bettman Archive

3. Title page of Harvey's book on the Circulation of the Blood

4. Harvey demonstrating his experiments to King Charles I. —Bettman Archive

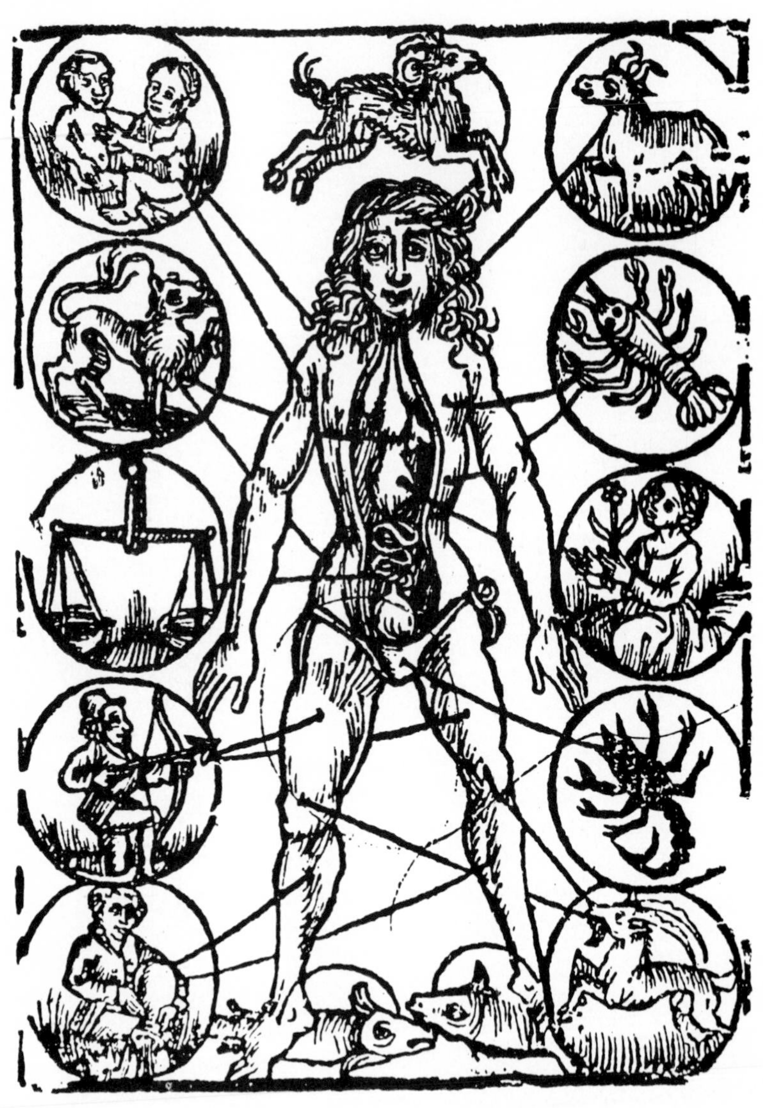

—Bettman Archive

5. Signs of the Zodiac as related to the organs of Man. From Mundinus Edition, 1513. The planets governed the various parts of the body indicated above.

My readers will smile perhaps to see me quoting Shakespeare among physicians and theologists but not one of all their tribe populous though it be, could describe so exquisitely, the marks of apoplexy conspiring with the struggles for life, and the agonies of suffocation deforming the countenance of the dead . . . .[2]

It is obvious here, that this is rather a tribute to his sense of observation than to his medical knowledge. And who can deny that Shakespeare's powers of observation and his genius for language are unsurpassed? That is what his greatness rests upon. But we must beware of falling into the error of confusing such abilities with actual medical knowledge, as so many of the commentators have done.

Continuing further, George Farren published a book on the medical knowledge of Shakespeare in 1826, in which there are "Observations on . . . Rates or laws of Mortality . . . Illustrations of the Progress of Mania, Melancholia, Craziness, and Demonomania as displayed in Shakespeare's characters of Lear, Hamlet, Ophelia and Edgar: on the comparative danger of first and subsequent births, etc., etc." This work falls into the category mentioned before; it contains references to medicine in the plays but little criticism.

The most important and dominant medical critic of the nineteenth century, however, is J. C. Bucknill. His two books, *The Medical Knowledge of Shakespeare* (1860) and *The Mad Folk of Shakespeare* (1867),[3] are still looked up to as authoritative works. In the first mentioned book, Bucknill gathers together all the references to the healing art present in each play and discusses them sanely, and more or less, from an historical standpoint. He affirms that Shakespeare had ". . . a mind imbued with medical thought,"[4] but he readily realizes that the times in which Shakespeare lived were markedly conducive to the acquisition of medical lore. Nevertheless, his enthusiasm bubbles over at times. Referring to the speeches in *The Comedy of Errors*[5] on the causation of melancholia by domestic trouble, he says that it "could scarcely be improved upon by the science of the present day," for it presents "a picture of medical etiology drawn with more knowledge than most members even of the profession of medicine could themselves display."[6] Referring to the mustering of the blood to the heart as described by Warwick in relating of the death of murdered Gloster,[7] he says, "it is perfectly in accordance with modern physiological science... in every way remarkable." However, in the final analysis, Bucknill feels ". . . that Shakespeare's theoretical knowledge of medicine closely corresponded to that prevailing at his time among its professors, . . ." He comes to the historical conclusion as follows: "I have arrived at the fullest conviction that the great dramatist had at least been a diligent student of all medical knowledge existing at the time,"[8] and that ". . . his mind was deeply imbued with the best medical information of his age,"[9] having ". . . authority even for his trivialities and most glaring absurdities."[10]

Following Bucknill's work, we have that of C. W. Stearn. In his *The Shakespeare Treasury* (1869), he devotes a good deal of space to Shakespeare's medical and psychopathological knowledge, gathering together the numerous references in his plays, under the heading of Anatomy, Physiology, Pathology, Practical Medicine, Medical Jurisprudence, Insanity, Medical Ethics, Hygiene, Dietetics and Materia Medica. Together with most medical men, he is, "with reason, astonished at Shakespeare's knowledge of their profession,—a knowledge which it has cost them both time and diligence to acquire."[11] Referring to Shakespeare's knowledge of the physical signs of death and pointing to the death-scene involving Falstaff,[12] Stearn says: "Here Shakespeare, with one penful of ink has given us what amounts to a whole class lecture or a dozen pages of an ordinary medical textbook."[13] It is interesting in this regard to note that Bucknill puts forth the suggestion that Shakespeare might have read Hippocrates, and that from this source he might have obtained a great deal of medical material, particularly in regard to the Falstaff death-scene; for he takes cognizance of the fact that "in a note to the Sydenham Society's edition of Hippocrates, Adams (the editor) remarks, "Shakespeare's description of the death of Falstaff contains images which have always appeared to me to be borrowed (at second hand no doubt) from this and other passages of the present work'[14] (Hippocrates)." "Of Shakespeare's conception of Sanitary, Dietetic and Hygienic influences," Stearn says that "there is evidence enough to show that, on those matters, as in all else, he was far in advance of the age in which he lived."[15] It is obvious here that Stearn has exercised his critical faculties very little. He echoes merely the idolatry of his period, and the quotations that he gives are nothing more than casual allusions to the healing art, that the average layman of the day might have been familiar with.

Another work, published in 1884, is *Shakespeare as a Physician* by J. Portsmouth Chesney. Here again, for the most part, we have a mere cataloguing of medical references under medical headings, together with a great deal of puerile moralizing, but little actual criticism. Chesney is most lavish in the praise of Shakespeare's medical knowledge. He considers that "It is . . . wonderful to note the accuracy of Shakespeare's knowledge even in . . . medical thought . . . ."[16] He attests to the accuracy of Shakespeare's therapeutics. Thus, referring to Shakespeare's descriptions of epilepsy, Chesney says, "These pictures of epilepsy, though terse, are yet very well drawn,—even a medical pen well skilled in portraiture could not do it better. . . . "[17] Referring to Shakespeare's description of the death of John of Gaunt,[18] he says, "Shakespeare . . . has managed the symptomatology of the case with such a masterly skill, that it might puzzle the most astute diagnostician of our time. . . ." Shakespeare's description of syphilis, especially, he considers "a marvel of accuracy."[19] Chesney says, "The ravages made by pock upon the osseous system seem to have been clearly comprehended by Shakespeare."[20] "Ricord, Videlle nor Bumstead [famous syphilographers of Chesney's time] could hardly paint a better pen picture of the ravages of syphilis than did . . . Timon."[21] He finally concludes on this subject: "There cannot be found in the writings of the ablest medical authority of this age, a more terse and truthful picture of syphilis than is seen" in Shakespeare. All this may be very true; but it can readily be seen that Chesney like many others has confused observation and exposition with true medical learning.

Chesney quotes the words of the clown Pompey in *Measure for Measure*:

> Why, very well. I telling you then, if you be remenb'red, that such a one and such a one were past cure of the thing you wot of, unless they kept very good diet, as I told you,—[22]

and adds

> The idea conveyed in the last paragraph, as to the necessity of good diet in the treatment of the "diseases you wot of" was ignored by the medical world until a period so recent as to come within the memory of our junior practitioners; and that its propriety, nay, necessity, should have forced itself upon the notice of a non-medical man three centuries and a half ago when no medical mind had grasped the idea, is only one among the thousand of evidences we have of Shakespeare's unequalled sagacity.[23]

Chesney was evidently unfamiliar with the therapeutics current in Elizabethan England, otherwise he could not possibly have been guilty of such a false statement. The fact is that diet was a well recognized and commonly used method of treating the sick. In the case of syphilis especially, it was "the tubfast and diet" combination which was in universal use. The references to this in the general literature as well as the medical literature of the day, are very numerous. Bullein's *New Boke of Phisicke* gave the three best physicians to cure sickness as follows: "The first was called Doctor Diet, the second, Doctor Quiet, the third, Doctor Merryman."[24] This same Bullein gives the following directions as to diet in syphilis:

> Also the sicke body must eate but little meate,
> And that kynde of meate as shall here after be prescribed,
> And at sutch time as shall be appoynted.[25]

Sir Thomas Elyot's *Castel of Helthe* (1541) has not less than two chapters on diet as a therapeutic measure, one "on the diete of colerike persons" and the other "on the diete of fleumatic persons."[26] Even Bacon in his "Essay on the Regimen of Health" does not fail to mention diet, for he says, "I commend rather some diet for certain seasons than frequent use of physic."[27]

But especially in Shakespeare's understanding of the parturient stage in woman does Chesney speak of the "wonderful accuracy of detail in which our author is so fertile . . . [for, continues he] See how he names the leading facts connected with labor."[28] What are these leading facts as pointed out by Chesney? They include nothing more than this: that Shakespeare describes labor as occurring in the night time, and particularly on dismal nights. On such a basis does he conclude that Shakespeare knew the facts of labor!

In a like category with Chesney is B. R. Field. In his book, *Medical Thoughts of Shakespeare* (1885), he asserts that "Shakespeare's . . . mighty mind seems to have teemed with the knowledge of . . . medicine. . . ."[29] Thus he refers to the "accuracy with which Shakespeare has written of apoplexy . . ."[30] and of "how concisely he describes epilepsy."[31] Speaking of sleep, he says, "Shakespeare certainly had the true idea of the great value of sleep, and he also knew of its importance in the treatment of brain diseases."[32] For the most part, Field's work is nothing more than a concordance of medical references.

It is refreshing now, to turn to a few critics who are more rational in their consideration of Shakespeare's medical learning. Such a one is Newton Hawley. Hawley (1892) feels, that in a general way, Shakespeare's "learning is not of the pedantic sort, too common with scholars, but is drawn from the book of nature and does not lead him into serious mistakes."[33] He is against those particularly, who consider that Shakespeare had any real medical knowledge. He grants the fact that "the poet was familiar with the theories of the older medical writers."[34] But as to his actual medical knowledge, he distinctly says, "It has seemed to me that the medical learning of the poet has been rather alleged than proved, . . . and I cannot see . . . any evidence of medical or scientific knowledge that would have been at all astonishing in an intelligent and observing layman."[35] With this Getchel (1907) agrees, for although he does not deny "the wonderful grasp that he (Shakespeare) had of the knowledge of the time. . ." nevertheless, he distinctly states that, primarily, "he was a playwright and not a scientist."[36] Griffiths also is in complete accord with these views. In his article "Shakespeare and the Practice of Medicine"[37] he lists numerous references to indicate Shakespeare's aquaintance with medical matters, but he does this logically and from the historical viewpoint.

In the same group belongs John Moyes (1896). His *Medicine and Kindred Arts in Shakespeare*[38] attempts to deal with Shakespeare's medical knowledge historically, in its relations to sixteenth century medicine. Under the headings, Physiological and Pathological Notions, Medicine, Materia Medica, Toxicology, Therapeutics, Surgery, and Midwifery, he quotes the passages bearing on the subjects, offering little comment here and there of an historical nature. The general import of of the book is that Shakespeare was well acquainted with the medical knowledge current at the time. Such a conclusion is also reached by Simpson, though at a much later date (1959): "All that can be said is that he (Shakespeare) in his writings was expressing contemporary thought."[39]

But the most logical work along this line in the early part of the twentieth century has undoubtedly been done by A. W. Meyers (1907). Meyers seems to be the only one of the medical commentators of his time with the true historical viewpoint, and with the adequate scholarship to properly and rationally adjudge the medical material in Shakespeare's plays. In his two articles on the subject he places Shakespeare's medical knowledge and his general attitude toward physicians in the proper historical light, showing that the poet reflected but the life about him. He sounds the key note of the best modern Shakespearean criticism when he says:

> Of some of the characteristics of the Medicine in Shakespeare, . . . the picture we obtain is . . . that which could easily be obtained from the life of that time by a layman of *such extraordinary genius* as Shakespeare's. The wonderfully accurate descriptions of death and old age are elo-

quent testimonials of his powers of observation, expression and portrayal.[40]

He concludes, "The characteristics of the Medicine of Shakespeare are . . . those of the medicine of the best physicians contemporary with him." Nevertheless, in a later book on the subject (1932) Dr. Harry Epstein seems to have been entirely unaffected by the skepticism that has prevailed in Shakespearean criticism in the last fifty years. The book only serves to illustrate further the uncritical approach and the expository methods of the medical commentators. Dr. Epstein continues along the same beaten paths as his predecessors whom we have already considered, merely listing passages in Shakespeare's works relating to the healing art, and accepting such as *prima facie* evidence of "the bard's great fund of knowledge in this field." He is so "impressed . . . with his (Shakespeare's) deep knowledge of medicine and its collateral sciences,"[41] that he considers such knowledge as most "comprehensive" and "nothing short of amazing." He concludes his book by saying that Shakespeare's medical lore, "considering the period in which he lived, fills us with wonder and admiration for medicine was decidedly disjointed."[42] We shall see later that it was precisely for this very reason that Shakespeare had so much medical knowledge.

But even later than this is the work of Dr. Herman Pomeranz, mentioned before. His research in the *Medicine in the Shakespearean Plays and Era,* (1934) is admirable especially when he is dealing with the status of medicine in the Shakespearean period. In this he has added a real contribution. However, when he considers the plays themselves, he falls hopelessly into the idolatrous trap, repeating undiscerningly the same errors of so many of the medical commentators. Thus, as quoted before, he considers "Shakespeare's knowledge of the general medical topics of his day . . . amazing . . . considerably in advance of current education and teaching."[43] He implies that "Shakespeare . . . knew that the blood . . . *circulated* throughout the body,"[44] citing the same lines referred to by all the idolatrous commentators on this point. Yet, on the very same page he admits that "all educated people in England and elsewhere before and after him knew that the blood was not a stagnant stream and circulated throughout the body."[45]

In this respect, it is most astounding to find Dr. Pomeranz making the statement that "Shakespeare, *before any scientist of his day,* realized that the blood stream also carried nutriment to the organs of the body."[46] This is the more amazing because Dr. Pomeranz is a student of the status of the medical knowledge of the Shakespearean Era and should have been aware, as we shall later show, that the best scientific opinion of the Elizabethan period held this view.

Dr. Pomeranz further repeats the idea, professed by many of the commentators, that Shakespeare "foreshadowed Newton"[47] on gravitation. Yet in his own research in the very same paper, but in relation to a different topic, he points out[48] that a prominent physician of the period, William Gilbert (1544-1603), at one time medical attendant to Queen Elizabeth, wrote a work "On the Magnet and Magnetic Bodies and the *Great Magnet the Earth.*" Even if we do not consider the probability that the earth's drawing power was vaguely suspected and perhaps mentioned by many before Newton, yet the idea of the concept of the *Great Magnet the Earth* which undoubtedly was prevalent at this time, is sufficient to explain the following from *Troilus and Cressida* mentioned by Dr. Pomeranz and others, as implying Shakespeare's knowledge of gravitation:

> Time, force and death
> Do this body what extremes you can
> But the strong base and building of my love
> Is the very center of the earth
> Drawing all things to it.

Obviously, we have here ". . . the very center of the earth/ Drawing all things to it" as the *Great Magnet the Earth.* It is more probable that Shakespeare and his contemporaries were referring to this idea rather than to gravitation as such, propounded by Newton much later. Other poets and dramatists can be shown to have been familiar with the same concept.

There are other claims of similar nature in Dr. Pomeranz's

work, such as, that Shakespeare foreshadowed the idea of immunity,[49] that Shakespeare was "an ultra modern psychiatrist,"[50] "considerably in advance of his age, in mental and nervous diseases."[51] These claims have no real foundation and reflect merely the blind acceptance of the previous idolators.

It is refreshing now to come to the latest book on the subject, R. R. Simpson's *Shakespeare and Medicine* (1959).[52] Simpson approaches his subject rationally and with little bardolatry, though he does remark that "Here indeed (in Shakespeare's works) is a large part of the art of medicine written for us by a layman."[53] As he himself states, "the material for this paper was taken largely from Bucknill's book of 1860"[54] which has already been considered.

Simpson records 712 medical references in Shakespeare, but hastens to state that "the number of medical references . . . is no indication that Shakespeare had any training in medicine,"[55] as some medical commentators had implied. He notes that Shakespeare was particularly good at (descriptions of) death from the medical point of view, and, referring specifically to the death of Falstaff, states, "In a few lines Shakespeare creates a masterpiece of clinical description."[56] He does conclude that Shakespeare's knowledge of medicine corresponded closely to that prevailing at his time among its professors and that he had authority even for his trivialities and absurdities, and further, he remarks, "that he was aware of the current thought, there can be little doubt."[57]

Simpson classifies his 712 medical references in Shakespeare into twenty categories including Shakespeare's Medical Aphorisms; Medical Knowledge in Shakespeare's Contemporaries; Shakespeare's Doctors Apothecaries and Quacks; Shakespeare and The Influence of His Son-in-Law; Shakespeare's Clinical Descriptions; Medical Problems in Shakespeare's Tragedies; On Wounds; On Public Health and Epidemics; On Shakespeare; On Pregnancy; etc. He comes to acceptable logical conclusions that Shakespeare had "accuracy of . . . observation . . . and the clinical pictures he leaves (as) . . . unsurpassed in clinical value in any medical writings . . ."[58] He further asserts, "that Shakespeare was well acquainted with the medical knowledge of his day and with the literature . . . and had some knowledge of the ancient medical writers . . . "and that in his writings he was "expressing contemporary medical thought."[59]

Surgery too, Obstetrics, Syphilology, Therapeutics, Materia Medica, Toxicology, all these branches of the healing art are well represented in Shakespeare's plays, all come in for laudatory commendation at the hands of the medical commentators. Thus John Knott remarks that Shakespeare's "knowledge of the principles of surgery and medicine was nowhere behind the professional knowledge of his day."[60] Field says that "Obstetrics was Shakespeare's favorite branch of the profession."[61] Max Kahn asserts that "Shakespeare everywhere evinces a marked knowledge of toxicology"[62] and that "a student of Shakespeare must inevitably become a good syphilographer."[63] Referring to the latter, J. F. Rogers writes that "Shakespeare paints the picture of the victim of venereal disease with no sparing of pigment and with no uncertain sweep of the brush."[64] There are others and others, but all run in the same uncritical vein, as we shall further see.

NOTES AND REFERENCES

CHAPTER III

1. Dryden in the eighteenth century did appreciate the greatness of Shakespeare but his point of view, of course, was not idolatrous.
2. Cited by Field, B. R., **Medical Thoughts of Shakespeare.** Easton, Pa., 1885, p. 25.
3. This book was first published at London, 1859, bearing the title, **The Psychology of Shakespeare.**
4. **The Medical Knowledge of Shakespeare.** London, Longman, 1860, p. 74.
5. **Comedy of Errors,** IV, 4.
6. **Op. cit.,** 4p. 12.
7. **II Henry VI,** III, 2, 160-179.
8. **Op. cit.,** 4 p. 12.
9. **Op. cit.,** 4 p. 13.
10. **Op. cit.,** p. 14.
11. **Shakespeare's Treasury.** N. Y., Putnam, 1878, p. 163.
12. **Henry V,** II, 3.
13. **Op. cit.,** 11 p. 169.
14. **The Medical Knowledge of Shakespeare,** p. 166.
15. **Op. cit.,** p. 175.
16. **Shakespeare as a Physician.** Chicago, Chambers, 1884, p. 42.
17. **Op. cit.,** p. 122.
18. **King John,** V, 7, 14-23.
19. **Op. cit.,** 16 p. 172.
20. **Op. cit.,** 16 p. 179.
21. **Op. cit.,** 16 p. 171.
22. II, 1, 113-116.
23. **Op. cit.,** 16 p. 21.
23. **Op. cit.,** 16 p. 21.
24. Page 155. Cited in Bucknill's **The Medical Knowledge of Shakespeare,** p. 27.
25. Bulwarke of Defence. London, **Booke of Compoundes.** Folio Cited in Moyes, **op. cit.,** p. 97.
26. Cited in Bucknill, **op. cit.,** p. 88.
27. **Op. cit.,** p. 286.
28. **Op. cit.,** p. 43.
29. **Medical Thoughts of Shakespeare.** Easton, Pa., 1885, p. 10.
30. **Op. cit.,** p. 17.

31. **Op. cit.,** p. 19.
32. **Op. cit.,** p. 15.
33. Hawley, R. N., "The Medical Lore of Shakespeare." **Medical Age.** 10: 740—753, 1892.
34. **Ibid.,** p. 741.
35. **Ibid.,** p. 753.
36. Getchell, A. G. "The Medical Knowledge of Shakespeare," **Boston M & S. J.,** 156: 65, 1907.
37. Griffiths, L. M. "Shakespeare and the Practice of Medicine," **Ann. Med. Hist.,** 3: 50, 1921.
38. Glasgow, MacLebose, 1896.
39. Simpson, R. R. **Shakespeare and Medicine,** E and S Livingston Ltd., Edinburgh and London, 1959, p. 15.
40. Meyers, A. W. "Some of the Characteristics of the Medicine in Shakespeare." **Bull. Johns Hopkins Hosp.,** 18: No. 190, 10, 1907. Yet 8 years later in 1915, Dr. John W. Wainwright in his book, **Shakespeare's Medical and Surgical Knowledge,** seems to have been entirely unaffected by these contrary and more rational currents of criticism. Speaking of Shakespeare as "the master of all time"[1] he writes that "The whole range of human knowledge and passion from science, anticipating research, to law and theology is within his grasp."[2] Further, he states that "Shakespeare . . . displays a marvelous acquaintance with physiology as well as with medicine" including "a knowledge of the circulation of the blood . . . in anticipation of Harvey."[3] All in all, Wainright, under medical headings, does what most of the other medical commentators have done. He lists references with only minor discerning criticism.

    [1]Introduction.

    [2]**Ibid.**

    [3]**Ibid.,** p. 61.
41. **William Shakespeare, M.D.,** Newark, Lasky, 1932, p. 2.
42. **Op. cit.,** p. 24.
43. **Med. Life,** 41: 493.
44. **Ibid.,** p. 497.
45. **Ibid.**
46. **Op. cit.,** p. 500. The italics are mine.
47. **Op. cit.,** p. 497.
48. **Op. cit.,** p. 487. Giordano Bruno in 1600 also published a book called **De Magneta, Magnetisque Corporibus et de magno magnete tellure** in which the globe of the earth was put down as a vast spherical magnet.
49. **Op. cit.,** p. 502.
50. **Op. cit.,** p. 511.
51. **Op. cit.,** pp. 509, 295.

52. Simpson, R. R. **Shakespeare and Medicine,** E. & S. Livingston, Ltd., Edinburgh and London, 1959.
53. **Ibid.,** p. 154. Quoted also in "M.Ds. Join Shakespeare Celebration," **Medical World News,** Aug. 14, 164, p. 106.
54. **Ibid.,** p. 1.
55. **Ibid.,** p. 9.
56. **Ibid., p. 55.**
57. **Ibid., p. 13.**
58. **Ibid., p. 154.**
59. **Ibid., p. 15.**
60. **Loc. cit., p. 436.**
61. **Op. cit., 2 p. 19.**
62. Kahn, M., "Shakespeare's Knowledge of Medicine," **N.Y. Med. Journ.,** 42: 863.
63. **Ibid.,** p. 863.
64. Rogers, J. F. "Shakespeare As a Health Teacher," **Scientific Monthly** 2: 589, 1914.

CHAPTER IV

THE ATTITUDE OF THE MEDICAL COMMENTATORS ON SHAKESPEARE'S KNOWLEDGE OF THE CIRCULATION

It must now be readily apparent that in no department of Shakespearean criticism have commentators erred so grossly or sinned so unforgivably as in the field of Shakespeare's medical and psychopathological knowledge. Idolatry seems to have rooted itself more deeply and persisted more stubbornly in the minds of the medical commentators than in those working in any other classification of Shakespearean criticism. And so Shakespeare has not only been raised to the pinnacle of physicianship, but, travesty of logic! Shakespeare has actually been credited with a knowledge of the circulation of the blood previous to the epoch-making discovery of William Harvey! Thus Dr. A. O. Kellogg (1859), discussing physiology in general, speaks of the "extraordinary amount of physiological knowledge possessed by Shakespeare,"[1] considering that "a very complete physiological . . . system . . . could be deduced from the writings . . . a system in complete accordance . . with that which we now possess as a result of the scientific research and experience of the last two centuries,"[2] including of course, the circulation of the blood; for he later remarks ". . . that many passages from his dramas seem to indicate a pre-existent knowledge of this great physiological fact."[3] Strangely enough, more than seventy-two years later, Dr. Harry Epstein, (1932) one of the later of the medical commentators, in general line with the idolatrous nature of all his comments, agrees with Dr. Kellogg in this matter, for in speaking of "the great master's knowledge of the general range of physiology and pathology as well as of general diseases,"[4] he is convinced that the evidence "clearly indicate (s) that the theory of the circulation of the blood was known . . . to Shakespeare . . .,"[5] definitely stating, "that Shakespeare seems to have had a knowledge of the circulation of the blood."[6]

The strongest proponent of the latter matter, however, is Dr. Orville W. Owen. Owen first set out to prove that Bacon was the author of the works attributed to Shakespeare. In common with all those who wish to make the plays teem with knowledge enough to make them worthy of Bacon, he envelops Shakespeare in the purple toga of actual medical knowledge and accords to him the credit of discovering the circulation of the blood in preference to William Harvey. He quotes many lines to prove his contention. Like many Shakespearean fanatics he does not quote the lines that show the fallacy of his belief. Dr. Owen says that Shakespeare "had a very good knowledge of the great discovery"[7] being "perfectly familiar with the experiments and proofs of the circulations of the blood,"[8] and stating further, that ". . . he was either the original discoverer of the great anatomical and physiological truth or knew intimately the experiments and dissections upon which it is based." He concludes that Shakespeare "...must either have dissected the human body or at least seen it done," and further that ". . . if William Shakespeare wrote the plays bearing his name, he discovered the circulation instead of Dr. William Harvey." Hence, "Harvey must have stolen the great discovery" from Shakespeare. In like manner, Dr. John Knott (1903) believes that "Shakespeare's ideas of the course of the vital fluid appear to be decidedly in advance of those of most, of even his medical contemporaries." And again, "there are various glimpses of some knowledge of the circulation scattered through the plays of Shakespeare . . . certainly enough to show that Harvey's discovery which was published after Shakespeare's death would not have been a startling discovery to him if he had lived."[9] All in all, Dr. Knott concludes that Shakespeare ". . . had an approximate conception of the circulation of the blood in the human body."[10] Thus too, Dr. J. W. Wainwright (1904) considers that "it is quite certain that Shakespeare anticipated Harvey in a knowledge of the circulation of the blood."[11] And Dr. David Cerna (1927) states that "the great dramatist appears to have been a general anatomist and physiologist," and to have "entertained more or less correct ideas about the circulation of the blood."[12] Of similar character, also, is the opinion of Dr. Samuel Dodek, who, writing of "Shakespeare's right to membership in the Guild of Medicine,"[13] affirms that a certain passage of *Hamlet*[14] "is indeed in anticipation of Harvey" as regards the circulation and that another passage in *Coriolanus*,[15] "Give (s) added confirmation of Shakespeare's knowledge of the circulation of the blood." He concludes in wonder that "it is most illuminating that before an experimental study of the circulation of the blood was given widespread recognition, Shakespeare should have definitely asserted himself on that score."[13] Referring to these same passages, Dr. Herman Pomeranz (1934) seems quite in agreement with Dr. Cerna, for he states that "the circulation of the blood" is distinctly referred to in *Hamlet,*" and that "Shakespeare . . . knew that the blood was not a stagnant stream but that it circulated throughout the body."[16]

We can excuse the earlier commentators for their serious considerations of this absurd claim. The idolatry of their period, perhaps, distorted their vision and obtused their judgment. But what of the later medical critics down to this very day? These seem to have been entirely unaffected by the skeptical and historical trend in the Shakespearean scholarship of the last forty years. These seem to have been quite oblivious of the newer facts relating to Shakespeare and his times. These critics keep on uttering hackneyed idolatrous phrases.

This does not mean that all the medical commentators ascribe to Shakespeare a knowledge of the circulation of the blood. Such an impression would be erroneous. On the contrary, a large group of them are of precisely the opposite opinion. And it would be a gross injustice to the high calibre and discerning judgment of the medical profession, and of the particular commentators themselves not to mention their viewpoints. Thus Dr. Bucknill (1859) remarks: "the circulation of the blood was not known to Shakespeare,"[17] and again: "There is not . . . in Shakespeare, a trace of any knowledge of the circulation of the blood."[18] Thus too, Dr. Gillespie (1875) says, "It is questionable whether Shakespeare was acquainted with the discovery of Harvey about the circulation of the blood."[19] Thus also, Dr. L. K. Hackman (1888) asserts ". . . that he knew nothing of the circulation of the blood . . ."[20] Likewise Dr. Moyes (1896) contends "that notwithstanding the frequent references in Shakespeare to the circulation of the blood, he had no notion of its course as understood since the discovery of Harvey."[21] And so too, Dr. B. R. Field maintains that, "There is not one thought to be found in Shakespeare in any way relating to the circulation of the blood, that is not applicable to the teachings of either Hippocrates, Galen, Servetus, or Sylvius."[22] Drs. Donnellan (1902), Getchell (1907), and Kahn (1914) come to an historical conclusion on this matter, the one holding that, "Regarding the true nature of the circulation of the blood, the great dramatist was without accurate knowledge,"[23] the second believing that ". . . his ideas were those current at the time,"[24] and the third saying, "It is doubtlessly true that the great dramatist knew as much as was known in his time about the circulation of the blood . . . (but) was not in advance of his contemporaries in that knowledge;"[25] while R. R. Simpson (1959) after a consideration of the evidence in the matter concludes that there is ". . . no evidence to be found in Shakespeare of any knowledge of the circulation of the blood."[26] All this serves but to illustrate how far Shakespearean idolators can stray from the path of logic and the atmosphere of reason.

However, even these who oppose the idolators have failed. Their comments represent merely impressions, feelings, opinions, and the medical idolators really stand factually unrefuted. Nowhere in the whole vast range of Shakespearean criticism has anyone taken up this matter and carried it to logical ultimate conclusions, in the light of modern enlightened Shakespearean scholarship;[27] We intend to fill this void once and for all; let us refute the medical idolators and settle this question beyond the possibility of further serious controversy.

NOTES AND REFERENCES

CHAPTER IV

1. Kellogg, A. O. "William Shakespeare as a physician and psychologist." **Am. J. Insanity,** 16: 129, 1859. Also in his "Shakespeare's Delineations," etc. **op. cit.,** p. 8.
2. **Ibid.,** p. 130. Also in "Shakespeare's Delineations, etc.," p. 3.
3. **Ibid.,** p. 131. Also in "Shakespeare's Delineations, etc.," p. 3.
4. **William Shakespeare, M.D.** Newark, Lasky, 1932, p. 16.
5. **Op. cit.,** p. 9.
6. **Op. cit.,** p. 8.
7. Owen, O. W., "The Medicine in Shakespeare," **Det. Med. & Lib. Assoc. Trans.** 1893, p. 109.
8. **Ibid.,** p. 105.
9. Knott, J. "The Medical Knowledge of Shakespeare," **Westminster Rev.,** 159: 437 (Apr. 1903); pp. 442, 438.
10. Knott, J. "The Bacon Shakespeare Controversy," **Westminster Rev.,** 158: 304 (Sept. 1902).
11. "Medical and Surgical Knowledge of Shakespeare," **Med. Rec.,** 56: 135, 1904.
12. Cerna, D. "Shakespeare and the Circulation of the Blood," **Med. Record & Ann.,** 24: 443 (Jl. 1927); see pp. 443-445.
13. Dodek, S. M. "Some Notes on William Shakespeare's Knowledge of Medicine," **Med. Ann. Dist. Col.,** I: No. 12, 1-3, 1932.
14. **Act I,** Sc. 5.
15. Act II, Sc. 2. As dear to me as are the ruddy drops/That visit my sad heart . . .
16. Pomeranz, H. "Medicine in the Shakespearean Plays and Era," **Med. Life,** 41: 496-7 (Oct. 1934).
17. **The Medical Knowledge of Shakespeare,** London, Longman, 1860, pp. 8-20.
18. **Op. cit.,** p. 215. Bucknill does some mild backsliding in this matter, for he says (p. 82) "Shakespeare may with the intuition of genius have guessed very near the circulation of the blood."
19. "Medical Notes About Shakespeare and His Times," **Edinb. M. J.,** 20: 1061, 1875.
20. Hackman, L. K. H., "Shakespeare and Harvey," **Lancet,** 2: 789, 1888.
21. **Medicine and Kindred Arts in Shakespeare,** Glasgow, MacLehose, 1896, p. 6.

22. "Medical Shakespearean-Fanaticism," N.Y. **Shakespeareana,** 6: 1-19, Jan. 1889.
23. "Medical Allusions in Shakespeare's Plays," **Am. Med.,** 3: 280, 1902.
24. Getchell, A. C. "The Medical Knowledge of Shakespeare," **Boston M. & S. J.,** 156: 65, 1907.
25. Kahn, M. "Shakespeare's Knowledge of Medicine." **New York M. J.,** 42: 863, 1910.
26. **Shakespeare and Medicine,** E and S Livingston Ltd., 1959, p. 20.
27. Dr. W. J. Bristow ("Shakespeare as a Physiologist," **South. Med. & Surg.,** 94: 274-6, May 1932), and C. C. Greenwood before him ("The Medical Knowledge of Shakespeare," **Westminster Rev.,** 159: 573, May 1903; and "Bacon, Shakespeare, Harvey and Dr. Knott," **Westminster Rev.,** 164: 552, No. 1905), have, in some degree, attempted to do this, but their work is incomplete and unconvincing, and hence falls far short of its mark.

CHAPTER V

SHAKESPEARE, HARVEY AND THE CIRCULATION OF THE BLOOD

The discovery of the true circulation of the blood was one of the most momentous discoveries in the entire realm of medical science. Like all other great advances in science it came only after a long period of preparation, slowly, laboriously, the result of trained thinking and scientific observation—Galen, Vesalius, Caesalpinus, Fabricius and finally Harvey—in such gradations and through the chemistry of such minds was the fact of the circulation opened to the world. To suppose, then, that a scientific discovery of such magnitude should spring Minerva-like from the head of Zeus-Shakespeare is certainly stretching the bounds of plausibility to the point of infinity. And yet, this is precisely what some of the medical commentators would have us believe, as already pointed out. To suppose further, that, having discovered the great anatomical-physiological process, Shakespeare should have merely and casually only dropped a line here and there throughout his plays appraising the world of his discovery, perhaps only in simile or metaphor,—this certainly rises to the height of grossest absurdity.

Let us look at this matter clearly and logically. Nowhere, neither in fact nor tradition, neither in the official documents of Shakespeare's England nor in the words of close contemporaries, not even in the voluble gossipings of an Aubrey or a Pepys, do we find one iota of a suggestion that Shakespeare knew anything of anatomy or physiology, or of the circulation of the blood, or cared to know about these things. Yet to this actor-poet-dramatist, busy revamping old plays or making new ones for court or pit,—to such a one would some ascribe the discovery of the circulation.

Is it not of some peculiar significance that not until the

deification of Shakespeare in the nineteenth century did anyone discover anything about the circulation in the poet's dramas? And yet we have every reason to believe that the plays were quite popular through all these years.

When Harvey published *Exercitatio Anatomica de Motu Cordis et Sanguinis in Animalibus* in 1628, the book created quite a surprise and also a great deal of controversy. Harvey and his doctrine were attacked in many quarters by Primrose, Parisanus, Hoffman, Vesling, Roilanus and others. In derision they named him the "circulator." Aubrey called him "the little choleric man." Many considered him a quack. Some considered him somewhat insane. As a result, "after his book on the *Circulation of the Blood* came out, he fell mightily in practice: 'twas believed by the vulgar that he was as crack-brained and all the physicians were against him."[1] But through all this controversy no one mentions Shakespeare in connection with the circulation. When the fact of the circulation was finally accepted, there were attempts to detract from Harvey's greatness by proving that others before him had known of the circulation. But nowhere is Shakespeare mentioned in this relationship. Not one single actor of the many who had to memorize Shakespeare's lines during the two hundred and fifty years following, seems to have recognized anything of the circulation of the blood in the dramas. Most certainly, they do not seem to have been puzzled by the lines which the idolators have pointed out as showing Shakespeare's knowledge of the circulation. But on the contrary, Dryden, who certainly knew Shakespeare's dramas, if anyone did in his day, gives Harvey proper credit for the discovery of the circulation:

> The circulation streams once thought but pools of blood,
> (Whether life's fuel or the body's food,)
> From dark oblivion Harvey's name shall save.[2]

Abraham Cowley too, singles out Harvey as the discoverer of the circulation:

> Thus Harvey sought for truth in Truth's own book
> –Creation–which by God himself was writ;

And wisely thought 'twas fit
Not to read comments only upon it,
But to th' original itself to look
Methinks in Art's great circle others stand
Lock'd up together hand in hand:
Every one leads as he is lead;
The same bare path they tread,
A dance like that of fairies, a fantastic round,
Had Harvey to this road confined his wit,
His noble circle of the blood had been untrodden yet.[3]

Neither Rowe, nor Upton, nor Dennis, nor Pope—biographers, critics, students of Shakespeare—none of these, nor the hundreds of lesser commentators, ever mention Shakespeare as having a knowledge of the circulation.

We do find, however, definite opinions expressed against such a notion. Zachary Gray (1754) quoting the following lines from Shakespeare,

Or if that surly spirit, Melancholy,
Had baked thy blood, and made it heavy-thick
Which else runs tickling up and down thy veins.

says, "Shakespeare wrote this, some time before the discovery of the circulation of the blood by the celebrated Dr. Harvey; which was about the year 1628. Had he lived till that time, he would have expressed his meaning with more propriety."[4]

No indeed, in spite of the fact that for over two hundred fifty years, Shakespeare was edited and reedited, prefaced, criticized, staged innumerable times,—search where we may, we can find no one crediting Shakespeare with a knowledge of the circulation. That the knowledge of this great physiological fact did begin to be ascribed to him in the nineteenth century leads us only to one conclusion: that it represents solely the exuberance of idolatrous minds, a manifestation of a wish that is merely father to the thought.

If Shakespeare did have the least idea of the true circulation of the blood, where could he have obtained such knowledge? He could not have read Servetus, or Caesalpinus, or Fabricius, to have gleaned any suggestion of the physiological process in question: their works were not available to him. Some have contended, however, that Shakespeare might have become acquainted with a true knowledge of the circulation of the blood directly through Harvey himself. In fact, one of these commentators, Dr. O. W. Owen, picking passages here and there throughout the plays of the poet and fitting them together supposedly by cipher, presumes to be able to draw out of such, the following actual meaning:

> I have oft seen Dr. William Harvey, the new doctor at Bartholomew hospital, in the presence of the learned doctors, force a purple, distilling liquor through the veins of a dead body, and after it had descended to the heart, liver, and lungs, the blood-coloured liquor returneth againe to the face which blacke and full of blood, or pale, meagre, and bloodless before doth blush and beautifie as if with life . . . The doctor was enrolled at Caius College.[5]

Dr. Owen, of course, is an extremist, the author of *The Story of Sir Francis Bacon's Cipher Book,* which attempts to prove Bacon the author of the plays attributed to Shakespeare. Nevertheless, there are others who are of similar opinion.[6] Let us therefore, examine this possibility.

William Harvey was born April 1, 1578, in Folkstone, England. After attending the school of his native town he went to King's School, Cambridge, and afterwards, in 1593 at the age of sixteen, he entered Caius College. He remained here four years and obtained the B.A. degree. The following year, 1598, Harvey betook himself to the continent and particularly to Padua, where he obtained his M. D. degree in 1602. He did not settle in London, however, until 1604. He was not elected to fellowship in the College of Physicians until 1607. It was in 1609 when he became Physician to St. Bartholomew's Hospital, and 1616 when he began his lectures on anatomy and surgery at the College of Physicians. Not until the year 1628 was his discovery given to the world in his book on the motions of the heart.

Shakespeare then, could not have been acquainted with Harvey's published work for he was dead fully twelve years when the work appeared.[7] He could not have attended any of Harvey's lectures at the College of Physicians for he died the very year Harvey began these lectures. He could not have become acquainted with Harvey at Court because the poet was dead fully two years when James I made Harvey his physician-in-ordinary. Nor could he have met Harvey at St. Bartholomew's Hospital, for by the year 1609, when Harvey became physician to the hospital, Shakespeare had ceased living in London. There are only the years then, between 1604, when Harvey settled in London, and 1609, when Shakespeare left London—only in these five years is there the remotest possibility that the paths of the two men could have even crossed. To suppose that they ever did meet during these years is pure conjecture; there is not the slightest evidence that the one had ever heard of the other. On the contrary, the weight of logic is definitely against such a possibility. For, as Dr. Harris remarks, ". . . the two great men may never have met. Harvey was a student of medicine at Padua from 1598 to 1602, the very time when Shakespeare was at the height of his activity."[8]

Furthermore, when Harvey settled in London in 1604, he was unknown—merely a medical practitioner setting up in practice. He also married in 1604. From what has come down to us of the character of the man, we can be assured that during these early five years of his life in London he was too much occupied with his own career to have frequented disreputable haunts of actors and playwrights where Shakespeare was wont to spend his time. The two men walked in such utterly different paths of life.

But supposing we concede that the two did meet, would Shakespeare, the actor-poet-dramatist, be likely to discuss with Harvey, the physician, the complexities of anatomy and physiology? Would he have propounded to such a one, the entirely new concept of the circulation? By all reason, no! ". . . the young doctor was not in the least likely to discuss with the great actor his revolutionary view of a matter of pure physiology. If Harvey discussed so technical a subject before he gave it to the world, it would have been exclusively with his medical brethren. We should expect from *a priori* considerations, without examining Shakespeare's works at all that their author was not acquainted with the new views."[9]

Having grasped a true idea of the circulation, would Shakespeare then be likely just to casually mention the matter here and there in his plays, and to place the exposition of the circulation in the mouths of laymen? Would those reading the plays—particularly the actors who also had to memorize the lines—would these accept this utterly new and radical conception of the circulation without question? Would not these, as well as the audience, be puzzled by lines purporting to disclose the true doctrine of the circulation? Yet none seems to have questioned the meaning of these lines either during Shakespeare's life or immediately after.

The fact of the matter is this: Had Shakespeare even been an intimate friend of Harvey during these five years, he could not possibly have learned of the circulation, for Harvey himself had not formulated this new conception of the circulation at so early a period. In the preface to his book, *An Anatomical Disquisition on the Motion of the Heart and Blood in Animals,* published in 1628, Harvey mentions the fact that for nine years previously he had experimented, dissected and lectured on the true circulation of the blood; this places his discovery back to 1619. But Harvey was lecturer in anatomy and physiology at the College of Physicians as early as 1615, so that even at this date Harvey had not a complete idea of the circulation. How then could Shakespeare have obtained from him an explanation of the true circulation as early as 1604 to 1609, the years in which the two great men possibly might have met?

But the idolators are not to be daunted. Comes Dr. David Cerna to the rescue in the year 1927, and attributes all of Shakespeare's medical knowledge to natural intuition and to mental telepathy! This commentator fully realizing that, as regards the circulation, "the dramatist did not acquire his knowledge of it from the work of Servetus, and much less from that of Harvey,"[10] inclines to the conclusion that he "did derive his medical knowledge, including, of course, his ideas about the circulation of the blood, from the individual mental observations or actual experimentations made by his contemporaries *through thought-transference*."[11] (The italics are mine.) Dr. David Cerna, of course, is both doctor of medicine and doctor of philosophy, and we fully respect his opinions, but we feel incompetent to argue the matter of mental telepathy about which Dr. Cerna probably knows more than the writer. Nevertheless, it must be remembered that Shakespeare died in 1616, before Harvey himself had a complete understanding of the circulation. So that even by thought-transference, it is extremely unlikely that Shakespeare could have been appraised of the circulation as early as 1607. But then, perhaps, Shakespeare's peculiar "receptivity" of mind made it posible for Servetus to speak from his grave through "unknown ether waves" appraising him, at least, of the pulmonary circulation; or perhaps the vague beginnings of the idea of the circulation, arising in the mind of Harvey while a student reached across from Padua to London to become synthesized in the mind of Shakespeare by some unknown gymnastics of subconscious thought into a complete conception of the circulation of the blood, before such a synthesis had taken place even in the mind of Harvey; for as Dr. Cerna says, Shakespeare "must have had strange visions from unknown powers, visions which his mighty pen would jot down on the spur of the moment, unconscious of whether those visions or conceptions were his own or belonged to others."[12] How grand and easy is the road of Science!

But to come down from the ethereal heights to solid ground again. The truth is, Shakespeare knew nothing of the real circulation of the blood as known after Harvey's discovery. All these commentators have grossly misinterpreted Shakespeare in this connection in order to comply with the rationalizations of their own idolatrous minds. Viewing Shakespeare through the magnifying lens of hero-worship, they have raised up merely the deified image of their own making, creating a Shakespeare all-pervading in genius, all judicial in art, all-comprehensive in knowledge. They have doted upon every word in his plays with such intensity that their very vision has become distorted, and, applying the standards and advanced knowledge of their century, have drawn out meanings which are not there at all. Yet, as far back as 1847, Dr. Robert Willis, who translated the works of Harvey at that time, being aware of those who attributed a knowledge of the circulation of the blood to Shakespeare, warned against just such a 'contemporization' of history when he stated that,

> "The interpretation which successive generations of men give to a passage in a writer some century or two old is very apt to be in consonance with the state of knowledge at the time, in harmony with the prevailing ideas of the day; and doubtless often differs signally from the meaning that was in the mind of the man who composed it. The world saw nothing of the circulation of the blood in Servetus, Columbus, Caesalpinus, or Shakespeare until after William Harvey had taught and written."[13]

In this matter of the circulation of the blood, a study of the passages dealing with it, in proper relationship to the times in which they were written, leads us irresistibly to but one conclusion; that Shakespeare had merely the current notions and only the current notions of the physiology of the circulation, and not our modern Harveian conception of it. Had these medical commentators, who hold that Shakespeare did have this conception—had they been at all familiar with the Elizabethan theories on the matter, and had they brought to their tasks minds cleansed of idolatry they could not possibly have fallen into so gross an error. For all the passages in Shakespeare's works dealing with human physiology can easily be explained upon the basis of the accepted theories of the times.

NOTES AND REFERENCES

CHAPTER V

1. Aubrey, John. **Lives of Eminent Persons,** London: 1813.
2. Dryden, John. **Epistle to Dr. Charleton.**
3. Cowley, Abraham. **Ode on Dr. Harvey.**
4. Grey, Zachary. **Critical, Historical and Explanatory Notes on Shakespeare,** London, Richard Manby, 1754, Vol. 1, p. 228. (I am indebted for this reference to Prof. R. W. Babcock of Wayne University, Detroit).
5. Owen, O. W., "The Medicine in Shakespeare," **Annual Proceedings** of the Detroit and Medical Library Association, 1892-3, p. 110.
6. See Thomas Mimmo, Esq., of New Amsterdam, "Berbice: On a passage in Shakespeare's **Julius Caesar,"** **The Shakespeare Society's Papers,** II, p. 109.
7. Dr. D. F. Harris is of the same opinion, for he says, "Seeing that Shakespeare died on April 23, 1616, it is at once apparent that he could have known nothing of the Harveian views on the circulation of the blood . . . Shakespeare could not have known of his great contemporary's discovery because he died twelve years too soon" **Discovery,** III (1922) p. 132.
8. **Loc. cit.**
9. **Loc. cit.**
10. "Shakespeare and the Circulation of the Blood," **Medical Records and Annals.** 24 (July 1927), p. 445.
11. **Ibid.**
12. **Ibid.** Chesney also felt Shakespeare knew things intuitively.
13. **Works of William Harvey, M. D.,** Tr. by Robert Willis (London, 1847), p. Lxiii (63), Quoted by Overholser, Winfred, in "Shakespeare's Psychiatry—And After" **Shakespeare Quarterly,** Vol. X, No. 3, p. 336.

CHAPTER VI

ELIZABETHAN CONCEPTIONS OF THE PHYSIOLOGY OF THE CIRCULATION AND SHAKESPEARE'S DRAMAS

I

The Liver and the Heart and Their Functions in Elizabethan Physiology and in Shakespeare's Dramas.

To really understand Shakespeare's dramas we must understand the times in which he lived. We must know not only the historical, political, economic and social backgrounds of the great dramatist, but also his intellectual armamentarium. What were the accepted systems of thought in his age?

In this matter of the circulation of the blood, the ideas that were current in Elizabethan England were nothing more than a conglomeration of Aristotelian, Praxagorasian and Galenic doctrines; for just as the ancients came to dominate in literature in this age, so did they come to dominate in science, and particularly so in medical science. Accordingly, there were three main organs in the body: the liver, heart and brain.[1] The liver was considered as the great blood-forming and nutrition-giving organ of the body from which also were supposed to arise the four humors and the natural spirits. The raw materials for these and for the general nourishment of the body were obtained from the alimentary canal "as from a manger,"[2] by means of the mesenteric blood vessels which were supposed to draw in the products of digestion as roots draw in nourishment from the soil.[3] The liver, furthermore, was also considered the origin of the veins which spread by ramifications throughout every part of the body. But these veins were not held as passageways for a continuously circulating fluid. They were considered rather as "vessels or receptacles [to] hold the blood . . . in safekeeping,"[4] since, as Aristotle expresses it, every liquid must have a vessel, or vase, to contain it. These "hollow and round like pipes arising from the liver . . . feed all the parts."[5] By means of the venae cavae, the venous system passes through and becomes continuous with the right side of the heart from whence branches enter the lung, not for circulation, as Servetus proved in his "Christianismi Restitutio" (1553), but rather for nourishment as to any other part of the body, and for the discharge of *fuliginous vapors.* Through the interventricular septum, furthermore, the Elizabethans believed with Galen that a small portion of the venous blood entered the left cavity of the heart by means of perforations in this septum. However, this did not occur as a continuous current but rather (as Galen takes pains to point out) as a distillation, transudation or osmosis, drop by drop "as a torch doth oil." Thus, it is apparent that in the Elizabethan conception of the circulation, the venous system with its origin in the liver and its ramifications throughout the body was practically a separate and closed system with the blood not in circulation in the sense of a continuously moving current under the propulsion of a central pump-organ, but rather in a static state or in an up-and-down movement, or more precisely, a movement similar to that of the ebb and flow of a tide. Or, as Vesalius and other sixteenth century anatomists taught, the three sets of fibers, longitudinal, transverse and oblique, comprising the structure of the veins, had the effect respectively of expanding the vessel, thereby drawing blood into it at a particular area from an adjacent portion of vessel, of contracting and partially expelling blood, and finally of holding the blood at rest, all of which would necessarily result in a form of mild peristaltic motion occurring at various portions of a vessel, the process making it possible to produce movement of blood momentarily in one direction and at the same time in the opposite direction in a different portion of vessel a short distance away in the same vein. The veins then were nothing more than reservoirs from which any local part of the body might draw its nourishment by transudation, replenishment, of course, coming always from the liver. Botallus (1583) expresses this conception as follows:

> As the stomach, when it has digested the food received by the Oesophagus, and delivered it to the intestines lower down, soon calls for more food, so the liver, transmitting to the veins chyle brought by the vena porta and converting it into blood for the continual nourishment of the body, at once demands, as if famished, a fresh supply of chyle. In like manner each particle of the body takes blood from the little veins, not indeed to transmit it to other parts, but to retain it for its own nourishment, and assimilate to its own substance; and the blood thus appropriated and assimilated is soon after resolved into vaporous excretions and disappears. So all parts of the body require new aliment, as the stomach must have new food, the liver new chyle, or the milk glands new blood.[6]

As is already apparent, Elizabethan physiologists considered the arterial system as separate from the venous system, both anatomically and functionally. The heart and more especially, the left side of the heart, was the center and seat of life, of vital heat, "the source as it were, the fireplace of the innate heat, by which the living organism is directed and controlled."[7] It was not merely an organ for the muscular propulsion of blood. Its function was rather one of coction and elaboration of the elements brought to it from the venous system and lungs for impregnation with animal heat. In its cavity (the left ventricle) by means of a "moving and smiting together of the parts of the heart," the natural spirits from the liver were refined into vital spirits. As the liver had its venous system to contain the thick blue venous blood for grosser nutrition, so the heart had, arising from it, the arterial system, ramifying throughout the body to contain the red light *spirituous,* aeriform blood impregnated with "vital spirits" and bringing "natural heate to the other members, and to give them vertue and strength to put in practice those actions and offices, which exercise the same heate."[8] The elements that went to make up the arterial blood came, as already stated, from the venous system,[9] through the perforations that were supposed to exist in the interventricular septum and from the lungs through respiration by means of the pulmonary vein (arteria venosa). But the process of respiration also had another important function. It served for the "refrigeration of the heart by means of the cool air,"[10] for Fallopius (1584) speaks of the vena arteriosa as "bringing air, already prepared in the lungs to the heart for its refrigeration," and Alpinus (1601) speaks of the lungs as receiving "from without cool air, which they communicate through the arteries [pulmonary veins] to the heart to cool and moderate its fiery spirit."[11] This was a conception, however, which Aristotle propounded:

> The animal organism in all cases requires a cooling influence, on account of the fiery kindling of the principle of life within the heart. In animals with both heart and lungs, this is supplied by the act of inspiration.[12]

Like the blood in the venous system, the blood in the arterial system was not considered as having a true circulation.[13] If it was in motion at all, such motion was nothing more than an agitation resembling the boiling in a cauldron. The rhythmic beating of the heart with the accompanying pulsations in the arterial system were held by sixteenth century physiologists to be a direct result of a quality in the blood itself, for it was the blood which palpitated in the vascular system from the internal force of its own vital heat, and not from the muscular action of the heart in the sense we know it today, the pulsations of the heart and blood vessels being merely the passive effect of this cause,[14] or, as Galen taught, the result also of a "pulsatile force" in the walls of the heart and arteries. Accordingly the heart and blood vessels expanded and contracted continuously, the expansion or diastole (contrary to modern knowledge) being the active stage and the contraction or systole being the passive stage. In this way all parts of the body were supplied with vital spirits from the arteries, and "fuliginous vapours" were expelled through the lungs.

The discouerie of witchcraft,

Wherein the lewde dealing of witches *and witchmongers is notablie detected, the* knauerie of coniurors, the impietie of inchan- *tors, the follie of soothsaiers, the impudent fals-* hood of cousenors, the infidelitie of atheists, *the pestilent practises of Pythonists, the* curiositie of figurecasters, the va- *nitie of dreamers, the begger-* lie art of Alcu- mystrie,

The abhomination of idolatrie, the hor- *rible art of poisoning, the vertue and power of* naturall magike, and all the conueiances *of Legierdemaine and iuggling are deciphered:* and many other things opened, which *haue long lien hidden, howbeit* verie necessarie to be knowne.

Heerevnto is added a treatise vpon the *nature and substance of spirits and diuels,* &c: all latelie written *by Reginald Scot* Esquire.

1. Iohn 4, 1.

Beleeue not euerie spirit, but trie the spirits, whether they are of God; for manie false prophets are gone out into the world, &c.

1584

—Bettman Archive

6. Title-page of Reginald Scot's *The Discoverie of Witchcraft*, 1584.

—Bettman Archive

7. Sir William Butts, a well known and highly respected physician of Shakespeare's England who appears in *Henry VIII*.

—Bettman Archive

8. Mandragora plant showing dog pulling plant from the ground (supposedly running mad thereafter on account of the plant's scream). Man supervising operation covers his ears to remain sound of mind. 15th century miniature.

"Give me to drink mandragora . . .
That I might sleep out this great geep of time
My Antony is away."

Anthony & Cleopatra

"Or have we eaten of the insane root
That takes the reason prisoner."

Macbeth

". . . not poppy, nor mandragora,
Nor all the drowsy syrups of the world,
Shall ever medicine thee to the sweet sleep
Which thou ow'dst yesterday."

Othello

—Bettman Archive

9. Charles II of England healing a subject of the "kings-evil" during court, 1679. Engraving.

The vital spirits in the arterial system were supposed to function more or less like our nervous system of today. They were considered the chief instrument of the soul. Accordingly, the heart was the seat of the affections and the emotions and also the source of all the perturbations of the soul.

As to the brain, it was considered as the center of the rational soul, the seat of reason, memory, imagination, etc., with the animal "spirits" as its instruments.

> In the brain vital spirits are:
>
> . . . concocted, refin'd, wrought off, and subtiliz'd, in exceeding fine Arteries, which like so many little Threads plaited and interwoved with each other, make a sort of Labyrinth, in which the Vital Spirit being kept by perpetual Motion, backward and forward, is exalted and refin'd till it becomes animal, that is, sublimated and spirituous to the last and highest Degree.[15]

The final picture we have, then, of the circulation of the blood, as conceived by the sixteenth century is one in which the liver is the central organ of sanguinification and nutrition, etc. Within the veins the blood has an "agitated" to-and-fro or tidal movement. The heart is the seat of life, of vital heat, of the emotions and affections. It acts as refiner and concocter of the natural spirits which it draws out of the blood in the veins, principally through the interventricular septum but also by means of transudation through anastomoses. In the arteries which have their origin in the heart there is the thinner, more refined, "spirituous," "frothy," "yellowish" blood, producing pulsations throughout the system because of alternate expansion and contraction of the blood itself, and not because of any continuous circulatory current with the heart as the center of propulsion as first taught by Harvey.

Upon the basis of these physiological notions (notions that the best Renaissance intellects professed, and to which Shakespeare was undoubtedly heir) we can readily explain all passages in the poet's dramas dealing with the physiology of the circulation. Thus to begin with, Shakespeare places proper, sixteenth-century importance on the three great organs of the body; for in *Twelfth Night* he speaks of the liver, brain and heart,

> These sovereign thrones . . .[16]

and again, in *Cymbeline;* Belarius, Guiderius and Arviragus are complimented for their bravery against the Romans by being called the "liver, heart and brain of Britain."

> To my grief, I am
> The heir of his reward; which I will add
> To you, the liver, heart and brain of Britain
> By whom I grant she lives.[17]

In these passages Shakespeare is merely echoing a general conception of the times. One might almost think that he had Robert Burton's *Anatomy of Melancholy* before him or certain other of the popular treatises of the period. Burton writes as follows:

> As first of the *head,* in which the animal organs are contained, and brain itself, which by his nerves gives sense and motion to the rest, and is (as it were) a Privy Counsellor, Chancellor, to the *Heart.* The second region is the chest, or middle *belly* in which the *Heart* as King keeps his court, and by his arteries, communicates life to the whole body. The third region is the lower *belly* in which the *liver* resides, as a hidden governor with the rest of those natural organs, serving for concoction, nourishment, expelling of excrements.[18]

In another passage he speaks of ". . . the heart . . .—[as] the Sun of our body, the King and sole commander of it . . . ."[19]

Shakespeare is particularly consistent in carrying out this conception of these organs as "sovereign thrones," especially in regard to the heart. He says:

> With tears as sovereign as the blood of hearts.[20]

And again:

> The kingly-crowned head, the vigilant eye,
> The counsellor heart, the arm our soldier

Our steed the leg, the tongue our trumpeteer.[21]

And further:

. . . and then the vital commoners and inland petty spirits muster me all to their captain, the heart.[22]

In *Troilus and Cressida,* Shakespeare writes of Agamemnon as:

Thou great commander, nerve and bone of Greece, Heart of our numbers, soul and only spirit.[23]

Again, when Achilles strikes down Nestor, Shakespeare puts these words into his mouth:

So, Ilion, fall thou next! now Troy, sink
Here lies thy heart, thy sinews and thy bone.[24]

But such similes and metaphors are far from being uncommon in the writings of the day. Thus Gower writes:

For as a King in his Empire
Above all other is lorde and sire,
So is the Herte principall
To whom Reason is speciall
Is Yove [given] as for the governaunce.[25]

Thus, also La Primaudaye definitely writes: "For the heart is . . . not unlike to a Prince or Captaine."[26] Even William Harvey likens the heart to a sovereign king. In the very dedication to King Charles in his momentous book, *De Motu Cordis,* in which is set forth the true circulation of the blood, Harvey does this very thing:

The Heart of creatures is the foundation of life, the Prince of all, the Sun of their Microcosm, on which all vegetation does depend, from whence all vigor and strength does flow. Likewise the King is the foundation of his Kingdoms, and the Sun of his Microcosm, the Heart of his Commonwealth, from whence all power and mercy proceeds.[27]

In this same book, also, Harvey likens the brain to the conductor of an orchestra, to a military commander, to an architect, even to a king. The muscles and nerves he likens to subordinate officers, etc. Witness such similitudes as follows:[28] "An Cerebrum rex" (whether the brain is king), "Musculi cives populus" (the muscles, the citizens or the people), "Nervi Magistratus" (the nerves his ministers), etc. Upon the same basis that at least one of the medical commentators considers Harvey as having stolen the discovery of the circulation of the blood from Shakespeare, we might just as well accuse him, with equal plausibility, of having appropriated his figures of speech from the same source, or perhaps from Burton. It is obvious, however, that Shakespeare was merely thinking in terms of the generally accepted ideas of his time, ideas that permeated the intellectual atmosphere all about him, forming the very basis of Elizabethan psychology. Shakespeare merely molded his language in the thought-patterns of his age. Had the medical critics interpreted Shakespeare in the light of such thought-patterns, had they viewed the great dramatist's medical knowledge in its true relationship to the general conceptions prevalent in Elizabethan England, they could not possibly have fallen into the gross errors that they have. We shall soon see how this bluntness of vision on the part of the commentators led them into the absurd notion that Shakespeare did discover the circulation of the blood.

To begin with, how can we reconcile Shakespeare's references to the liver with any true conception of its function in the circulatory system? Shakespeare mentions the liver only in connection with psychological notions current in his time, based, of course, upon the supposed physiology of the organ current in his time. The liver was considered the seat of blood-formation, of heat-generation. In the psychology of the Elizabethan these are connected with courage and its opposite, cowardice; love also springs out of the heat-generating function of the liver. Shakespeare only voices these Elizabethan notions with regard to the liver. Thus Sir Toby Belch in disparagement of Sir Andrew's courage, says:

> For Andrew, if he were opened, and you find so much blood in his *liver* as will clog the foot of a flea, I'll eat the rest of your anatomy.[29]

Kent calls Oswald, "lily-livered, action taking, whoreson, . . ."[30]

> Thou lily-livered boy . . .
> . . . those linen cheeks of thine
> Are counsellors to fear.[31]

says Macbeth. Bassanio says:

> How many cowards, whose hearts are all false
> As stairs of sand, wear yet upon their chins
> The beards of Hercules, and frowning Mars;
> Who, inward search'd, have livers white as milk![32]

Similarly, Troilus remarks:

> Reason and respect
> Makes livers pale and lustihood deject.[33]

Again Ferdinand, speaking of love, says:

> The white-cold virgin snow upon my heart
> Abates the ardour of my liver.[34]

Says Falstaff:

> You do measure the heat of our livers
> With the bitterness of your galls.[35]

Says Pistol:

> My knight, I will inflame thy noble liver
> And make thee rage.[36]

Says Friar Francis:

> . . . then shall he mourn,
> If ever love had interest in his liver.[37]

John Lyly, before Shakespeare, makes similar references to the liver in connection with love:

> *Top*. I brook not this idle humor of love; it tickleth not my liver from whence the love-mongers in former Ages seemed to infer they should proceed.

And again farther on:

> *Dares.* Now say you, Favilla, is not love a lurcher that taketh men's stomach away that they cannot eat their spleen, that they cannot laugh their hearts, that they cannot fight . . . and leaveth nothing but livers to make nothing but lovers?[38]

Wine is also set down as heating the liver, and increasing courage; and this too is in accordance with Elizabethan ideas of physiology. When the soothsayer says to Charmian, "you shall be more beloving than beloved," she retorts, "I would rather heat my liver with drinking."[39] A similar meaning is implied in Gratano's words to Antonio, "And let my liver rather heat with wine."[40] Falstaff says:

> The second property of your excellent sherries is the warming of the blood; which before cold and settled left the liver white and pale which is the badge of pusillanimity and cowardice.[41]

Most of the writers of the period express similar views on this matter. La Primaudaye says this of wine in relation to blood and courage:

> For it engendereth very pure blood
> converted into nourishment, it helpeth to make digestion in all parts of the body, it giveth courage . . . quickeneth the spirits . . . augmenteth naturall heate . . . maketh good colour . . . .[42]

Thus it is readily apparent that, as far as the liver is concerned, there is not a single passage in all of Shakespeare's dramas that would indicate the poet knew its proper function in the circulation of the blood, but that on the contrary, all his references to the organ merely confirm the fact that he held only the current ideas of his period in this connection.

But it is in the interpretation of the passages in Shakespeare dealing with the blood and circulatory system proper that the medical commentators have gone astray the farthest. In the first place, they have confused Shakespeare's references to the motion of the blood with an actual circulation. No one can deny that the great poet knew that the blood had motion within the veins. Witness but the following passages:

The blood and courage that renowned them
Runs in your veins.[43]

Stands at guard with envy; scarce confesses
That his blood flows.[44]

When presently through all thy veins shall run
A cold and drowsy humour . . .[45]

A dram of poison, such soon-spreading gear
As will disperse itself through all thy veins.[45]

I freely told you, all the wealth I had
Ran in my veins, I was a gentleman.[46]

Runs not this speech like iron through your blood.[47]

And by the royalties of both your bloods
Currents that spring from one most gracious hand.[48]

The veins unfill'd, our blood is cold, and then
We pout upon the morning, are unapt
To give or forgive; but when we have stuffed
These pipes and these conveyances of our blood.[49]

And all the conduits of my blood froze up.[50]

Sluiced out his innocent soul through streams of blood.[51]

But surely, based on such a type of reference to the blood one cannot by any stretch of the imagination claim for Shakespeare any knowledge of the true circulation. There is not one single word here that even suggests our modern conception of the blood vascular system.

That blood flowed within the body must have been evident to the most primitive of men, let alone educated Elizabethans. Bleeding from a wound naturally led to the conception of "streams" of blood. Blanching of the face, blushing, congestions of any portion of the body—these gave all too vivid evidence of blood movements within the body for men not to recognize it. And especially must this have been so in Shakespeare's England, what with all the venesection prevalent and all the psychological treatises based on the external evidences of the emotions. In fact, as we have previously pointed out, the physiology of the day readily admitted of blood movements within the body. And many of Shakespeare's contemporaries refer to such movements. Thus Spenser in his *Faerie Queene* writes:

> Sudden cold did roone through every vayne.
> A gushing river of blacke gory blood.
>
> . . . through every vaine.
>
> The cruddled cold ran.[52]

Beaumont and Fletcher write:

> How the blood runs to the vein
> That erst was empty!
>
> Keep her near here in the wood
> Till I have stopt these streams of blood.[53]

Thomas Dekker writes:

> If ever whilst frail blood through my veins run.
> Shall my blood-streams by a wife's lust be barred?[54]

Chapman writes:

> With damask eyes the ruby blood doth peep,
> And runs in branches through her azure veins.[55]

Massinger writes:

> You will grant
> The blood that runs in this arm is as noble
> As that which fills your veins.[56]

Lyly in *Euphues* wrote, "one droppe of poyson dispenseth itself into every vaine."[57] And there are numerous other examples of similar nature. Yet no one has considered these dramatists as having a knowledge of the true circulation of the blood. It is but obvious here that Shakespeare knew no more than his fellows about the motion of the blood. Far from implying any type of true circulation, the great dramatist rather expressed the current knowledge of his time in this regard, knowledge that seems to have been the common property of everyone in Shakespeare's class.

Elizabethans all knew that blood had motion. But in their system of physiology, this motion resembled that of a tide in a sea, a backward and forward, a to-and-fro movement. This is precisely what Shakespeare believed.[58] He says:

> The tide of blood in me
> Hath proudly flowed in Vanity till now.[59]

And again:

> As true we are as flesh and blood can be:
> The sea will ebb and flow.[60]

Thomas Dekker says exactly the same thing about the motion of the blood:

> Art sure the soporiferous stream will ebb,
> And leave the crystal banks of her white body.[61]

And again:

> You are the powerful moon of my blood's sea,
> To make it ebb and flow into my face,
> As your looks change.[62]

But Shakespeare is even more empathic and decisive on this matter, for he definitely places the movement of the blood "as [an] up and down" movement within the veins, and not as a circulation. He puts these words into the mouth of King John:

> Or if that surly spirit melancholy,
> Had bak'd thy blood and made it heavy thick
> Which else *runs tickling up and down the veins.*[63]

A declaration as definite as this upon the subject is most certainly incompatible with a knowledge of the true circulation.

And such evidence should be plain enough to rise up and refute the idolators.

But more than this. In accordance with Renaissance theories, Shakespeare considers the blood as always *within the veins;* in not one single instance does he speak of the blood as in the arteries. The arteries he reserves for the vital spirits.

> Why, universal plodding prisons up
> The nimble spirits of the arteries.[64]

> Makes each petty artery in this body
> As hardy as the Nemean lion's nerve.[65]

In fact, these are the only two references in all of Shakespeare's works that even mention the arteries. The veins he mentions forty-one times. Why even Marlowe, in the play, *Tamburlaine the Great,* alone, speaks of the arteries at least three times:

> Your arteries, which alongst the veins convey
> The lively spirits which the heart engenders
> Are parch'd and void of spirit. . . .

> May never spirit, vein, or artier, feed
> The cursed substance of that cruel heart.

> And death . . .
> Sucks every vein and artier of my heart.[66]

Massinger refers to them at least twice in the single play, *The Roman Actor*:

> My veins and arteries emptied with fear,
> Would fill and swell again.[67]
>
> When cunning chirurgeons ripped his arteries.

Moreover, Shakespeare likens a "petty artery" to a "Nemean lion's nerve." No one having a knowledge of the true circulation of the blood can liken an artery to a nerve. But an Elizabethan, professing Elizabethan conceptions, could not do otherwise; for, actually, the arterial system was a type of nervous system to sixteenth century anatomists and physiologists. And Shakespeare, an Elizabethan through and through, expressed these views. Had he had a true conception of the relationship of artery and vein in the circulatory system, he would not have spoken of blood only in the veins and as moving "up and down" within these "pipes," "conveyances," "conduits." Nor would he have placed only "nimble spirits" in the arteries.

The more one studies the significance of Shakespeare's references to medical-scientific matters in relationship to his time, the more convincing does it appear how truly and completely the great poet was the child of his age.

But some medical commentators still insist that Shakespeare had knowledge of the circulation of the blood; and they point to the following two passages in his dramas as evidence of the circulatory flow:

> O heavens! why does my blood thus muster to my heart?
> See how the blood is settled in his face.
> Oft have I seen a timely parted ghost,
> Of ashy semblance, meagre, pale, and bloodless,
> *Being all descended to the labouring heart;*
> Who in the conflict that it holds, with death
> Attracts the same for aidance against the enemy
> Which with the heart there cools and ne'er returneth
> To blush and beautify the cheek again.[68]

Here again, these commentators have misinterpreted a movement of blood towards the heart as signifying a circulation; and they have placed upon the word, "labouring," the significance of regular heart-pump action. Nothing can be farther from the truth. These critics, apparently unfamiliar with sixteenth century physiology-psychology, have simply superimposed modern conceptions upon Renaissance doctrines. Why, upon the same basis of reasoning, what shall we say of the words of Shakespeare's contemporary, Philip Massinger (*The Fatal Dowry,* Act II, Sc. 2):

> See, see how her blood drives to her heart and straight
> Vaults her cheek again.

Presto! Take the crown of Harvey and place it not upon the brow of Shakespeare but upon that of Massinger! For in

Massinger's lines the blood not only "drives to" the heart but also "vaults" away from the heart to the cheek! It is much easier to place an interpretation of this type upon these lines than upon those of Shakespeare. The truth, however, is this: neither Shakespeare nor Massinger, nor any other dramatist of the period knew anything of the circulation of the blood. The physiological-psychological treatises popular in Shakespeare's day, especially the *Microcosmos* of Sir John Davies of Hereford, Nicholas Coeffeteau's *A Table of Humane Passions* (1621), Thomas Wright's *The Passions of the Minde in General* (1601), Burton's *Anatomy of Melancholy,* La Primaudaye's *The French Academy* (1594), Charron's *Of Wisdom* (1601), and others—all these readily explain all the passages in question upon a Renaissance basis much more satisfactorily than the medical critics do from the modern standpoint. Thus, according to these works, the heart is the center of all the affections and emotions—joy, hope, anger, hate, fear, sorrow, despair, etc. Burton writes of the function of the "Heart, . . . the seat and fountain of life . . . in joy to send the blood outwardly,"[69] and agrees with Melanchthon who "holds the mountain of these spirits to be the *heart.*"[70] Laurentius speaks of ". . . the heate and moisture influent, which come from the heart, as from a lively fountaine and are conveyed along by the arteries, as through certain pipes. . ."[71] recalling Shakespeare's lines in similarity,

> . . . my heart . . .
>
> The fountain from which my current runs
> Or else dries up;[72]
>
> the *fountain* of your blood
> Is stopped; the very source of it is stopped.[73]

Joy, furthermore, expands the heart enabling it "to concoct a goodly store of spirits and to disperse them throughout the body."[74] Should this joy, however, be too strong it may destroy the heart. Grief, sorrow and fear all of which are present in "a timely parted ghost" at death, cause blood, spirits and the melancholy humour of *descend* and "muster" to the heart from the peripheral parts of the body. As a result, the heart labors and languishes, the melancholy humor quenching the natural heat and extinguishing the spirits to produce death. This *mustering* of the blood to the heart under the emotion of fear is aptly expressed by Davies:

> As spiders touched seek their webs' inmost part,
> As bees in storms into ther hives return
> *As blood in danger gathers to the heart.*[75]

La Primaudaye sets forth more clearly the psychology-physiology involved here. He is discussing the effect of the passions upon the heart, particularly that of fear:

> . . . first of all it draweth in and shutteth up the heart, and so weakeneth the same. Whereupon nature being desirous to relieve and succour it, sendeth heate upon it from upper parts: and if that be not sufficient, she draweth away that heate also which is in the neather parts. By which doing she suddenly calleth backe the bloud and spirits unto the heart, and then followeth a generall palenesse and colde in all the outward parts and chiefly in the face, with a shivering throughout the whole body . . . whereupon it followeth, that by reason of the great beating and panting of the heart, the tongue faltereth and the voice is interrupted. Yea, it commeth to pass sometimes that present death followeth a great and sudden feare, because *all the blood retiring to the heart* choaketh it, and utterly extinguisheth naturale heate and spirits, so that musts needs ensue thereof.[76]

It is obvious that all this *mustering, descending, gathering, retiring* of the blood to the heart referred to by Shakespeare has no significance whatsoever as far as the circulation of the blood is concerned as the medical commentators would have us believe. Shakespeare talked but the language of his day, in the thought-patterns of his age.

From this standpoint, the following passages become simple of explanation:

> I have a faint cold fear thrills through my veins,
> That almost freezes up the heat of life.[77]

Reference here is to the "general paleness and colde in all the outward parts" as a result of the rush of "bloud and spirits unto the heart" under the emotion of fear.

> Seeing too much sadness hath congealed your blood.[78]

> Or if that surly spirit, melancholy
> Hath bak'd thy blood and made it heavy thick.[79]

> Dry sorrow drinks our blood. . . .[80]

In these passages Shakespeare is enunciating the commonly accepted Elizabethan theory that the humor, melancholy, heats and thickens the blood in the literal sense, as a result of the very physical nature of this humor. La Primaudaye, describing the humours in the blood, says: "For the muddy dregs, which commonly thicken and settle in the bottom of it" ("like to the lees of wine in a vessel") "are of the nature of the earth and are called Melancholy." He goes on to say what Shakespeare here says, that this humor thickens the blood.[81] Batman expounds the same ideas.[82] And Christopher Marlowe says exactly the same thing when he puts into the mouth of Faust:

"My blood congeals, and I can write no more."[83]

> Sorrow concealed, like an oven stopp'd.
> Doth burn the heart to cinders where it is.[84]

> The tackle of my heart is crack'd and burn'd
> And all the shrouds where with my life should sail
> Are turned to one thread one little hair
> My heart hath one poor string to stay it by,
> Which holds but till thy news is uttered.[85]

> . . . but his flawed heart,
> Alack, too weak the conflict to support!
> 'Twixt two extremes of passion, joy and grief,
> Burst smilingly.[86]

> *Nor.* He is vexed at something.
> *Sur.* I would 'twere something that would fret the string,

The master-cord on's heart.[87]

My heart for anger burns; I cannot brook it.[88]

My tongue will tell the anger of my heart
Or else my heart concealing it will break.[89]

But break my heart for I must hold my tongue.[90]

. . . throw my heart
Against the flint and hardness of my fault;
Which being dried with grief, will break to powder.[91]

Here again our great poet is expressing the actual physical effects of emotion. In the Elizabethan physiological-psychological systems, the heart expanded and contracted, drawing air from the lungs through the Venosa artery to cool and fresh itself, or, as Burton puts it "to refrigerate the heart," and expelling "smoking excrements" through the same channels, "for the heart hath his filaments or small threads apt and convenient for that purpose."[92] These "filaments" or *chordae tendinae* of the heart were believed to "crack" under strong emotion. The psychologist and contemporary of Shakespeare, Sir John Davies of Hereford, expresses this when he says:

Worke on my Hart, sterne Griefe, and do thy worst;
Draw it together till his strings do crack.[93]

James Shirley expresses a similar notion, only here the emotion is not grief but a mighty joy:

My heart that call'd my blood and spirits to
Defend it from invasion of my fears
Must keep a guard about it still lest this
Strange and too mighty joy crush it to nothing.[94]

Christopher Marlowe, similarly, voices the physical effects of anger upon the heart:

May never spirit, vein or artier, feed
The cursed substance of that cruel heart
But wanting moisture and remorseful blood,

Dry up with anger, and consume with heat![95]

Dekker expresses the effects of grief:

It will so overcharge her heart with grief
That like a cannon when her sighs go off
She in her duty either will recoil
Or break in pieces and so die.[96]

Chapman does likewise in the following line:

And grief's a natural sickness of the blood.[97]

Shakespeare has many more references to the psychological-physiological effects of the emotions on the heart:

The broken rancour of your high-swoln hearts,
But lately splintered, knit, and join'd together.[98]

The execution of my big-swoln heart
Upon that Clifford, that cruel child-killer.[99]

Some devil whisper curses in mine ear
And prompt me, that my tongue may utter forth
The venomous malice of my swelling heart.[100]

The king, thy sovereign, is not quite exempt
From envious malice of thy swelling heart.[101]

Measureless liar, thou hast made my heart
Too great for what contains it.[102]

These passages represent the heart as swelling with the emotion of hate and anger. This is also in accordance with Elizabethan psychology, for as La Primaudaye teaches, the heart swells and puffs up when it is enraged and there is a great milling and boiling about it. Relief for the heart, however, may be obtained by sighing, sobbing, groaning, etc., even though these consume the blood. Witness the following:

Might liquid tears or heart-offending groans
Or blood-consuming sighs recall his life,

I would be blind with weeping, sick with groans
Look pale as primrose with blood-drinking sighs.[103]

When my heart, as wedged with a sigh would rive in
twain.[104]

And stop the rising of blood-sucking sighs.[105]

And let my liver rather heat with wine
Than my heart cool with mortifying groans.[106]

All fancy-sick she is, and pale of cheer,
With sighs of love, that cost the fresh blood dear.[107]

Here also, we have an expression of Elizabethan physiological-psychological reactions. Actually, sighing, groaning, weeping, sobbing were considered by physiologists of Shakespeare's day as affording relief from the effects of passion on the heart.

> For howsoever griefe shutteth up the heart . . . yet by groaning, sighing and weeping the heart doth in some sort open it selfe, as if it would come forth to breathe, least being wholly shut up with sorrow it should be stifled.[108]

Timothy Bright says:

> Sighing hath no other cause of moving then to coole and refresh the heart, with fresh breath and pure ayre which is the nourishment and food of the vitall spirits, besides the cooking which the heart itselfe receiveth thereby.[109]

Thomas Lodge expresses this as follows:

The horrors, burning sighs by cares procured
Which forth I send whilst weeping eyes complaineth
To cool and heat the heart containeth.[110]

Should the sighing and groaning, however, be vehement it might react unfavorably to make these "blood-consuming," "blood-sucking," "heart-offending," as these quoted passages from Shakespeare's contemporaries similarly suggest. Christopher Marlowe writes:

Witness this heart, that sighing for thee breaks.[111]

Chapman says:

. . . I will . . . kiss

Spirit into thy blood, or breathe out mine
in sighs and kisses and sad tunes to thine.[112]

Dekker speaks of:

. . . such heart swol'n big

With sighs and tears.[113]

And Middleton writes:

His sighs drink life-blood in this time of feasting.[114]

Thus Shakespeare was very much at one with his contemporaries in his conceptions about the physiology of the heart and knew no more than they did.

As Ruth L. Anderson concludes from her study of Elizabethan psychology:

> All these passages from Shakespeare possess a literal quality which we have not often attributed to them, for in the works of writers whose interests lie definitely in the field of psychology there is an abundant reference to the power of passion to overcome the actual substance of the heart.

Shakespeare has done nothing more than put into poetic language the commonly accepted tenets of Elizabethan psychology. And all these passages take their proper place in interpretation as directly and literally referring to Renaissance doctrines and not to modern facts of science.

II

The Circulation of The Blood in Shakespeare And in the 'Scientific' and General Literature of Elizabethan England.

But the passages in Shakespeare's drama upon which most of the medical commentators have based their contention that the great dramatist knew the true circulation of the blood are the following:

You are my true and honourable wife,
As dear to me as are the *ruddy drops*
That visit my sad heart.[115]

The tide of blood in me
Hath proudly flow'd in vanity till now;
Now doth it turn, and ebb back to the sea,
Where it shall mingle with the state of floods,
And flow henceforth in formal majesty.[116]

Note me this, good fellow
Your most grave belly was deliberate
Not rash like his accusers, and thus answer'd:
"True it is, my incorporate friends," quoth he,
"That I receive the general food at first
Which you do live upon and fit is,
Because I am the storehouse and the shop
Of the whole body; But if you do remember
I send it through the rivers of your blood,
Even to the court, the heart, to the seat of the brain;
And through the cranks and offices of man,
The smallest nerves and the small inferior veins
From me receive the natural competency
Whereby they live."[117]

Thus as far back as 1845 Thomas Nimmo, who, referring to the first quotation, holds that it "contains . . . a distinct reference to the circulation of the blood,"[118] and Dr. B. Rush Field, although ascertaining that "none of the quotations from Shakespeare express this idea [circulation]" yet cites the second quotation as the one "perhaps" worthy of "excepting"[119] in this regard. And such a recent commentator as Dr. S. M. Dodek considers these passages as "indeed in anticipation of Harvey" and as giving "added confirmation of Shakespeare's knowledge of the circulation of the blood."[120] Even Dr. W. Bristow who definitely states that "Shakespeare did not have any superior knowledge along this line" distinctly considers these passages "the strongest evidence that Shakespeare really understood something about physiology."[121] Dr. David Cerna in referring to the first of the above passages makes the following statement: "We may take for granted that the ruddy drops spoken of here represent the blood itself, and even admit that their visiting the heart implies a sort of going around and around, an encircling phenomena."[122]

Dr. Herman Pomeranz, as previously pointed out, referring especially to the latter of these passages, deduces the added conclusion that "Shakespeare, *before any scientist of his day,* realized that the blood stream also carried nutriment to the organs of the body."[123] Yet Pomeranz himself takes note of the fact that North's *Plutarch* with which Shakespeare was undoubtedly familiar, suggests this in these very words: "It is true I first receive all meats that nourish man's body; but afterward I send it again to the nourishment of other parts of the same."[124] Similarly Burton states:

> Veins are . . . like pipes, arising from the liver, carrying blood and natural spirits; they feed all the parts. . . . That *Vena Porta* is a vein coming from the concave of the liver and receiving those meseraical veins, by whom he takes the chylus from the stomach and guts, and conveys it to the liver. The other [*Vena Cava*] derives blood from the liver to nourish all the other dispersed members.[125]

In defining blood Burton further emphasizes this point as follows:

> Blood is a hot . . . red humour prepared in the meseraic veins, and made of the . . . chylus in the liver, whose office is to nourish the whole body, . . . being dispersed by the veins through every part of it."[126]

Botallus, in the passage previously quoted,[127] adds further definite evidence of the absurdity of the above statement of Dr. Pomeranz and others of the medical commentators on this point of the circulation.

But even Rabelais (1550) discussing this same physiological process writes that:

> . . . the messaraick Veins suck out what is good and fit . . . thereafter it is comed to the Liver . . . becomes Blood

> . . . What joy conjecture you, will then be founded amongst those officers when they see this rivulet of Gold . . . *through the veins is sent to all the parts.*[128]

Indeed, this famous metaphor told in *Aesop,* retold by Plutarch and told again by Camden in his *Remains* (1605), finds repetition in this same Rabelais:

> These fellows . . . I do hate . . . , and if, conforme to the pattern of this grevious, peevish and perverse world which laudeth nothing, you figure and lighten the little world, which is man, you will find in him a terrible justting coyle and clutter. The head will not lend the sights of his eyes to guide the feet and hands; the legs will refuse to bear up the body; the hand will leave off working anymore for the rest of the members; the heart will be weary of its continued motion for the beating of the pulse, and will no longer lend his assistance; . . . the liver will desist from conveying any blood through the veins for the good of the whole . . . The brains . . . will fall into a raving dotage and withhold all feeling from the sinews . . .[129]

This is so close to Shakespeare that one wonders whether he actually got it from Rabelais or the other sources mentioned. At any rate, there certainly can be no question about Shakespeare's consistent dependence on the accepted knowledge of his day. As to the last quoted passage, it can readily be seen as has already been explained that it refers to the blood as of a "tide," a "to and fro" movement, a flow forward and an "ebb back to the sea" in strict accordance with Elizabethan doctrines of the macrocosm and microcosm.

Those that have previously taken upon themselves the task of refuting these medical commentators on this issue have failed completely for they have been lacking in a true appreciation of Shakespeare's background. They have not taken into consideration the extent of knowledge current in this period and most likely to affect Shakespeare. Hence their arguments are specious, inadequate and unconvincing.

In referring to the first quoted passage, Dr. D. Fraser-Harris simply waves aside all argument as to ". . . the ruddy drops that visit my sad heart" by saying that "all that this asserts could be known from observing slaughtered animals, namely, that blood is in the heart."[130]

Had Dr. Fraser-Harris been more cognizant of the significance of Elizabethan doctrines as to the circulation and had he examined Shakespeare's utterances in the light of these doctrines he would have been more successful in his arguments.

In the first place, we note that Shakespeare speaks only of "ruddy drops," and these as merely *visiting* the heart and nothing more. Can any one today who has ever seen the heart in action and who understands the circulation of the blood—can such a one speak of the constant regular torrential flow of blood through the heart and its valves as of "drops that visit . . . [the] sad heart"? Could Shakespeare, having a true Harveian conception of that swirling, eddying, milling circulation, speak of *drops visiting the heart?* Any true knowledge of the circulation is incompatible with metaphorical language of this type. Furthermore, why should Shakespeare speak of these particular "ruddy drops" as especially "dear" and "dearest heart blood"?[131] Again, why should he speak of the "belly" as sending food throughout the entire body, *even* to the heart? Why *even* to the heart? That word has significance here. Had Shakespeare had the least conception of the true circulation he would have known that anything entering the "rivers" of the blood would reach the heart almost immediately and completely. He would not have placed special emphasis on the fact that drops of blood reach *even* to the heart. Moreover, Shakespeare carries this conception further in such lines as the following:

> The blood weeps from my heart.[132]
> My heart drops blood.[133]
> I am sure my heart weapt blood.[134]
> These words of yours draw life blood from my heart.[135]

The meanings here have reference to the definite functions as understood during the period. The weeping of the heart has to be in "drops" by the very nature of the metaphor involved. The eyes also weep "drops." Furthermore, the "heart drops blood" directly in the sense of the very small amount of blood that was actually supposed to enter and leave the heart as precious "life blood from [the] heart."

All these questions indeed can readily be answered by reference to the Elizabethan theories of physiology, theories undoubtedly held by Shakespeare. Only upon such a basis can we arrive at a true interpretation of the passages in Shakespeare dealing with the circulation.

It will be remembered, that according to Renaissance theories, the greatest portion of the blood remained in the venous system which included the right side of the heart. From the right ventricle, however, a very small portion of the blood passed through the supposed perforations in the septum into the left ventricle where it became refined and incorporated with the vital spirits generated in this ventricle to form the frothy blood, carrying "the nimble spirits in the arteries." "But the passage of the blood through these communications was not a circulation; it was a transudation or distillation, drop by drop."[136] From this standpoint we can now understand what Shakespeare meant. The "ruddy drops" of blood that are so "dear" are actually drops of blood and of a better, finer, dearer quality than the rest. And they but *visit* "even to the court, the heart." That Shakespeare likens the heart to a "court" is further evidence that the poet thought only in terms of the Elizabethan physiological-psychological system, for the likening of the heart to a "court," a "counsellor," a "king" is based on actual Elizabethan conceptions as to its functions. The heart was the seat of the affections, the passions, the emotions. All action was supposed to depend upon the judgment of the heart. Ruth Leila Anderson sums up this Elizabethan conception as follows:[137]

> When the imagination has judged an impression from the external senses or from memory, animal spirits flock through certain "secret channels" from the brain to the heart, where they "pitch at the dore" and make known whether the object is good or bad. Immediately the sensitive appetite strives to effect the soul's desire and through

> contracting or expanding the heart either calls in or disperses the humours or spirits . . . if the heart is agreeably disposed it responds readily. . . .

In this fashion did Shakespeare consider the heart a court, all of which is in general accordance with the rest of his beliefs as to the functions of the heart in the circulatory system.

But furthermore: that Shakespeare held the current ideas as to the heart and not the Harveian conceptions of it is evidenced by the following passage:

> But even the very middle of my heart
> Is warm'd by the rest, and takes it thankfully.[138]

From the modern Harveian standpoint how shall we interpret the words, "the very middle of my heart"? Nobody knowing the true circulation of the heart can speak of a "middle" of this organ. And did Shakespeare know of the true circulation he could not have spoken in such terms. However, Shakespeare was perfectly innocent of any true conception of the circulation. In the use of these terms he was merely referring to a theory taught and accepted in all the scientific centers of Europe. This theory considered the septum of the heart containing the perforations as taught by Galen, as a middle ventricle. Mundinus, whose book *De omnibus humani corporis intercoribus membris anathomia* was a widely used textbook in Europe in Shakespeare's day "and the standard guide to anatomy for two hundred and more years after it was written,"[139] actually describes a "middle ventricle" in the cardiac septum where venous blood is refined into arterial blood.[140] Thus does Shakespeare speak of a "middle of the heart," having in mind here, as everywhere else where he mentions the circulation, the Renaissance doctrines of his times and not modern facts of science.

And so we are brought down now to the last-quoted passage in Shakespeare about which controversy has arisen as regards the circulation of the blood. In reality this concerns but the one line,

> I send it through the rivers of your blood.

Because Shakespeare uses the words, "rivers of . . . blood" some of the commentators have assumed that this signified a continuous current propelled by a "central motive power" in one direction. Thus Dr. Knott writes as follows:

> Accordingly, the latter [the veins] are in precise metaphorical language the *rivers of the blood.* And accordingly, too, if Shakespeare had used . . . the term *veins,* as I represented him, he would have displayed an "approximate conception" of the knowledge of the present day on the subject. But if his application of the word *rivers* can be received with exactness, he knew that the central motive power of the circulation propelled the blood *in a definite direction* through the *veins* (the true *rivers*) properly so-called; and his knowledge of the *general* circulation of the blood was complete—there was nothing left for Harvey's discovery to teach him on that head.[141]

He concludes:

> If this passage does not indicate a distribution of pabulum by the circulatory fluid to the various tissues of the body—distinctly foreshadowing the outline of what is known at the present day— I cannot suggest any other interpretation.

And again: "Shakespeare's ideas of the course of the vital fluid appear to be decidedly in advance of those of most of even his medical contemporaries."[142]

Such a level-headed commentator as Dr. Fraser-Harris, even though he definitely states that Shakespeare "held the views which had been taught in the medical schools of Europe for 1400 years—the views of Claudius Galen" nevertheless conceded that this passage indicates some knowledge of the true circulation, for he remarks, "If we had none other than this passage to go upon, we might admit that Shakespeare had before him the Harveian notion of a flow only in one direction."[130] Nothing can be farther from the truth as we shall see. And this seems only to show how such able investigators as Dr. Fraser-Harris and others of his kind have failed to bring to their task the full weight of their capabilities and the broad extent of their knowledge. Why even such an erudite scholar as G. C. Greenwood has failed utterly in his purpose and allowed himself but to become involved in the wrangle of that puerile, superfluous Greenwood-Knott controversy.[143]

Greenwood merely cites the fact that the source of this controversial passage Shakespeare found in North's *Plutarch* or in Camden's story "The Belly and the Members" printed in his *Remains* (1605) and that the poet simply paraphrased this in poetic language; hence Shakespeare could not have known the true circulation of the blood, for he concludes: ". . . it seems quite clear that no particular knowledge beyond that of his contemporaries—no prophetic 'foreshadowing' or anticipation of Harvey's great discovery—can be claimed for the poet on the strength of this quotation."[144] All this is very true, but such speciousness of argument remains inconclusive for North's *Plutarch* does not speak of "rivers of blood" and Dr. Knott rightfully takes the better of the controversy. But there is ready proof at hand to show that when Shakespeare wrote of "rivers of blood" he was not referring to the veins as part of the circulatory system. He was merely using metaphorical language, language common to the day, and quite suited to the thought-patterns of Renaissance England. Even Bacon in his essay on "Empire," refers to merchants as the *Vena Porta* of a nation in the sense of a river. He carries this metaphor even further in his *History of Henry VII* in this manner: "Being a King that loved wealth and treasure he could not endure to have trade sick nor any obstruction to contrive in the gate-vein which disperseth that blood."[145]

Indeed, if Shakespeare is to be invested with the royal toga of knowledge belonging to Harvey then we must do the same for Beaumont and Fletcher, for these also liken the veins to rivers:

> Is it not strange, among so many a score
> Of lusty bloods I should pick out these things,
> *Whose veins, like a dull river* Springs.
> Is still the same slow, heavy and unfit

For stream or motion, though the strong winds hit
With their continual power upon his sides?[146]

We must honor Thomas Dekker similarly for he writes:

That pair of stars that gave her body light,
Darkened and dim forever; *all those rivers*
That fed her veins with warm and crimson streams
Frozen and dried: if these be signs of death,
Then she is dead.[147]

Likewise, on the same grounds, the anatomical physiologist Caesalpinus deserves recognition, for he speaks of "rivulets" in relation to veins: "As, therefore, *rivulets* derive their water from a fountain, so do the veins and the arteries from the heart."[148]

And also Fabricius, for this great anatomist in describing the valves of the veins says that they are "so constructed, in order that they may in some measure retard the blood and prevent *its running pell-mell, like a river,* into the feet, hands or fingers and being impacted there."[149]

Why, Shakespeare himself does this very thing directly when he puts these words into the mouth of *King John* (V, 7):

There is so hot a summer in my bosom
Poison'd,—ill fare; dead forsook, cast off:
And none of you will bid the winter come,
To thrust his icy fingers in my maw;
Nor let my kingdom's rivers take their course
Through my burn'd bosom;

in which words also, is evident the metaphorical microcosm-macrocosm conception of the age, which we shall presently see dominated Elizabethan thinking.

The fact is this: With what the average Elizabethan knew of anatomy and physiology, with what he observed with his own eyes in the stream of blood flowing from a wound, the flushing and paling of the countenance, etc., the most natural thing in the world for an ordinary intelligence to have done, would have been to liken the veins to "rivers of blood." But even more than this, far more important than this, is the fact that the doctrine of the microcosm was accepted as completely by the Elizabethan as we accept the doctrine of evolution today. And:

> To the literary artist of the Renaissance the doctrine of the microcosm, with its intricate series of relationships between the world of man and the universe, was peculiarly attractive. It became the basis of such poems as John Davies of Hereford's "Microcosmos" and Phineas Fletcher's "The Purple Island."[150]

It permeated all the processes of his thinking and pervaded all the complexities of his psychological system. And consistently, quite consistently, in all the descriptions of man in this relationship—man, this "universe in one small volume,"[151] this "world's abridgement"[152]—I say in all these descriptions, the veins are always likened to rivers.

Sir Walter Raleigh has this to say about man as a microcosm:

> Man thus compounded, became a Model of the Universe, having a Rational Soul, with ability fit for the Government of the World, an Intellectual Soul, common with Angels and Sensitive with Beasts; thus he became a little World in the Great, in whom all Natures were bound up together; our Flesh is heavy like Earth, our Bones hard as stones, *our Veins as the Rivers,* Breath as the air. . . .[153]

And again:

> His blood which disperseth itself by the branches of veins through all the body, may be resembled to *those waters which are carried by brooks and rivers* over all the earth.[154]

Rabelais (1550) writes:

> . . . the Messaraick Veins suck out what is good and fit . . . thereafter it is carried to the Liver . . . becomes Blood . . . What Joy conjecture you, will then be founded amongst those officers, when they see this *rivulet of Gold* . . . through the veins is sent to all the parts.[155]

David Person in his *Varieties* (1635) also carries out the idea of the microcosm. He compares the body of man to the earth:

> . . . the rocks and stones whereof are his bones, the *brookes and rivers serpenting through it, the veynes and sinews conveying moistnesse from their fountaines unto all the members;* the hollow of our bowells and of the trunke of our bodies to the vast and spacious cavernes and caves within the body of this earth.[156]

One could probably go on and on quoting references of this character. Is it any wonder that Shakespeare used the terms "rivers of . . . blood"? Can there be any question as to what he meant? Why, it was one of the commonest similitudes of Shakespeare's England, as clear in its Renaissance implications to the audiences as to the poet himself. And yet, this is the type of evidence upon which idolatrous commentators, distorted in vision by hero-worship—it is upon such evidence that they base their contention that Shakespeare knew the true circulation of the blood.

But be that as it may, there are other references in Shakespeare that point toward Renaissance conceptions of physiology. Thus in *The Rape of Lucrece* Shakespeare describing the blood issuing from Lucrece's self-inflicted knife-pierced breast says:

> Some of her blood still pure and red remain'd
> And some look'd black, and that false Tarquin stain'd.

> And *blood untainted still doth red abide.*

Whether this is a poetic flight of the imagination or not is hard to tell but it implies here that the black blood was the result of the staining of her honor by Tarquin's act of rape, the red blood still being pure and "untainted." This brings to mind the point that Elizabethan physiology had not accounted for the fact that the flow of blood from a wound might be red or black, for it must be remembered that they considered the arteries as carrying mainly air. Even Harvey in his *Second*

Disquisition explains this phenomenon on the basis of the size of the orifice from which the blood flows, a small one allowing a brighter color since "it is strained as it were, and the thinner and more penetrating portion only escapes."[157] One explanation is as good as another.

Nor was the true physiology of the coagulation of the blood known in the time of Shakespeare. Harvey in his *On Generation* explains it thus:

> As it [the blood] lives and is a very principal animal part consisting of these juices mingled together, it is composed of a body and a vital principle. When this living principle of the blood escapes however in consequence of the extinction of 'native' heat, the primary substance is forthwith *corrupted* and resolved into the parts of which it was formerly composed . . . Into such a serum does the blood almost wholly resolve itself at last. But these parts have no existence severally in living blood; it is that only which has become *corrupted* and is resolved by death that they are encountered.[158]

The blood then that "false Tarquin stain'd" is *corrupted* blood in accordance with Harvey's explanation. This is further brought out in the following lines from the same work:

> About the mourning and congealed face
> Of that black blood a watery rigol goes,
> Which seems to weep upon the tainted place:
> And ever since, as pitying Lucrece's woes,
> *Corrupted* blood some watery token shows.

And again in *King John* (V, 7):

> It is too late; and life of all his blood
> Is touch'd corruptly . . .

For the "watery rigol" and the "watery token" mentioned here are of *corrupted blood* or of blood "touch'd corruptly" and the end result of coagulation.

Apropos of this, it is well to mention here that it was generally believed in Shakespeare's day that when a murderer was brought into the presence of the murdered and an incision made, the body would bleed. Burton states definitely that a corpse will bleed "when the murderer is brought before it." Sure enough, Shakespeare refers to this in *Richard III* (1, 2) when he puts these words to the lips of Anne:

> O, gentlemen, see, see! dead Henry's wounds
> Open their congeal'd mouth and bleed afresh.
> Blush, blush, thou lump of foul deformity;
> For 'tis thy presence that exhales this blood
> From cold and empty veins, where no blood dwells;
> Thy deed, inhuman and unnatural,
> Provokes this deluge most unnatural.

Many an innocent man was convicted for murder by this test. But the possible explanation for such a thing actually happening may be based on the formulation of the "watery rigol," "watery token" as the result of the coagulation and separation of *corrupted* blood into serum and coagulum, the serum portion possibly actually flowing out of the blood vessel and giving semblance of bleeding.

Shakespeare, also, in at least two passages, writes of "thick blood," with pathological implication which certainly has no place in any post-Harveian conception of the physiology of the circulation but is readily explainable on the basis of Elizabethan conceptions. He puts into the mouth of King John (III, 3):

> Or if that spirit, melancholy,
> Hath bak'd thy blood, and made it heavy thick

And he has Lady Macbeth utter these words:

> . . . Come, you spirits
> That tend on mortal thoughts, unsex me here,
> And fill me, from the crown to the toe, top-full
> Of direst cruelty! Make thick my blood

Of similar significance perhaps are the words of Timon of Athens (II, 2):

> Their blood is cak'd, 'tis cold, it seldom flows;
> 'Tis lack of kindly warmth they are not kind;
> And nature, as it grows again toward earth,
> Is fashion'd for the journey, dull and heavy.

If we take also into consideration the following words of the ghost in *Hamlet* (I,5) with its implication of the normality of the blood as "thin and wholesome,":

> And was a sudden rigour, it doth posset
> And curd, like sour droppings into milk,
> *The thin and wholesome blood*: so did it mine

then we have further emphasis in juxtaposition of the intended meaning in these quotations.

Indeed, all three passages refer to the actual thickening of the blood by the humour, melancholy—"sable-colored melancholy, the black-oppressing humour"[159]—which, as has already been pointed out, thickens the blood in a very literal sense as the Elizabethans believed, since it is "of the nature of earth," "cold, dry, thick, black"[160]; and the "spirits that tend on mortal thought" here are the actual spirits concocted in the heart and brain and liver and present in the blood.

III

The Spleen in Shakespeare and in Elizabethan Physiology and Psychology

It is obvious that Shakespeare handles the aforementioned sovereign organs of the body in a way that any intelligent layman of his day would do, and, indeed, as his contemporaries certainly did do. But along with these organs he also brings in the spleen and implies its functions as understood by Elizabethans. It was the "office" of the spleen to digest and filter off the black *choler* and *melancholy* humour—to purify it as it were. Thus the spleen helped determine disposition and tempera-

—Bettman Archive

10. Henry VIII granting a charter to the Barber-Surgeons. (Painting after Holbein.)

—Bettman Archive

11. DR. CAIUS, who appears in *The Merry Wives of Windsor* as a comic character (unsheathing sword in drawing above), has little connection with the historic Dr. John Caius (below), physician to three English rulers. Shakespeare's Caius is believed to be patterned after a French charlatan named Theodore Mayerne, expelled from Paris College of Physicians. In play he is referred to as "Master Caius, that calls himself Doctor of Physic."

—Bettman Archive

12. EDMUND I giving a touch-piece to a leper.

'Tis called the Evil;
A most miraculous work in this good King
Which often since my here-remayn in England,
I've seen him do. How he solicits heaven
Himself knows best; but strangely-visited people,
All swo'ln and ulcerous, pitiful to the eye,
The mere despair of surgery, he cures
Hanging a golden stamp about their necks
Put on with holy prayers; and it is spoken,
To the succeeding Royalty he leaves
The healing benediction.

Macbeth

—Bettman Archiv

13. Portrait of Paracelsus (1493-1541) alchemist and physician. Copper engravin

ment, and hence entered very definitely into the physiological-psychological system current at the time. Rabelais writes that "The spleen draweth from the blood its terrestrial part, viz, the ground lees or thick substance, settled in the bottom thereof, which you term melancholy"[161]. Burton writes that "the spleen from which is denominated *hypochondriacal melancholy*"[162] [extracts] "melancholy . . . draws this black *choler* to it . . . and feeds upon it."[163] Laughter, gaiety, sadness, anger, envy, even madness, can readily be seen as influenced by the function of this organ in the development of the humours. Shakespeare carries these ideas in his dramas. He writes in *Troilus and Cressida* (I, 3):

> Or give me ribs of steel! I shall split all
> In pleasure of my spleen.

in *Twelfth Night* (III, 2, 72):

> If you desire the spleen, and will laugh yourself
> into stitches, follow me.

in *The Taming of the Shrew* (Ind. 1, 137):

> Haply, my presence may well abate the over-merry spleen.

in *Coriolanus* (IV, 5):

> . . . for I will fight
> Against my canker'd country with the spleen
> Of all the under fiends.

in *Titus Andronicus* (II, 3, 191):

> Ne'er let my heart know merry cheer, indeed,
> Till all the Andronici be made away
> And let my spleenful sons this trull deflower.

in *1 Henry IV,* (V, 2, 20):

> A hare-brain'd Hotspur, govern'd by a spleen.
> All his offences live upon my head. . .

Again in *Richard III* (V, 3, 350) Shakespeare writes:

> Inspire us with the spleen of fiery dragons. . .

in *1 Henry VI* (IV, 6, 13):

> Leaden age, Quickened with youthful spleen
> and warlike rage.

and in *As You Like It* (IV, 1, 217):

> Begot of thought, conceived of spleen, and born of madness.

There are many more references of this nature, but these quotations are sufficient to indicate Shakespeare's knowledge of this particular organ and similar references could be mustered from the contemporary playwrights of this same period, to prove that these too expressed similar views.[164]

The liver, the spleen, the heart, the four humours,—"which four . . . be comprehended in the mass of blood"[165] and distributed by the veins to nourish all the parts, "Even to the court, the heart"[166] where the precious drops of blood are formed into spirits and distributed throughout the body by the arteries, —the brain, "the soul's frail dwelling house,"[167] the seat of the faculties, the noblest and sovereign organ of the body—out of these and their functions the Elizabethans, as reflected in the writings of the period and in Shakespeare, had developed a comprehensive physiological-psychological system that explained everything to their satisfaction.

NOTES AND REFERENCES

CHAPTER VI

1. Robert Burton adequately summarizes this in the following: "As first of the head, in which the animal organs are contained, and brain itself, which by his nerves gives sense and motion to the rest and is (as it were) a Privy Counsellor, Chancellor, to the Heart. The second region is the chest or middle belly in which the heart as King keeps his court, and by his arteries, communicates life to the whole body. The third region is the lower belly in which the liver resides, as a hidden governor with the rest of those natural organs, serving for concoction, nourishment, expelling of excrement." **Anatomy of Melancholy.** N.Y., Farrar & Rinehart, 1927, p. 131.
2. Aristotle. **Opera Omnia.** 3: 234.
3. "While plants accordingly have roots fixed in the soil, in animals the stomach and bowels furnish a kind of soil, from which their nourishment is to be drawn; and for that is provided the structure of the mesentery, with its blood vessels like so many roots." (Ibid., p. 276.)
4. Andreas Laurentius. Historia anatomica humani corporis. Parisis, 1600, lib. IV, cap. II. Cited by Dalton, J. C., **Doctrines of the Circulation.** Phila., 1884, p. 157.
5. Burton, R. **Anatomy of Melancholy.** Lond., Bell, 1896, 3 vols.; see I: 171.
6. Botallus, De Curatione per sanguinis missionem. Antverpiae, 1583, cap. I, p. 17. Cited in Dalton, **op. cit.** (ref. 4), p. 155.
7. Galen. **Opera Omnia.** 4: 472.
8. De La Primaudaye, P., The French Academy: **Fully Discoursed and Finished in Foure Bookes.** Lond., 1618. p. 564.
9. Galen believed that there were actual anastomoses between the small venules and the arterioles, but he taught that any communication between the venous and arterial system from this source was through transudation or osmosis rather than by direct circulatory current. La Primaudaye (**French Academy,** p. 564) echoes Galen's views when he states: "To conclude, the arteries and veins are joined together, to the end that the vital spirits might draw and receive from the veins convenient matter for their nourishment as also that by their heat they might warm the blood that is within them."
10. Colombo. Realdi Columbi Cremonensis in almo Gymnasio Romano Anatomici celeberrisii, De Re Anatomica, Libri XV. Venetiis, Ex Typographia Nicolai Beuilacquae, MDLIX, p. 223.

Cited in Dalton, **op. cit.** (Ref. 4); p. 215.

11. Cited by Dalton, **op. cit.** (Ref. 4); see pp. 133, 135.
12. Aristotle. **Opera Omnia.** 3: 547.
13. Both Servetus (1563) and Colombo (1559) proved the presence of the pulmonary circulation. This was not generally accepted in their century.
14. "In the heart there is a continual accession of liquids from the nourishment; and there expansion by heat extending to the walls of the organ causes its pulsation." (Aristotle. **Opera Omnia**, 2: 550).
15. Charron, P. **Of Wisdom.** Trans. by George Stanhope. London, 1647, 3 books. The original **De La Sagesse** was printed at Bordeaux, 1601. There is a translation by Samson Lennord, contemporary with Shakespeare.
16. Act I, Sc. 1, 37-40.
17. Act V, Sc. 5, 11-14.
18. **Anatomy of Melancholy.** N.Y., Farrar & Rinehart, 1927, p. 131.
19. Burton, Robert. **Anatomy of Melancholy.** London: Chatto and Windus, Piccadilly, 1883, p. 97.
20. **Antony and Cleopatra,** Act IV, Sc. 1, 41.
21. **Coriolanus,** Act I, Sc. 1, 120.
22. **II Henry IV,** Act IV, Sc. 3, 120.
23. **Troilus and Cressida,** Act I, 354-56.
24. **Ibid.,** Act V, Sc. 8, 12.
25. Quoted by Pomeranz, **op. cit.,** p. 495.
26. **The French Academy,** pp. 496-7. Cited by R. L. Anderson in **Elizabethan Psychology and Shakespeare's Plays,** p. 85.
27. Harvey, W. **De Motu Cordis.** London, Nonesuch, 1653.
28. See Dempster, J. H. "Pathfinders of Physiology." Detroit, **Detroit M. J.,** 1914, p. 8.
29. **Twelfth Night,** Act III, Sc. 2, 65-67.
30. **King Lear,** Act II, Sc. 2, 17.
31. **Macbeth,** Act V, Sc. 3, 15-16.
32. **The Merchant of Venice,** Act III, Sc. 2, 83.
33. **Troilus and Cressida,** Act II, Sc. 2, 50.
34. **The Tempest,** Act IV, Sc. 1, 55.
35. **II Henry IV,** Act I, Sc. 2, 197.
36. **II Henry IV,** Act V, Sc. 5, 33.
37. **Much Ado About Nothing,** Act IV, Sc. 1, 233.
38. **Endymion,** Act I, Sc. 3, 9-12, and Act II, Sc. 2, 12-17.
39. **Antony and Cleopatra,** Act I, Sc. 2, 22-3.
40. **The Merchant of Venice,** Act I, 1, 812.
41. **II Henry IV,** Act IV, Sc. 3, 110-114.
42. **Op. cit.,** p. 810. See also Timothy Bright, **A Treatise of Melancholy,** London, 1613, p. 43, and Sir John Davies of Hereford, **Microcosmos,** p. 33.

43. **Henry V,** Act I, Sc. 2, 118.
44. **Measure for Measure,** Act I, Sc. 3, 52.
45. **Romeo and Juliet,** Act IV, Sc. 1, 95, and Act V, Sc. 1, 61.
46. **Merchant of Venice,** Act III, Sc. 2, 258.
47. **Much Ado About Nothing,** IV, 1, 124.
48. **Richard II,** Act III, Sc. 3, 107.
49. **Coriolanus,** Act V, Sc. 1, 54.
50. **Comedy of Errors,** Act V, Sc. 1, 313.
51. **Richard II,** Act I, Sc. 1, 103.
52. I, VI, 37, 2 and XI, 22, 4; 52, 1.
53. **Valentinian,** Act IV, Sc. 2, 375; Act V, Sc. 3, 394.
54. **I The Honest Whore,** Act I, Sc. 1, 97 and **II The Honest Whore,** Act III, Sc. 1. 233.
55. **Hero and Leander,** Sestaid III, 383.
56. **A New Way to Pay Old Debts,** Act I, Sc. 3.
57. "Medicine in the Shakespearean Plays and Era," **Med. Life,** Part I, July 1934; Part II, Oct. 1934, p. 500.
58. Dalton (**Op. cit.,** pp. 151-152) summarizes sixteenth century conceptions on this subject as follows: "The idea of a continuous current, carrying all before it, and moving, under the heart's impulse . . . had no place in their conception of the vascular apparatus. To them it was rather like the slow swelling of the tide, in an inlet already nearly full." Dr. David Cerna (**op. cit.,** p. 444) also summarizes the ideas of the ancients and those of the anatomist-physiologists of the sixteenth century: "They held . . . that the movement of the blood could properly be compared to the rising and ebbing of the tide."
59. **II Henry IV,** Act V, Sc. 2, 129.
60. **Love's Labour's Lost,** Act IV, Sc. 3, 306.
61. **I The Honest Whore,** Act I, Sc. 3, 103.
62. **The Witch of Edmonton,** Act II, Sc. 2, 421.
63. **King John,** Act III, Sc. 3, 42.
64. **Love's Labour's Lost,** Act IV, Sc. 3, 306.
65. **Hamlet,** Act I, Sc. 4, 82.
66. **II Tamburlaine,** Act V, Sc. 2; Act IV, Sc. 1; and **I Tamburlaine,** Act II, Sc. 7.
67. Act III, Sc. 2 and Act V, Sc. 2.
68. **Measure for Measure,** Act II, Sc. 4, 20; and **II Henry VI,** Act III, Sc. 2, 160-8.
69. Burton, **Anatomy of Melancholy,** ed. Floyd Dell. Tudor Publishing Co., N.Y., p. 133.
70. **Ibid.,** p. 129.
71. Shakespeare Association Facsimile No. 15 **A Discourse of the Preservation of the Sight; of Melancholike Diseases; of Rheumes, and of Old Age,** by M. Andreas Laurentius, etc., p. 170.
72. **Othello,** IV, 2.

73. Macbeth, Act II.
74. Davies, J. (of Hereford) Microcosmos. In: Complete Works. Edinb., 1878, p. 38.
75. Nosce Teipsum (1599). In: Poetry of the English Renaissance. N.Y., Crofts, 1930, p. 361.
76. Op. cit., p. 471.
77. Romeo and Juliet, Act IV, Sc. 3, 15-16.
78. Taming of the Shrew, Act II, Sc. 2, 134.
79. King John, Act III, Sc. 3, 42-43.
80. Romeo and Juliet, Act II, Sc. 5, 59.
81. Op. cit., pp. 524 and 341, p. 530.
82. Batman uppon Bartholome, Bk. IV, ch. ii.
83. The Tragical History of Doctor Faustus. In: The Plays of Christopher Marlowe, Everymans Library, Lond., Dent, 1929, p. 132.
84. Titus Andronicus, Act II, Sc. 4, 37.
85. King John, Act V, Sc. 7, 52-6.
96. 2 The Honest Whore, Act II, Sc. 2, p. 221.
87. Henry VIII, Act III, Sc. 2, 106.
88. Henry VI, Act I, Sc. 1, 60.
89. The Taming of the Shrew, Act IV, Sc. 3, 77.
90. Hamlet, Act I, Sc. 2, 159.
91. Antony and Cleopatra, Act IV. Sc. 1, 34.
92. La Primaudaye. Op. cit., p. 451.
93. Wittes Pilgrimage (1599). In: Works in Verse and Prose. Ed. Grosart, 1869, 3 vols., 2: No. 68, 15.
94. The Cardinal, Act II, Sc. 3, 44-5.
95. Elizabethan Psychology and Shakespeare's Plays. Univ. Iowa Humanistic Studies, 3: No. 4, 87.
96. 2 The Honest Whore, Act II, Sc. 2, p. 221.
97. Bussy D'Ambois, Act IV, Sc. 1, p. 185.
98. Richard II, Act II, Sc. 2, 117.
99. 3 Henry VI, Act II, Sc. 2, 111.
100. Titus Andronicus, Act V, Sc. 3, 13.
101. 1 Henry VI, Act III, Sc. I, 26.
102. Coriolanus, Act V, Sc. 6, 103-4.
103. 2 Henry VI, Act III, Sc. 2, 60-63.
104. Troilus and Cressida, Act I, Sc. 1, 34.
105. 3 Henry VI, Act IV, Sc. 4, 22.
106. Merchant of Venice, Act I, Sc. 1, 81-2.
107. Midsummer Night's Dream, Act III, Sc. 2.
108. La Primaudaye. Op. cit., p. 468.
109. A Treatise of Melancholy, Containing the Causes Thereof. Lond., 1413, p. 190.
110. Like Desert Woods. In: R. S. Phenix Nest (1593), in: Poetry of

the English Renaissance. N.Y., Crofts, 1930, p. 160.

111. **King Edward II,** Act IV, Sc. 1, p. 185.
112. **The Revenge of Bussy D'Ambois,** Act I, Sc. 1, p. 24.
113. **Old Fortunatus,** Act IV, Sc. 1, 353.
114. **The Witch,** Act I, Sc. 1, p. 121.
115. **Julius Caesar,** Act II, Sc. 1, 288-290.
116. **2 Henry IV,** Act V, Sc. 2.
117. **Coriolanus,** Act I, Sc. 1, 131-144.
118. **The Shakespeare Society's Papers.** Vol. II.
119. **Medical Thoughts of Shakespeare,** op. cit., p. 78.
120. "Notes on William Shakespeare's Knowledge of Medicine," **Med. Ann. Dist. Col,** I, No. 12, 1-3, 1932.
121. Shakespeare as a physiologist. **Southern Med. & Surg.,** 94: No. 5, 274. (May) 1932.
122. "Shakespeare and the Circulation of the Blood," **Med. Record & Ann.,** 24: 433, (Jl., 1927). See pp. 443-445.
123. Op. cit., p. 500. The italics are mine.
124. Op. cit., p. 497.
125. Op. cit., p. 95.
126. Op. cit., p. 93.
127. See chap. VI, Botallus, **De Curatione per Sanguinis Missionem.** Antverpiae, 1583 cap. 1, p. 17. Cited in Dalton, **op. cit.,** p. 155.
128. Works of Rabelais. Czell's ed., 1733, Phillip Crampton, printer. Cited by Knott: "Bacon, Shakespeare and Harvey," **Westminster Rev.,** 164: 198, 1905.
129. Quoted in Bucknill, **The Medical Knowledge of Shakespeare,** op. cit., p. 204.
130. **Discovery,** 3: 132, 1922. See p. 134, 132.
131. **3 Henry VI,** Act V, Sc. 1, 1. 223.
132. **2 Henry IV,** Act IV, Sc. 4. 58.
133. **Cymbeline,** Act V, Sc. 5. 148.
134. **Winter's Tale,** Act V, Sc. 2. 97.
135. **Henry VI,** Act IV, Sc. 6. 43.
136. Dalton, **Op. cit.,** p. 92. This sentence represents Dalton's summary of Renaissance ideas on the passage of blood from the right ventricle to the left ventricle through the septum.
137. **Op. cit.,** p. 80. See Robert Burton, **op. cit.,** I:290 also Thomas Wright, **The Passions of the Minde in Generall,** pp. 45-46. I am greatly indebted to Miss Anderson for much of the material used here. However, I have not neglected to consult original sources.
138. **Cymbeline,** Act I, Sc. 6, 27.
139. Dempster, W. T. European anatomy before Vesalius. **Ann. Med. Hist.,** n. s. 6: 450 (Sept.) 1934.
140. See Dalton, **op. cit.,** p. 97; also Dempster, **op. cit.,** p. 452.

141. Bacon, Shakespeare and Harvey. **Westminster Rev.,** 164:52 (July) 1905.

142. "The Medical Knowledge of Shakespeare." **Westminster Rev.,** 159: 437, (Apr. 1903), see pp. 442 and 438.

143. See **Westminster Rev.,** 158:304; 683 (Sept.) 1902; 159:437-448; 161-166; 573 (April, May) 1903; 164: 46-52; 195; 552 (July, Nov.) 1905.

144. North's **Plutarch** reads: "It is true," says the belly, "I first receive all meats that nourish man's body; but afterwards I send it again to the nourishment of other parts of the same." Cited by Greenwood: The Medical Knowledge of Shakespeare. **Westminster Rev.,** 159: 573 (May) 1903.

145. I am indebted for this reference to Dr. Pomeranz, **op. cit.,** p. 497.

146. **The Faithful Shepherdess,** Mermaid Series, Act I, Sc. 3, p. 339.

147. **1 The Honest Whore** (Mermaid Series), Act I, Sc. 1, p. 94.

148. **Ut igitur rivuli ex fonte aquam haurivent, sic venae et arteriae ex corde.** Quoestiones Peripatetecoe, Lib. v, Quoest. iii, p. 116 A. Cited by Dalton, **op. cit.,** p. 146. See also Appendix, No. 72.

149. **Ibid.,** p. 149.

150. Anderson, R. L., **op. cit.,** p. 63.

151. Charron, **op. cit.,** Book I, p. 16.

152. Davies, Sir J. **Nosce Teipsum,** pp. 97-98.

153. An Abridgment of Sir Walter Raleigh's History of the World. 5 books, London, 1698, pp. 12-15. Cited by Prof. J. D. Rea, Jacques on the Microcosm, **Phil. Quart.,** 4: 346, 1925.

164. Ben Jonson in **Every Man in His Humour** writes: "My spelen is

155. Works of Rabelais. Ozell's ed., 1733, Philip Crampton, printer. Cited by Knott: "Bacon, Shakespeare and Harvey," **Westminster** Rev., 164: 198, 1905.

156. Varieties: **Or a Surveigh of Rare and Excellent Matters. London,** 1635, p. 27. Quoted by Anderson, R. L., op. cit., p. 63.

157. Bucknill, **op. cit.,** p. 284.

158. **Ibid.**

159. **Love's Labours Lost, I,** Sc. 1.

160. Burton, **op. cit.,** p. 128.

161. **The History of Gargantua and Pantagruel,** Book III, Chapt. 3.

162. **Op. cit.,** p. 131.

163. **Op. cit.,** p. 133.

164. Ben Johnson in **Every Man in His Humour** writes: "My spelen is great with laughter," and in Penates: "This draught shall make him a petulant spleen. But how is he loose or costive of laughter?"

165. Burton, **op. cit., p. 128.**

166. **Coriolanus,** I, 1. p. 130.

167. **King John V, 7. p. 3.**

CHAPTER VII

MEDICAL PRACTICE AND THE PHYSICIAN IN ELIZABETHAN ENGLAND AND IN SHAKESPEARE'S DRAMAS

I

The Doctrines in Shakespeare's Dramas and the Status of Medical Practice in Elizabethan England

From all the mass of laudatory opinion heaped upon Shakespeare by the medical commentators what actual position shall we take with regard to his true accomplishments in this field of medical knowledge? Shall we succumb to the same idolatry so glaringly evidenced in the large proportion of the medical commentators of the past one hundred years? Shall we term Shakespeare "Apothecary," "Physician," "Surgeon," "M.D.," "Neuropsychiatrist"? Shall we throw up our hands in despair of explanation and ascribe to genius the wonder of miracles?

There is a rational road to a clear understanding of Shakespeare's medical and psychiatric knowledge, as already indicated on previous pages. We need but avoid the paths and pitfalls of the preceding century of commentators. Their greatest mistake has been this: they have taken Shakespeare out of the habitat of his century and examined him with the magnifying glass of modern conceptions only to arrive at myopic conclusions. They have removed him entirely from the relationship of his own environment and thereby failed to reach a true estimate in the various fields of knowledge which he displays. Heredity and environment shape life. The forces which moulded Shakespeare's thought-patterns, his attitudes, and his works are to be sought in his intellectual heritage and the environment of his century. It is in Renaissance England that we must place Shakespeare. We must view him as an Elizabethan among Elizabethans, reflecting only the times in which he lived and nothing more. For Shakespeare was truly the product of his age, myriad-faceted with all its aspects and endowed with all its complexities.

If then, Shakespeare astonishes us by his sallies into every field of knowledge, particularly those of medicine and psychiatry, we must realize that it is only the underlying current of curiosity, so characteristic of the age, welling forth in its most appropriate channel. Did not the Renaissance free the human mind from the scholastic prison of Medievalism to send it forth with feverish activity into a thousand paths of intellectual exploration? And does not the blind man who suddenly sees examine and explore everything about him with the greatest enthusiasm?

In this matter of Shakespeare's medical and psychiatric knowledge especially, most of the commentators have strayed from the path of reason because they have failed to take these factors into consideration. Because medical knowledge is abundant throughout the plays of Shakespeare, does that mean that he had any unusual learning in this field for the times in which he lived? Sixteenth century Englishmen were occupied a great deal more with medical matters than we are today, and for very compelling reasons as we shall see. The presence of so much medical material in Shakespeare's works is nothing unique or unusual among dramatists of his day, as so many commentators seem to imply. Dr. Arthur W. Meyers has aptly pointed this out, but it seems that credulous physicians have not taken cognizance of his work.[1] The fact of the matter is this: medical knowledge is also abundant throughout the plays of Shakespeare's contemporaries. Physicians and other medical characters were commonly introduced into the plays of nearly all Elizabethan dramatists—and perhaps with even greater freedom than in Shakespeare's. It seems to have been a characteristic of the time. Thus many of the folk plays delighted in presenting doctors, as for example, the *Oxfordshire St. George Play* which contains "Old Doctor Ball" and also the *Leicestershire St. George Play,* which has a "noble doctor."[2] Thus Heywood's, *The Playe of the Foure P. P.* introduces a "Poticary." Thus Massinger's *A Very Woman* contains one physician, two surgeons and one apothecary; his *Duke of Milan* has two doctors; his *Bashful Lover,* one doctor; his *Emperor of the East,* a surgeon and an empiric; and his *Parliament of Love,* a court physician. So, also Jonson's *Sejanus* contains a physician; Dekker's *The Honest Whore, Benedict,* a doctor; Webster's *Duchess of Malfi,* a doctor; Chapman's *All Fools,* Francis Pock, a surgeon; Ford's *The Lovers' Melancholy,* Corav, a true physician; Marlowe's *Massacre of Paris,* an apothecary and a surgeon; Marston's *The Wonders of Women,* a surgeon, Gisco. Further, Beaumont and Fletcher's *Thierry and Theodoret,* contains Lecure, a physician and several doctors; their *Valentinian* has several physicians; in their *The Chances* is a surgeon. Again Middleton's *The Changeling* contains Alibius, a doctor who understands the cure of fools and madmen; his *The Family of Love* has Glister, a doctor of physic, and Purge, a jealous apothecary; his *Inner-Temple Masque,* Dr. Almanac; and his *A Fair Quarrel,* a physician and surgeon.

Shakespeare's plays contain seven physicians, only four of whom he remembers to name—Cerimon, Cornelius, Caius and Butts, the remaining three, the physician in *King Lear* and the two doctors in *Macbeth,* being anonymous. There are neither surgeons nor apothecaries in his plays, although these are referred to again and again.

Nor are these medical characters, as Shakespeare depicts them, of too high esteem or worth as some of the medical commentators would have us believe; as for example, Dr. Bucknill, who speaks of the "high honor and worth with which Shakespeare invests the physician. . ."[3] saying that ". . . it would be easy to prove . . . that throughout Shakespeare's writings there is no character held in more honour than that of the physician,"[4] and also Dr. Field who agrees with this by saying that Shakespeare ". . . has furnished some of the finest specimens of the medical character that have ever been drawn by any writer,"[5] as well as Dr. Kahn who says that "Shakespeare held the physician in marked esteem."[6] But even as late as 1933, Dr. Macleod Yearsley speaks of "The consistently honourable mention which

Shakespeare assigns to physic and physicians . . . in strong contrast with those of his contemporaries."[7] Yet the very quotation which he mentions proves nothing of the sort. The fact is, the doctor in Shakespeare's plays is not so noble as these imply. On the contrary, he is pictured as a grasping individual, impotent in the face of disease. What of the English doctor in *Macgeth* evincing a belief in witchcraft and the cure of the King's Evil, "that despair of surgery," by the touch of the hand of Edward the Confessor because "such sanctity hath heaven given his hand"? What of the Scotch doctor in this same play with his tactlessness and his mercenary spirit admitting that

> Were I from Dunsinane away and clear
> Profit again should hardly draw me forth.[8]

What of Dr. Butts in *Henry VIII* without any medical role whatever, and Dr. Caius of *The Merry Wives of Windsor* serving merely as "an indiscreet love maker, a rival of the imbecile, Slender,"[9] "a thoroughly farcical eccentric pronouncing everything awry."[10]—the Monsieur Mock-water, the butt of ridicule and the object of cozenage? What of the words that Shakespeare puts into *Timon of Athens*

> His friends, like physicians
> Thrice give him over;[11]
>
> Trust not the physician;
> His antidotes are poison, and he slays,
> More than you rob.[12]

and into the mouth of *King Richard* in prayer,

> Now put it Heaven into his physician's mind
> To help him to his grave immediately.[13]

and into the mouth of *Cymbeline,*

> Whom worse than a physician
> Would this report become?[14]

What of the lines in *King Lear,*

> Kill thy physician, and the fee bestow

Upon the foul disease.[15]

Those in the *Merry Wives of Windsor,*

. . . Nay, said I, will you cast away your child
on a fool, and a physician.[16]

Those in *Pericles*

Thou speaks't like a physician, Helicanus;
That minister'st a potion unto me,
That thou would'st tremble to receive thyself.[17]

What of the lines in *All's Well that Ends Well*

He hath abandon'd his physicians, madam, under
whose practices he hath persecuted time with
hope, and finds no other advantage in the process
but only the losing of hope by time.

and

We thank you maiden
But may not be so credulous of cure
When our most learned doctors leave us, and
The congregated college have concluded . . .
I say we must not
So stain our judgment . . .
To prostitute our past-cure malady
To emprics.[18]

and

A poor physician's daughter my wife! Disdain
Rather corrupt me ever.[19]

and those in *The Rape of Lucrece,*

The patient dies while the physician sleeps.[20]

What again of the line in *Cymbeline* speaking of "the sure physician death,"[21] and those in *Othello* implying the same thing: "and have we a prescription to die when death is our physician."[22]

No, indeed, Shakespeare's allusions to physicians are far

from complimentary. It is true Cerimon was a noble character, and so was Gerard de Narbon, but the latter is merely referred to and plays no part at all.[23] In fact, Helena, the "doctor She" of this play, was taken over bodily from the ninth novel of the third day of Boccaccio's *Decameron,* through the medium of Painter's *Palace of Pleasure* (1566). She is none other than the Giletta of this novel. The truth is that Shakespeare, as well as his contemporaries, depicts his medical characters as no better and no worse than the tradition of his age called for.

What better proof could be had of the attitude of Elizabethan England toward the medical profession than a character study of the principals in this profession, if such could be found? *Character* books were very common in Shakespeare's England and certainly very popular. Sure enough, our search discloses that in the popular *Microcosmography, or a piece of the World Discovered in essays and characters* (1628) written by John Earle, Bishop of Salisbury, both the physician and the surgeon are fully satirized:

"His practice (the physician's) is some business at bedsides and his speculation is Urinall. He is distinguished from an Empericke by a round velvet cap, and doctor's gowne, yet no man takes degrees more superfluously, for he is Doctor howsoever. He is sworn to *Galen* and *Hypocrates,* as University men to their statutes, though they never saw them, and his discourse is all Aphorisms, though his reading be only *Alexis* of Piedmont, or the *Regimen of Health.* The best cure he has done is upon his own purse, which from a leane sickness, he hath made lusty, and in flesh. His learning consists much in reckoning up the hard names of diseases, and the superscriptions of Golypots in his Apothecaries Shoppe; which are rank't in his shelves and the Doctors memory. He is indeed only languag'd in diseases, and speaks Greeke many times when he knows not. If he had beene but a bystander at some desperate recovery, he is slandered with it, though he be guiltless; and this breeds his reputation, and that his Practice; for his skill is merely opinion. Of all odors he likes best the smell of Urine, and holds *Vespatian's* rule that no gaine is unsavory.

If you send this once to him, you must resolve to be sick howsoever, for he will never leave examining your Water till he have shakt it into a disease. Then follows a writ to his drugger in a strange tongue which he understands though he cannot conster. If he see you himselfe, his presence is the worse visitation; for if he cannot heale your sicknesse, he will bee sure to helpe it. Hee translates this Apothecaries shop into your chamber and the very windowes and benches must take physicke.

"A surgeon is one that has some business about his Building or little house of man, where Nature is as it were the Tyler, and hee the Playsterer. It is ofter out of reparations than an old Parsonage, and then he is set on worke to patch it againe. Hee deales most with broken Commodities, as a broken Head, or a mangled face, and his gaines are very ill-got, for he lives by the hurts of the Common-Wealth. He differs from the physitian as a sore do's from a disease or the sickle from those that are not whole, the one distempers you within, and the other blisters you without. He complains of the decay of Valour in these daies and sighs for that Slashing Age of Sword and Buckler, and thinkes the law against Duels was made merely to wound his Vocation. Hee had long since beene undone, if the Charities of the Stewes had not relieved him, from whom he ha's his Tribute as duely as the Pope or a wind-fall some-times from a Taverne, if a quart Pot hit right. The rareness of his custome maks him pittelesse when it comes: and he holds a patient longer than our Courts a Cause. Hee tells you what danger you had been in if he had staide but a minute longer, and thought it be but a prick't finger, hee makes of it much matter."[24]

The Guls Hornbook, a popular book of the day, has this to say on the matter:

> Physicians, I know (and none else) took up the bucklers in their defence, railing bitterly upon that venerable and princely custom of long lying-abed. Yet, now I remember me I cannot blame them; for they which want sleep (which is man's natural rest) become either mere *Naturals,* or else fall into the Doctor's hands, and so con-

sequently into the Lord's: whereas he that snorts profoundly scorns to let Hippocrates himself stand tooting on his Urinal, and thereby saves that charge of a groats worth of *physic*. . . . Insomuch that even their sick grunting patients stand in more danger of M. Doctor and his drugs, than of all the Cannon shots which the desperate disease itself can discharge against them. Send them packing, therefore, to walk like *Italian Mountebanks,* beat not your brains to understand their parcel-Greek, parcel-Latin gibberish.[25]

Burton in his *Anatomy of Melancholy* says this of physicians and surgeons of his day: "Many of them, to get a fee, will give physic to everyone that comes . . . when there is no cause . . . stirring up a silent disease, and making a strong body weak . . . or, as an hungry Chirurgeon . . . Harpylike to make a prey of his patient . . . often produce and wife-draw his cure, so long as there is any hope of pay."[26] Likewise, Latimer severely censures the mercenary physicians of his day: "But now in our days physick is a remedy prepared only for rich folks, and not for poor, for the poor man is not able to wage the physician. . . . Physicians in our time seek only their own profits . . . But God will find them out one day, I doubt not."[27] Stubbes says of some physicians that "if they hope for any preferment by their patient's death, will give them such medicines, such potions and drinks as will soon make an end of them."[28]

Lord Bacon, also, in *The Advancement of Learning,* takes his fling at the physician of the day: "In the enquiry of diseases, they do abandon the cure of many, some as in their nature incurable, and others as past that period of cure, so that Sylla triumvira never prescribed so many men to die as they do by their ignorant edicts."[29] Thomas Dekker, too speaks depreciatingly of the physician when he says that during the plague of 1603 they "hid their synodical heads." Again, Barnaby Rich, a contemporary of Shakespeare, who in his *Appollonius and Sylla,* provided Shakespeare with the principal events for *Twelfth Night,* says of the physician that ". . . if he cannot speedily cure you, he will yet quickly kill you."[30]

Examples of this nature can be multiplied many times from

the contemporary literature and indicate definitely that Shakespeare was only following the general tradition of the times, in making the physician not "noble," but ignoble.

Why, even Chaucer, several centuries back, lampoons the physician, and, numerous are the dramatists that follow his lead. Chaucer characterizes his "noble Doctor of Physic" thus:

And yet he was but easy to dispense,
He kepte what he won in pestilence
For gold in physic is a cordial
Therefor he loved gold in special

In "The Marriage of Witt and Wisdom," an anonymous interlude written in 1579, the physician is also chastised. Idleness, representing vice, says this of him:

Now shall you heare how kindly Master Doctor
Can play the outlandish man,
Ah, by Got, me be the Doctor
Me am the fine knave, I tell you.

The bee have no so many herbes
Whereout to suck hony,
As I can find shifts whereby to get money.[31]

In Middleton's *A Fair Quarrel,* the physician plays the part of villain and is denounced by Jane, his patient,

Away, you are a blackamoor! . . .
. . . Are you the man
That in your painted outside seemed so white?
O' you're a foul dissembling hypocrite!
You saved from a thief that yourself might rob me;
Skinned over a green wound to breed an ulcer:
Is this the practice of your physic-college?[32]

And again:

Torment me not,
Thou lingering executioner to death,
Greatest disease to Nature, that striv'st by art
To make men long a-dying! Your practice is

Upon men's bodies, as men pull roses
For their own relish, but to kill the flower,
So you maintain your lives by other's deaths.
What eat you then but carrion?[33]

Beaumont and Fletcher seem to be particularly fond of ridiculing medical men as pretenders, pedants, mercenary scoundrels:

I'll send you a doctor of mine own and after
Take order for your funeral.[34]

The doctors are our friends; let's please them well;
For, though they kill but slow, they are certain, Diego.[35]

Drink, drink, ye dunces!
What can your doses now do, and your scrapings,
Your oils, and mithridates? If I do die
Your only words of health, and names of sicknesses,
Finding no true disease in many but money,
That talk your patients into revenues—Oh!
And, ere ye kill your patients, beggar em
I'll have ye flayed and dried![36]

Thomas Dekker, too, adds many a diatribe against the physicians of his day:

Meet you, Sir? he might have met with three
fencers in his time, and received less hurt than by
meeting one doctor of Physic.[37]

Duke. Who told me that Hippolite was dead?
Cas. He that can make any man dead, the doctor.[38]

. . . hunger is an excellent physician
For he dares kill anybody.[39]

So does Ben Jonson:

Most of your doctors are the greater danger
And worse disease to escape.[40]

I often have heard him protest that your
physician should never be his heir.[41]

You make no more haste now, than a beggar upon
palters; or a physician to patient that has no
money.[42]

and Webster:

physicians thus
With their hands full of money, use to give o'er
Their patients.[43]

She'll use some prepared antidote of her own
Lest the physicians should re-poison her.[44]

and John Ford:

... thou takest upon thee the habit of a grave physician, but thou art indeed an impostorous empiric. Physicians are the cobblers, rather the botchers of men's bodies.[45]

and Chapman:

As fat
As a physician, and as giddy-headed.[46]

She talks to tinkers, pedlars, porters
Chimney-sweepers, fools and physicians. ...[47]

Thus, on and on. In the words of Dr. Fletcher "... the average doctor of the sixteenth century was a compound of ignorance and knavery, with an occasional dash of pedantry. In all the literatures of the period in question I cannot call to mind a decided instance to the contrary. If he be not a charlatan or a pedant he is merely a lay-figure in a doctor's gown and cap, like the physician in *Macbeth.*"[48]

Indeed, as Creighton says, "it would have been anachronism in England by more than two hundred years to have represented a physician as caring for any but paying patients or as regarding an epidemic sickness from any other point of view than as a source of income."[49] Why even in an Act of Parliament to regulate the practice of Surgery in 1542 "the Company and Fellowship of Surgeons of London" are branded as "... minding only their own lucres, and nothing the profit or ease of the diseased or patient...."

As mentioned before, the only physician in Shakespeare's works whom we may term really noble is Cerimon in *Pericles.* Since *Pericles* was written after Shakespeare acquired Dr. Hall as his son-in-law, (and Dr. Hall was a physician of repute), it has been suggested that he supplied the main features of this only noble doctor. Perhaps this is so. Perhaps Shakespeare knew of them. Perhaps he was familiar with most of the members of the Royal College of Physicians. Or perhaps, even, he had in mind, Edmund, Earl of Denby, who "was famous for chirurgerie, bone-setting, and hospitalitie," as Ward says in his Diary, or the Marquis of Dorchester, who was a Fellow of the Royal College of Surgeons.[50] However, is there not some significance in the fact that the only doctor in Shakespeare that we may term of "high honor and worth" is the only doctor given a noble rank—that of "Lord Cerimon"? And may not Shakespeare have made him "noble" in deference to Lordship rather than to physician-ship? Actually, the dramatis personae lists him as Lord Cerimon and not as Doctor Cerimon.

Dr. Butts of *Henry VIII* and Dr. Caius of the *Merry Wives of Windsor,* as the names seem to imply, have been suggested as referring to historical personages. If this is the case, either Shakespeare was ignorant of their true qualities and reputations or else set out deliberately to burlesque them. Or, as a third possibility, he may have made them to comply with public expectations of the medical character.

The real Dr. Butts was a man of note—physician to Henry VIII and Princess Mary, friend of Wolsey, Grammer, and Latimer. That he was held in high honor is evidenced by the fact that he was knighted Sir William Butts, that his portrait is included in Holbein's famous painting of Henry VIII, and that in the *Annals of the Royal College of Surgeons* he is recorded as follows: "Vir gravis; eximia literarum cognitione, sigulari judicio, summa experientia, et purdenti consilio doctor." [51]

There is an even greater incongruity between the irascible French Dr. Caius, the "Master Doctor Caius, the renowned physician" of Shakespeare and the real Dr. Caius of Shakespeare's day. The real John Caius was a versatile individual, naturalist, linguist, antiquary, distinguished physician to Edward VI, Mary and Elizabeth. He was the first to introduce the study of practical Anatomy into England. He is the author of *A Boke of Consseill against the Sweatynge Sickness,* and of numerous books on the Greek and Latin medical authors. Fuller in his *English Worthies* couples him with Linacre, "I may call these two doctors the two phenixes of their profession in our nation."[52] It was of this Dr. Caius too, that Osler said, "Johannes Caius is one of the great figures in our history."[53] Brandes suggests that Shakespeare used Dr. Caius as a vehicle for the production of comic effects through his broken English, having availed himself of the same device in *Henry V,* through a Welshman and a Frenchman.[54] However because the Dr. Caius of Shakespeare is made comic by virtue partly of his French accent, it has been suggested that this doctor was really meant to be a take-off on the famous French physician Sir Theodore Turquet de Mayerne (1573-1655), a refugee and expatriate from France. This Dr. Mayerne, considered by many to be the most famous physician of Shakespeare's day, was involved in the then heated controversy of the Galenists and anti-Galenists or followers of Paracelsus who advocated the use of antimony and other metals in treatment. It was this Dr. Mayerne who introduced calomel into practice. He had formerly been physician to Henry IV of France and had attended him in his last illness, the history of which he wrote. Partly because of his anti-Galenism and partly perhaps because he was a Protestant, he found himself expelled from the profession by an Aesculpian "bull" of the University of Paris faculty and he fled to England in 1607 where he soon became physician to Charles I. It was during Shakespeare's life and later that the controversy raged among the medical men of England and France—focused on the so-called "antimonyall cup"—with Mayerne as one of the centers of this controversy. Dr. Mayerne, expatriate of France, had a French accent. In a London of 150,000-200,000 population, Shakespeare probably saw and heard him. He undoubtedly knew of the controversy of the physicians and probably looked at it with the amusement expected of a layman. It certainly could not add to his already low general opinion of the medical profession. Perhaps Dr. Mayerne represented one element only in the composite picture

Shakespeare drew in the person of Dr. Caius. At any rate, Shakespeare does refer in accepted casualness to the controversy mentioned above. He speaks of the "schools" involved thus:

> How shall they credit
> A poor *unlearned* virgin when the *schools*
> *Embowell'd of their doctrine,* have left off
> The danger to itself.[55]
>
> *Par.* Why, 'tis the rarest argument of wonder, that
> hath shot out in our latter times
> *Ber.* To be *relinquished of the artists,*—
> *Par.* So I says, both of *Galen and Paracelsus*
> *Laf.* Of all the *learned and authentic fellows,*[56]

It is interesting to note as to the eventual outcome of this controversy and the importance of our Dr. Mayerne that in 1645 the House of Commons received from the House of Lords, and passed, the following resolution:

> The Lords desire that the House of Commons would join with them in expressing their esteem of a man whose extraordinary abilities would make him welcome in any part of Christendom; and, as he is singular for his knowledge in his profession so he may be singular in being by favor of the House exempted from all payments which others are subject to; it being but a continuation of that favour which he hath enjoyed for about thirty years without interruption.[57]

The inscription on Mayerne's tomb calls him the "second Hippocrates, health-bringer to the whole world, ornament of his age, the shamer of his opponents and exemplar to his successors. . ." Mayerne's portrait hangs in the National Portrait Gallery.

However, be that as it may, there was a physician in the sixteenth century that might have suggested Caius to Shakespeare. It was Dr. Andrew Borde, "a learned genial and sensible doctor" possessing "a rambling head and an inconstant brain."[58] It was this same doctor, author of the *Breviary of Health, The Dietary of Health* and *The Book of the Introduction to Knowledge,* who rightfully earned the appropriate title, "Merry Andrew," as a result of his hilarious conduct and buffoonery at the innumerable fairs and revels he attended. If we must have a prototype for the Caius of the *Merry Wives of Windsor,* then let it be "Merry Andrew" Borde and not John Caius. Or better still let it be our Andrew Borde with the French accent of Dr. Mayerne.

Shakespeare's doctors all play minor roles. They are entered into the plays merely as incidentals and are rarely made the instruments for the greater portion of the poet's medical utterances: "Indeed, it would be impossible to recognize the physicians themselves from the utterances which they express."[59] It is the laymen in his plays that show the greatest medical knowledge as we shall presently see. Surely if Shakespeare had wanted to exalt the physicians, he would certainly have done so in a more flattering manner. But then, as already pointed out, he was picturing the age in which he lived.

The very fact that Shakespeare composed similes and metaphors involving medical terms, such as names of diseases, anatomic parts of the body, etc., the very fact that he even built comedy dependent on medical materials, is proof enough that his audience, from Lord to groundling, was familiar with such medical terms and such medical materials, and that these were on everyone's tongues. Thus in *Henry V* there is a deliberate attempt at comedy in the coupling of the term "quotidian" and "tertian." From the frequency of malaria or ague in Shakespeare's day it was well known by everyone that in the one type of the disease the fever occurs every day, where as in the other, it occurs every other day. But Dame Quickly in Shakespeare's play, wishing to impress upon her hearers the gravity of Sir John's illness, is made to use the two terms in conjunction:

> As ever you come of woman, come in quickly to
> Sir John: Ah, poor heart He is so shake'd of a
> burning *quotidian tertian* that it is most lament-
> able to behold. Sweet men, come to him.[60]

If the audience had not been familiar with the quotidian and tertian fevers would Shakespeare have jested with them about it? Similarly, in *Much Ado About Nothing* Shakespeare produces humor through the means of a play on medical material.

> O Lord, He will hang upon him like a disease:
> *he is no sooner caught than the pestilence and*
> the taker runs presently mad. God help the noble
> Claudio! *If he have caught the Benedick,* it will
> cost him a thousand pound ere he be cured.[61]

Again in *Henry IV* Shakespeare composes a metaphor based on the incurability of consumption:

> I can get no remedy against this consumption
> of the purse: borrowing only lingers and lingers
> it out, but the disease is uncurable.[62]

Likewise, in *Henry VI*:

> As fester'd members rot but by degrees
> Till bones, and flesh, and sinews, fall away,
> So will this base and envious discord breed.[63]

There are other lines of similar character. All tend to show how very familiar the medical material involved must have been to the Elizabethan audience. Certainly, the fact that similar medical materials appear as frequently in other contemporary dramatists' works as in Shakespeare's is further proof of this assertion, and indicates that Shakespeare knew no more than his fellows as regards medical matters. Thus, in Thomas Middleton's *The Widow* (V, 2) palsy, gout, fistula in ano, ulcer, megrim, rupture, imposthume, gangrene, squinancy (quinsy), canker, pricking aches, hernia in Scrotum, apostemates—all these and more are mentioned in the casual dialogue of the regular characters. "We shall have thee . . . look like quartan ague and the black jaundice," says Ben Jonson in *Bartholomew Fair* (I, 1). ". . . I have a special friend with a quartan ague. . ." remarks a character in Beaumont and Fletcher's *A King and No King* (III, 2). Philip Massinger in the *Roman Actor* (II, 1), is responsible for the following lines bearing on this matter:

> *Parth.* But you destroy her in your want of care
> (I blush to see and speak it) to maintain her

In perfect health and vigour; when you suffer—
Frighted with the charge of physic-rheums, catarrhs,
The scurf, ache in your bones, to grow upon you
And hasten to your fate with too much sparing:
When a cheap purge, a vomit, and a good diet,
May lengthen it. Give me but leave to send
The emperor's doctor to you.

Phil. I'll be born first
Half rotten, to the fire that must consume me!
His pills, his cordials, his electuaries,
His syrups, juleps, bezoar stone, nor his
Imagined unicorn's horn, comes in my belly;
My mouth shall be draught first, 'tis resolved.

"This incision is not deep, nor the orifice exorbitant, the *pericranium* is not dislocated. . ." says Pock in George Chapman's *All Fools* (III, 1).

And here he feels me
With rotten ends of rocks and drowned chickens
Stewed *pericraniums* and *pia maters*.

says Antonio in Beaumont and Fletcher's *The Chances* (III, 2). Thus, on and on—even terms which would today be considered tcehnical are freely used and placed in the mouths of ordinary characters. Such examples can be multiplied manifold from other dramatists of the period. The medical knowledge involved represents the general knowledge of the average intelligent layman of the day.

Medical knowledge, in fact, was diffused among laymen to a much greater extent in Shakespeare's day than it is today. The reason for this is obvious. There was a great deal more of sickness in Shakespeare's day than there is today. Since medicine had not yet become scientific, since it had not yet freed itself from the trammels of superstition, magic and authority, since the doctor was not held in high esteem and was rarely called upon, at least by the masses, medical knowledge and medical practice remained in the hands of anybody and everybody. Empiricism was the order of the day. As a matter of fact, the first Act of the English Parliament dealing with the medical profession, 1511, puts into the preamble:

"For as much as the science and cunning of Physick and Surgery . . . is daily within this realm exercised by a great multitude of ignorant persons, of whom the greater part have no manner of insight in the same, nor in any other kind of learning; some also can read no letters on the book, so far forth that common artificers, as smiths, weavers and women, boldly and accustomably take upon them great cures, and things of difficulty in which they partly use sorcery and witchcraft, partly apply such medicines unto the disease as be very noxious . . . to the grievous hurt, damage and destruction of many of the king's liege people. . . Be it . . . enacted: That no person within the city of London . . . take upon him to exercise and occupy as a physician or Surgeon except he be first examined, approved and admitted by the Bishop of London. . ."[64]

But in 1542, the English Parliament reversed itself because it conferred the right to practice the healing art on "Every person being the King's subject having knowledge and experience of the nature of herbs, roots and waters, or the operation of the same by speculation or practice."[65] And this was done because medical men were "minding only their own lucres." In accordance with this we read that the Company of Barber-Surgeons after the proper examination licensed "James Vanetten and Nicholas Bowlden . . . to practice for the couchinge of catarack, cuttinge for the rupture, stone and wenne," allowing Edward Stutfeyld to set up as "a practitioner in bone settinge," and Joseph Johnson as "a practitioner in the cure of a fistula."[66] Similarly we find Queen Elizabeth, through her prime minister Walsingham requesting of the Royal College of Physicians that they allow "one Margaret Kennix, a poor woman, to quietly practice and minister to curing of diseases and wounds by means of certain simples, in the applying whereof it seemeth God hath given her especial knowledge."[67]

Dr. John Halle, possibly the father of Shakespeare's son-in-law, in his book *An Historical Expostulation Against the Beastly Abuses both of Chirurgery and Physyke in our Tyme* (1565), says: "Why is every rude, rusticke, braynsicke beast, fond fool, indiscrette idiots; ye every scoldinge drabbe suffered thus . . . to abuse this worthy arte upon the body of man? . . . What meaneth it, I saye . . . that so many sheepe heads, unwytly, unlearned . . . dronkards, beastly gluttons . . . envious, evill mannerred, shall thus myserably be suffered to abuse so noble an arte."[68]

From an old book entitled *Tom of All Trades, or the Plaine Pathway to Preferment* (1631), by Thomas Powell, we get further evidence of the practitioners of Shakespeare's day:

"And here I remember me of an old tale following, viz., at the beginning of happy raigne of our late good Queen Elizabeth, divers Commissioners of great place, being authorized to enquire of, and to displace, all such of the Clergie as would not conforme to the reformed Church, one amongst others was convented before them who being asked whether he would subscribe or not, denied it, and so consequently was advised to lose his benefice and to be deprived his function; whereupon, in his impatience, he said, 'That if they (meaning the Commissioners) held this course it would cost many a man's life' . . . And being asked whether hee spake these words or no, he acknowledged it, and took upon him the justification thereof; for, said he 'yee have taken from me my living and profession of the Ministrie; Schollership is all my portion, and I have no other means left for my maintenance but to turn Physition; and before I shall be absolute master of that Misterie (God he knows) how many mens lives it will cost. For few physitions use to try experiments upon their owne bodies. With us, it is a Profession can maintain but a few. And divers of these more indebred to opinion than learning, and (for the most part) better qualified in discoursing their travailes than in discerning their patients malladies. For it is growne to be a very huswives trade, where fortune prevailes more than skill."[69]

In Nicholas Gyer's *The English Phlebotomy,* published in 1592, we have the complaint that phlebotomy "is greatly abused by vagabond horse-leaches and travailing tinkers, who find work almost in every village through which it comes (having in truth neither knowledge or witte, nor honesty), the sober practitioner and cunning chirurgeon liveth basely, is despised and accounted in every abject among the vulgar sort."[70] Similarly Dr. Thomas Gale who was a surgeon during the wars of Henry VIII, complained in 1563 of the "great rabblement there, that took upon them to be surgeons. Some were pig-doctors, some were horse-doctors, some tinkers and cobblers."[71]

Nor was the practice of the healing art in Shakespeare's day limited to the laymen of the lower classes. Bulleyn mentions many medical and surgical amateurs among the nobility, such as Sir Thomas Eliot, Sir Philip Parras, Sir William Gasgoyne, Lady Taylor and Lady Darrel, and especially that "goodly hurtlesse Gentleman, Sir Andrew Haveningham, who learned a water to kill a canker of his own mother."[72] Even James IV of Scotland was "such a cunning Chirurgeon that none of his realm who used that craft but would take his counsel in all their proceedings."[73]

We need only add to this, the testimony of Dr. Caius, second president of the Royal College of Physicians, who enumerates "simple women, carpenters, pewterers, braziers, soap-ball sellers, apothecaries, and avaunters themselves,"[74] as practicing the healing art; and the testimony of Dr. Cotta who in his *Short Discoverie* (1612) mentions "midwives, cooks, priests, witches, conjurers, jugglers and fortune tellers,"[75] as practicing medicine, and finally that of the famous surgeon of Shakespeare's day, William Clowes who speaks of "tinkers, tooth-drawers, peddlers, catlers, carters, porters, horse-gelders, and horse-leeches, idiots, apple-spires, broom-men, bawds, witches, conjurers, soothsayers and sow-gelders, rogues, rat-catchers, runagates and procters of spittle houses,"[76] as practicing surgery,—to realize why Shakespeare puts practically all the medical knowledge in his plays into the mouths of laymen. With such a state of affairs existing is it any wonder that medical knowledge was more folklore than fact, more superstition than science—as much of the concern of the layman as of the doctor—as much the subject of ordinary conversation as the weather, or the outcome of the crops, or the beauty of this or that mistress? Is it any wonder that Shakespeare represents almost every walk of life as possessing medical knowledge? It is not Dr. Caius, Butts, Cornelius, or the other regular physicians in the plays, but it is Doll Tearsheet,[77] Mrs. Quickly,[78] Boult,[79] Falstaff,[80] Speed,[81] Biron,[82] Jaques,[83] Ulysses,[84] Iago, Menenius,[85] Holoferness,[86] Thersites,[87] Brutus,[88] Leontes,[89] Young Marcius,[90] Friar Laurence,[91] Troilus, Titania,[92] Casca,[93] Caesar, King Richard, Helena,[94] and others —these are the ones in whose mouths Shakespeare puts his medical learning. Why, one of the most highly praised passages in Shakespeare, from the medical standpoint, that is, the description of Falstaff's death[95] is put into the mouth of none other than Dame Quickly. The two passages containing the most medical material are also utterd by ordinary laymen. Timon curses his fellowmen in medical terms:

> Give them diseases, leavning with thee their lust.
> Make use of the salt hours; season the slaves
> For tubs and baths; bring down rose-check'd youth
> To the tub-fast and the diet.[96]

> Consumptions sow
> In hollow bones of man; strike their sharp sins,
> And mar men's spurring. Crack the lawyer's voice
> That he may never more false title plead,
> Nor sound his quillets shrilly; hoar the flamen,
> That scolds against the quality of flesh
> And not believe himself; down with the nose,
> Down with it flat; take the bridge quite away
> Of him that, his particular to foresee,
> Smells from the general weal; make curl'd plate
> ruffians bald;
> And let the unscarred braggarts of the war
> Derive some pain from you.[97]

Thersites playing the role of slave and fool exclaims against Patrocolus: ". . . Now, the rotten disease of the south, the guts-gripping, ruptures, catarrhs, loads o'gravel i' the back, lethargies, cold palsies, raw eyes, dirt-rotten livers, wheezing lungs, bladders full of impostume, sciaticas, limekilins i' the palm incurable boneache, and the rivelled fee, simple of the tetter, take and take again such preposterous discoveries!"[98]

To this also may be added Biondello's utterance full of veterinary knowledge[99] and we have a third passage containing much medical lore from the tongue of an inferior character, a mere servant to Lucentio.

Even the few technical terms present in the plays, are put to the tongues of laymen. Thus, *pia mater* occurs three times in the dramas, and each time this technical term is uttered by a layman: "These are begot in the ventricles of memory, nourished in the womb of *pia mater,* and delivered upon the mellowing of occasion" says the schoolmaster Holoferness.[100] "One of thy kin has a most weak *pia mater,"* says the clown in *Twelfth Night;*[101] and "I will buy nine Sparrows for a penny, and his *pia mater* is not worth the ninth part of a sparrow" says Thersites.[102]

Similarly, the technical term *Hysterica Passio*[103] is spoken by Leon and not by a physician. The drug Coloquintida is spoken of by Iago.

> Fill thy purse with money; the food that to him
> now is as luscious as locusto, shall be to him
> shortly as bitter as *Coloquintida.*[104]

Iago[105] and Cleopatra[106] speak of Mandragora. The Ghost in *Hamlet* speaks of "cursed Hebenon."[107] It is interesting to note in this respect, (and as further evidence that these drugs were commonly known) that Spenser in his *Faerie Queene* also mentions hebenon, "Lay now thy deadly heben bowe apart."[108] Again, the term *Serpigo* comes from the mouth of the Duke, Vincentio:[109]

> For thine own bowels, which do call thee sire,
> The mere effusion of thy proper loins,
> Do curse the gout, *serpigo,* and the rheum
> For ending thee no sooner.

In all this, Shakespeare was doing nothing more than representing the sixteenth century. The doctors, the surgeons, the apothecaries, the mountebanks, the quacks, the high and the low, all mouthing medical knowledge are here in the dramas. The plays really give us a better composite of medical practice in this century than all the authorities quoted.

II

Medical Education and Licensure in Elizabethan England and in Shakespeare's Dramas

But apropos of all these considerations, we must ever keep in mind that medical practice in the sixteenth century was limited not only by the general level of medical knowledge, even at its best, but also by the level of medical education and licensure. It has already been pointed out that to meet the conditions prevalent in the healing art at the time, a law was passed in 1511 by Henry VIII empowering the Bishop of London and the Dean of St. Paul's, together with an examining board of four Doctors or surgeons, to grant degrees and licenses to candidates to practice the healing art. This law was not too well enforced and what is more, the holders of such licenses issued in the name of God and the Church were little trusted. It was actually not until the Medical Act of 1858, in spite of the fact that in the Elizabethan period the College of Physicians had already begun to refuse to license the clergy to practice medicine and surgery, that this remnant of the union of Medicine and the Church was abolished.

This College of Physicians was founded, in fact, as far back as 1518 by Cardinal Wolsey and the famous Linacre. At first, they were only a qualifying and licensing body examining only graduates of the medical schools of Universities. Hence the men they licensed were really competent physicians equivalent to our Fellows of the American College of Physicians today. But in 1582 the College also instituted medical education with provisions for lectures, public demonstrations and dissections; and professorships were established in Medicine at Oxford, Cambridge and Gresham Colleges at various times.

That the College of Physicians in Shakespeare's day had already become an accepted part of the milieu of the Elizabethan is attested to by the fact that Shakespeare speaks to his audience of "the congregated college,"[1] and Ben Jonson of the "learned College of Physicians" at least three times,[2] while Beaumont and Fletcher tirade with "A college on you"[3] and "Ten colleges of doctors shall not save you"[4] and Middleton with "Is this the practice of your physic-college?"[5] It is likely that many more references of this nature could be found among the other dramatists of the period all of which emphasizes that the average person of this period knew of the Royal College of Physicians and of the company of Barber-Surgeons formed in 1540 as the average man today knows of the Mayos or of the American Medical Association. We can be sure therefore, that any unusual happenings or deliberations involving this "College," or Company in Shakespeare's day would be news of importance for the dramatists to notice and to use as topical material to bring to their audiences. And, if perchance this material also involved personages of high station, we can be doubly sure that such material would be bound to infiltrate into the dramas of the time. Thus Shakespeare definitely refers to a celebrated case involving a Jewish physician, Dr. Ruy Lopez, and his attempt on the life of Queen Elizabeth. He makes Gratiano rant at Shylock, the Jew:

> Thou almost makest me waver in my faith,
> To hold opinion with Pythagoras,
> That souls of animals infuse themselves
> Into the trunks of men; thy currish spirit
> Govern'd a wolf, who hang'd for human slaughter,
> Even from the gallows did his fell soul fleet,
> And, whilst thou lay'st in thy unhallow'd dam,
> Infused itself in thee; for thy desires
> Are wolvish, bloody, starved and ravenous.[6]

Ben Jonson mentions this same doctor as "Signor Lupo, the physician"[7] as does also Marlowe in the "Dr. Lopus" of his *Dr. Eaustus,*[8] as well as Beaumont and Fletcher when they speak of

> . . . a don of Spain . . . prescribes

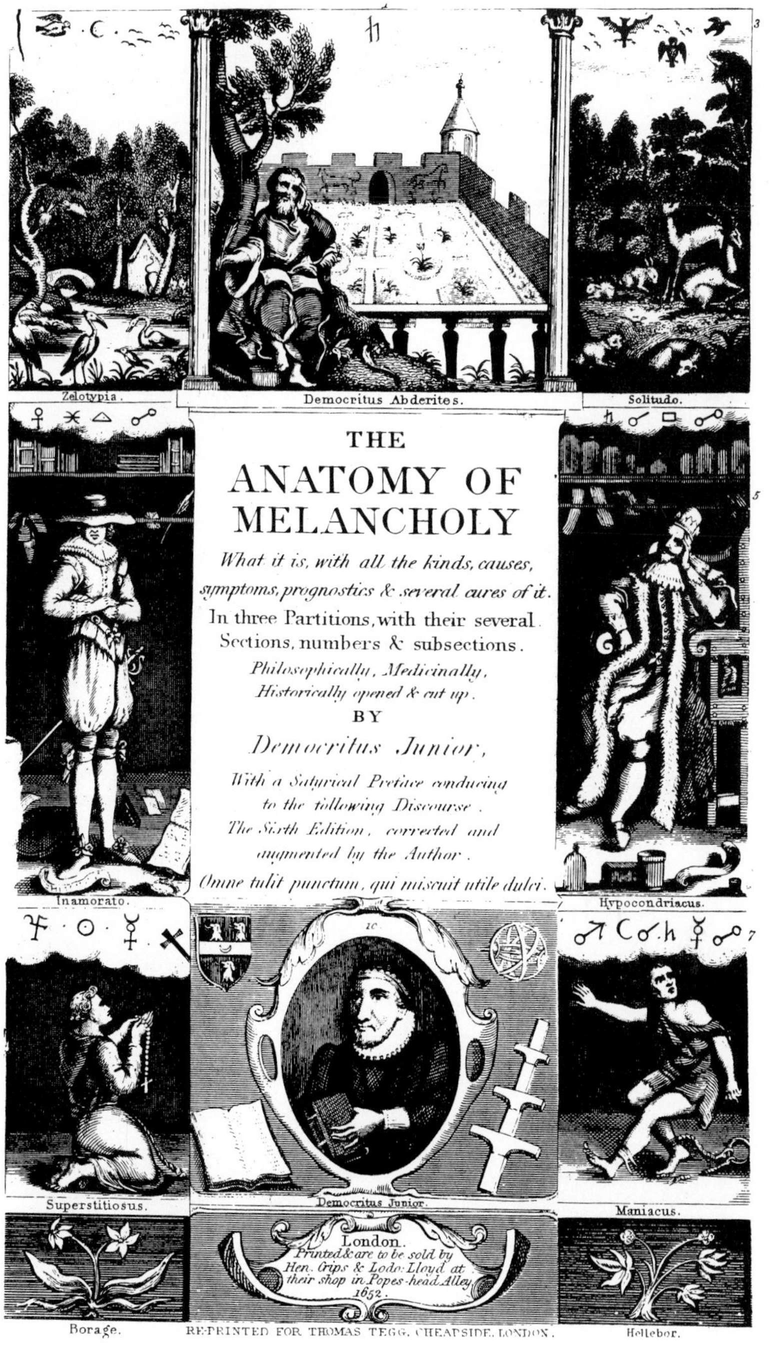

Zelotypia.

Democritus Abderites.

Solitudo.

THE

ANATOMY OF MELANCHOLY

What it is, with all the kinds, causes, symptoms, prognostics & several cures of it.

In three Partitions, with their several Sections, numbers & subsections.

Philosophically, Medicinally, Historically opened & cut up.

BY

Democritus Junior,

With a Satyrical Preface conducing to the following Discourse.

The Sixth Edition, corrected and augmented by the Author.

Omne tulit punctum, qui miscuit utile dulci.

Inamorato.

Hypocondriacus.

Superstitiosus.

Democritus Junior.

Maniacus.

London.
Printed & are to be sold by Hen. Crips & Lodo: Lloyd at their shop in Popes-head Alley.
1652.

Borage.

RE-PRINTED FOR THOMAS TEGG, CHEAPSIDE, LONDON.

Hellebor.

—Bettman Archive

14. Engraved Title-page of The Anatomy of Melancholy by Democritus Junior.

Phlegmatic

Melancholic

Sanguine

Choleric

—Bettman Archive

15. THE FOUR HUMORS

These illustrations of the humoral theory, were taken from a medieval manuscript. The sanguine person, who had a predominance of "blood," was supposed to love "mirth and musick, wine and women," whereas the phlegmatic man preferred "rest and sloth." "A heavy looke, a spirit little daring" characterized the melancholy type. And the choleric individual was identified as being "all violent, fierce and full of fire," Since the humors also corresponded to the elements, the various temperaments were supposedly related to a surplus of a particular element. Thus an individual with a sanguine temperament would have an over-balance of air; the phlegmatic, of water; the melancholy, of earth; and the choleric, of fire.

—Bettman Archive

16. **OBSERVING LADY MACBETH** in her sleepwalking act, the physician (rear) diagnoses her illness. "Foul whisperings are abroad," he says. "Unnatural deeds do breed troubles; infected minds to their deaf pillows will discharge their secrets; more needs she the divine than the physician."

—Bettman Archive

17. Hamlet learns his father's fate in the famous battlements scene. The ghost tells the young Prince of Denmark of the poison "that did posset and curd, like eager droppings into milk."

—Bettman **Archive**

18. PRESCRIBING FOR KING LEAR, the physician summoned to the monarch's aid by Cordelia, recommends music, the voice of the daughter who loves him and a hypnotic in the form of a "simple" Medicinal herb.

"Our foster-nurse of nature
is repose,

The which he lacks;
that to provoke in him,

Are many simples operative,
whose power

Will close the eye of anguish."
King Lear, Act IV; Scene IV.

More cooking opium than would kill a Turk.[9]

It was a celebrated case worthy of Shakespeare's notice. This Dr. Ruy Lopez was a Portuguese Jew in the famous Spanish Armada. Having been taken prisoner by the English and having impressed the Queen most favorably he soon became physician in the royal household. However, in the State Rolls of 1594 we find that this Lopez—"old doctor—is in the Tower for intelligence with the King of Spain . . . he conspired the death of the Queen in 1590 . . . treacherously accepted a jewel from the King of Spain . . . undertook to poison the Queen February 20, 1593 . . . undertook to kill the Queen for 50,000 crowns, to be paid by the King of Spain September 30, 1593."[10] In spite of the gallant defense of Strachey, and a delay of four months by the Queen herself, Dr. Ruy Lopez was hanged at Tyvum June 7, 1594.

Another such item of similar nature appearing on the State Rolls, May 1575 is also worthy of notice because it involves a person of high station and hence might have attracted much attention: "Dr. James was confined to the Tower and examined on account of some medicine sent to the Scottish Queen for her health which was paid for by the French Ambassador."

Another case that created quite a furore in the London of Shakespeare's youth was that of Peter Piers. On October 28, 1586, he was arrested and haled before the College of Physicians "for administering antimony and sublimated mercury by which he killed several persons," and for which he was found guilty and imprisoned. This latter case perhaps represents part of the controversy then raging between the "Paracelsists and Galenists" in which the College of Physicians took an active part in its controversy against the "antimonyall cup" previously mentioned.

There are other cases of like nature. Perhaps all this helps account for the distrust of the physician pointed out in previous pages so common in the dramas of the period. Perhaps this also accounts for the interest in poisons also evident so abundantly in the dramas of the times, including certainly those of Shakespeare.

III

The Medical Superstitions in Elizabethan England and in Shakespeare's Dramas

But further, that Shakespeare was only a child of his age is also glaringly evident by his numerous references to the particular conceits, superstitions and beliefs of his period, manifesting themselves in the accepted medical practice of the day. One such practice concerns the treatment of scrofula, the tuberculous involvement of the lymphatic glands, usually of the neck. It was called the "King's Evil" and was supposed to be cured by the King's touch. Shakespeare gives lines to it in *Macbeth* (IV, iii, 146):

> Ay, Sir, there are a crew of wretched souls
> That stay his cure; their malady convinces
> The great assay of art; but at his touch,
> Such sanctity hath heaven given his hand,
> They presently amend.
> *Macduff*: What's the disease he means?
> *Malcolm*: . . . 'Tis called the evil;
> A most miraculous work in the good king;
> Which often, since my here-remain in England,
> I've seen him do. How he solicits heaven
> Himself knows; but strangely visited people,
> All swoll'n and ulcerous, pitiful to the eye,
> The mere despair of surgery, he cures;
> Hanging a golden stamp about their necks,
> Put on with holy prayers; and 'tis spoken,
> To the succeeding royalty he leaves
> The healing benediction.

The best medical and surgical authorities believed in it and supported it. William Clowes, one time surgeon to Queen Elizabeth, in one of his widely read books on *Proved Practice for Young Surgeons* writes of "the king's or the queen's evil (as) a disease repugnant to nature; which grievous malady is known to be miraculously cured and healed by the sacred hands of the Queen's most royal majesty even by Divine inspiration and wonderful work and power of God, . . ." And one William Tookes, wrote a whole book on Queen Elizabeth's "touching for the evil": "Charisma; sine Domum Sanationis." Dr. James Primrose in his *De Vulgi in Medicina Erroribus,* in arguing against the "Popular Error of curing the King's Evil by the touch of the seventh sonne," which was also a superstition of the time, states that the "power of curing the King's-Evil [being] by the blessing of God granted to the Kings of Great Britaine and France," only, "the privilege is only vouchsafed to the . . . Kings and hence not to any 'seventh sonne.'" Incidentally this same Dr. Primrose also argues Harvey's discovery of the circulation of the blood as another of the "Popular Errors."

This practice of touching for the "King's Evil" was common long before Shakespeare's day, certainly during Shakespeare's life, and long afterwards. More factually, it was begun by Edward the Confessor, in 1058 and by all the succeeding rulers until William III, who discontinued it. Queen Anne resumed the practice but it was finally completely stopped by George I. Between 1662 and 1682, records show that more than 100,000 people were touched for this illness. Samuel Johnson went through (much later . . . .) the procedure himself. The laying on of hands in one form or another has lasted to this very day.

Another superstition of the period that finds expression in Shakespeare is that connected with the mandrake or mandragora root. This herb was known to the ancients and is mentioned by many classic writers, since the gods of mythology frequently used it and such famous authorities in Shakespeare's day as Bullein in his *Bulwark of Defence,* and Sir Thomas Browne in his *Vulgar Errors,* supported it. In the form of a wine of Mandragora it was used as a poison, an aphrodisiac, a narcotic and anaesthetic. Thus Shakespeare has Cleopatra say (I, v):

Give me to drink mandragora.
That I might sleep out this great gap of time
My Anthony is away.

and he has Iago say of Othello (III, ii):

Look where he comes! Not poppy or mandragora,
Nor all the drowsy syrups of the world,
Shall even medicine thee to that sweet sleep

But it was supposed to have enhanced and special properties if made from the plant growing over buried bodies and particularly over the remains of executed criminals. The root also had a peculiar form, being forked and asuming somewhat the shape of a man, which added to the superstition. However, if this plant was pulled out of the earth over the dead a loud shrieking and groaning would ensue. Those nearby and in the hearing of it would go insane and die.

Shakespeare puts these words into the mouth of the Duke of Suffolk (2 Henry VI, [III, 22, 310]):

Wherefore should I curse?
Would curses kill, as doth the mandrake's groan,
I would invent as bitter searching terms,
As crust, as harsh, and horrible to hear.

He has Juliet (IV, iii, 47) utter these words:

So early waking,—what with lothesome smells,
And shrieks like mandrake torn out of the earth,
That living mortals, hearing them run mad.

Nor was Shakespeare the only dramatist who refers to mandrake in this relationship. Philip Massinger in *Believe As You List* (III, 3) writes of:

The mandrake's shrieks, the aspic's deadly tooth
Kill not so soon, nor with that violence,
As he, who, in his cruel nature, holds
Antipathy with mercy

And again in *The Virgin Martyr* (III, 1) he writes:

The Stygian damps, breeding infectious airs
The mandrakes' shrieks, the basilisks' killing eye

The dreadful lightning that does crush the bones,
And never singe the skin, shall not appear
Less fatal than my zeal. . .

IV

Astrology and Medical Practice in Shakespeare's Dramas

Astrology too, as part of medical practice, also finds its place in Shakespeare's dramas in accordance with the best accepted authorities. The causation of disease, the time for treatment, the time for the gathering of herbs and the compounding of drugs, etc., etc, all were related to celestial geography. Shakespeare writes (*Othello,* V, ii, 109),

It is the very error of the moon,
She comes more nearer earth than she was wont
And makes men mad.
No natural exhalation in the sky
No scope of nature, no distemper'd day,
No common wind, no customed event,
But they will pluck away his natural cause
And call them meteors, prodigies and signs,
Abortions, presages and tongues of heaven,
Plainly denouncing vengeance on John.[1]

Therefore the moon, the governesse of floods,
Pale in her anger, washes all the air,
That rheumatic diseases do abound.[2]
This we prescribe though no physician. . .
Our doctors say this is no month to bleed.[3]

In this the heavens figure some event.[4]
And therefore is the glorious planet Sol
In noble eminence enthroned and spher'd
Amidst the ether; whose medicinable eye
Corrects the ill aspects of planet's evil,
but when the planets
In evil mixture, to disorder wander,

What plagues, and what portents, what mutiny,
What raging of the sea, shaking of earth,
Commotion in the winds, frights, chances, horrors.[5]

Likewise in Middleton's *The Changeling,* (III, iii) one Lollio tells Francissus that "Luna" made him mad. And the "Parson" in Fletcher's *The Pilgrim* (III, vi) must be "tied short" because "the moon's i' th' full." Brome in his *City Wit* (V, i) writes "Sure I was planet-struck." Chapman in *Biron's Conspiracy* (III, iii) has the astrologer, La Brosse, say:

This hour, by all rules of astrology,
Is dangerous to my person, if not deadly.

and Biron:

Spite of the stars and all astrology
I will not lose my head.

Massinger in the *Roman Actor* (IV, i) writes:

. . . condemned of treason,
For calculating the nativity
Of Caesar, with all confidence foretelling,
In every circumstances, when he shall die
A violent death

But, as indicated, high medical authority, as well as long tradition was the basis for the above beliefs. Vicary, chief surgeon at St. Bartholomew's Hospital (1548-1562) writes in his *Anatomie of the Bodie of Man,* that "the Brayne hath this propertie that it moveth and followeth the moving of the moone; . . . and this is proved in men that be lunaticke or madde . . . that he moste greeved in the beginning of the newe moone and in the latter quarter of the moone."[6]

The Reverend John Ward, the clerical physician of Shakespeare's own parish in his *Diary* quotes the famous Herbalist Nick Culpepper as saying, "that a physition without astrologie is like a lamp without oil."

More directly, Paracelsus taught that the planet Saturn influenced, to a great degree, human longevity. It was also generally accepted that the great plagues that struck England were caused by the conjunction of Mars and Saturn or of Saturn and Jupiter, and that the proper conjunction of Venus and Jupiter was of special benefit to sufferers from tuberculosis and "slow fever." Mars was considered as causing the tertian fever; Saturn, the quartan type; and the moon as ruling over the quotidian variety; while Phoebus influenced diseases of the skin and the fluctuations of pestilences. The famous physician Ramazzini taught that serious danger of death threatened the sick during an eclipse and that an epidemic petechial fever was more fulminating just after the full moon. The physician Baillow wrote in 1591 that "congestions, apoplexies and sudden deaths" were more likely towards the winter solstice, and that during one particular night in December of that year "the influences of the sun, the moon and of the heaven" produced "sudden delirium . . . unexpected convulsions. . ."[7]

It was also accepted astrological-medical doctrine that each organ of the body was ruled over by a particular metal, which metal had a remedial effect on the organ in question. In this wise, the heart, governed by the sun and by the metal gold, was to be treated by pharmacological mixtures in all of its diseases. Silver was specific for diseases of the brain, since the moon and silver ruled this organ. Mars was in relation to the liver with iron; Venus: the kidneys and copper; Jupiter: the lungs and tin; Mercury: the reproductive organs and quicksilver, etc., etc. And, as was to be expected, a particular therapeutics developed on this premise. A solution of gold especially was supposed to have extensive curative value since it was in association with the heart, and many an alchemist spent time and fortune in trying to develop the "sovereign" remedy, an *Aurum Potable*. Even contact with the pure metal itself made for good health in the wearer. In the "Secrets of Axia" translated by John Wight we find directions on how "to dissolve and reduce golde into a potable liquid which conserveth the youth and healthe of a man and *will heale any disease that is thought incurable* in the space of seven daies at the furthest."[8]

Surely enough, Shakespeare refers to this "grand liquid" in the *Tempest* (V, i):

Find the grand liquid that hath gilded 'em

Again, in *2 Henry IV* (IV, iv) he speaks of this "medicine potable":

Other, less fine in carat, is more precious
Preserving life in med'cine potable

and also in *All's Well* (V, iii):

Plutus himself
That knows the tinct and multiplying medicine
Hath not in nature's mystery more science
Than I have in this ring.

Shakespeare has a direct reference to this organic astrology in his *Twelfth Night* (I, iii):

Sir Toby: What shall we do else: Were we not
born under Taurus?
Sir Andrew: Taurus! That's sides and heart.
Sir Toby: No, sir; it is legs and thighs.

The Astrological prognostication of epidemics is mentioned in *Venus and Adonis*:

Long may they kiss each other for this cure!
O, never let their crimson liveries wear!
And as they last, their verdure still endure,
To drive infection from the dangerous year!
That the star-gazers, having writ on death,
May say, the plague is banished by their breath.

The prediction of the cause and means of Suffolk's death is indicated in *2 Henry VI* (IV, i):

A cunning man did calculate my birth
And told me that by water I should die

He did die by the seashore, beheaded.

Indeed, astrological medicine permeated, in varying degrees, the whole healing art from the times of Hippocrates until long after Shakespeare's day. It is no wonder that Chapman makes Orlando say (*Charlemagne,* II, i):

> I am the verye foote-ball of the starres,
> Th' anathomye of fortune whom she dyssects
> With all the poysons and sharpe corrasyves
> Stylled in the lymbecks of damde polycie

It is no wonder there is so much of this in Shakespeare and his contemporaries.

Associated with these factors also were the beliefs in sorcery, magic, witchcraft, demonology and the like, as causative elements in disease and hence influential elements in treatment. These had a serious part in the life of the Elizabethan and manifest themselves in the literature of the times, the scientific writings, as well as the dramas of Shakespeare and his contemporaries.

It is difficult for an educated man of the twentieth century, let alone a physician, to contemplate objectively the tenacious hold that the supernatural etiology of disease had on mankind, almost to the nineteenth century. Its roots, of course, reach deep into the evolutionary soul of man in primitive psychology. Disease is due to devils, spirits, demons, gods, witches, sorcerers; and these must be combatted by appropriate means —incantations, charms, talismans, prayers, white magic, and numerous other similar means. These dominated medicine till recent times. In Shakespeare's England, along with a beginning science and a few mild dissenting voices, the supernatural still had a dominant place. To doubt supernatural causation was to doubt the Bible,[9] the Church and the best medical authority of the day. Pope Innocent VIII declared such doubt, especially in relation to demoniacal possession as "unblushing effrontery."[10] Sir Thomas Browne, a Shakespeare contemporary, holder of degree from numerous universities, famous physician author of *The Religio Medici* helped greatly the continued hold of the belief in witchcraft upon the mind of man in Elizabethan England. He makes the statement that "I have ever believed, and do now, that there are witches!"[11] Actually, there are records of a famous trial of two witches at the Bury St. Edmunds

Assizes of 1664 in which our Dr. Browne testified professionally that the "fits" suffered by certain children were "heightened by the Devil co-operating with the malice of witches at whose instance he did the villainies."[12] A book written by one William Perkins that seems to have influenced Sir Thomas Browne while at Cambridge states that,

> Witchcraft is a rife and common sinne in these daies an very many are entangled with it, being either practitioners . . . or at least, yielding to seeke for helpe and counsell of such as practice it.[13]

King James I wrote in his treatise on *Demonologie* that

> The fearful abounding at this time (1597) . . . of these detestable slaves of the devil, the witches or enchanters hath moved me . . . to dispatch this . . . treatise of mine . . . to resolve the doubting hearts of many; . . . that such assaults of Satan are . . . practiced . . . I have divided it into three books; the first speaking of magic in general, and necromancie in special; the second of sorcerie and witchcraft; and the third contains a disclosure of all these kinds of spirits, and spectres that appear and trouble persons . . . Witches ought to be put to death . . . Yea . . . not to strike . . . is . . . treason against God . . .

Accordingly, in the very first year of his reign, with the help of a Parliament that included Francis Bacon and numerous other of the intellectual luminaries of this period, King James enacted the statute (1541) which in part reads:

> . . . If any person or persons shall use, practice, or exercise any invocation, or conjuration of any evil and wicked spirit, or shall consult, covenant with, entertain, employ, feed or reward, any evil and wicked spirit, to or for any intent and purposes: . . . or shall use, practice or exercise any witchcraft, inchantment, charm or sorcery, whereby any person shall be killed, destroyed, wasted, consumed, pained or lamed . . .; that then such . . . offenders . . . aiders, abettors, and counsellors . . . shall suffer . . . death . . . as

felons, and shall lose . . . benefit of clergy and sanctuary.

During Queen Elizabeth's day (1563) also, laws were enacted against "those who shall use, practice, or exercise any witchcraft, enchantment, or sorcerie. . ." Nevertheless, some years later (1589) in the presence of the Queen herself Bishop Jewell sermonized that "Your Grace's subjects pine away even unto death; their colour fadeth, their flesh rotteth; their speech is benumbed; their senses are bereft; . . ." all due to the increase of witches and sorcerers within her Grace's realm.

Dr. John Cotta, a contemporary of Shakespeare whom we have already referred to, wrote a treatise dealing with "The Troll of Witch Craft. Shewing the True and Right Methods of Discovery with a Confutation of erroneous ways."

Shakespeare and his contemporary dramatists reflect all these influences in their dramas. Thus the delineation of Jeanne d'Arc in *I Henry VI* is in strict accordance with the supposed behavior of witches in Shakespeare's day, for she speaks of feeding her "Familiars" with her own blood, just as Mother Sawyer in Dekker's *Witch of Edmonton* feeds her familiars with her own blood too.

The *Tempest* is full of the supernatural. Prospero has the magic power to produce cramps and numerous pains in the characters. Prospero says (I, ii):

. . . I'll rack thee with old cramps;
Fill all thy bones with aches; make thee roar

For this be sure, tonight thou shalt have cramps,
Side stitches that shall pen thy breath up . . .

. . . Thou shalt be pinched
As thick as honey-comb, each pinch more stinging
Than bees that made them.

Again in the same play (IV, i) Prospero similarly says:

Go, change my goblins, that they grind their joints
With dry convulsions; shorten up their sinews
With aged cramps; and more pinch-spotted make them
Than pard or cat o'mountain.

A Midsummer Night's Dream also is involved with much magic, spirits, fairies; and the transformation of Bottom in this play finds actual authority in the famous Albert Magnus' *Of the Wonders of the World*, in which exact directions are given as follows: "If you wish that a man's head should appear as an ass's head take the parings of [the hoofs of] an ass, and rub the man's head with them." And, of course, we must not forget the witches in *Macbeth* in the form of the Three Weird Sisters.

In the *Comedy of Errors*, the character of Pinch is that of a typical conjuror or sorcerer, with supposed medical powers. In the same play (IV, iii), an example of "contagious magic" is mentioned:

> Some devils ask but the parings of one's nail,
> A rush, a hair, a drop of blood, a pin,
> A nut, a cherry-stone.

while earlier in the *Comedy* (I, ii) reference is made to "Dark-working sorcerers that change the mind" as a cause of insanity. In *2 Henry VI* (I, iv) the historical charge of sorcery against Eleanor, the Duchess of Gloster is repeated. In *1 Henry IV* (III, i) Glendower referring to his astrological nativity at birth presumes supernatural powers when he says: "I can call spirits from the deep."

In *King John* (V, iv), Shakespeare gives us a good example of so-called "Puppet Magic," in which an image of wax or clay is made of the individual to be harmed, stuck through with pins or nails and placed in the chimney. Melun in this play says:

> Have I not hideous death within my view
> Retaining but a quantity of life,
> Which bleeds away, even as a form of wax
> Resolveth from his figure 'gainst the fire?

And again, in *Two Gentlemen of Verona* (II, iv), Shakespeare has Proteus remark:

> . . . for now my love is thaw'd;
> Which, like a waxen image 'gainst a fire,
> Bears no impression of the thing it was.

That such "puppet magic" was taken seriously in Shakespeare's day is evidenced by the fact that Queen Elizabeth, having found a wax image of herself in Lincoln's Inn Fields, hired the notorious Dr. Die Sr., "the arch conjuror of this whole Kingdom," who succeeded in counteracting this malevolent influence by his own white magic. In all this too, Shakespeare reflected but another facet of the multi-faceted character of the age and certainly was something less than a "master" in the healing art as so many have called him, but a human being rooted in his own generation partaking of its cultural nutriment and rising no higher than the best of his age—the Robert Burtons, the Thomas Brownes, the Timothy Brights.

V

'Scientific' Medical Practice and Shakespeare's Dramas

While belief in the supernatural, with its numerous and various ramifications, as has already been shown, dominated the healing art and expressed itself in Shakespeare's dramatic works, yet a medical practice did exist based on Hippocratic-Galenic-Arabian-Paracelsian foundations with all the limitations, we know today, that this implied. Our poet here also, pictures directly this facet of medical knowledge and medical practice in his literary productions, but only as a literary artist dealing wth an integral part of the teeming life of Elizabethan England about him, and not as a professional man ahead of his time. His knowledge of anatomy was only that of an intelligent layman of his day in spite of the fact that some have pointed to certain technical terms in his works to prove otherwise. Thus Shakespeare writes:

> I have tremor cordis on me.[1]

He mentions the term *pia mater*[2] three times, once in association with "the ventricle of memory," and the technical term *Hysterica Passio*[3] once. As a matter of fact these terms were commonly used words in Elizabethan England and, as already pointed out, Shakespeare put these supposed technical terms into the mouths of laymen as evidence of this. Indeed, such terms can most likely be found, perhaps even to a greater degree, in Shakespeare's contemporaries. Beaumont and Fletcher in *Monsieur Thomas* (II, 5) write:

> 1st phys.: A pleurisy, I sie it.
> 2nd phys.: I rather hold it
> For *tremor cordis*

Thomas Nashe[4] writes:

> Thou turmoil'st thy *pia mater* to prove base births better than the offspring of many descents.

Beaumont and Fletcher in *The Chances* (III, 2) write of "stewed pericraniums and *pia maters.*" The term *pia mater,* named such because this membranous covering "is so softe and tender over the brayne, that it nourisheth the brayne and feedeth it as doth a loving *mother* unto her tender child"[5] had also come vulgarly to mean the brain in Shakespeare's day. Hence Shakespeare in intended ridicule, speaks of a "weak *pia mater*" and of a "*pia mater* . . . not worth the ninth part of a sparrow," as well as of "the womb of *pia mater.*"

As to Shakespeare's "ventricle of memory" here too was current usage. Vicary, discussing the brain, writes:

> In the foremost Ventricle are the Five Wits: also the Fancy and the Imagination. In the 2nd or Middle Ventricle is Thought. In the Third Ventricle is the Memory.[6]

Laurentius also writes:

> beholde also his foure closets or cels, wherein the principall powers of the minde (if we will believe the *Arabians*) are lodged, as for example, the imagination in the two foremost, the reason in the middlemost, and the memorie in that which is hindermost.[7]

Similarly, Burton writes of the "fourth creek behind the head . . . the place where they say the memory is seated."[8]

However, Edmund Spenser in his *The Faerie Queene* (2.9.47ff) in very beautiful and poetic language imaginatively describes the three ventricles personified as three rooms in the House of Temperance, the abode of the three master faculties, imagination, judgment, and memory, the last being the "Ventricle of Memory" of Shakespeare.

With regard to the term *Hysterica Passio,* now known as Hysteria meaning "The Mother—a Fit of the Mother"[9] ". . . the Disease called otherwise Hysterick . . . or Melancholy"[10] or "fits of the Mother,"[11] we need go no further than the fact that Shakespeare's own daughter Sussana Hall, at one time suffered from "fit of the Mother" as noted down by his son-in-law, Dr. John Hall.[12] We can be sure that on this basis alone among others, he was familiar with the term, leaving aside the probability that Hysteria was as common in Shakespeare's day as in later centuries.

Shakespeare's concepts of physiology-psychology, as shown in his works, were based on the theories of the four elements and their derivatives the four humours, which we have already amply discussed in previous pages. Health, briefly, was a proper balance of these humours, disease was but a varying degree of imbalance. The etiology of disease, then, was related to all the factors that caused such imbalance aside from the supernatural forces already noted. These included poisons mentioned many times in the dramas. Thus aconite is referred to when King Henry (*2 Henry IV,* IV, 4) says:

> . . . though it do work as strong
> As aconitum or rash gunpowder.

Ratsbane or arsenic is referred to many times. Edgar (*King Lear,* III, 4) says:

> Set ratsbane by his porridge

In *1 Henry VI* (V, 4) we have:

> I would the milk
> Thy mother gave those when thou suck'd her breast,
> Had been a little ratsbane for thy sake!

Iago (*Othello,* III, 3) says:

> Dangerous conceits are, in their natures, poisons,

Which at the first are scarce found to distaste,
But with an act upon the blood
Burn like the mines of sulphur

In *King John* (V, 6) Shakespeare writes:

The king, I fear, is poisoned by a monk
Whose bowels suddenly burst out....

and also (*King John,* V, 7):

There is a hot summer in my bosom,
That all my bowels crumble up to dust:

Within me is a hell; and there the poison
Is as a fiend confined to tyrannize
An unreprievable condemned blood.

"The leprous distillment" "juice of cursed hebenon" was the poison that killed Hamlet's father (*Hamlet,* I, 5). Although there has been some controversy[13] as to what drug hebenon refers to, some considering it the same as henbane or hyocyamus "the insane root" (*Macbeth,* I,3) others calling it *Nicotiana tabacum* or the poison, nicotine, and still others considering it as hemlock, most commentators agree that it refers to the yew. This, perhaps, is confirmed by the fact that Spenser uses the word "heben" in a similar relationship as does Shakespeare indicating current usage. Spenser in his *Faerie Queene* (Book I, Introduction III) writes:

Lay now thy deadly heben bowe apart

Shakespeare (*Richard II,* III, 2) writes:

to bend their Bowes
Of double fatall Eugh.

He also refers to the "insane root" as an etiological factor in madness in the following lines (*Macbeth,* I, 3):

Have we eaten of the insane root
That takes the reason prisoner

The "insane root" here is undoubtedly henbane or hyocine as we know it today, and it is mentioned in Batman's Upon *Bartholomew de Proprietatibus Rerum* (Lib. XVII, Ch. 87):

> Henbane is called *Insana,* mad, for the use thereof is perrilous; for if it be eaten or drunke, it breedeth madnesse, or slow lykeness of sleepe . . . it taketh away wit and reason.

In addition, Shakespeare speaks of

> these most poisonous compounds,
> Which are the movers of a languishing death.[14]

> She doth think she has
> Strange lingering poisons. . . .
> Will stupefy and dull the sense awhile;[15]

> I have drugged their possets,
> That death and nature do contend about them,
> Whether they live or die.[16]

> She did confess she had
> For you a mortal mineral, which, being took,
> Should by the minute feed on life, and ling'ring
> By inches waste you. . .[17]

In all this, let us emphasize again, this apparent knowledge of poisonous drugs by Shakespeare was not unique. It was common current knowledge and all the dramatists of the time seemingly delighted to introduce poisons into their plays sometimes of a fantastic character. Let it suffice to quote only Marlowe in this respect. He writes in *The Jew of Malta* (V, p. 265):

> I drank a poppy and cold mandrake juice;
> And being asleep, belike they thought me dead.

In *Edward the Second* (Everyman's Edit., 1950, p. 351) he writes:

> I learn'd in Naples how to poison flowers:
> Or, whilst one is asleep, to take a quill

And blow a little powder in his ears

Again in *The Massacre at Paris* (p. 367) he has the Old Queen, poisoned by perfumed gloves, say:

> . . . the fatal poison
> Works within my head; my brain-pan breaks;
> My heart doth faint; I die.

Shakespeare, furthermore, in referring to the numerous diseases of his day, in his dramas mentions many of the accepted etiological factors of these diseases, but only as an observing layman. Bad weather, marshy areas, contagion and infectiousness, in addition to the supernatural and astrological factors all come in for casual comment. Thus in *1 King Henry IV* (IV, 1), Shakespeare writes:

> . . . worse than the sun in March
> This praise doth nourish agues

In *Julius Caesar* (II, 1) Portia, says:

> Is Brutus sick, and is it physical
> To walk unbrac'd, and suck up the humours
> Of the dank morning? What! is Brutus sick
> And will he steal out of his wholesome bed,
> To dare the vile contagion of the night,
> And tempt the rheumy and unpurged air
> To add unto his sickness?

In *The Tempest* (II, 2) we find these words of Caliban:

> All the infections that the sun sucks up
> From bogs, fens, flats, on Prosper fall, and make him
> By inch-meal a disease

Again Shakespeare gives these words to King Lear (II, 4):

> . . . Infect her beauty,
> You fen-suck'd fogs, drawn by the powerful sun.

In addition, our poet mentions again and again the idea that "sickness is catching,"[18] "their diseases are grown so catching"[19] and that "one infect another."[20] But such ideas, in relation to the "red plague," the red pestilence, the French disease, etc., were common knowledge and they appear in the writings of his contemporaries, also.

There are many other causes of disease in man which Shakespeare mentions such as are "sick that surfeit with too much,"[21] and "the sick hour that (his) surfeit made"[22] and the too much eating of beef "that does harm to (the) wit"[23] and "over-roasted flesh, burnt and dried" that "engenders choler, planteth anger,"[24] etc., etc. All these causes were matters of common conversation and Shakespeare mirrors them well enough.

In Shakespeare's works are also reflected the diagnostic procedures common in Elizabethan England but they are expressed only as would interest a layman. Aside from direct observation, which the Elizabethan physician must have developed to a great degree, Shakespeare refers to the examination of the pulse[25] many times and to the expectoration as well as to the urine. But the words are practically always put into the mouths of laymen and often are used in metaphorical language indicating certainly a common usage and a common knowledge on the part of the audience. Thus in *Hamlet* (III, 4) we have the words:

> My pulse, as yours, doth temperately keep time
> And makes as healthful music. . .

King John (IV, 2) says,

> Have I commandment on the pulse of life?

In *Macbeth* (II, 3) Shakespeare writes,

> Some say the earth was feverous and did shake

In *1 Henry IV,* (III, 1) he writes:

> Diseased nature oftimes breaks forth
> In strange eruptions; oft teeming earth
> Is with a kind of colic pinch'd and vex'd
> By the imprisoning of unruly wind
> Within her womb; which for enlargement striving
> Shakes the old bedlam earth and topples down

Steeples and moss-grown towers. At your birth
Our grandam earth, having this distemperature
In passion shook.

In both the above quotations it is evident that our poet is speaking figuratively and comparing the human being to the earth in the manner of microcosm and macrocosm which permeated Elizabethan thinking.

In the matter of the urinalysis of the Elizabethan called "water-casting," which was certainly open to the attention of every layman judging by some of the paintings of the period depicting such "water casting," we have the words in *Macbeth* (V,3):

If thou couldst, doctor, cast
The water of my land, find her disease,
And purge it to a sound and pristine health.

Likewise, Shakespeare, in his *Two Gentlemen of Verona* (II, 1)

. . . You are so without these follies, that
these follies are within you, and shine through you
like the water in the urinal.

The diseases which Shakespeare mentions most frequently are the plagues and pestilences, the "sweating sickness," ague, rheumatism, fevers, measles, leprosy and the "pox." This is just what we would expect. These are the very diseases that prevailed most frequently in Shakespeare's England. His allusions to them, however, merely indicate an observing layman's familiarity with them and not any technical knowledge of their nature, even as understood by the regular physicians of his own day. Indeed, when we go through the plays of Shakespeare, the medical expressions found there that can be called technical and unfamiliar to the laymen of the day are extremely few.

As to Therapeutics in Elizabethan England, it consisted mainly of purging, bloodletting, dieting and numerous drugs and herbs, as well as surgery. Shakespeare could not help referring to these treatment measures, for he and his family must have undergone many of these therapeutic procedures, and must have witnessed many more. And here too, the fact that Shakespeare and his contemporaries combine such procedures in figurative language, points most decidedly to common usage in the daily life of the people. And to invest Shakespeare with unusual knowledge equal to the physicians of his day and even in advance of his day is a gross error made possible only by the self-hypnosis of idolatrous commentators.

NOTES AND REFERENCES

CHAPTER VII

I

1. "The Physician and Surgeon in Shakespeare," **Bull. Johns Hopkins Hosp.**, XVIII No. 200 (1907), pp. 430-438. "Some Characteristics of the Medicine in Shakespeare," **Bull. Johns Hopkins Hosp.**, XVIII, No. 190 (1907), pp. 1-11.
2. J. Q. Adams, **Pre-Shakespearean Dramas.** (New York: 1924), 353-356. See also, "The Physician and Surgeon in Shakespeare," **Bull. Johns Hopkins Hosp.**, XVII No. 200 (1907), pp. 430-438; and "Some Characteristics of the Medicine in Shakespeare," **Bull. Johns Hopkins Hosp.**, XVIII No. 190 (1907), pp. 1-11.
3. The Mad Folk of Shakespeare, **op. cit.**, p. 227.
4. **Ibid.**, p. 228.
5. **Medical Thoughts of Shakespeare, op. cit.**, p. 10.
6. **Op. cit., New York Med. Jour.**, LXXXXII (1910), p. 865.
7. **Doctors in Elizabethan Drama, London:** John Bale Sons, Ltd., 1933, p. 25.
8. **Macbeth,** V, 3, 61.
9. A. W. Meyers, "The Physician and Surgeon in Shakespeare." **op. cit.**, p. 435.
10. Geo. Brandes, **William Shakespeare,** A Critical Study (New York: 1898), quoted in A. W. Meyers', "The Physician and Surgeon in Shakespeare," **Bull. Johns Hopkins Hosp.**, XVIII, No. 200, p. 436.
11. III, 3, 11.
12. **Timon of Athens,** IV, 3, 434-36.
13. **Richard II,** I, 4, 59.
14. **Cymbeline,** V, 5, 28.
15. I, 1, 165.
16. III, 4, 99.
17. I, 3, 67-69.
18. II, 1.
19. II, 3, 122.
20. Line 996.
21. V, 4.
22. I, 3.
23. **All's Well That Ends Well,** I, 1, 30.
24. See R. Fletcher, M.D., "Medical Lore in the Older English

Dramatist "(Exclusive of Shakespeare)" **Bull. Johns Hopkins Hosp.**, VI, Nos. 50-51 (May-June 1895) pp. 73-84.

25. Quoted in Yearsley, M., **Doctors in Elizabethan Drama**, p. 19.
26. Quoted in W. Andrews' **The Doctor in History, Literature and Folklore** (London: Hull Press, 1896), p. 259.
27. Quoted in Andrews, **op. cit.**, p. 280.
28. Quoted in A. H. S. Doran "The Physician," (Chap. 14) **Shakespeare's England** (Oxford: 1918).
29. Quoted in W. Andrews, **op. cit.**, p. 86.
30. Barnaby Rich, **"The Honestie of This Age,"** (London: 1614).
31. Scene III.
32. III, 2.
33. V, 1.
34. **The Spanish Curate**, I, 1.
35. **Ibid.**, II, 1.
36. **Valentrican**, V, 2.
37. **I The Honest Whore**, IV, 4.
38. **I The Honest Whore**, V, 2.
39. **Old Fortunatus**, II, 2.
40. **Volpone**, I, 1.
41. **Ibid.**, I, 1.
42. **Poetaster**, V, 1.
43. **Duchess of Malfi**, III, 5.
44. **Ibid.**, II, 1.
45. **The Lovers Melancholy**, I, 2.
46. **All Fools**, III, 1.
47. **May-Day**, II, 1.
48. "Medical Lore in the Older English Dramatics (Exclusive of Shakespeare)" **Bull. Johns Hopkins Hosp.**, VI (1895), pp. 73-84.
49. O. C. Creighton, **A History of Epidemics in Great Britain**, (Cambridge University Press, 1891), p. 208.
50. Quoted in W. Andrews, **op. cit.**, p. 88.
51. Quoted in A. W. Meyers' "The Physician and Surgeon in Shakespeare," **Bull. Johns Hopkins Hosp.**, XVII No. 200, (1907), p. 435.
52. Quoted in J. C. Bucknill, **The Medical Knowledge of Shakespeare**, (London: 1867), p. 30.
53. Cited in A. W. Meyers' "The Physician and Surgeon in Shakespeare," **op. cit.**, p. 436.
54. **Ibid.**, p. 437.
55. **All's Well**, I, 3.
56. **All's Well**, II, 3.
57. I am indebted for this quotation to Dr. H. Pomeranz, **op. cit.**
58. E. Berdoe, **op. cit.**, p. 358.

59. A. W. Meyers, op. cit., XVIII No. 190 (1907), p. 5.
60. Henry V, II, 1, 122.
61. I, 1, 86.
62. Part II, 1, 2, 264.
63. I Henry VI, III, 1, 192.
64. Quoted in E. Berdoe, op. cit., p. 353.
65. Ibid., p. 353.
66. South's Memorials of the Craft of Surgery, p. 161, quoted in J. Moyes, op. cit., p. 5.
67. Meyers, op. cit., XVIII (No. 200), 431.
68. Quoted in Lanier, Shakespeare and his Forerunners (N.Y.: Doubleday Page & Co., 1903), p. 181.
69. Quoted in Berdoe, op. cit., p. 369.
70. Quoted in J. Jeafferson's, A Book About Doctors (N.Y., 1861), p. 227.
71. Lanier, op. cit., p. 186.
72. Quoted in J. C. Jeafferson, op. cit., p. 166.
73. Ibid., p. 167.
74. Quoted in Moyes, op. cit., p. 4.
75. Ibid.
76. F. H. Garrison, History of Medicine (Phila.: 1924), p. 232.
77. II Henry IV.
78. Merry Wives of Windsor, II Henry IV & Henry V.
79. Pericles.
80. Merry Wives of Windsor.
81. Two Gentlemen of Verona.
82. Love's Labour's Lost.
83. As You Like It.
84. Troilus and Cressida.
85. Coriolanus.
86. Love's Labour's Lost.
87. Troilus and Cressida.
88. Julius Caesar.
89. Winter's Tale.
90. Coriolanus.
91. Romeo and Juliet.
92. Midsummer Night's Dream.
93. Julius Caesar.
94. All's Well That Ends Well.
95. Henry V, II, 3, 10.
96. Timon of Athens, IV, 3, 83.
97. Ibid., IV, 3, 151-163.
98. Troilus and Cressida, V, 1, 20.
99. Taming of the Shrew, III, 2, 45-64.
100. Love's Labour's Lost, IV, 2, 70.
101. I, 5, 122.

102. Troilus and Cressida, II, 1, 78.
103. King Lear, II, 4, 57.
104. Othello, I, 3, 335.
105. Othello, III, 3, 329.
106. Antony and Cleopatra, I, 5, 4.
107. I, 5, 62.
108. Book I, Introduction, III.
109. Measure for Measure, III, 1, 31.

II

1. All's Well, II, 1.
2. Volpone, II, 1; II, 3; Cynthia's Revels, II, 1.
3. Thierry and Theodoret, I 1.
4. The Custom, V, 2.
5. Fair Quarrel, III, 2.
6. Merchant of Venice, IV, 1, 130.
7. Volpone, II, 3.
8. Scene II.
9. Thierry and Theodoret, V, 2.
10. Quoted in Pomeranz, op. cit., p. 359.

IV

1. King John, III, 4.
2. Midsummer Night's Dream, II, 1.
3. Richard III.
4. Henry VI, II, 1.
5. Troilus and Cressida, I, 3.
6. Quoted by Pears, E. A., Elizabethan Drama and Its Mad Folk. op. cit., p. 13.
7. See Yearsley, M., op. cit., p. 114.
8. Quoted by Field, B. R., op. cit., p. 41.
9. See Gen. 6:4; Exod. 22:18; Levit. 19:31; 20:6,27; Deut. 18:10; I Sam. 18:10; 28:3-20; Matt. 4:24; 8:16, 28:33; Mark 16:9; Luke 4:14; 8:2, 27-36; Acts 16:16-18; Gal. 5:20; et passim.
10. Zilboorg, G., A History of Medical Psychology, p. 150.
11. Quoted in Pomeranz, op. cit., p. 370.
12. Ibid., p. 371.
13. Ibid.

V

1. Winter's Tale, I, 2, 110.
2. Love's Labour's Lost, IV, 2, 70; Twelfth Night, I, 5, 122; Troilus and Cressida, II, 1, 28.
3. King Lear, II, 4, 57.
4. Four Letter Confut. Wks. (Grosart) II, 272.

5. **Vicary's Anatomie, (1548), op. cit., IV.**
6. **Anatomie of the Bodie of Man (1548). See Early Text Society,** 1888, Extra Series, LIII, p. 31.
7. **Op. cit.,** p. 15.
8. **Op. cit.,** Floyd Dell Edition, **p. 135.**
9. See Dr. Nedham in his **Medela Medicinae (1665), p. 48.**
10. Harris, **J. Lex. Techn., (1704).**
11. Crooke, **Body of Man (1615),** 326.
12. Observation 33. "Select Observations on English Bodies; etc." in British Museum. Egerton MSS 2065.
13. See: Nicholson, Brinsley "Hamlet's Cursed Hebenon," **Transactions of the New Shakespeare Society,** Nov. 14, 1879 (Transactions, 1880-86, p. 21). Also Harrison, W. A., **Transactions,** May 12, 1882, p. 295. Also Grindon's **Flora of Shakespeare.**
14. **Cymbeline, I, 5.**
15. **Ibid.**
16. **Macbeth, II, 1.**
17. **Cymbeline, V, 5.**
18. **Midsummer Night's Dream, I, 1.**
19. **Henry VIII, 1, 3.**
20. **Coriolanus, I, 4.**
21. **Merchant of Venice, I, 2.**
22. **Richard II, II, 2.**
23. **Twelfth Night, I, 3.**
24. **Taming of the Shrew, IV, 1.**
25. **For quotations, see Moyes or Fields.**

CHAPTER VIII

THE ACQUISITION OF SHAKESPEARE'S MEDICAL AND PSYCHIATRIC KNOWLEDGE

I

The Sources of Shakespeare's Medical and Psychopathological Knowledge

Shakespeare's dramas do contain what seems to us today a vast amount of medical material. Because of this he has been credited with an unusual amount of medical knowledge. In fact, the Shakespearean idolators have gone so far as to make of him a "master of medicine," a "physiologist," a "great physician," etc., and they have attributed to him scientific knowledge which only later generations could possibly have had. The reason for this, as has been pointed out, is that the medical commentators have failed to take into consideration the age in which the dramatist lived, and have interpreted him on the basis of modern standards. The result, of course, has been a grand travesty of logic, which has led to foolish extravagances in respect to the poet, utterly beyond the pale of reason. Surely these commentators should have known the importance of environment in life. They should have attached proper significance to the historical background in which Shakespeare moved.

Now, in the first place, it has been proved in the previous pages that medical knowledge was much more widely diffused among laymen in Shakespeare's day than it is today. Such medical knowledge consisted mainly of Aristotelian and Galenic teachings brought into the limelight by the Renaissance. It was possible for an intelligent layman like Shakespeare to acquire an acquaintance with it. Secondly, since the Elizabethans had no newspapers or periodicals, the Elizabethan stage assumed, more or less, the functions of these. The stage was undoubtedly an avenue for the dissemination of all kinds of knowledge, political, social, economic, medical. Not only are Shakespeare's dramas full of medical matter, as most of the medical commentators seem to infer, but the dramas of practically all of Shakespeare's contemporaries are full of medical references.

But, aside from all this, Shakespeare had ample opportunity to acquire the medical knowledge that he shows. The fact that Shakespeare's son-in-law was a doctor certainly contributed to his interest in the subject. And "it is not unreasonable to suppose," as Dr. Hawley points out (1892), "that he had become acquainted with the theories of the older medical writers through conversations with his son-in-law, the physician of Stratford, Dr. John Hall," and that some of his wealth of clinical observation may be attributed to this close relationship."[1] Dr. Bucknill (1859), earlier than Dr. Hawley, also felt that it was "scarcely possible but that some influence should have been exercised upon the impressionable mind of the poet, by the husband of his favorite daughter, living with him in the same house,"[2] while Dr. Donnellan, at a later date (1902), agreed with both: "It is reasonable to suppose he was assisted in his researches by his son-in-law, Dr. Hall . . ."[3] However, be that as it may, we must not lose sight of the fact that Dr. Hall married Susannah Shakespeare in 1607, that is, at a time when Shakespeare had completed most of his works. Hall's influence on Shakespeare therefore, in the matter of medical knowledge, must have been very little if any.

In addition, Shakespeare's supposed medical knowledge might have been derived from books of a medical character. Dr. Hackman says "That he was possessed of such knowledge as could be gained by reading the available anatomical treatises of the period is proved."[4] Thus, Dr. W. B. Richardson and others believe that Shakespeare studied Helkiah Crookes' book on anatomy, *Microcosmographia* (1615),[5] "for the closer this book and the book of the plays are read together the more clearly is it detected where and how the dramatist became the student of anatomy."[6] Similarly, Dr. Moyes attributes to Shakespeare a knowledge of the book *Batman upon Bartholme his Booke De proprietatibus rerum,* published in 1582.[7] At least, the view of digestion and nutrition expressed in the famous metaphor in *Coriolanus* seems to be but an amplification of that in *Batman upon Bartholme his Booke De proprietatibus rerum.* Shakespeare puts this into the mouth of Menenius:

Note me this, good friend;
Your most grave belly was deliberate
Not rash like his accusers, and thus answered:
"True is it, my incorporate friends," quoth he,
"That I receive the general food at first
Which you do live upon; and fit it is,
Because I am the store-house and the shop
Of the whole body. But if you do remember,
I send it through the rivers of your blood,
Even to the court, the heart, to the seat o' the brain;
And through the cranks and offices of man,
Strongest nerves and small inferior veins
From me receive that natural competency
Whereby they live. And through that all at once,
You, my good friends,"—this says the belly, marke me.

Batman upon Bartholme his Booke De proprietatibus rerum reads:

> The stomach is the purveyor and husband of all the body, and the stomach taketh feeding for all the members and serveth all the members thereof as it needeth, as saith Constantine. (Book V. Chap. 38).

The similarity in idea here is too close to require further comment.

In addition, Shakespeare might have had access to Galen and Paracelsus and perhaps to Hippocrates and others (at second hand no doubt), or, at least, he was familiar with some of their teachings. "I have read the cause of its effects in Galen," says Shakespeare's Falstaff (*2 Henry IV.*, 1, 2, 133); "the most sovereign prescription in Galen be but empiricutic. . ." says his Menenius (*Coriolanus,* II, 1, 127). "He [Caius] has no more knowledge of Hippocrates and Galen—an he is a knave besides," says his Evans (*Merry Wives of Windsor,* III, 1).

> Thou almost maketh me waver in my faith
> To hold opinion with Pythagoras

says his Gratiano (*Merchant of Venice,* IV, 1, 30). Aristotle is mentioned twice,[8] Galen, two more times than already quoted,[9] five times in all, and Paracelsus[10] once. Contemporary dramatists practically all mentioned the above famous men and many others.

But it is not necessary to make Shakespeare a reader of medical treatises, and "a diligent student of all medical knowledge existing in his time,"[11] nor yet a purposive seeker of medical knowledge in the association with physicians, to account for the abundance of medical material in his plays. As already mentioned, the laity generally knew more of medical matters in Shakespeare's day than they do today. There was no real scientific medicine. Even the medical profession itself had not risen above the pall of the Dark Ages. It was Galen, Aristotle and Hippocrates, and Hippocrates, Aristotle and Galen. These bound medicine with the cords of traditional doctrine; these ruled over science with the tyranny of accepted authority. The healing art was bound up with philosophy, astrology, religion, natural science, magic. Consequently, books of all types, from those on metaphysics to those on cookery, from books of poetry to books of sermons—all abounded in the medical knowledge of the day. Thus, Burton's *Anatomy of Melancholy* (1612), Timothy Bright's *Treatise of Melancholy* (1586), Thomas Wright's *Passions of the Minde in Generall* (1601), Bacon's *Novum Organum* (1620), Wilson's *Arte of Rhetorique, Knowledge which maketh a Wise Man* (1533), and also his *Castel of Helth,* Sir John Davies' *Microcosmos,* Huarte's *Examen de Ingenios* (1594), La Primaudaye's *French Academy* (1594), Charron's *De la Sagesse* (1601), Ludovicus Vives' *Introduction to Wisdom* (1540), Andrew Boorde's *Dietary of Health* (1542), and many others—in all these do we find the intellectual arcana of the day. Indeed, many of these popular books were written for laymen and went through many editions as best-sellers.

Might not Shakespeare have absorbed these from the very atmosphere about him, let alone from the books themselves directly, and with them the medical materials which he uses in his plays?

As a matter of fact, some scholars have pointed out that ". . . the greatest dramatist of all times was under obligations to Timothy Bright's most popular work [*A Treatise of Melancholy*]." In his paper, "On the Physiological Basis of Shakespeare's Psychology,"[12] Professor Richard Leoning of Jena University, declares it to be highly probable that Shakespeare knew and made use of the book ("Es ist sehr Wahrscheinlich, das der Dichter dieses Buch gekannt und benutzt hat"); and argues that in his masterly portrayals of the melancholic temperament in *Hamlet* and other plays the poet has drawn largely upon his knowledge of the *Treatise of Melancholy*. Indeed, he finds it the key to Shakespeare's entire physiological psychology, the atmosphere in and under the influence of which his works had their birth.[13] Dr. Curt Deunscheit affirms that "it is now established beyond doubt that Shakespeare read this book . . . It was through Bright that Shakespeare first obtained a profound insight into physiological psychology."[14]

More specifically, "It has been pointed out that the phrase 'discourse of reason' to which Hamlet gives utterance (I, 2, 150) and 'generally supposed to be exclusively Shakespearean' occurs in Bright's *Epistle Dedicatorie* where he remarks: 'I have interlaced my treatise besides with disputes of philosophie that the learned sort of them, and such as are of quicke conceit & delited in *discourse of reason* in naturall things, may find to pass their time with.' "[15] As William Blades remarks, "It would be an interesting task to compare the Mad Folk of Shakespeare, most of whom have the Melancholy fit, with *A Treatise of Melancholy* [Bright's] which was probably read carefully . . . by the youthful poet."[16]

Surely enough, Mary I. O'Sullivan[17] has done just this with the character of Hamlet, for she states that ". . . the treatise influenced Shakespeare and more particularly Hamlet." She comes to the conclusion that "Shakespeare used the *Treatise* in his task of fitting a ready made destiny with a convincing character." In addition, Shakespeare must also have been acquinted with Reginald Scot's *Discoverie of Witchcraft* (1584), for the "ass's nowl" of Bottom's head seems definitely derived from it as are references in *Hamlet, Twelfth Night, I Henry VI, I Henry IV, Midsummer Night's Dream, Macbeth* and *Love's Labour's Lost.*[18]

In this respect, we must not lose sight of the fact that Elizabethan England was a restless, expanding Renaissance England, with a rising middle class, filled with a passion for learning and education. This gave tremendous stimulus to reading and the printing of books with a large increase in booksellers and publishers so that it became an important industry that by 1557 was incorporated into a Stationer's Company consisting of 97 stationers with the privilege of printing and selling books. Shakespeare could easily have been one among the many browsing among the books and pamphlets in the stalls of Paul's Walk—such books including numerous and various publications, encyclopedias of useful knowledge, novels, pamphlets, best sellers of the period, etc. The books and treatises mentioned previously were undoubtedly in Shakespeare's reach. It is interesting to note that in a letter that one Robert Laneham, a mercer of London, wrote to a friend concerning the library of one Capt. Cox, a mason of Coventry, a list of books of various types is mentioned, among them being "doctor Broode's breviary of health"[19] that we have referred to many times.

That Shakespeare actually was familiar with these books of the period and the doctors of the period may perhaps be gathered not only from the fact that he mentions all the accepted authorities in his dramas and shows a familiarity with the "schools" of controversy, but also from the intrinsic implications of one particular passage. He puts into the mouth of the noble physician, Cerimon, the following words:

> 'Tis known, I ever
> Have studied physic, through which secret art,
> By turning o'er authorities, I have
> Together with my practice made familiar

To me and to my aid, the bless'd infusions
That dwell in vegetives, in metals, stones;
And I can speak of the disturbances
That nature works; . . .[20]

No one who has not actually read such treatises as Laurentius' *Of the Diseases of Melancholie,* Timothy Bright's, *A Treatise of Melancholy,* Burton's *Anatomy of Melancholy* and the other similar popular medical books of the day, could possibly have used the words "by turning o'er authorities." This characterizes most significantly these books of the period, for essentially that is all they are—a rehashing, a "turning o'er [of] authorities"—Aristotle, Plato, Avicenna, Pythagoras, Galen, Hippocrates, etc., etc. That is all medicine was at this stage and the writers of the period actually prided themselves on this "turning o'er authorities." Actually, Burton in his *Anatomy* quotes over a thousand authors, the greater part of whom are medical writers of the past centuries. And it is even with apparent pride that he writes, "I have laboriously collected this Cento out of divers writers. . ." Whether Shakespeare, after becoming familiarized with these numerous books, merely used poetic descriptive English or intended satire, is problematical, but it certainly indicates an acquaintance with the character of the books mentioned in the Elizabethan era.

Then too, we must not forget that Shakespeare was the friend of university men, companion to Ben Jonson, Heminges, Condell, Marlowe, etc., an acquaintance of Jaggard, possibly Bacon, the Earl of Southampton, and others. Might not he have gleaned from these the intellectual heritage of the day? Surely if Shakespeare himself did not have recourse to the books of the day, then Ben Jonson and the others of the coterie certainly did. In this regard it might be of some significance to note that Thomas Lodge,[21] the contemporary of Shakespeare, was a physician, and in 1603 published *A Treatise on the Plague;* also that Thomas Dekker,[22] another contemporary dramatist, wrote two treatises dealing with the plague. Can it be stretching the limits of possibility too far to suppose that

Shakespeare might have shown an interest in such treatises, if not for the subject matter, then for the very fact that contemporaries and perhaps friends of his were their authors?

Furthermore, there were popular Herbals in Shakespeare's day which undoubtedly accounts for the fact that "Shakespeare . . . shows a surprising knowledge of the therapeutic effects of various herbs and drugs."[23] Indeed, as previously implied, knowledge of herbs and plants was fostered for centuries as a necessary part of everyone's education, what with the poor status of medical practice, and the poverty of the people. Philemon Holland's *Pliny,* which was very popular in Shakespeare's day urges people "to go a simpling into the desarts and forrests to seeke and gather herbs at all seasons of the yere. . ."[24] Andrew Boorde wrote "There is no Herbe, no weede, but God have gyven vertue to them to helpe man."[25] Shakespeare implies the influence of such a concept when he has Cordelia say (*King Lear,* IV, 5):

All blest secrets,
All you unpublish'd virtues of the earth,
Spring with my tears! be aidant and remediate
In the good man's distress! Seek, seek for him

and Friar Laurence (*Romeo and Juliet,* II, 3):

O, mickle is the powerful grace that lies
In herbs, plants, stones, and their true qualities;
For naught so vile that on the earth doth live,
But to the earth some special good doth give

and Jessica (*Merchant of Venice,* V, 1):

In such a night
Medea gather'd the enchanted herbs
That did renew old Aeson

and Laertes (*Hamlet,* IV, 7):

Where it draws blood no cataplasm so rare
Collected from all simples that have virtue
Under the moon, can save the thing from death

Dekker carries the meaning in his *Belman of London*:

> If the practice of physic delight thee what Aphorisms can all the Doctors in the world set down more certain? . . . What virtues can all their Extracted Quintessences instill into our bodies more sovereign than those which the earth of her own bounty bestows for our preservation, . . .?[26]

All this indicates how knowledge of herbs, plants, drugs, must have seeped into the consciousness of the Elizabethan to find expression and general acceptance in the Herbals of the day. John Taylor, the "Water Poet" speaks of

> The Paracelsists and Galenists
> The philosophical Herbalists[27]

There was the great Herbalist Peter Treveris (Southwark, 1516) who wrote the popular "The Grete Herball." There is the famous philosopher Herbalist Richard Banckes whose Herbal was the first printed in England in 1525 and went through several editions. There was the *Niewe Herball or Historie of Plants* (1578) of Henry Lyte, the Herbal entitled "Adversaria" of Matthios Lobel, for whom the drug, lobelia, is named. Finally, it is well to mention what was probably the most popular of the Herbals in Shakespeare's day, the one of Rembert Dodoens, translated from the Dutch in 1595, entitled

> An New Herbal or Historie of Plants: Wherein is contained the whole discourse and perfect description of all sorts of Herbs and Plants: . . . their Names, Natures, Operations and Vertues; . . . commonly used in physicke . . .[28]

Add to this the fact that it was the universal practice in Elizabethan England to scatter various herbs throughout their homes as a possible accepted preventative of the terrible plague, and we have another essential reason why the common man used Herbals and knew so much of herbs and drugs, so clearly reflected in the dramas of the period.

There were almanacks and versified versions of medical tracts, as well as broadsides and advertising handbills of nostrum mongers.

On many a post I see Quacksalver's bills
Like fencers challenges to show their skill.

writes Taylor, "The Water Poet," about 1603.[29] One such handbill "imprinted" by H. Hills in Black-Fryers near the Waterside runs as follows:

See Sirs, see here
A Doctor rare,
Who travels much at home,
Here take my bills,
I cure all ills,
Past, present and to come;
The Cramp, the Stitch,
The Squirt, the Itch
The Gout, the Stone, the Pox;
The Mulligrubs
The Bonny Scrubs
And all Pandora's box.
Thousands I've dissected
Thousands new erected,
And such cure effected
As none e'er can tell
Let the Palsie shake you
Let the Chollik rack ye,
Let the Crinkums break ye
Take this and ye are well.
Come wits so keen
Devour'd with spleen;
Come beaus who sprain'd your backs,
Great Belly'd Maids,
Old Foundered Jades,
And pepper'd Vizard cracks.
I soon remove the pains of Love,
And cure the Love-sick maid;
The hot, the cold

The young, the old
The living and the dead;
I clear the lass,
With Wainscot face
And from pimginets free,
Plump ladies red
Like Saracen's Head
With Toaping Rat affia
This with a jerk
Will do your work,
And scour your O're and O're,[30]

Dr. John Halle in his "An Historical Expostulation Against the Abuses both of Chirurgery and physyke in Oure Tyme" (1565), cites many examples of such advertising handbills of the day[31] one of which follows:

> If any manne, womanne, or childe bee sicke, or would be let blood, or bee diseased with any manner of inworde or outworde grefes, as al maner of agues, or fevers, pluri-ses, cholyke, . . . goutes . . . bone ache . . . and payne of the joints . . . let them resorte to the sygne of the Sarazen's Hedde, in the easte lane . . and they shall have remedie,
>
> By me, Thomas Luffkin

Dekker in *Lanthorne and Candlelight* wrote:

> Upon this scaffold, also might be mounted a number of Quack-Salving Empiricks, who arriving in some country town clap up their *Terrible Bills,* in the Market Place, and filling the Paper with such horrible names of diseases . . . . Yet these Beggarly Mountebanks are mere Cozeners and have not so much skill as Horseleeches.[32]

The Library of the Royal College of Surgeons possesses one of such handbills printed about 1525. Part of it reads:

> The Canker or the Colyck and the Skarre in the lyppe or other diseases in the mouth . . . Also, if any man hade any

dysease in his eyen, who be with Spurblindnes or a Wem or any other Skynne over the Syghts. These and other much lyke disease can this aforesaid Mayster avoyde and Heale by the grace and help of God. Moreover if any be diseased with the Pockes or other pryoy diseases or have sore leggs of old or new greves, let him come to the forsayde Maister Gernaes . . . and he wyl heale him with the grace of God. . .[33]

Ben Jonson in his *Volpone* (II, 1) puts into the song of the Mountebank Nano what any Elizabethan might hear in the public places of London any day:

You that would last long, list to my song,
Make no more coil, but buy of this oil

Want you live free from all diseases?
Do the act your mistress pleases?
Yet fright all aches from your bones?
Here's a med'cine for the nones.

Thomas Middleton in his play, *The Widow* (1608), portrays a quack hanging out the following poster at his place of business:

Here within this place is cured
All the griefs that were ever endured.
Palsy, gout, hydropic humour
Breath that stinks beyond perfumer,
Fistula in ano, lucer, megrim,
Or what disease soe'er beleaguer 'em,
Stone, rupture, squinancy, imposthume,
Yet too dear it shall not cost 'em.
In brief, you cannot, I assure you,
Be unsound as fast as I can cure you.

(Act IV, sc. 2)

From such sources at least Shakespeare might have acquired the names of diseases, if nothing else. These quacks and mountebanks putting on spectacular medicine shows were numerous. In a London, with a population of only about 150,000, and being himself a frequenter of taverns and of all the other popular haunts of London,[34] consorter with all manner and types of people, from groundling to lord, could Shakespeare have helped picking up the general medical knowledge of his day?

But even if we set aside all this as mere conjecture, yet Shakespeare could not have escaped the evidence of his own senses. We must not forget that Shakespeare's England was a plague-ridden England. Disease and death were all about the poet. Houses were quarantined, stamped with the red cross and the words "God have Mercy Upon Us," to warn the passers by. The signs and symptoms of the disease were common knowledge and common household words. And, indeed, Shakespeare takes due notice of all this in his plays. He says (*Love's Labour's Lost,* V, 2):

> Write *Lord have mercy on up* on those three;
> They are infected, in their hearts it lies;
> They have the plague and caught it in your eyes.

And again (*Troilus and Cressida,* II, 3):

> He is so plaguy-proud, that the death tokens
> of it cry
> No recovery.

And further (*Antony and Cleopatra,* III, 10):

> On our side, like the token'd pestilence,
> Where death is sure

And in *Coriolanus,* (IV, 1):

> Now the red pestilence strike all the trades in Rome

These passages and others referring to "the infectious pestilence," "red pestilence," "token'd pestilence" had much more meaning for those in Shakespeare's day than for us today. Those who had the plague and who presented a reddish petechial rash were given up as marked for certain death. Therefore the petechial making up the rash were called "God's tokens" and, as mentioned before, their houses were closed.

Abraham Holland, a minor poet of the period in his "Posthuma" (1626), gives us vivid evidence of what Shakespeare undoubtedly witnessed:

A noon in Fleet Street now can hardly show
That press which midnight could, not long ago
Walk through the woeful streets (whoever dare
Still venture on the sad infected air)
So many marked houses you shall meet
As if the city were one Red-Cross Street.[35]

There were bodies in the streets and continual processions of funerals.[36] John Taylor, the "Water Poet," takes notice of this

In some whole street, perhaps, a shop or twain
Stands open for small takings and less gain
And every closed window, door and stall
Makes everyday seem a solemn festival.
All trades are dead, or almost out of breath,
But such as line by sickness and by death.[37]

Of the sick, Taylor writes,

Some franticks raving, some with anguish crying
Dead corpses carried and recarried still
Whilst fifty corpses scarce one grave doth fill.

John Davies, of Hereford, in his "The Triumph of Death; or the picture of the plague, according to the Life, as it was in A. D. 1603" adds graphic details to our picture of the plague as Shakespeare probably saw it.

Cast out your dead, the carcass-carrier carries,
Which he by heaps in groundless graves inters...
The London lanes, themselves thereby to save,

Did vomit out their undigested dead,
Who by cart-loads are carried to the grave
Each village free now stands upon her guard . . .
The haycocks in the meads were oft oprest
With plaguey bodies, both alive and dead,
Which beings used confounded man and beast.[38]

During these plagues business was paralyzed, civil courts were closed, and there were exoduses of the rich from London. What was of even more immediate importance to Shakespeare was the closing of the theatres and their removal to the outskirts of the city.[39]

All these factors must have been forced on his attention. For him to have failed in the acquisition of the general medical knowledge involved in such would have been no compliment certainly to his sense of observation or to his genius as a moulder of language. Moreover, we must not forget that the districts about James Burbage's "The Theatre" and "The Globe" to the very stage doors and the theatres themselves were notorious rendezvous for the gangsters of the day, the ruffians, horse-thieves, rogues, hoboes, deserters, disbanded soldiers, skid-row characters, beggars, prostitutes, etc. There must have been knifings, stranglings, homicides. Things had come to such a pass that in 1595 the Lord Mayor of London petitioned the Privy Council to take note how the theatres had become the center of all "Masterless" men and vagabond persons who haunted the highways causing trouble. We can be sure that Shakespeare had ample opportunities to see, among other things, violent deaths of all types. Add to this, the fact that there were public hangings always well-attended,—and we can readily explain our dramatist's familiarity with deaths of all types, about which so many of the medical critics have exclaimed in puzzlement and in idolatrous wonder. These critics particularly point to the following lines in *2 Henry VI,* (III, 2):

But see, his face is black and full of blood,

His eyeballs further out than when he lived,
Staring full ghastly like a strangled man;

His hair up-rear'd, his nostrils stretched with struggling:
And tugg'd for life, and was by strength subdu'd.
Look on the sheets, his hair, you see, is sticking;
His well proportioned beard made rough and rugged.

and come up with the statement that "In medical jurisprudence his knowledge of the symptoms of violent and sudden death must have been remarkable for his day. . ."[40] and again "it is really surprising to read Shakespeare's differential diagnosis between cases of natural and violent deaths—the post-mortem appearance."[41] Had these critics given true significance to Shakespeare's environment, they would have better understood where the poet gained his medical knowledge.

Further, Shakespeare knew human nature, and he observed it in all its intricate forms. Besides his intuitive insight into the human mind, his opportunities for observation of human action, particularly in the mentally deranged, were indeed numerous. The insane in Shakespeare's day were not confined to asylums. Except in the case of those that became dangerously maniacal the insane were allowed to mix in society. Some however, were kept in jail. Shakespeare's father was judge, bailiff and jailer of Stratford at one time. It is reasonable to suppose that the youth, William, might have had direct contact with the insane.[42] It is well to mention here also that Susanna Hall, Shakespeare's daughter, probably suffered from a neurosis as a complication of scurvy for we find the following observation of her husband, Dr. John Hall:

> *Observation XXXIII*: Wife was troubled with the scurvy, accompanied with . . . Melancholy, wind, cardiac passion, Laziness, difficulty of breathing, fear of the Mother . . .[43]

Since, also, it was the custom to board out the more mildly deranged among the householders of a town, this offered further opportunity for direct observation. Thus, Shakespeare must have observed all the degrees of mental derangement, as well as of emotional instability. With the ability of a literary master he reproduced these for us in his plays.

II

Madness In Elizabethan England and in Shakespeare's Dramas

It is true as the critics hold that Shakespeare paid special attention to the abnormal states of mind and even of madness. But here again, this is certainly not unique with Shakespeare. We must remember to consider him in the light of his own times. The Shakespearean audience loved to see madness on the stage. Shakespeare's contemporary playwrights often introduced mad scenes and madness into their dramas with, perhaps, even greater frequency that did Shakespeare. There are numerous maniacs, melancholias, imbeciles, morons and feigners of madness introduced by most of the Elizabethan dramatists. Hieronimo of Kyd's *Spanish Tragedy,* Memmon of Fletcher's *Mad Lover,* Penthea of Ford's *Broken Heart,* Venelia of Peele's *Old Wives Tale,* Sir Giles Overreach of Massinger's *A New Way to Pay Old Debts,* Trouble-All of Ben Jonson's *Bartholomew Fair,* Lucibiella of Chettle's *Tragedy of Hoffman,*—these are only a few of the psychotic characters in general Elizabethan drama. As Allison Peers so aptly points out, "the subject of lunacy was so commonplace that the dramatist who like Shakespeare mirrored the life and speech of everyday, would find himself, even against his will, borrowing figures from Bedlam."[1]

Madmen, in fact, were exhibited for amusement in the asylums for a penny or two admission; and Shakespeare certainly must have attended these. Although our poet himself has no such actual scenes in his plays but only refers to them, this does not necessarily mean that he had a compassionate understanding of the insane ahead of his time, but rather that he was a better dramatic artist. Ben Jonson in his *Epicence* (II, 1) has one of his characters announce,

> Mad folks and other strange sights to be seen daily,
> private and public

In Middleton's *The Changeling* (III, 3) Dr. Alibius, together with his assistant Lollio, trains his "brainsick" patients to perform at entertainments such as weddings, in order

> . . . to make a frightful pleasure.
> To finish as it were, and make the fag
> Of all the revels, the third night from the first

In Webster's *The Duchess of Malfi,* (IV, 2) we find a scene in which madmen dance and sing. Thomas Dekker, in one of his plays, writes in relation to all this:

> Yet they do act
> Such antics and such pretty lunacies
> That spite of sorrow they make you smile

Many other quotations could be cited from different dramatists. Suffice it to say that, in general, "the subject was regarded rather as one for mirth than for solemnity."[2] How could it be otherwise when even Dr. Andreas Laurentius in his serious work on *Melancholie* writes in relation to certain cases of insanity ". . . it behoveth me now in this chapter, (*to the end I may somewhat delight the reader*) to set down some examples of such as have had the most fantastical . . . imaginations. . . ."[3] and Robert Burton likewise, in dealing with case histories, shows similar levity.

If we add to this the already mentioned fact that Bedlam beggars, the feeble-minded, and the harmlessly insane were common everyday sights in Shakespeare's day—then is it any wonder that our poet evinces what seems to us today a great interest and knowledge of the mentally ill? And the statement of Dr. Isaac Ray, agreed to by some of the later commentators, that Shakespeare's "opportunities for observing the insane were scanty and imperfect"[4] has no validity whatsoever.

But, further, be that as it may, the important reason that Shakespeare was so interested in the abnormal states of mind is not that there was so much madness all about him, or that it was a custom of the dramatists of the time, but rather because these abnormal states gave him greater play for his abilities in psychological delineations. Would you have the states of mind and the interaction of petty motives of the ordinary humdrum every day life depicted, you will have only gross comedy. Shakespeare was too good a psychologist not to have availed himself of the wide range for psychological delineations present in the abnormal states of mind. But he did not choose actual maniacal madness, for that would have made an end to his purpose. He chose rather to depict the borderline between madness and normality. He took that wavering twilight of the mind between sanity and insanity, to which so many of us, under stress, are so subject, and he painted for us the stirring dramas we have in *Macbeth, Othello, King Lear* and *Hamlet.* There are very good reasons, then, why Shakespeare should have introduced so much medical and psychiatric material into his works, and made laymen, not physicians, the instrument for the utterances of such medical lore.

But what in actuality can we truthfully say of the real character, the quality, of the medical knowledge in Shakespeare's plays? Is it such that we must attribute to the poet an actual study of the healing art, as so many of the commentators seem to think? And should we credit him with knowledge that even physicians lacked in his day? The truth is that in this, as in everything else, Shakespeare was necessarily limited by the horizon of his century and the limits of his education. The medical knowledge in his plays is of a general character, such as any intelligent observing layman of his day might have acquired in a similar environment. Much has been made of the fact that Shakespeare shows an acquaintanceship with the chief medical theories of the times, especially those of Galen and Paracelsus. But how could he have escaped such knowledge? Aside from the fact that the teachings of Galen, Hippocrates, Aristotle, Paracelsus, Avicenna, Rhazes, and others have crept into the general literature and language of the day, bitter controversies raged regarding those various schools of medicine, particularly one between the Galenists and the Paracelsians. Shakespeare, in fact, refers to this, for he speaks of being "relinquished of the artists . . . both of Galen and Paracelsus" (*All's Well that Ends Well,* II, 3, 10-11). He also flouts the empiricism of the medical practice of the day. He puts into the mouth of Menenius the following (*Coriolanus,* II, 1, 124-130):

> It gives me an estate of seven years' health in which time I will make a lip at the physician; the most sovereign pre-

scription of Galen is but empiricutic, and, to this preservative, of no better report than a horsedrench.

Ben Jonson, intimate friend of Shakespeare, also did not fail to notice the two contending schools. In *The Alchemist* (II, 1) he satirizes a type of physician as

> A rare physician . . .
> An excellent Paracelsian, and has done
> Strange cures with mineral physic. He deals all
> with spirits, he; he will not hear a word of
> Galen, or his tedious recipes.

Thomas Middleton in his *A Fair Quarrel* (II, 2), also shows acquaintance with these matters, for one of his characters is made to say,

> Can all your Paracelsian mixtures cure it?

Marlowe, too, in his *Doctor Faustus,* says,

> Bid economy farewell, and Galen come.

To challenge the infallibility of Galen in Shakespeare's day, further, "to make a lip" at him, as Shakespeare expresses it, was fraught with serious consequences. Sir Theodore Mayerne, Court physician to James I and also to most of the monarchs of Europe, of whom Shakespeare might have direct knowledge, as already pointed out, was forced to flee France in 1607 and to settle in England because he was a follower of Paracelsus. The Royal College of Physicians of London severely reprimanded any of their members who dared question the teachings of Galen. Thus we read of one Dr. Geynes being suspended from the College in 1559 for such a crime. Only "on his acknowledgement of error and humble recantation, signed with his own hand, was he received into the College."

The London of Shakespeare's day was not too large, nor yet the tongues of gossip-purveyors and scandal-mongers too dulled, for such matters of interest to have escaped the notice of the frequenters of Shakespeare's haunts. We can be sure that, in the course of the conversations, such matters as the medical theories of Galen and Paracelsus would certainly come up. Might not Shakespeare have gained a great deal of his medical knowledge in just such a fashion?

The mistake of the 19th century and of most modern commentators on Shakespeare has been this: they have confused a keen sense of observation and a genius for language in Shakepeare with actual medical and psychiatric knowledge. Thus vivid descriptions of the apopletic stroke, the epileptic fit, the facies of death from strangulation, the general effects of alcohol upon the system, the states of senility and madness, etc.—all these have been cited as proof of Shakespeare's unusual medical knowledge rather than of his dramatic ability.

We need go no further than a recent book (1932) *William Shakespeare, M.D.* by Harry Epstein, M.D., to realize this method of approach so evident in practically all medical critics. Dr. Epstein quotes the famous lines of Jaques, with respect to the seven ages of man (*As You Like It,* II, 7, 140-166); and he adds, "In commenting upon this passage, can one, today, improve upon this excellent description of the sequences taking place in one's lifetime?" Certainly not. Not a physician today, nor one in Shakespeare's day, could do half as well. But does that prove anything about Shakespeare's medical knowledge? Does the observation that an infant "mewls and pukes," that a school-boy "whines," and that "second childishness" is, "Sans teeth, sans eyes, sans taste, sans everything," prove anything but that Shakespeare was a good observer and a master of poetic language?

Dr. Epstein quotes from *II Henry IV* (I, 2, 200-208):

> Have you not a moist eye, a dry hand, a yellow cheek, a white beard, a decreasing leg, and increasing belly? Is not your voice broken, your wind short, your chin double, your wit single, and every part about you blasted with antiquity, and will you yet call yourself young?

and he says, "Could there be a more complete manner of expressing a beginning or an established senility?" Certainly not. But wherein is there any true medical knowledge involved? In like manner, Dr. Epstein quotes a passage from the same play (IV, 3, 103-122), showing Shakespeare's knowledge of "the glowing effects of alcohol" and also another passage showing Shakespeare's knowledge of insomnia (III, 1, 4-31). But one can challenge any member of the Royal College of Physicians and Surgeons, even of today, who could describe "the glowing effects of alcohol" or the tortures of insomnia, who has not himself imbibed of "sherris-sack," or himself has lived through endless nights of insomnia. That Shakespeare described all these sensations so beautifully only proves that perhaps he himself had spent many a hilarious night in convivial drunkenness, and many a tortured night in lonesome sleeplessness, and that he had had the power that few physicians have of setting these sensations to language; or, at least, that Shakespeare had the power of imagination to write about these states. Clearly then, such types of evidence to prove Shakespeare's knowledge of medicine (and most medical commentators are guilty of their use) fall far short of fulfilling their aim.

But even the actual passages that deal with authentic medical material in Shakespeare, and that have been used by commentators to prove Shakespeare's medical knowledge, prove nothing of the kind. Thus in the matter of syphilis, Shakespeare has been given much credit for an unusual knowledge of this disease, since he has numerous references to it in his works. Dr. Epstein quotes the following passage from *As You Like It* (II, 7, 64-70) to prove this point:

> Most mischievous foul sin, in chiding sin:
> For thou thyself hast been a libertine,
> As sensual as the brutish sting itself;
> And all the embossed sores and headed evils,
> That thou with license of free foot hast caught,
> Wouldst thou disgorge into the general world.

and adds,

> Shakespeare in these few lines shows an understanding of the way in which syphilis is contracted by sinning, and indicates that promiscuity begets venereal disease.... Shakespeare clearly describes the sores, and the headed

evils accompanying the disease. He refers to the tendency of syphilis to show itself on the forehead, and, when neglected to cause an increase in the size of the bone of the head, as seen in cranio tabes and in exostoses found at the temporo-frontal angles.

All this is merely tribute again to Shakespeare's wide-awake, intelligent observations of the environment in which he lived, for we must not lose sight of the fact, as already pointed out, that in Elizabethan England the average layman knew more of medical matters, saw more of diseases, than the average layman today, and that it was a common thing for all playwrights of the time to refer to medical subjects with much frequency. Syphilis, especially, because of its wide distribution in London in Shakespeare's day, and because of its social nature, was bound to receive particular attention at the hands of everyone. Shakespeare has the clown in *Hamlet* (V, 1) say:

> I' faith, if a' be not rotten before a' die—as we have *many pocky corses* now-a-days, that will scarce hold the laying in—a' will last you some eight year or nine year: a tanner will last you nine year.

In *2 Henry IV* (I, 2) Shakespeare writes:

> A man can no more separate age and covetousness, than he can part young limbs from lechery; but the gout galls the one, and the pox pinches the other.

In *Timon of Athens* (IV, 3) we have the following words:

> Be a whore still . . .
> . . . Season the slaves
> For tubs and baths; bring down rose-cheeked youth
> To the tub-fast and the diet.

Again in *Henry V* (II, 1) we have:

> To the spital go,
> And from the powdering tub of infamy
> Fetch forth the lazar-kite of Cressid's kind

Similarly, we find references to tubs, baths and diet which was the common treatment of syphilis in Shakespeare's day, in numerous other plays of the period.[5] Thus in *Monsieur S'Obue* (1606) we find the following lines:

> Our embassage is into France, there may be employment for thee
>
> Hast thou a tub?

In *A Family of Love* (1608) we have:

> O for one of the hoops of my Cornelius' tub
> I shall burst myself with laughing else

Again in *Jasper Maenis* (1639) we read:

> — You had better match a ruin'd bawd,
> One ten times cur'd by sweating and the tub

In fact, the phrases, "the tub, the sweat and diet on you" and "a pox on you" were common oaths of Shakespeare's day and entered into ordinary conversations in the same way as the oaths "damn you," "to hell with you," etc., enter into the everyday language of our own times. Shakespeare, as well as his contemporaries, uses these phrases or oaths frequently.

Bullein in his *Bulwarke of Defence*[6] (1579), a popular book of the day, describes the current treatment of syphilis and throws much lights on these passages. Thus, the so-called "tub" was a wooden vessel, similar to that used in corning or curing beef in which process also the meat was powdered with salt and hence the name "powdering tub of infamy" in relation to curing syphilis for, according to Bullein also, herbs were powdered into the treatment tub. This, no doubt, satisfactorily accounts for the following line in *Measure for Measure* (III, 2) associating beef and the tub of treatment:

> She hath eaten up all her beef, and she is herself in the tub.

Following are part of Bullein's directions from this treatise:

> Eighthly, after ix or x dayes be past, once in three days, let the sicke bedye bee bathed on this sort. Set fayre running

water on the fyre, and put thereto a great deale of ground Ivie leaves, and red Sage and Fenell also, and by a good fyre when the sicke body is going to Bed, put the water and herbs into a vessel of wood, and let the sicke Body stand upright in it, by the fyre, and take up the herbes and rubbe the body of the sicke pacient dounewards, and then dry him with warme cloathes, use this, iii weekes. . . .

As to diet, which Shakespeare and his contemporary dramatists mention many times, Bullein says,[7]

> Also the sicke body must eate but little meate, and that kynde of meate as shall hereafter be prescribed, and at sutch time as shall be appoynted.

The average layman of the period was well aware of this treatment for the French disease.

The fact that Shakespeare even jests about some of the symptoms of syphilis shows that the disease was well known in all its aspects by his audience. Thus the baldness (alopecia) of syphilis, referred to as the "French Crown" in Shakespeare's day, allows him several more opportunities for plays on the word "crown" as a piece of money. In *King Henry V* (IV, 1, 242-246), King Henry is made to say,

> Indeed, the French may lay twenty French crowns to one, they will beat us, for they bear them on their shoulders; but it is no English treason to cut French crowns, and to-morrow the king himself may be a clipper.

Similarly, the following occurs in *Measure for Measure* (I, 2, 36-42) with the added pun on the word "dolours":

Lucio. Behold, behold where Madame Mitigation comes!
First Gent. I have purchased as many diseases under her roof as come to—
Sec. Gent. To what, I pray?
First Gent. Judge.
Sec. Gent. To three thousand dolours a year
First Gent. Ay, and more
Lucio. A French crown more.

Likewise in *A Midsummer Night's Dream* (I, 2, 95-100):

Bot. I will discharge it in either your straw-colour beard, your orange-tawny, beard, your purple-in-grain beard, or your French-crown-colour beard, your perfect yellow.
Quin. Some of your French crown have no hair at all, and then you will play barefac'd.

Thomas Dekker in *The Honest Whore* makes a similar attempt at such humour (Part I, 1, 5):

Castruchio . . . pox on't 'tis rough.
George. How? is she rough? but if you bid pox on't, Sir, 'twill take away the roughness presently.
Fluello. Ha, signor; has he fitted your French curse?

and it is certain that similar material could be found in practically all of Shakespeare's contemporary playwrights. Another lesion of syphilis which Shakespeare uses to produce humour is the breakdown of the bridge of the nose, with its concomitant alteration of the voice. The clown in *Othello,* chiding the musicians for their music says

Why, masters, have your instruments been in Naples, that they speak i' the nose thus.

Referring to this lesion Dr. Walter E. Vest (1941) remarks that "Shakespeare appears to have been the original observer of the sunken nose"[8] in syphilis. Again in 1950 he states that "here is she the first reference to the sunken nose of syphilis, as far as I can determine in medical or any other type of literature."[9] The fact is that Thomas Dekker in *The Honest Whore* (1604) refers several times to this lesion of syphilis before Shakespeare did. In Part I (III, 3) occur the following lines:

How; marry with a punk, . . .
I'll be burnt through the nose first.

In Part II (I, 2) one of the characters is made to say, "a pox a' de horse's nose"; and again (V, 2) "Pox ruin her nose for't."
Philip Massinger in *The Guardian* (IV, 3) also makes refer-

ence to this lesion when he puts into the mouth of Calypso the following words:

> . . . and I will build
> An hospital for noseless bawds.

Again in his *The Virgin Martyr* (IV, 2) we also find reference to this lesion in the following lines:

> *Theo.* . . . see, my lord, her face
> Has more bewitching beauty than before
> Proud whore, it smiles! cannot an eye start out,
> With these?
> *Hir.* No, sir, nor the bridge of her nose fall.

As to treatment of this disease, Shakespeare is not only not in advance of the opinions of his scientific contemporaries but he is far behind, for nowhere does he mention the use of guaiacum or mercury, the former in the form of the "holy wood," lignum vitae and the latter in the form of the liquid metal, used therapeutically since 1497 and mentioned often in the literature of the Elizabethan period.

But even on the merits of these passages there is nothing to prove a physician's knowledge of syphilis. Is it so remarkable that Shakespeare recognized "that promiscuity begets venereal disease"? The communicability of syphilis through venereal contact was common knowledge in Shakespeare's day, referred to, all too frequently, in the general literature as the French, Italian or Spanish Pox, depending, of course, upon the country to which one was antagonistic. Perhaps such communicability was even more apparent to the layman than to the physician. The jolly milkmaids in Jenner's day knew cowpox from smallpox and recognized the immunity produced by the one against the other long before Jenner was born. Would you credit them with extraordinary medical knowledge on that account and particularly with a knowledge of immunity? Indeed, some of the medical commentators,[10] as previously pointed out attribute to Shakespeare a knowledge of immunity on much lesser grounds, in fact based merely on the following lines in *Romeo and Juliet,* (I, 2):

Take thou some new infection to the eye
And the rank poison of the old will die

Thus, referring to these lines, Dr. Wainright remarks that "Here unquestionably is an allusion to the antitoxic effect of one septic substance when brought in contact with another."[11] Had these commentators studied Shakespeare more objectively they would have found that he was merely referring to the philosophical doctrine current at the time that you fight like with like. Our poet refers to this concept many times in various forms. Note but the following quotations:

And falsehood falsehood cures; as fire cools fire
Within the scorched veins of one new burn'd
(*King John,* IV, 1)

One fire drives one fire; one nail, one nail;
Rights by rights founder, strengths by strengths do fail
(*Coriolanus,* IV, 7)

One fire burns out another's burning
One pain is lessen'd by another's anguish
(*Romeo and Juliet,* I, 2)

Even as one heat another heat expels
Even as one nail by strength drives out another
So remembrance of my former love
Is by a newer object quite forgotten
(*Two Gentlemen of Verona,* II, 4)

It is readily evident here that the taking of a new infection to the eye so that "the rank poison of the old will die" was meant by Shakespeare merely to be in line with the idea that "one fire burns out another's burning," ". . . one heat another heat expels," etc., and not in accord with the modern conception of immunity as these commentators would have it. And this further serves to highlight the prejudices and the reasoning of idolatrous critics.

As to the knowledge of the lesions of syphilis described by Shakespeare, no one can deny his observant acquaintance with them. He probably knew more about them than the most educated of laymen today. We may even go further than this. One can venture to say that Shakespeare knew more of "the headed evils" "as seen in craniotabes and in the exostoses at the temporo-frontal angles" than most physicians of today. What is the answer to this? It is a simple one. The average individual in Shakespeare's environment probably saw more lesions of syphilis, especially of the terrible types, in one week than the average physician today sees in a lifetime of practice. And there was probably more craniotabes in London of Shakespeare's day than in the entire United States today. William Clowes, surgeon at St. Bartholomew's Hospital, in his "A Short and Profitable Treatise Touching the Cure of the Disease called Morbus Gallicus by Unctions" (1579) gives the following picture of the Gargantuan proportions of the syphilis epidemic in Elizabethan London:

> It is wonderful how huge multitude there be of such as be infected with it, and that dayly increase to the great daunger of the common-wealth and the stayne of the whole nation. . . . In the hospital of Saint Bartholomew in London, there hath been cured of this disease by me, and three (3) others, with in this fyve yeares, to the number of one thousand and more, I speake nothing of Saint Thomas Hospital and other howses about this citye, wherein an infinite multitude are dayly in care . . . among every twentye diseased persons that are taken in fifteen of them have the pocks.[12]

The lesions of syphilis were as common and offensive to the eye as the stinks of London were to the nose. For a man of the type of Shakespeare not to have noticed them would seem to us a matter of far greater wonder and amazement than his actual acquaintance with them. And the same holds true for many of the descriptive passages bearing on medical knowledge and offered as evidence of the poet's extraordinary learning in this field. Shakespeare's description of violent death in *Henry VI* is held up as showing his understanding "of the pathological changes that take place in the body." But it shows nothing more than that Shakespeare saw more hangings coldly, observantly, in one month than all the physicians in the United States see in their lifetime, for hangings were frequent and open to the public as holiday spectacles, such spectacles also including the subsequent disemboweling of the victims, at which procedure the hangman had become quite adept.

Shakespeare's reference to scrofula in *Macbeth* (IV, 3, 147-159) is quoted by Dr. Epstein (loc. cit.) as showing that "Shakespeare was well aware of this historical fact that the early Saxon kings were believed capable of curing scrofula by the laying on of hands." With the chronicle histories at his disposal, with this very laying on of hands taking place in his own day, he would have had to have been stupid not to have known this. Shakespeare saw more of the "swoln and ulcerous" scrofula in a day than the physician of today sees in many years.

Dr. Epstein quotes passages from *Julius Caesar* to prove that "all this thoroughly demonstrates that Shakespeare understood the nature of epilepsy." If this is the case, then his knowledge was more thorough than that of the greatest neurologists of today, for the true nature of epilepsy is not yet completely known. In line with Dr. Epstein and other medical commentators Dr. W. E. Vest (1941), feels that "It is hard to realize that a layman untrained in medicine could have known so many of the symptoms of epilepsy."[13] However that Shakespeare knew epilepsy from the objective standpoint is neither questionable nor yet a matter for wonder. Certainly one cannot call Shakespeare a physician for this knowledge. He witnessed epileptic seizures many times, no doubt, for in a city the size of London there must have been numerous epileptics, who, not being confined in sanitaria, gave many opportunities to the poet to observe them. And who, having witnessed an epileptic seizure, can forget the swooning, the foaming at the mouth, the biting of the tongue, etc. And what Shakespeare's eyes saw, his pen could put to language in unforgettable English.

Dr. Epstein quotes many passages referring to childbirth and intimates that Shakespeare had an unusual knowledge of obstetrics. In this respect, Dr. Chesney previous to Dr. Epstein goes even further, actually calling Shakespeare a "master in the science of Obstetrics" and exclaiming in great wonder,

"How Shakespeare could have become possessed of a knowledge so accurate in regard to scenes and incidents in the lying-in-chamber is a problem. . . . It was another of his intuitions."[14] The truth is, Shakespeare did not know the technique of labour, but with obstetrics in the hands of old wives, with deliveries being carried on in the home, with Shakespeare himself being the father of children, how could he possibly have escaped knowing the anguish of childbirth and referring to it as "a night of groans"? The most ignorant savage cannot escape such knowledge. Furthermore, there are prints in existence depicting the lying-in-chamber of the sixteenth century, Singer in his *Short History of Medicine* (p. 163), reproduces one such contemporary print. And what do we find here? The woman is in labor. There are five women, two men and two children in the room, and one dog. Drinking and feasting are going on. And this scene represents the average upper-class lying-in-chamber of Shakespeare's England. It was a common enough scene as medical history proves. Is it any wonder then that the average layman including Shakespeare was "possessed of a knowledge so accurate in regard to scenes and incidents in the lying-in-chamber"? In a similar manner, there are very few passages in Shakespeare's works, of a medical character, that cannot be explained on the same principles as outlined above.

NOTES AND REFERENCES

CHAPTER VIII

I

1. Hawley, R. N., Medical Lore of Shakespeare, **Medical Age,** 1892, 10: 755.
2. Bucknill, J.C., **The Medical Knowledge of Shakespeare,** Longman Co., London, 1860, p. 36.
3. Donnellan, P. S., "Medical allusions in Shakespeare's plays," **Am. Med.,** 1902, 3: 279.
4. Hackman, L.K.H., "Shakespeare and Harvey," **The Lancet,** 1888, 2:789.
5. Because this work was published in 1615 Shakespeare could not have seen the printed work. However, since Jaggard published both Crookes' and Shakespeare's works it has been considered by Richardson that he saw it in manuscript form. See B. W. Richardson, Shakespeare and the **pia mater, The Lancet,** 1888, 2: 757.
6. Green-Armytage, V. B., "Gynecology and Obstetrics in Shakespeare," **J. Obst. Gyn.,** 1930, 37: 272.
7. Garrison, F. H., **History of Medicine,** Saunders, Phila., 1924, p. 195. See also Dr. J. F. Payne for a consideration of early books of a medical character in the English vernacular, **Brit. M. J.,** 1889, 1: 1085.
8. **Taming of the Shrew,** I, 1; **Troilus and Cressida,** II, 1.
9. **Merry Wives of Windsor,** II, 3; **All's Well,** II, 3.
10. **All's Well That Ends Well,** II, 3.
11. Bucknill, **op. cit.,** p. 290.
12. **Jahrbuch der Deutschen-Shakespeare-Gesellschaft,** Jhrug. 31 (1895), pp. 4, 5.
13. Quoted in Carlton, William J., **Timothe Bright, Doctor of Phisicke,** London: Elliot Stock, 1911, p. 56.
14. Shakespeare und die anfange der englischen Stenographie (1897), p. 38 et seq.; **Jahrbuch der Deutschen-Shakespeare-Gesellschaft.** Jhrg. 35 (1898), p. 216.
15. Notes and Queries, first series, Vol. 7, p. 546 (June 4, 1853).
16. **Shakespeare and Typography** (1872), p. 35. Quoted in Carlton's **Timothe Bright,** op. cit., p. 55.
17. "Hamlet and Dr. Timothy Bright," **P.M.L.A.,** XLI, 1926, pp. 667-679.

18. See Pomeranz, H., **op. cit.**, p. 372.
19. See Wright, Louis, B. **Middle-Class Culture in Elizabethan England.** Chapel Hill, Univ. of North Carolina Press, 1935, p. 84.
20. **Pericles**, III, 2.
21. Shakespeare made use of Lodge's **Rosalynd** (1509) in the composing of **As You Like It.** He might also have been interested in Lodge's treatise on the plague.
22. Following is an extract from "The Wonderful Yeare 1603," wherein is showed the picture of London Lying sick of the Plague by Dekker. The treatise gives us a very vivid and graphic account of London during a pestilence. Shakespeare witnessed such pestilences. The particular extract quoted is cited by Creighton in his **History of Epidemics in Great Britain** and illustrates the impotence of the physicians against disease.

    "Never let any man ask me what became of our phisitions in this massacre. They hid their synodical heads as well as the proudest, and I cannot blame them, for their phlebotemies, losings and electuaries, with their dicacathelicans, diacodiens, amulets and antideres had not so much strength to hold life and soul together as a pot of Pinder's Ale and a nutmeg. Their drugs turned to durt, their simples were simple things. Galen could do no more good then Sir Giles Gooescap, Hippocrate, Avicen, Paracelsans, Ferne-lius, with all their succeeding rabble of doctors and water-casters, were at their wits end, for not one of them durst keep abroad."
23. Pomeranz, H., **op. cit.**, p. 503.
24. **The Historie of the World. Commonly called, The Natural Historie of C. Plinios, Secundus**, 1634.
25. **A Dyetary of Helthe**, 1542, Chap. XX, (Ed. F. J. Furnivall), 1870, p. 282.
26. Yearsley, M., The Doctor in Elizabethan Drama.
27. Quoted in Creighton, **op. cit.**, p. 575.
28. Quoted in Pomeranz, **op. cit.**, **Medical Life XXXI**, p. 372.
29. Quoted in C. Creighton (**op. cit.**, footnote, p. 515).
30. Quoted in Pomeranz, **op. cit.**, pp. 352-3.
31. Lanier, S., **Shakespeare and His Forerunners**, N.Y., 1902, p. 183.
32. Quoted in Yearsley, **op. cit.**, p. 103.
33. **Ibid.**, p. 104.
34. Shakespeare well knew where the center of the London drug trade flourished in his day. In **The Merry Wives of Windsor**, Falstaff refers to "these lisping hawthorn buds, that come like women in men's apparel, and smell like Bucklersbury in simple time," (III, 3, 76). Bucklersbury actually was the

center of the drug trade in Elizabethan England.

35. Quoted in C. Creighton (**op. cit.**, footnote, p. 514).

36. See also Pepys' and Evelyn's diaries and also Defoe's "Journal of the Plague Year." Their descriptions of the pestilences are applicable to those Shakespeare witnessed.

37. Taylor, J., **Work** (ed. by C. Hindly), London, 1872, p. 491.

38. **Ibid.**, p. 491.

39. "Plaies are banished for a time out of London" says Harrison in 1572, "lest the resort unto them should ingender a plague, or rather disperse it being already begone"—Extracts from Harrison's M. S. Chronologie, by Furnivall in appendix (p. 268) to **Elizabethan England**, Camelot Series 1890.

"Behold the sumptuous theatre-houses, a continual monument of London's prodigal folly! But I understand they are now forbidden because of the plague."—T. W. in a sermon preached at Paul's Cross on Sunday, November 3, 1577.

I am indebted for these quotations to Creighton, (**op. cit.**, footnote p. 17) pp. 494-5.

40. Walter J. Bristow, "Shakespeare as a Physiologist," **Southern Med. & Sur.**, 94: 274-276, May, 1932.

41. Pomeranz, H., **op. cit.**, p. 493.

42. I am indebted for this suggestion to C. E. Phelps, His (Shakespeare's) School of Insanity in "Falstaff and Equity," N.Y.: Houghton, Mifflin & Co., 1901, pp. 104-112.

43. British Museum Egerton MSS 2065, in his "Select Observations on English Bodies: Or Cures both Empirical and Historicall performed upon very eminent persons in Desperate **Diseases** . . . "

II

1. **Elizabethan Drama and Its Mad Folk, op. cit.**, p. 177.
2. Peers, E. A. **Elizabethan Drama and Its Mad Folk**, p. 50.
3. **Op. cit.**, p. 101.
4. **Contributions to Mental Pathology, op. cit.**, p. 485.
5. The following three quotations are cited in Johnson and Stephens edition of Shakespeare's works and quoted by Field, **op. cit.**, p. 52.
6. Chapter one, "A Treatise of the Pockes."
7. **Op. cit.**, chapter on **Books of Compounds**, Folio 43.
8. "Old Doc Shakespeare," **The Quarterly of the Phi Beta Pi Medical Fraternity**, May, 1941, p. 20.
9. "Shakespeare's Knowledge of Chest Diseases," **J.A.M.A.**, Dec. 1950, p. 1332.
10. See footnote No. 43, Chapt. I.

11. **The Medical and Surgical Knowledge of William Shakespeare,** New York, 1915, p. 12.
12. Quoted in C. Creighton, **op. cit.,** p. 424. See also Burnet, "History of His Own Time," I (1823), 395-6, for an account of the prevalence of syphilis among the nobility.
13. "Old Doc Shakespeare," **The Quarterly of the Phi Beta Pi Medical Fraternity,** May, 1941, p. 6.
14. **Op. cit.,** p. 50.

PART II

THE PSYCHOPATHOLOGY IN SHAKESPEARE'S DRAMAS

CHAPTER IX

THE NEUROPSYCHIATRY IN SHAKESPEARE'S DRAMAS

I

A Preliminary Survey of Critical Commentary

William Shakespeare was a great poet, he was a great dramatist; perhaps the greatest of all time. Few deny this. But his greatness rests almost entirely upon his vivid sense of observation, upon his deep psychological insight into human nature and upon his genuine ability as the true creative artist to synthesize, by means of his imagination, the play of the human emotions into living poetry and living drama. Shakespeare encompassed with understanding all that was about him—the good and the bad, the beautiful and the ugly, the fanciful and the real, the comic and the tragic.

Because the abnormal states of mind came within the range of his mighty vision, and because he endowed his delineations of these states of mind with truth, intensity, and power, Shakespeare has been falsely raised to the pinnacle of special knowledge in psychiatry in the same manner, as we have seen, as in the other fields of medicine, and this from medical men, neuropsychiatrists, superintendents of mental hospitals. And although the wind of historical criticism engendered in the last half century, as pointed out previously, has swept clean Shakespearean idolatry in their respective fields, yet in the field of medical psychiatry, bardolatry seems to have remained undisturbed and perhaps unchallenged. Indeed, as recently as 1964, Dr. Robert A. Ravich in "A Psychoanalytic Study of Shakespeare's Early Plays" comes to the sweeping conclusion "that Shakespeare's theories of mental illness, as expressed in his early plays were in advance of his time,"[1] while Dr. Walter A. Meek (1952) evaluating the doctor's treatment of King Lear also calls it "very advanced" and labels the doctor, "as master of his psychiatric art"[2] and there are many other voices raised of a similar nature in this area of Shakespearean commentary.

Thus, Dr. Orville W. Owen, already cited, in posing the rhetorical question, "Was he a neurologist?" answered it by saying, "It might be called his specialty . . . his wonderful descriptions and delineations in this great field of our science . . (shows that he had) thoroughly mastered the subject in all its branches."[3] Similarly, Dr. T. A. Ross intimates that "One feels that unless Shakespeare was engaged in psychiatric practice—which I admit is possible from his immense knowledge of the subject" he could not draw his character as he did, naming as one, Antonio's depression (*Merchant of Venice*), a "clinical description of the highest order."[4] Dr. Pomeranz too, calls him "an ultra modern psychiatrist," who "intimated that insanity was due to disease of the brain and . . . could be alleviated or cured by . . . medical means."[5] Dr. P. R. Vessie calls him "the outstanding psychopathologist of all time"[6] and points out "that when a psychiatrist reads *Measure for Measure*, he finds many passages which seem almost like having a conversation with a colleague."[7] Dr. Karl A. Menninger says that "His delineations of insanity unfold many a deep truth in mental pathology"[8] and he quotes Sir Harry Maudsley as saying of Shakespeare, "I am apt to think that we may learn more of the real causation of insanity by the study of a tragedy like *Lear* than from all that has yet been written thereupon in the guise of science,"[9] in which he echoes an even earlier commentator, William Farren (1824), who writes that ". . . Shakespeare displays not only a perfect knowledge of the disease under which Lear labors but an intimate acquaintance with the course of medical treatment."[10] Dr. J. Rogers considers that "As a minister to the mind . . . he has no peer."[11] Dr. Max Kahn feels that Shakespeare's knowledge of insanity was immense . . . [12] Dr. G. E. Price, speaking of Shakespeare as a neuropsychiatrist, says that ". . . his insight and analysis of the workings of the human mind is something at which to marvel . . . nowhere do we find so many and such remarkable descriptions of senility as we find in the writings of Shakespeare,"[13] while R. Alexander points out that, "The myriad-minded Shakespearean writer had an intimate knowledge of the truly mentally diseased."[14] In truth, every new advance in the field of psychology finds conformity in the characters of Shakespeare. No one points this out more clearly than Dr. Ira S. Wile who exemplifies at length that "various portions of the text may be used to illustrate almost any or all of the current theories of psychology," and that "it is not difficult to consider the interpretation of *Hamlet* according to Freud or solve the meaning of *A Midsummer Night's Dream,* or to appreciate Caliban and Ariel . . . in the light of Jung's *Collective Unconscious,* or to hold *Richard III* as an exposition of Adlerian Doctrines."[15] On this point, in fact, the psychoanalyst, Dr. Abenheimer, too, states that "Shakespeare's best plays are truly symbolic in Jung's sense, i.e., they are the best possible expression of some insight for which no more rational formulation had yet been found. Shakespeare was the creator of a mythology of Modern Man."[16] And, indeed, many psychiatrists, as we shall later see, have followed these very lines, and have created and are creating a whole body of Shakespearean criticism. For, as emphasized previously, Shakespeare knew human nature and he depicted it with truth. And the basic psychological mechanism, the motivating forces, the aims, and goals of Elizabethan man are not much different than that of 20th century man. Therein lies the greatness of Shakespeare. There are portions of all of ourselves in the characters of Shakespeare. Each generation interprets his delineations according to its own experiences and its own knowledge. Controversy involves only these interpretations. For as mentioned before, practically all critics agree that Shakespeare knew the human mind and could depict the play of the passions, even unto delineations of the psychoneuroses and psychoses. Let us listen to the voices of some of these critics, doctors, specialists in pathological psychology, physicians to the insane.

II

Doctors Amariah Brigham, Isaac Ray and Shakespeare

First let us consider Doctors Amariah Brigham and Isaac Ray in this field of Shakespearean criticism.

Doctors Amariah Brigham, and Isaac Ray are deservedly well known as important figures in the history and progress of American psychiatry. Both were medical superintendents of famous psychiatric hospitals. Both are numbered among the thirteen original founders of the *Association of Medical Superintendents of American Institutions* for the insane, which developed into the present *American Psychiatric Association.* Both held high office in this Association, Dr. Brigham being Vice President in 1848 but dying in 1849 before he could attain to the presidency, while Dr. Ray served in both capacities between 1851 and 1859. Both traveled extensively for further psychiatric education through the medical centers of Europe. Both contributed much to the psychiatric literature of their day, Amariah Brigham actually being the founder and first editor of the *American Journal of Insanity,* forerunner of the present *Journal of The American Psychiatric Association,* and Isaac Ray publishing many articles in the issues of this *Journal* as well as elsewhere. Both added much to the advancement of American Psychiatry.[17]

What is less well known and certainly of more than mere passing interest is the fact that both men also occupy a place in the history of Shakespearean Criticism. Being Psychiatrists with broad educations and wide humanistic interests, both men focused on Shakespeare's dramas in terms of psychopathology. And both their contributions in this field of psychiatry and Shakespearean criticism first appeared in the *American Journal of Insanity.*

Dr. Brigham wrote his commentary on Shakespeare's characters in a paper entitled "Insanity—Illustrated by Histories of Distinguished Men and by the Writings of Poets and Novelists." It appeared as the first formal article in the first issue of *The*

American Journal of Insanity in July 1844, and ran from pages 9-49, pages 27-41 being devoted exclusively to Shakespeare's dramas. Dr. Isaac Ray entitled his paper, "Shakespeare's Delineations of Insanity" and it appeared in the *Journal,* April 1847, and ran extensively from pages 289 to 332. It is interesting to note that this paper somewhat enlarged was later included in Dr. Ray's then very important book—*Contributions to Mental Pathology* which appeared in 1873[18] and which ran through many editions.

It should be kept in mind that while there were a few previous publications in this field of psychiatry and Shakespearean criticism, these were by laymen and mainly in Europe, so that Brigham's paper was the first of its kind to appear in America (1844), while Dr. Ray's contribution (1847) was the second to be published here—both in the *Journal of Insanity.*

Doctors Brigham and Ray then, may be considered the first psychiatrists in America to write in this area of Shakespearean Criticism. They are the pioneer commentators in this country, who dealt with the psychiatric aspects of Shakespeare's dramas, leading the way for many others that were to follow thereafter.

However, both these men were but children of their century, living in the frame of reference of their own times and molded by the streams of thought flowing through the intellectual atmosphere of their day. They succumbed only too readily to the cult of Shakespeare idolatry then in vogue, and added much to its influence in their particular field of Shakespearean Criticism. This idolatry caused these two psychiatrists, among many others, to raise Shakespeare to a most false pinnacle of special knowledge in psychopathology. Thus Dr. Brigham, referring to Shakespeare's "remarkable ability, . . . accuracy, . . . immensity and correctness of his knowledge" in delineating insanity says, "There is scarcely a form of mental disorder he had not alluded to and pointed out the causes and treatment"[19] and that he "seems to have understood all its varieties and all its causes;" and further, that "his knowledge of insanity was not only great and varied . . . but his views were very far in advance of the age in which he lived."[20] He writes of "the mental disorder of Hamlet (as) most exquisitely drawn . . . finely portrayed, . . . a full history of a case of insanity from the beginning to the end . . . a real case . . . correctly reported . . . a faithful history of a case of senile insanity from the beginning to the end . . . a real case . . . correctly reported . . . a faithful history of a case of senile insanity."[21] Dr. Brigham goes on to prove point by point that Shakespeare "believed the following facts, all of which were in advance of the general opinions of his age and are now deemed correct:

1. That a well formed brain, a good shaped head, is essential to a good mind.
2. That insanity is a disease of the brain.
3. That there is a general and partial insanity.
4. That it is a disease which can be cured by medical means.
5. That the causes are various, the most common of which he has particularly noted"[22]

He concludes by saying, "In this extensive establishment (New York Lunatic Asylum, Utica, of which he was superintendent) are all the insane characters described by Shakespeare."[23]

In similar vein, does Dr. Isaac Ray raise Shakespeare to undeserved pinnacles of special knowledge in psychopathology. Speaking of ". . . the extraordinary merit of Shakespeare's representations of insanity"[24] and of "the unapproachable preeminence of Shakespeare in the delineation of insanity,"[25] he affirms that Shakespeare's "knowledge . . . could hardly have been expected from any but a professional observer,"[26] and ". . . was in advance of his own and succeeding generations;"[27] and further, that "in the pages of Shakespeare are delineations . . . of insanity that may be ranked with the highest triumphs of their masterly genius,"[28] . . . "greatly in advance of the current notions of his own and perhaps the present times."[29] Referring specifically to *King Lear,* he states, "that the development of the early stage of Lear's insanity, or its incubation, as it is technically called, is managed with masterly skill. . ."[30] Referring to the scene on the heath between Lear, Edgar and the fool he exclaims," . . . who can finish this scene without feeling that he has read a new chapter in the history of mental disease of most solemn and startling import?"[31] Pointing to Edgar's feigned insanity in the same scene, he remarks that, "The management of Edgar's simulation, strikingly evinces the accuracy and extent of Shakespeare's knowledge of mental pathology."[32] Speaking of the skill of the poet's delineation of Hamlet's insanity he refers to it as a "great skill . . . founded on what would seem to be a professional knowledge of the subject." He considers Shakespeare as having "a most thorough mastery of the phenomena of insanity and the most consummate skill in . . . displaying them in action;" and as ". . . unfolding many a deep truth in mental science."[33] With regard to the treatment in vogue in his own times, Dr. Ray comes to the conclusion: "Would that we were able to say that courts of our own times studied the influence of insanity upon human conduct by the light of Shakespeare . . . and of nature than of metaphysical dogmas and legal maxims."[34]

As already noted both Drs. Brigham and Ray are viewing Shakespeare's psychiatric knowledge in a very uncritical and unhistorical way. They fail to place him in the milieu in which he moved, the historical horizons by which he was limited. Hence the picture we have is distorted and false and remains but bardolatrous rhetoric. (It has already been shown by the author that Shakespeare's apparent knowledge in the broad field of medicine and psychiatry was actually but a reflection of the general medical knowledge current at the time).[35]

Dr. J. C. Bucknill (1859), English Chancery Visitor in Lunacy and head of a large hospital for the insane, likewise goes into veritable rhapsodies of praise over Shakespeare's ability in developing psychological situations, for, says he "Shakespeare not only possesses more psychological insight than all other poets but more than all other writers."[36] He speaks of the poet's "intimate knowledge of the normal state of the mental functions in every variety of character."[37] And further than this: "The consistency of Shakespeare is in no characters more close and true than in those most difficult ones wherein he portrays the development of mental unsoundness,"[38] for, continues Bucknill, "In his hands the laws of mental aberration are as sure as those of the most regular development."[39] His unbounded enthusiasm and idolatry takes him to the height of saying,

> Our wonder at his profound knowledge of mental diseases increases, the more carefully we study his works; here and elsewhere, he displays with prolific carelessness a knowledge of principles, half of which would make the reputation of a modern psychologist.[40]

Dr. A. O. Kellogg, physician of the State Hospital for the Insane at Poughkeepsie, N. Y., too, speaks of Shakespeare's intuitive psychological knowledge,[41] for, "To suppose that Shakespeare obtained his knowledge of insanity and medical psychology from his contemporaries, or from works on these subjects extant in his day, is simply absurd."[42] Referring to the "Extraordinary accuracy and facility manifested by the great dramatist in the delineations of mind as warped and influenced by disease,[43] Dr. Kellogg says that "...he understood insanity in all its varied forms, and it would not be more difficult to show that Shakespeare was once physician-in-chief to Bedlam Hospital, than to establish many other things that have been asserted respecting his early career."[44] He points out that contrary to the practices and beliefs of the time with regard to insanity, Shakespeare ". . . believed that insanity was a disease of the brain and could be cured . . . by judicious care and management, all of which he, Shakespeare, points out as clearly as it could be done, by a modern expert,"[45] for ". . . after nearly two centuries and a half we have little to add to what Shakespeare appears to have known of these intricate subjects."[46] He quotes Dr. Brigham, head of an asylum in Utica, N. Y., to the effect that all of Shakespeare's insane characters could be found in his institution and further, that there was "little to add, to his method of treating the insane."[47] With regard to certain phases of insanity, Dr. Kellogg is struck with wonder and astonishment, that one man (and he a layman) "should have known more of this most obscure subject than all the physicians of his time," and should have, "exhibited a knowledge of the operations of the mind . . . far beyond that of his own times and quite equal to that of the most accomplished psychologists of our own."[48] Finally, a consideration of Shakespeare's fools and clowns leads Dr. Kellogg to speak of the "Galaxy of fools such as nowhere else is to be found," and of "every shade of folly, imbecility and mental obtuseness . . . represented, . . . with a truthfulness and vigor, which has never been equaled, . . ."[49] "so extensive, varied and rich is Shakespeare in his illustrations of the almost endless forms of mental imbecility."[50]

NOTES AND REFERENCES

CHAPTER IX

1. Ravich, A.A. "A Psychoanalytic Study of Shakespeare's Early Plays," **The Psychoanal. Quart.**, 33:386-410, p. 409.
2. Meek, Walter A. "Medicine in Shakespeare," **Texas Reports, Biology and Medicine.** 10: 372-398, Summer 1952, p. 377.
3. "The Medicine in Shakespeare," **Detroit Medical and Library Assoc. Trans.**, (1892-1893) p. 104.
4. Ross, T.A., "A note on The Merchant of Venice," **Brit. J. of Med. Psychol.** 14: 303-311, (1934).
5. "Medicine in the Shakespearean Plays and Era." **Med. Life**, 41: 511.
6. "An Interpretation of Shakespeare's Sex Play, **All's Well That Ends Well.**" Med. Rec., 146: 14-16, p. 14.
7. "Psychiatry Catches Up With Shakespeare," **Med. Rec.**, 144, p. 141. (Aug. 5, 1936).
8. "The Insanity of Hamlet," **Journ. Kansas Med. Soc.**, 35: 337.
9. **Ibid.**, p. 337.
10. "Madness of King Lear," **London Mag.**, X (Jl., 1824), p. 82.
11. "Shakespeare as Health Teacher," **Scient. Month.**, II (July 1916) p. 592.
12. "Shakespeare's Knowledge of Medicine," **N.Y. Med. Journ.**, XCII, p. 864 (Oct. 29, 1910).
13. "William Shakespeare as a Neuropsychiatrist," **Ann. Med. Hist.**, (1928), p. 159.
14. "Hamlet—Classical Malingerer," **Med. Journ. and Record**, CXXX (1929), 287.
15. "Some Shakespearean Characters in the Light of Present Day Psychologies," **Psychiat. Quart.** 16: 62-90 (Jan. 1942), p. 67.
16. Abenheimer, K.M., "Shakespeare's **Tempest**: A Psychological Analysis," **Psychoanalytic Review**, 33: 399-415 (Oct. 1946).
17. **One Hundred Years of American Psychiatry**, Columbia University Press, 1954.
18. Ray, Isaac: **Contributions to Mental Pathology.** New York: Little Brown Co., 1873.
19. "Shakespeare's Illustrations of Insanity," **Amer. Journ. of Insanity**, I (1884), p. 27.
20. **Ibid.**, p. 27.
21. **Ibid.**
22. **Ibid.**, p. 78.
23. **Ibid.**, p. 79.

24. Contributions to Mental Pathology, p. 482.
25. Ibid., p. 529.
26. "Shakespeare's Delineations of Insanity." Amer. Journ. of Insanity, III (1847), p. 486.
27. Ibid., p. 289.
28. Ibid., p. 290.
29. Ray, I. Contributions to Mental Pathology, op. cit., p. 525.
30. "Shakespeare's Delineations of Insanity," Amer. Journ. of Insanity, III (1847) p. 293.
31. Ray, Isaac. Contributions to Mental Pathology, op. cit., p. 494.
32. Ibid., p. 500.
33. Ibid.
34. "Shakespeare's Delineations of Insanity," Amer. Jour. of Insanity, III (1847), p. 293.
35. Edgar, I: Ann. Med. Hist., 6: 150,1934.
— Ann. Med. Hist., 7: 519, 1935.
— Ann. Med. Hist., 8: 355, 456, 1936.
— Med. Life, 41: 331, 1934.
— J. Abn. & Soc. Psychol., 30: 70, 1935.
— Canad. Med. Assoc. J., 33: 319, 1935.
— Med. Record, 144: 37, J1, 1936.
— J. Mich. St. Med. Soc., J1., 1956.
36. The Mad Folk of Shakespeare. London: Macmillan & Co., 1869, p. 165.
37. Ibid., p. 164.
38. Loc. Cit.
39. Ibid., p. 166.
40. Ibid., p. 197.
41. Shakespeare's Delineations of Insanity, etc., N.Y.: Hurd & Houghton, 1868, p. 14.
42. Ibid., p. 9.
43. Kellogg, A. O. "Shakespeare's Delineations of Mental Imbecility as Exhibited by his Fools and Clowns," Amer. Journ. of Insanity, XVIII (1861), p. 97.
44. Ibid., p. 98.
45. Shakespeare's Delineations, etc., N.Y.: Hurd & Houghton, 1868, p. 11.
46. "Shakespeare as a Physician & Psychologist," Amer. Journ. of Insanity XVI (1859), p. 135.
47. Ibid., p. 147. Shakespeare's Delineations, etc., op. cit., p. 27.
48. "Shakespeare's Delineations of Mental Imbecility," etc., op. cit., XVIII (1861), p. 97.
49. Ibid., p. 99.
50. Ibid., p. 101.

CHAPTER X

AN EVALUATION OF THE NEUROPSYCHIATRY IN SHAKESPEARE'S DRAMAS

Manifestly, these commentators are viewing Shakespeare's psychiatric knowledge in the same uncritical way, as we have pointed out, they viewed his general medical knowledge. They fail to place him in the milieu in which he moved, the frame of reference by which he was surrounded, the historical horizons by which he was limited. Hence the picture we have is distorted and false and remains but bardolatrous rhetoric.

Even a superficial perusal of the intellectual atmosphere that Shakespeare breathed, readily explains much more simply and satisfactorily the psychiatry in his dramas. And this leads but to one conclusion: Shakespeare in this respect, was only a child of his age and not ahead of it, and reflects only the ideas and conceptions current in Elizabethan England, the thought-patterns of which were woven by him into words of such unforgettable dramatic and poetic English as his plays really are. Let us therefore now bring direct question and into open challenge the assertions of our idolatrous neuropsychiatric commentators relative to Shakespeare's psychiatric knowledge. In the first place, Dr. Amariah Brigham, (and most of these commentators echo his opinions in this respect) quotes three passages[1] to show that our poet referred to low foreheads disparagingly, and hence, that he recognized "the excellence of a high forehead," and that a well-formed brain is essential to a good mind." Presto! He comes to the conclusion that on this basis Shakespeare was "in advance of the general opinions of his age."[2] As a matter of fact, all this was common knowledge for centuries and certainly during Shakespeare's day. The most simple observer had noticetd that of all of the vertebrates, man was distinguished by a comparatively large forehead and heavy brain, and that even among humans an unusually low forehead often went hand in hand with low intelligence. Common reference to this can be found in much of the literature of the period. We need go no further than Laurentius in his Discourse on *The Diseases of Melancholie* . . . (1599), a very popular book in Shakespeare's day and quoted by Burton in his *Anatomy* many times, to recognize this. He says the following on the whole subject:

> Philosophers that have written of Physiognomie, say that such as have the hinder part of the head hanging out much, have a good memorie; that such as have large and high foreheads . . . are of pleasant imagination; and that such as in whom these two eminences are wanting, are blockish, without imagination, and without memorie.[3]

Burton (Memb. I, Subs. 4) considers with the "physiognomers" that *"much hair on the brows* . . . and a little head" "argues natural melancholy." It can be shown that other dramas of the period have similar references, but we need stretch this point no further.

Secondly, these same commentators, particularly stress the fact that Shakespeare refers "to insanity as a disease of the brain" and that on this basis he was "in advance . . . of his age" and "an ultra-modern psychiatrist."[4] It is incredible that such an opinion should be so tenacious when even a superficial perusal of the literature of Elizabethan England would here too readily indicate that every intelligent layman, let alone the physicians of the time, knew that insanity had its source in the brain. Vicary, chief surgeon of St. Bartholomew's Hospital (1548-62), writes in his *Anatomie of the Bodie of Man*[5] that "the Brayne . . . followeth the moving of the moon . . . the Brayne shrinketh . . . and is not obedient to the spirit of feeling and this is proved in men that be lunaticke or madde . . . . Wherefore when . . . the Brayne is too drye or too moyst . . . then followeth feebleness of the wittes . . ."

Robert Burton writing ("Of the part affected" in Melancholy [insanity] states that "Most are of opinion that it is the *brain* . . . . It cannot otherwise be but that the *brain* must be affected . . . the *brain* must needs primarily be misaffected, as the seat of *reason*"[6] "for the body works upon the mind, by his bad humours . . . sending gross fumes into the brain, and so, disturbing the soul, and all the faculties of it . . ."[7]

Laurentius, before Burton, expresses similar views. Speaking of "melancholie which hath his proper seate in the braine"[8] and of "The Melancholike Man . . . (I mean him which hath the disease in the braine)"[9] he affirms that ". . . the minde is not at rest, the braine is distempered . . ."[10] and concludes definitely that "The braine then is the part grieved and hurt . . . it is become too drie and colde . . . the onely and sole fault of the braine; . . ."[11] Timothy Bright likewise considers that unnatural melancholy "destroyeth the braine with all his faculties. . ."[12]

But we need only turn to some of the contemporary dramatists of the Elizabethan period to confirm this further. Thus, John Ford in his *The Lovers Melancholy* (III, 1) writes:

> Melancholy
> Is not, as you conceive, indisposition
> Of body, but the mind's disease
> A mere commotion of the mind, o'ercharged
> With fear and sorrow; *first begot i' the brain,*
> *The seat of reason*. . . .

In the same play (II, 1910-1912) the character Meleander speaks of himself as "franticke" and that "throngs of rude divisions huddle on, and doe disranke" his "braines from peace and sleepe." Again, in Ford's *The Fancies* (II, 1858-1895), Morosa, Secco's wife, seeing him rage and fume, asks "Are thy mad braines in thy mazar now, thou jealousy Bedlam." Massinger in his *A New Way to Pay Old Debts* (V, 1) has Sir Giles Querreach, the madman, cry out, "my brain turns." Middleton in his *The Changeling* (I, 2) has Dr. Albius speak of,

> The daily visitants that come to see
> My brain-sick patients . . .

And Fletcher in his *The Two Noble Kinsmen* has the doctor say,

> How her brain coins
> How she continues this fancy! 'Tis not an engraffed madness, but a most thick and profound melancholy.

Similarly, Shirley, in his *Coronation* (III, 2) has Arcadius say "my uncle is something craz'd; there is a worm in's brain," and in *The Ball* (I, 1) he has Winfield say, "He has a worm in's brain which . . . doth ravish him into perfect madness." And even Edmund Spenser writes:

> As one . . . whose dryer *braine*
> Is tost with troubled sights.[13]

and again,

> To breake his sleepe and
> waste his ydle *braines.*[14]

It is thus readily evident that the brain, being considered the seat of reason, was the seat of the disease in insanity. This was a platitude of the times. It is therefore puzzling to find Professor D. Fraser-Harris,[15] acting as though he had discovered something new in the greatness of Shakespeare, when he says that if we are to interpret in anything resembling the modern meaning the line in *Antony and Cleopatra* (IV, 8), "Yet we have a brain that nourishes our nerves," Shakespeare seems to have had the conception of the brain as preeminent in the nervous system. After quoting other similar passages he comes to the conclusion that "From all we can gather, Shakespeare seems to have appreciated the functional pre-eminence of the brain in a manner far beyond the writers of his time."[16] "Here and there he seems actually prophetic."[17]

The fact is, that the brain was considered as the preeminent organ of the entire body in the past centuries as well as in Shakespeare's day. Robert Burton calls "the brain . . . the most noble organ under heaven, the dwelling house and seat of the soul, the habitation of wisdom, memory, judgment, reason . . ."[18] and he considers that "the nerves . . . proceed from the brain and carry the animal spirits for sense and motion."[19] Likewise, Laurentius calls the "braine . . . the most noble part of the whole body . . ."[20] and, waxing lyrical, continues:

> This is that magnificent and stately turret of the soule, this is that goodly royall palace, the confederate house of *Pallas,* this is the impregnable fort, environed with bones, as with strong walles, wherein is lodged the sovereigne power of the soule.[21]

It is interesting to note that there had been some controversy as to the seat of the soul and that this controversy was common knowledge enough to have seeped down through Shakespeare into his dramas. In *King John* (V, 7, 2) Prince Henry says:

> . . . and his pure brain,
> Which *some suppose the soul's frail dwelling house,*
> Doth by the idle comments that it makes
> Foretell the ending of mortality

Again in *The Merchant of Venice* (III, 2, 63) Shakespeare writes:

> Tell me where is fancy bred,
> Or in the heart, or in the head?
> How begot, how nourished

Laurentius summarizes this controversy. After mentioning many of the numerous ancients' opinions, he writes that Aristotle ". . . thought that the soule had his proper seat in the heart"[22] and that "It is . . . the heart, according to the Peripatetikes, which is the true mansion of the soule, the onely prince and governour, in this so excellent and admirable disposing of all things in the government of the bodie."[23] After refuting these at length, Laurentius himself comes to the conclusion thus, "I say then that the principal seate of the soule is in the braine."[24] "Let us then acknowledge the braine to be the principall seate of the soule, the originall of moving and feeling and of all the other most noble functions of the same."[25] Burton is apparently in agreement with Laurentius on this point for he writes of "the brain . . . the dwelling house and seat of the soul."[26]

Shakespeare thus uses almost the identical words of Burton in referring to the "brain . . . the soul's frail dwelling house." And his rhetorical question as to "where is fancy bred . . . the heart or . . . head"[27] certainly points to the controversy in question. We might also mention, in passing that the famous poet John Donne, (1573-1631) also writes of "the braine, the soule's bedchamber" which is a variation of its previous usage. It is certain that this platitude of Elizabethan England could be found in many other of Shakespeare's contemporary literary men and does not represent any grand knowledge that Shakespeare exclusively possessed in advance of his age, which, of course, also includes the idea already disposed of, that Shakespeare, in considering "insanity . . . a disease of the brain" was thereby "in advance of the general opinions of his age."[28]

Professor Fraser-Harris in a great admiration of the poet's psychiatric knowledge also points to these words in *II King Henry IV* (IV, 4): And now my sight fails and my brain is giddy and says, "Not everyone in Shakespeare's day would have referred the sensation of giddiness to the brain. Shakespeare not only does so but he couples it with the failure of sight..."?[29] As a matter of fact, the relation of dizziness to the brain was common knowledge, for the sensation of dizziness in the human organism is necessarily related to the senses, especially that of sight. Bartholomew,[30] already referred to as popular reading in Elizabethan England describes two kinds of giddiness, one, the result of fumes proceeding from the stomach to the *brain* and the other from the *brain itself*. Marlowe, in his *Edward The Second* (Everyman's Library, 1950 p. 295) also implies that dizziness is connected with the brain, when he has King Edward say,

> My heart is an anvil unto sorrow,
> Which beats up it like the Cyclops' hammers
> And with the noise turns *my giddy brain*

Nor is it true, as Dr. Epstein and certain others of the medical commentators imply "that Shakespeare's portrayal of the symptoms of insanity was undimmed by the theological and scholastic myths of his time,"[31] and more particularly, as Dr. R. A. Ravich puts it, that "he consistently rejected these concepts . . . of demoniacal possession, witchcraft and bewitchment that were the accepted popular explanations of mental illness."[32]

Witness the famous scene on the heath in *King Lear* (III, 4) where Shakespeare, in portraying the simulated madness of Edgar, does bring in "the theological and scholastic myths" of demonological possession in insanity. For it is "the *foul fiend* follows" Edgar "leading him through fire and through flame, through ford and whirlpool, o'er bog and quagmire; that hath laid knives under his pillow and halters in his pew; set ratsbone by his porridge." And our dramatist even names these demon friends direct out of "the Popish Impostures" of Horsnet including

> . . . Hobbididence, prince of dumbness; Mahu of stealing; Modo, of murder; Flibbertigibbet, of mopping and mowing; who since possesses chambermaids and waiting-women[31] . . . he begins at curfew and walks till the first cock; he gives the web and the pin squints the eye and makes the harelip; mildews the white wheat and hurts the poor creatures of earth.[33]

Witness further the scenes in *Twelfth Night* where "Malvolio the lunatick" "tainted in's wits," with "midsummer madness," in whom "the fiend speaks" "hollow" "within him," who "does nothing but smile," "sure, possessed" "with devils of hell . . . and Legion himself" is placed "in a dark room and bound," and visited by the clown in the guise of Sir Topas who attempts to exorcise "out" the "hyperbolical fiend" "the dishonest Satan" that "vexest . . . this man." Add also to these the words that Shakespeare puts into the mouth of Banquo in Macbeth (I, 3)

> Have we eaten on the insane root
> That takes the reason prisoner

and in the mouth of Othello (V, 2)

> It is the very error of the moon;
> She comes nearer earth than she was wont
> And makes men mad.

and into the mouth of the Abbess in the *Comedy of Errors* (V, 1, 34)

> How long hath this possession held the man.

and we have sufficient evidence certainly to refute these idolatrous commentators on this point of the modernity of our poet. No, indeed, Shakespeare, did not rise above Burton, Laurentius, Sir Thomas Browne, James, King of England and others who expressed and sincerely believed in the numerous supernatural causes of madness.

However, comes a more recent psychiatrist commentator (1964), Dr. Robert A. Ravich already mentioned and holds that . . . "Shakespeare's attempts to understand psychopathology and psychodynamics are evident throughout his earliest plays" and that while "He made dramatic use of the theories of demoniacal possession, witchcraft and bewitchment that were the accepted popular explanations of mental illness," that nevertheless, "he (Shakespeare) consistently rejected these concepts and expressed support for the more humane naturalistic view of psychopathology first propounded in 1563 by the physician Johannes Weyer."[34]

In support of this, Dr. Ravich, mentioning the capture and conviction of Joan of Arc for witchcraft (*First Part of King Henry VI*) hastens to state that "Shakespeare carefully dissociated himself from those who attributed her power to supernatural causes and demoniacal possession."[35] He gives as proof for this the following lines spoken by Joan, (*First Part of King Henry VI*),

> I never had to do with wicked spirits
> But you, that are . . . tainted with a thousand vices
> You judge it straight a thing impossible
> To compass wonders, but by help of devils.
> (V. iv: 42-48)

In the first place these are the lines that Shakespeare puts into the mouth of a purportedly historic character, who is pleading 'not guilty' to a charge of witchcraft, who is actually fighting for her life, and Shakespeare is simply giving her the appropriate words of denial, "I never had to do with wicked spirits" in accordance with the historical needs of the play and for the fulfillment of an actor's character. His words cannot be construed as necessarily representing the convictions and beliefs of Shakespeare himself. If such an argument were to be taken as valid, then the lines of every character in his plays, no matter how contradictory, could be accepted as Shakespeare's own real beliefs.

Dr. Ravich further goes on to point out that in the *Second Part of King Henry VI,* Eleanore Cobham, the Duchess of Gloucester "is exiled for consorting with witches and conjurers,". . . but that Shakespeare depicts her as a bedlam 'brain-sick duchess', not as a witch,[36] (III, 1:51) and that presumably therefore Shakespeare was in advance of his time. This argument falls into the same category as mentioned previously and cannot be accepted as valid.

Again Dr. Ravich points to the tragedy of *King Richard III* in which Richard now, himself, the Duke of Gloucester, accuses Hastings of protecting Jane Shore, claiming she has withered his arm through witchcraft (III, IV: 68-72). To this Dr. Ravich states that "Shakespeare, seeking a psychodynamic explanation of Richard's distorted self-image and psychopathic behavior, attributed both to rejection by his mother which began before he was born."[37] And he mentions as proof of this the words of Richard's mother,

> I have stay'd for thee . . . in torment and agony,
> Thou comest on earth to make the earth my hell
> A grievous burden was thy birth to me
> Tetchy and wayward thy infancy,
> Thy school days frightful, desperate, wild and furious.
> (IV, iv, 162-169)

How this proves that Shakespeare rejected witchcraft but instead directly offered a modern psychoanalytic concept as to the causation of personality disorder, is hard to conceive, for the mother is merely making a statement of fact so that through her words Shakespeare is able to add greatly to the drawing of Richard's character. To pick one group of words of Shakespeare's characters as his true belief as against many other groups of words with conflicting meanings as not Shakespeare's true beliefs is illogical, to say the least. It is valid for psychoanalytic criticism to deduce insights from the poetry of Shakespeare's dramas only when viewing them as the complex dream-phantasy-like products of his mind fulfilling its own psychoanalytic dynamic needs, but to intimate that Shakespeare intended directly to do so is to invest Shakespeare with conscious concepts that Freud promulgated several centuries later.

Apropos of this, Dr. Winfred Overholser, Superintendent of Saint Elizabeth Hospital, Washington, D. C. is much more logical in viewing "Shakespeare's psychiatry" when he states, "It seems likely that when Shakespeare used such expressions as, "He is sure possessed Madam" (*Twelfth Night*) or "How long has this possession held the man" (*Comedy of Errors*) or "For nature so preposterously to err sans witchcraft could not be" (*Othello*) he was using something more than a figure of speech.[38]

Dr. Overholser goes on to assess the numerous psychiatric references in Shakespeare's writings in a rational and acceptable manner and he comes to the following conclusions when he states,

> The question naturally arises how much of astrology, of witchcraft, and of humoral pathology did Shakespeare himself believe? He was perhaps the most accurate mirror ever held up to mankind, a keen observer, one who knew human nature, and who depicted it with truth. He was a dramatist well-attuned to the tastes and the knowledge of those who saw and would read his plays. He was in every way a man of his time . . . From anything in his writings we cannot estimate the extent to which he believed in the legends of his time.[39]

In a like category with the above idolatrous assertions is the idea expressed by so many of the medical commentators, especially by Amariah Brigham already alluded to, that Shakespeare was ". . . far beyond that of his own time"[40] "a modern expert,"[41] as it were, because he "intimated that insanity . . . could be alleviated or cured like other diseases by medical means"[42] such as "wholesome syrups and drugs,"[43] "simples operative (to) . . . close the eye of anguish"[44] and music "the comforter of an unsettled fancy"[54] "that hath help madmen to their wits,"[46] in contradiction supposedly to those who would manacle, whip, keep the insane in dark dungeons, and pray, charm and exorcise the demons possessing these insane.

In the first place, side by side with this humane treatment, Shakespeare expresses acceptance, by the evidence of his own words, of the common treatment of the insane in his day. He says,

> Love is merely a madness; and, I tell you, *deserves as well a dark house and a whip as madmen do.*[47]

> Both man and master is possess'd . . .[48]
> They must be bound and laid in some dark room

> Not mad, but bound more than a madman is;
> Shut up in prison, kept without food
> Whipt and tormented . . .[49]

> If 'gainst yourself you be incensed, we'll put you
> (Like one that means his proper harm) in manacles[50]

> To fetch my poor distracted husband hence
> Let us, come in that we may bind him fast
> and bear him home for his recovery.[51]

But Shakespeare goes even further than this when he actually derides those who

> Would give preceptial medicine to rage
> Fetter strong madness in a silken thread
> Charm ache with air and agony with words[52]

And again, in *Twelfth Night* (III, 4) when Fabian advises in the treatment of Malvolio's madness:

> No way but gentleness; gently, gently; the fiend is rough and will not be roughly used

Sir Toby rants:

> . . . what, man! 'tis not for gravity to play at cherry-pit with Satan: hang him, foul collier!

No indeed, Shakespeare felt, in line with one of Hippocrates' aphorisms, that

Diseases desperate grown
By desperate appliance are reliev'd
Or not at all[53]

and he evidently meant this also to apply to the treatment of certain types of insanity in line with the general method of treatment current in Elizabethan England.

But even if it were specifically true, that Shakespeare did advocate particularly kind and modern treatment for the insane this most certainly does not place him ahead of his time. Why any standard History of Medicine could have revealed the fact that Dr. Felix Platter (1563-1614) advocated and fought for mild treatment of the insane. And here too we must express astonishment at the medical neuropsychiatric commentators, for even the most casual acquaintance with Elizabethan literature makes such an assertion immediately untenable. Thus in Bartholomew's *De Proprietatibus Rerum* which was a popular encyclopedia of medicine written by a non-physician in the thirteenth century, considered "the most read book after the Bible down to the middle of the sixteenth century . . . (and) the favorite reading of Shakespeare and a number of the Elizabethan writers,"[54]—in this favorite "popularization of medicine" surprisingly, not only "is . . . there . . . not a word about possession by spirits" as a cause of insanity with the usual expected concomitant treatment but it is stated that "the insane must be bound so that they hurt not themselves and others, their environment must be changed, they must be gladded with instruments of music and some deal occupied," in addition to "purging and electuaries and feeding them well and refreshing them."[55] Similarly Andrew Boorde in his popular *Dyetery of Helth* (1542) advocates the confinement of the insane in dark rooms devoid of objects with which they might harm themselves. He would also be gentle towards them and provide them with a good diet.

Andreas Laurentius also, in his then well-known *Discourse of the Diseases of Melancholie* (1599) advocates in the treatment of the insane a "good order of dyet," "an ayre as is temperate," "claret wine . . . indifferently delaied," "sleepe, the meanes to doe it," "moderate exercise . . . in pleasant and delightsome places

. . . with rest . . . oft," "Musicke in all melancholike diseases," "baths," "Faire words and cunning speeches" in addition to "either letting of bloud, or purgation of numerous types," "many sorts of opiates" for "sleepe" etc., etc.

Needless to say, Robert Burton too in much greater elaboration[56] advises all the above means of treating melancholy, "the disease of the brain," in addition to much else.

As a matter of fact, we need only consult some of Shakespeare's contemporary dramatists to realize even more fully that our poet was not unique in his treatment of madness. Thus in Philip Massinger's *A Very Woman,* Dr. Paulo diagnoses the case of Cardenes as follows (II, 2):

> His senses are distracted,
> Not one, but all; and if I can collect them
> With all the various ways invention
> Or industry e'er practised, I shall write it
> My masterpiece

and he proceeds to restore him to health by a regimen of fresh air and generally humouring him. In his *The Virgin Martyr* (IV, 1), Massinger has his doctor advocate treating Antoine for "deep melancholy" with music, also ordering him to,

> Take again your bed, sir;
> Sleep is a sovereign physic,

which, of course, brings to mind the words of the doctor in *King Lear* (IV, 4)

> The foster nurse of nature is repose

In William Broome's *Antipodes,* Dr. Hughball, the physician, cures no less than three persons, Joyless, Martha and Perigrine of madness by humouring them. In Fletcher's *The Two Noble Kinsmen* (IV, 2) also, the doctor, called in to treat a girl with "a most thick and profound melancholy" of a sexual etiology, at first remarks, in similarity to Macbeth's doctor:

> I think she has a perturbed mind which
> I cannot minister to

but later devises a treatment wherein her lover impersonates Palamon whom the girl secretly and passionately loves. The treatment is successful for after her wooer reports to the doctor that he has succeeded in kissing the girl twice, he remarks, (V, 2)

> Twenty times had been far better, for there
> the cure lies mainly.

Apropos of such a method of "cure" it is well to mention that "melancholie which cometh by the extremitie of love" was a well recognized form of madness in Shakespeare's day, and one way of treating it, as advocated by Burton and Laurentius and others was by "the enjoying of the thing beloved . . . the principal cause of the disease which is the burning desire, being taken away, the diseased partie will find himself marvellously relieved."[57]

However, it is in John Ford's *The Lover's Melancholy* (1628) that we find the treatment of madness handled in a manner certainly equal to, and in many respects superior to that of Shakespeare, so that we can say with greater validity that Ford not Shakespeare, was portraying the treatment of madness according to the best professional opinion of the day and perhaps "far beyond that of his own times." In this drama, Dr. Corax, who "need (s) no prince's favour"[58] and who is characterized as a high-minded, capable and honest physician in these words (IV, 2):

> Corax, to praise thy art were to assure
> The misbelieving world that the sun shines
> When 'tis i' the full meridian of his beauty.

this Dr. Corax is called on to treat the melancholy of Palador and the madness of the aged Meleander.

In the case of Prince Palador, having prescribed exercise as part of his regimen of treatment, Dr. Corax shows his irritated disapproval, when he finds his patient solitarily reading a book. He excoriates him

> A book! is this the early exercise,
> I did prescribe? instead of following health,
> Which all men covet, you pursue disease.

Where's your great horse, your hounds, your set at tennis,
Your balloon-ball, the practice of your dancing,
Your casting of the sledge, or learning how
To toss a pike? All changed into a sonnet

He finally cures him in accordance with one of the methods prescribed by the best professional authorities of the period. He presents before the Prince a "Masque of Melancholy" in which different forms of prescribed madness pass before him and orate upon their individual attitudes toward life, allowing Dr. Corax to comment on each form of madness. It is in this manner, under Laurentius' and Burton's heading of "Faire words and cunning speeches"[59] in treating such melancholy, that he helps Palador realize the foolishness and futility of his own feelings toward the world and helps effect the cure.

Shakespeare did not portray such means of treatment and therefore it can actually be said here that he was not familiar with the best accepted professional knowledge of his day or at least was deficient in his portrayals in this respect. In Dr. Corax's treatment of Meleander too John Ford certainly equals Shakespeare from the standpoint of the psychotherapy of his day. Indeed, with little exception, it is quite close to the treatment of Lear. Essentially, this treatment consists of humouring the old man, pacifying him with gentleness, allowing for his "repose" with a narcotic, changing his clothes after trimming and combing his hair and beard, and the singing of a song.

Thus "To produce sleep and to quiet the mind by medical and moral treatment, to avoid all unkindness . . . to guard against . . . a relapse . . ."[60] which words Dr. Brigham applies to Shakespeare's portrayal of the treatment of the insane, as though it were the poet's exclusive discovery,—was really one of the accepted forms of treatment of certain types of madness in the Elizabethan period.

Furthermore, that Shakespeare was "in advance of the general opinions of his age"[61] because he knew the causes of insanity to be various and that there are several varieties of insanity, is also an invalid assertion. Aside from the exhaustive dissertations on the subject by Timothy Bright, Burton, Laurentius and others to which Shakespeare certainly had access and which refute this, we find Shakespeare's contemporary dramatists portraying this phase of madness with even greater fidelity than our poet, though with less literary art. Thus Ben Jonson in *Epicence* (IV, w) writes of "insania, furor, vel ecstasis melancholica, that is aggressio, when a man ex melancholico evadit fanaticus . . . . But he may be but 'phreneticus,' yet, mistress, and 'phrenesis' is only delirium or so." Thomas Dekker in *The Honest Whore* (V, 1) writes of the type that speaks "fantastically," "of a thousand matters and all to no purpose." John Ford in his *The Lover's Melancholy* (III, 1) writes of "Ecstasy, Fantastic Dotage, Madness, Frenzy, Rapture." And the various mad characters with their varying degrees of madness in the dramas of Shakespeare and the causes thereof including melancholy, love, watchfulness, irritation, jealousy, worry, heredity, etc., can easily be matched in the dramas of his contemporaries. Ben Jonson in the *Alchemist* (II, 1) has these words:

> She is a most rare scholar,
> And is gone mad studying Broughton's works.
> If you but name a word touching the Hebrew
> She falls into her fit and will discourse
> So learnedly of genealogies,
> As you would run mad, too, to hear her, sir.

In the *Emperor of the East* (III, 4) also we find,

> Grant heaven, your too much learning
> Does not conclude in madness.

Marlowe writes (Everyman's Edit., p. 355):

> So that for want of sleep and sustenance
> My mind's distemper'd

All of which brings to mind Shakespeare's words (*2 Henry IV*, I, 2, 132):

> It hath its original from much grief, from
> Study and perturbation of the brain.

In the final analysis, it is obvious then that Shakespeare, as well as his contemporaries, both literary and scientific, definitely considered most madness as an affliction centered in the brain with causes that were many and various. And, in addition to this, our poet also expressed the generally accepted pathological physiology of the period—the modus operandi, the basic mechanism working on the brain, leading to the development of mental illness. This mechanism, as already pointed out, was simply a disorganization in the balance of the four humours with effects upon the spirits, rising to the brain resulting in the pathological physiology manifesting itself in madness.

NOTES AND REFERENCES

CHAPTER X

1. **Antony and Cleopatra** (III, 3, 36); **Two Gentlemen of Verona,** (IV, 4, 198); **The Tempest** (IV, 1, 249).
2. **Op. Cit.** Brigham, Amariah.
3. Laurentius, Andreas. **A Discourse of the Preservation of the Sight; of Melancholike Diseases; of Rheumes, and of Old Age,** trans. by Richard Surphlet (1599). Shakespeare Assoc. Facsimile No. 15, p. 79.
4. Pomeranz, H. "Medicine in the Shakespearean Plays and Era," **Med. Life,** 41: 511. (Oct. 1934).
5. Quoted in Peers, Allison **Elizabethan Drama and its Mad Folk.** p. 13.
6. **The Anatomy of Melancholy,** edit. Floyd Dell, 1938, p. 149.
7. **Ibid.,** p. 217.
8. **Op. cit.,** p. 89.
9. **Ibid.,** p. 81.
10. **Ibid.,** p. 95.
11. **Ibid.,** p. 88.
12. Quoted by O'Sullivan, Mary "Hamlet and Dr. Timothy Bright," **PMLA,** XLI, 1926, pp. 667-679.
13. I, 1.42.7.
14. H. L. 256.
15. "Thought and Brain: A Guess by Shakespeare" **Cornhill Mag.,** N. S. 64, pp. 671-677, p. 675.
16. **Ibid.,** p. 675.
17. **Ibid.,** p. 671.
18. **Anatomy of Melancholy.** 1883, p. 97.
19. **Ibid.,** 1938 edition, p. 130.
20. **A Discourse . . . Of Melancholike Diseases, etc., op. cit., p. 5.**
21. **Ibid.,** p. 6.
22. **Op. cit.,** p. 2.
23. **Op. cit.,** p. 3.
24. **Ibid.**
25. **Ibid.,** p. 5.
26. **Anatomy,** 1883 edit., p. 97.
27. **Merchant of Venice** (III, 2, 63).
28. Brigham, Amariah, **loc. cit.**
29. "Thought and Brain: A Guess by Shakespeare," **Cornhill Mag., U. S. 64, pp. 671-677, p. 675.**

30. Walsh, James, "Medicine in the Middle Ages, Bartholomew's Proprietatibus Rerum", Med. Life, 39: 365-82, July 1932, p. 367.
31. William Shakespeare, M. D., p. 17.
32. "A Psychoanalytic Study of Shakespeare's Early Plays," The Psychoanalytic Quart., 33: 388-410, 1964, p. 394.
33. King Lear, III, 4.
34. Ravich, R. R. "A Psychoanalytic Study of Shakespeare's Early Plays," Psychoanal. Quart., 33: 388-410, 1964, p. 394.
35. Ibid.
36. Ibid.
37. Ibid., p. 395.
38. Overholser, Winfred. "Shakespeare's Psychiatry—And After." Shakespeare Quart., Vol. X, No. 3, 1959, 335-352, p. 340.
39. Ibid., p. 349.
40. Kellogg, A. O., Shakespeare's Delineations, etc., op. cit., p. 97.
41. Kellogg, A. O., Ibid., p. 11.
42. Pomeranz, H., op. cit., p. 511.
43. Comedy of Errors, V, 1.
44. King Lear, IV, 4.
45. King Lear.
46. King Richard II, V, 5.
47. As You Like It, III, 2, 420.
48. Comedy of Errors, IV, 4, 95.
49. Romeo and Juliet, I, 2, 54.
50. Coriolanus, I, 9, 56.
51. Comedy of Errors, V, 1.
52. Much Ado About Nothing, V, 1, 24.
53. Hamlet, IV, 3.9.
54. Walsh, James, Clinical Medicine in the Middle Ages. Bartholomew's De Proprietatibus Rerum. Med. Life. 39: 365-82, July 1932, p. 367.
55. Ibid., p. 377.
56. Anatomy of Melancholy, "The Second Partition" The Cure of Melancholy, pp. 381-601.
57. Op. cit., p. 121.
58. III, 1.
59. Op. cit., p. 122.
60. Brigham, A. "Illustrations of Insanity," Amer. Journ. of Insanity, I, p. 36.
61. Ibid.

CHAPTER XI

HUMORAL PHYSIOLOGY-PSYCHOLOGY AND SHAKESPEARE'S DRAMAS

I

The Elizabethan World Outlook and Shakespeare

The Elizabethans had developed a comprehensive psychological-physiological system of man based on the teachings of the ancient Greek philosophers, and highly elaborated by the later Arabian thinkers—all to be further synthesized with the beliefs of the Church. This synthesis gave them an all-encompassing philosophy of life, a complete *Weltanschauung* that satisfactorily explained all universal phenomena. Man was God's masterpiece, his noblest creation, "the best furnished and most perfect of all other living creatures, having . . . in his soule the image of God, and in his bodie the modell of the whole world."[1] He was the microcosm, the abridgment of the universe which was the macrocosm—all guided by the hand of God. Their system of psychology-physiology accounted for all man's activities in the world much like the psychoanalytic psychology of today encompasses all of man's activities.

Specifically, it has already been shown how their world outlook influenced the Elizabethan view of the circulation of the blood and of the place of the organs of the body in this system. But not only did they liken man to the earth in the gross and superficial sense,—speaking of his veins as rivers, his bones as rocks, his heart as the sun, his brain as the governor, etc., but they went deeper in this fundamental conception. For in addition, the whole world was made up of the four elements, earth, water, fire and air; and this was also true of man. The humoral physiology, psychology and pathology that dominated the healing art for so many centuries was but an extension of the concept of these elements, inherent in their qualities of *heat, moistness, dryness, coldness;* further developed into the more complex psychology of the four humours, *complexions,* constitutions, and of the *passions* of the mind. It is within such a frame of reference that the Elizabethans fitted their thinking.

Man was composed of the four elements, earth, water, air, and fire, each of which was characterized by two of the four qualities, coldness, moistness, heat and dryness. Man also functioned by means of the four humours, blood, phlegm, choler and melancholy which were analogues of the four elements and partook of the same qualities. Health, both mental and physical, was determined by the proper proportions of these humours, and disease by their improper proportions. All medical diagnosis was aimed at determining the status of this humoral mixture in the body; and diet, purging and blood-letting were the chief therapeutic measures used to effect changes in this humoral mixture. Normal and abnormal psychology was based on the relative proportions of the four elements or humours; and the personality types, temperaments, constitutions or complexions, as Elizabethans called them, were directly derived from these humours and further elaborated with qualities of color. In consequence Elizabethans thought and wrote quite literally in terms of the elements and the humours with their qualities, and of the complexions with their characteristics and colors. They thought in terms of *earthiness, grossness, heaviness, airiness, lightness, thickness, moistness, dryness, coldness* and *hotness.*

Interwoven and elaborated into this pattern of physiology-psychology were the vital spirits, "the chiefe and principall instrument of the minde,"[2] concocted in the heart and sent like vapours through the arteries to the various parts, particularly the brain, as a sort of nervous system helping to maintain proper functioning. If we add to this the effects of the emotions, which the Elizabethans called the passions of the mind, upon man's actions we have then all the components to complete their system of thinking.

The scientific literature of the period is permeated with these concepts. Andreas Laurentius, a famous physician of the period, summarizes some of these ideas. He writes that

> . . . there are foure humours in our bodies, Blood, Phlegme, Choler and Melancholie; and that all these are to be found at all times, in every age, and at all seasons to be mixed and mingled together within the veins, though not alike much of everyone: for even as it is not possible to finde the partie in whom the foure elements are equally mixed; and as there is not that temperature in the world in which the foure contrarie qualities are in the whole and every part equally compounded . . . but there must be someone evermore which doth exceed the other: even so it is not possible to see any perfect living creature in which the foure humours are equally mixed, there is alwaies someone which doth over rule the rest and of it is the partie's complexion named: if blood doe abound, we call such a complexion, sanguine; if phlegme, phlegmatike; if choler, cholerike; and if melancholie, melancholike.[3]

He speaks of "phlegmatike persons" as "blockish" ". . . because the substance of their braine is too thicke and the spirits laboured therein too grosse;"[4] of "sanguine persons," as having "the best complexion for health and long life . . . because . . . it hath the two main pillars of life . . . naturall heate and moysture in greatest measure,"[5] of "cholerike persons" as being hot and drie;"[6] and of "the many sorts" of "the melancholike" ". . . one . . . grosse and earthie, cold and drie . . . another . . . hot . . . another mixed with some small quantitie of blood, and yet . . . is more drie than moyst . . ."[7] He concludes that "the qualities of the minde doe follow the temperament of the bodie."[8] He repeats platitudes of the times when he says that "gay and cheerfulness proceed from heate and moisture . . . Heaviness and sadness from the two contrarie;"[9] that, "Heate maketh men bolde, quicke of motion and headlong in their actions . . .;"[10] that "the instrument of these noble faculties is the braine . . . whose health and welfare consisteth of a good temperature;"[11] the commonest form of melancholy being due to "a cold and drie distemperature of the braine."[12] He states the causes of some of the symptoms of melancholy in terms of that humour:

> The melancholike humour . . . being blacke, causeth the animall spirits, which ought to be pure subtile, cleere and lightsome, it maketh them . . . grosse, darke . . . smoked. But the spirits being the chiefe and principall instrument of the minde, if they be blacke and overcooled also, doe double her most noble powers[13]
>
> because that the spirits and blacke vapours continually passe by the sinews, veins and arteries, from the braine . . .[14]

While Laurentius deals very little with the passions of the mind in their effects on human functioning, Thomas Wright has devoted a whole treatise to it and Robert Burton discussed it at length in his *Anatomy*. We quote a passage from each one as valid to our purpose.

Burton writes:

> For as the Body works upon the mind, by his bad humours, troubling the spirits and sending gross fumes into the Brain; and so *per consequens* disturbing the Soul, and all the faculties of it . . . with fear, sorrow, etc. . . . so . . . the mind effectually works upon the Body, producing by his passions and perturbations, miraculous alterations; as Melancholy, despair, cruel diseases, and sometimes death itself.[15]

Thomas Wright says that

> . . . there is no passion very vehement but that it altereth extremely some of the four humours of the body; and all physitians commonly agree that among divers other extrinsicall causes of disease, one, and not the least is, the excess of some inordinate passion. The physitians therefore, knowing by what passions the maladie was caused, may well inferre what humour aboundeth, and consequently what ought to be purged.[16]

We have then a picture of a man as a replica of the universe, made up of the four elements. The four humours, equivalent to the elements, arise from the chyle of the gastro-intestinal tract and are elaborated by the spleen and liver and contained in the composite blood mass to maintain life in the whole body. Some of this blood is further refined in the heart to form the spirits which are contained in the arteries. and, with the brain which is the seat of the faculties, help rule man's activities. The passions of the mind influence the body humours and in this way produce changes in the body and in the mind.

Shakespeare and his contemporaries reflect all this in their works, and only in being aware of this milieu in which they moved can we truly understand them. In Sonnets 44 and 45 Shakespeare writes:

> But that, so much of *earth* and *water* wrought
> I must attend time's leisure with my moan;
> Receiving nought by *elements* so *slow*
> But *heavy* tears, badges of eithers woe.
>
> The other two, *slight air* and *purging fire,*
> Are both with thee wherever I abide;
> The first my thought, the other my desire,
> These present-absent with *swift* motion slide.
> For when these *quicker elements* are gone
> In tender embassy of love to thee,
> My life, being made of *four,* with *two* alone
> Sinks down to death, *oppressed* with *melancholy.*

in *Twelfth Night* (II, 3, 10):

> Does not our life consist of four *elements?*

and again in the same play (I, 5, 294):

> . . . O, you should not rest
> Between the *elements* of *air* and *earth*

In *I Henry IV* (III, 1, 237) he says:

> You are altogether governed by *humours*

In *Much Ado About Nothing* (II, 1, 357) we have the following line:

> There's little of the melancholy element in her.

In *Richard II,* (III, 3, 35):

> Methinks King Richard and myself should meet
> With no less terror than the *elements*
> Of fire and water, when their thundering shock
> At meeting tears the cloudy cheeks of heaven.

in *King Henry V* (III, 7, 23):

> He's of the *colour* of the *nutmeg.*
> And of the *heat* of the ginger . . . He is pure *aire* and *fire*
> And the *dull* elements of *earth* and *water* never appear in him.

in *Troilus and Cressida* (I, 3, 41):

> Bounding between the two *moist elements*
> Like Perseus' horse

in *Julius Caesar* (V, 5, 53):

> His life was gentle, and the elements
> So mix'd in him that Nature might stand up
> And say to all the world 'This was a man!'

and in *Antony and Cleopatra* (V, 2, 292):

> I am *fire* and *air;* my other elements I give to baser life.

Likewise, Sir Philip Sydney in his *The Arcadia* writes:

> O elements by whose (men say) contention,
> Our bodies be in living power maintained,
> Was this man's death, the fruit of your dissension?
>
> Great be physicians' brags, but aide is beggarly,
> When rooted *moisture* fails, or groweth *drie*

Christopher Marlowe writes (*I Tamburlane,* II, 7):

> Nature, that fram'd us of four elements
> Warring within our breasts for regiment

and further in the same scene:

> The heat and moisture which did feed each other

Are dry and cold; and now doth ghostly Death
gripe my bleeding heart

And again (*II Tamburlane,* IV, 1):

In sending to my issue such a soul
Created of the *massy dregs of earth*
The scum and *tartar* of the *elements*

Similarly, John Ford writes:

Like four straight pillars the *four elements*
Support the goodly structure of mortality;
Then shall the *four complexions* like four heads
Of a clear river, streaming in his body,
Nourish and comfort every vein and sinew[17]

and again:

This will not doe, I read it on thy forehead
The graine of thy *complexion* is quite altered
Once 'twas a comely *browne,* 'tis now of late
A perfect *green* and *yellow;* sure prognosticate
Of th' over flux o' th' gall, and *melancholy,*
Symptoms of love and jealousie, poor soule[18]

Shakespeare carries through many more of these concepts that mirror his times. Thus in the matter of the complexions he writes down the following conversation between Moth and Armado (*Love's Labour's Lost,* I, 2, 82):

Moth: A woman, master.
Armado: Of what *complexion?*
Moth: Of all the four, or the three, or the two, or one of the four.
Armado: Tell me precisely of what *complexion.*
Moth: Of the sea-water green, sir.
Armado: Is that one of the four complexions?
Moth: As I have read, sir; and the best of them too.

The basic principle of the disequilibrium of the humours or complexions as a cause of mental illness in the Elizabethan sense is well stated in *Hamlet* (I, 5). Hamlet says to Horatio:

So, oft it chances in particular men,
By the o'ergrowth of some *complexion,*
Oft breaking down the pales and forts of reason
Shall in the general censure take corruption
From that particular fault.

In the *Merry Wives of Windsor* (IV, 2, 25) we have:

So curses all Eve's daughters, of what *complexion* soever

From *Measure for Measure* (II, 4, 129) we get:

Nay call us ten times frail
For we are as soft as our *complexions* are

and from *Julius Caesar* (I, 3, 128):

The *complexion* of the *element*
In favour's like the work we have in hand
Most bloody, *fiery* and most terrible

In regard to the humours Shakespeare has many, many passages too, some of which have already been quoted. In *I Henry IV* (III, 1, 237) he writes:

You are altogether governed by *humours*

In *Twelfth Night* (II, 4, 116), we have:

With a *green* and *yellow* melancholy she sat like patience
On a monument, smiling at grief

In *Taming of the Shrew* Shakespeare puts these words from Petruchio (IV, 1):

For it engenders *choler,* planteth *anger;*
And better 'twere that both of us did fast,
Since of ourselves, ourselves are *choleric.*

In *Hamlet* (III, 3) when Guildenstern tells the prince that the king is distempered with *choler* Hamlet answers:

Your wisdom should show itself more richer to signify

this to his doctor; for, for me to put him to his *purgation*
would perhaps plunge him into far more *choler*.

while in *Taming of the Shrew* (Ind., 2, 135) Shakespeare speaks of the humour melancholy as being "the nurse of frenzy."

The passions of the mind including grief, anger, hate, love, joy, etc., get their full share of Elizabethan meaning in the dramas. Shakespeare (*Pericles,* IV, 4,24) speaks of

The *passions of the mind*
That have their first conceptions by mis-dread,

of (*As You Like It,* IV, 3, 72) the

great testimony in your *complexion* that it was
a *passion of earnest*

that (*I Henry VI,* V, 2, 18):

Of all base *passions,*
Fear is most accurst

He speaks of "the hot passion of distemper'd blood" (*Troilus and Cressida,* II, 2, 169); of the "two extremes of passions, joy and grief" (*King Lear,* V, 3, 198) and of "Idle merriment, a passion hateful to my purposes" (*King John,* III, 3, 47). He has one of his characters ask the question (*Much Ado About Nothing,* II, 1, 83): "What effects of *passion* shows she?" and another character is described as "Free from gross passion, or of mirth or anger" (*Henry V,* 2, 132).

In the matter of the *spirits,* there is also much to exemplify Shakespeare's literal usage of the term as part of the physiological system of the period. In his *Old Wives Tale* (I, 2, 72), he writes:

And our weak *spirits* ne'er been higher rear'd
With stronger *blood.*

in *The Tempest* (I, 1, 486):

My *spirits,* as in a dream, are all bound up.

and in *Love's Labour's Lost* (IV, 3, 306):

Universal plodding prisons up

The nimble *spirits* in the arteries

Of similar nature are Shakespeare's references to the fumes or vapours rising up to the brain and producing definite effects as referred to previously in Burton and others. Thus in *Cymbeline* (IV, 2, 301) he writes:

'Twas but a bolt of nothing, shot at nothing
Which the brain makes of *fumes*

in *The Tempest* (V, 1, 59):

And as the morning steals upon the night,
Melting the darkness, so their rising senses
Begin to chase the ignorant *fumes* that mantle
Their clearer reason.

while in *II Henry IV* (IV, 3, 106), in referring to sherris:

It ascends me into the brain; *dries* me there
All the foolish and *dull* and *crudy vapours*

He further speaks of the brain "as dry as the remainder biscuit" (*As You Like It,* II, 7, 38), of "boiled brains" of "a bot braine," of a "heat-oppressed brain," etc. When Laertes sees Ophelia in her mad state, he thirsts for active and quick vengeance; he cries out (*Hamlet,* IV, 5):

O heat, dry up my brains!

By heaven, thy madness shall be paid by weight
Till our scale turn the beam

recalling the doctrine of the period that "Heate maketh men bolde, quick of motion and headlong in their actions."[19]

A great many more quotations could be cited of similar nature to further prove how much of a child of his age our poet really was and how truly he reflected the general knowledge of his period. However, we shall pursue this point later but only in relation to other aspects of the medicine and psychiatry of his age.

II

Astrology and Humoral-Physiology-Psychology In Shakespeare's Dramas

Interwoven also, as a large part of the world outlook of Shakespeare's England, was the influence of the heavenly bodies on this microcosmic man we have been considering—involving all of his activities and functions. This took the form of astrology, and more particularly of astrologic medicine and psychology.

While we shall take up this whole matter of astrology in Shakespeare and in Elizabethan England in a later chapter, we shall here briefly show the relationship of the astrology of the period to the humoral physiology-psychology we have been considering. The planets influenced the humors from birth and throughout man's life, and in this way, affected his temperament or 'complexion'—whether sanguine, choleric, phlegmatic or melancholic—dependent on the dominance of any one of the four humors. Thus Saturn tended to cause an excess of black bile promoting melancholy; the planet Jupiter was in relation to blood, the sanguine humor, which was considered appropriate to princes, accepted lovers, and to the jovial and fortunate. Venus was in relation to the phlegmatic humor and was thought proper to women, children and voluptuaries, and under the moon, . . . "belonged to simpletons and fools."[20] The sun was in relation to the humor, yellow bile, appropriate to rulers and self-willed women, and, in conjunction with Mars, to soldiers, roisterers and drunkards. The moon especially was held important in the causation of mental illness. The very use of the word "lunacy" is certainly evidence of this; and Shakespeare and his contemporaries used this concept of the moon's influence as a part of the everyday language of the period, and their literary productions have many passages dealing with it. As a matter of fact, Shakespeare's works contain over one hundred astrological allusions. As to the 'scientific' attitude in this matter it can be said that practically all doctors and educated laymen accepted astrology and astrological medicine as a general part of their general belief and education. Burton in his *Anatomy of*

Melancholy, Thomas Viczry in his *Anatomie of the Man's Bodie,*[21] A. Boorde in his *Breviary of Healthe,*[22] Sir Thomas Browne in his *Pseudodoxia Epidemica*[23] and other popular works of a similar nature—all deal with astrology and astrological medicine and psychology as an accepted part of the intellectual environment of their times. As Dr. Overholser points out, "It was true in the time of Shakespeare . . . that astrology played an important part in the training of the physician," and he quotes Robert Burton as stating that "the constellation alone many times produceth melancholy."[24]

As indicated previously, Shakespeare, as a child of his age automatically was bound by this humoral, astrological medicine and psychology prevalent at the time; and it can easily be shown that all the characters in his plays are drawn in terms of such humoral astrological psychology. Thus, John W. Draper considers King Lear as "based on the humoral alterations in Lear who now over eighty years old, was changed from the choler proper to kingship and maturity to the melancholy weakness of old age."[25] He considers "Hamlet . . . naturally sanguine, but the stress of misfortune and uncertainty have changed him to the opposite complexion."[26] In the same way Draper categorizes most of the characters in the tragedies of Shakespeare. This does not mean however, that Shakespeare wrote his plays and drew his characters consciously and deliberately to exemplify humoral astrological psychology; nor does it mean, that because the characters do fall within the bounds of this Elizabethan psychology, that, therefore it is mutually exclusive in relation to the modern neuropsychiatric and psychoanalytic approaches. Both these approaches have validity within their frames of reference, as we shall soon see.

NOTES AND REFERENCES

CHAPTER XI

1. Laurentius, op. cit., p. 80.
2. Laurentius, op. cit., p. 91.
3. **A Discourse of the Preservation of the Sight: of Melancholike Diseases: of Rheumes, and of Old Age.** Shakespeare Association Facsimiles, No. 15. Oxford University Press, 1938, p. 84.
4. Ibid., p. 85.
5. Loc. cit.
6. Loc. cit.
7. Loc. cit.
8. Ibid., p. 91.
9. Ibid., p. 93.
10. Ibid., p. 90.
11. Ibid., p. 83.
12. Ibid., p. 88.
13. Ibid., p. 91.
14. Ibid., p. 92.
15. **The Anatomy of Melancholy**, part I, Sect. 2, Memb. 3, Subject. 1.
16. Quoted in Laurentius, op. cit., p. XXI.
17. "The Sun's Darling" (II, 437), **The Dramatic Works of John Ford**, ed. Gifford, 1827, p. 54.
18. Quoted in Sensabaugh, **The Tragic Muse of John Ford.**
19. Laurentius, op. cit., p. 90.
20. Draper, John W., "The Humors," **Journ. Amer. Med. Assoc.**, Vol. 188, No. 3, April 20, 1964. p. 259.
    See also—C. A. Mercier, **Astrology in Medicine** (London 1914). C. Comden, Jr. "Elizabethan Astrological Medicine," **Annals of Med. Hist.**, H. S., II (1930), 217.
21. **True Anatomie of the Man's Bodie** (London, 1587).
22. **Breviary of Healthe** (London, 1952), folio 73.
23. **Pseudodoxie Epidemica** (London 1646), p. 231 (Book IV, Ch. 13).
24. "Shakespeare's Psychiatry—And After," Vol. X, No. 3, Summer 1959. p. 337.
25. See "The Humors, Some Psychological Aspects of Shakespeare's Tragedies," p. 261. **Journ. Amer. Med. Assoc.**, Vol. 188, No. 3, Apr. 20, 1964. pp. 259-262.
26. Ibid., p. 260.

CHAPTER XII

KING LEAR: AN HISTORICAL SURVEY OF CRITICISM AND INTERPRETATION

I

The Seventeenth and Eighteenth Centuries and *King Lear*

King Lear has been considered by many critics as the greatest achievement of Shakespeare. Some even go further than this, and accept it as one of the greatest pieces of work in the entire realm of literature. Thus Shelley considers it "the most perfect specimen of the dramatic art in the world;"[1] and the bardolators of the nineteenth century generally echo this judgment. H. N. Hudson calls it "the greatest and noblest achievement of the greatest and noblest of poets."[2] Dowden calls it "the greatest single achievement in poetry of the Teutonic or Northern genius."[3] Karl Young finds it to be the "greatest of all dramas,"[4] Allardyce Nicoll points it out as Shakespeare's "most beautiful work of art from the poetic point of view."[5] Dover Wilson calls it "the greatest monument of human misery and despair in the literature of the world."[6] While Hardin Craig is not averse to calling it "possibly the greatest of Shakespeare's tragedies."[7] And yet controversial criticism is far from lacking on the various aspects of *King Lear*. Is it a great drama? What of its gross improbabilities? Is Lear the picture of an insane man throughout the play? Is it the medium of symbolic mythology of political import? Has it as its aim the picturing of tragedy resulting from the violation of Elizabethan ethics and moral standards? It is upon these, among other less important problems, that the attention of critics has been focussed. It shall be our purpose here to consider *King Lear* in the light of its various interpretations and deduce from all this, perhaps, not only a more rational attitude toward the play itself, but toward all of Shakespeare's works.

It is a well known fact that the mood of an individual often determines his appreciation and his interpretation of a work of art. Likewise the mood of an age, determines the appreciation and the interpretation of its works of art. Shakespearean criticism, to a greater or lesser degree, is characterized and colored by the moods and tendencies of the centuries. Thus the seventeenth and the greater part of the eighteenth centuries with their adherence to the Aristotelian unities, their passion for poetic justice, their desire for refinement, looked upon Shakespeare as vulgar, and barbarous, and unlearned. Nevertheless, they recognized the comprehensiveness of his soul and the universality of his genius; and such a strong hold had he, that they set about to improve his faults in order to make him more acceptable to the mood of the times. No better commentary as to the attitude of these centuries towards *King Lear is necessary* than this: that from 1631 to 1838, for fully 207 years, Nahum Tate's altered version of *King Lear* was the accepted form of the play.[8] In this adaptation of the play, there is a happy ending. Lear does not die, but is restored to his sanity and to his kingdom. Cordelia is not murdered, but is united in marriage and happiness to Edgar, and made reigning queen of England. And the Fool, whom later critics praised to the very heavens, is entirely omitted. The play ends with justice distributed wherever due, and closes with the following words of Edgar.

> Our drooping Country now erects her Head,
> Peace spreads her balmy wings, and plenty blooms,
> Divine Cordelia, all the Gods can Witness
> How much thy Love to Empire I prefer!
> Thy bright example shall convince the world
> (Whatever Storms of Fortune are decreed)
> That Truth and Virtue shall at last succeed.[9]

Let us place beside this the last words of Shakespeare's Lear. Lear, bearing the dead Cordelia in his arms says:

> And my poor fool is hang'd! No, no, no life!
> Why should a dog, a horse, a rat have life,
> And thou no breath at all? Thoult come no more,
> Never, never, never, never, never!

Pray you, undo this button. Thank you, sir.
Do you see this? Look on her, look, her lips,
Look there, look there!

And Lear dies. Compare these two; and we realize more fully the biased and perverted interpretation of an age that was willing to forego the poignant passion and tragic pathos for the sugary sentimentality of a poetic justice of the previous version. Indeed, the insertion of the apparently calm simple line, "Pray you, undo this button. Thank you, sir." amidst the soul-stirring cries in the other lines has in it far more of genius, far more of effectiveness, far more of dramatic value, than volumes of moralizations can possibly have. "A happy ending!" says Lamb, "As if the living martyrdom that Lear had gone through, the flaying of his feelings alive, did not make a fair dismissal from the stage of life the only decorous thing for him . . . as if at his years, and with his experience anything was left but to die."[10]

John Dryden, even though an adapter of one of Shakespeare's plays, himself, and although calling him "many times flat, insipid"[11] in a flash of intuitive foresight says, "Therefore, let not Shakespeare suffer for our sakes; 'tis our fault who succeed him in an age which is more refin'd if we imitate him so ill, that we copy his feelings only, and make a virtue of that in our writings, which in his was an imperfection."[12]

Joseph Warton in 1754, believing that general criticism with respect to Shakespeare was absurd, takes up the "origin and progress of the distraction of Lear," "step by step, and scene by scene."[13] According to his interpretation, Lear's distraction begins with the rage engendered in him by Goneril in proposing to reduce the number of knights in his train. This is increased to tumultuous passion by the actions of Regan in driving him forth into the storm on the heath. The contemplation of the ingratitude of his daughters, the fury of the elements, and the meeting with the Fool and the mad-feigning Edgar in the hovel—these finally bring him to definite insanity. And "the first plain indication of the loss of his reason," according to Warton, "is his calling Edgar a 'learned Theban';"[14] Joseph Warton gives due recognition and praise to Shakespeare for the "perfect picture of the secret workings and changes of Lear's mind,"[15] but he also points out the many imperfections in the play. Thus he considers the Gloucester sub-plot as distracting the attention and destroying the unity of the drama. He considers the extinction of Glo'sters eyes as too horrid to be exhibited on the stage, and finds the cruelty of Lear's daughters, "painted with circumstances too savage and unnatural."[16] The delusion of Gloucester, as having leaped down Dover cliff, he points out as highly improbable; and he finds it impossible to excuse the "passages that are too turgid and full of strained metaphors."[17]

Samuel Johnson, foreshadowing the historical method of criticism common among the Twentieth century skeptics, explains and excuses the improbabilities in *King Lear* mainly on historical grounds. The conduct of Lear may be improbable but then we must realize that he "is represented according to histories at that time vulgarly received as true."[18] The cruelty of Lear's daughters may appear too savage and too unnatural, but then we must remember, according to Johnson, that such cruelty "is an historical fact, to which the poet has added little."[19] The gouging out of Gloucester's eyes is shocking and horrid. "Yet let it be remembered that our author well knew what would please the audience for which he wrote."[20] Granted, that the addition of the sub-plot complicates and destroys the simplicity of the main action but then this is "abundantly recompensed by the addition of variety, by the art with which it (he) is made to cooperate with the chief design, and the opportunity which it (he) gives the poet of combining perfidy with perfidy, and connecting the wicked son with the wicked daughters . . . ."[21]

As to the tragic fate of Cordelia, Johnson feels that it is "contrary to the natural ideas of justice, to the hope of the reader, . . . and to the faith of chronicles."[22] As far as he was concerned Cordelia's death was so shocking to him that he could not endure to read again the last scenes of the play. What a tremendous compliment it is to Shakespeare, that he could produce on the printed page, action, so real and so tragic, as to evoke such emotion in the level-headed Samuel Johnson.

Generally speaking, then, the seventeenth and eighteenth centuries looked upon *King Lear* with sane critical eyes. They recognized the expression of tremendous genius in the development of the character and the passions of Lear. But they also recognized the faults and the absurdities in the play. And though, both Johnson and Pope considered and explained these absurdities and these faults in the light of the historical method, yet they must have been supporters of Nahum Tate's perversion of the play. It is interesting to note here that all the elements of Shakespearean criticism that were to bloom out so luxuriantly in the nineteenth and twentieth centuries, are already present here. There is a note of suppressed idolatry in the consideration of Shakespeare's depiction of the character of Lear and in the conflict of his emotions. And there is the germ of skepticism in the due attention paid to Shakespeare's faults evidenced in *King Lear*, and to a consideration of these faults in the light of Shakespeare's times.

II

The Nineteenth Century and *King Lear*

And now, we come to an important phenomenon in the trend of Shakespearean criticism, which we have already discussed in relation to Shakespearean criticism in general, but which we shall now apply especially to *King Lear*. The nineteenth century, as a furious reaction to the rationalism and classicism of the previous century, was swept off its feet into a maelstrom of emotional romanticism. The pendulum swung completely to the other extreme. The mood was set in this age to a raising of Shakespeare unto a veritable godhood. The critics touched their own spirits to the works of Shakespeare and raised out of them their own emotions and their own sentimentalism. They clothed Shakespeare in the purple toga of all-comprehensive-knowledge. They named him a great philosopher, a great poet, a great dramatist, a great physician, a great lawyer, a learned scholar, an astronomer, a psychiatrist, etc., etc. As already mentioned they approached him with bated breath and reverenced awe; uttering ecstatic rhapsodies and metaphorical confusions. And woe to him who dared be heretic, for in the words of Coleridge, "The Englishman, who without reverence, a proud and affectionate reverence, can utter the name of William Shakespeare stands disqualified for the office of critic."[23] and in the words of Hazlitt, "those who are not for him are against him."[24]

With such a mood prevailing, we can readily understand the idolatrous nature of the interpretations of *King Lear* in the nineteenth century.

Charles Lamb, believing "that the plays of Shakespeare are less calculated for performance on a stage than those of almost any other dramatist whatever,"[25] feels particularly, that "the Lear of Shakespeare cannot be acted."[26] for the "play is beyond all art."[27] "The greatness of Lear is not in corporal dimension but in intellectual; the explosions of his passion are terrible as a volcano; they are storms turning up and disclosing to the bottom that sea, his mind, with all its vast riches."[28] To Charles Lamb *King Lear* represents mainly the picture of an old man "turned out by his daughters in a rainy night."[29].

And in general, it may be said of most of the early idolators, that they considered the characters in *King Lear* and the conflict of the passions, as supremely painted. They did not bother much with its improbabilities and its absurdities, and its dramatic faults. For according to Coleridge, the play "is merely the canvass for the characters and passions."[30] Granting the improbabilities in the first scene,

> "Let the first scene of this play have been lost and let it only be understood that a fond father had been duped by hypocritical professions of love and duty on the part of two daughters to disinherit the third, previously, and deservedly, more dear to him—and all the rest of the tragedy would retain its interest undiminished, and be perfectly intelligible."[31]

Coleridge considers the trial of professions as a trick; "and that the grossness of the old king's rage is in part the natural result of a silly trick suddenly and most unexpectedly baffled and disappointed."[32] It was accepted by the audience because it was "an old story rooted in the popular faith."[33]

As to Edgar's assumed madness, Coleridge feels that it "serves the great purpose of taking off part of the shock which would otherwise be caused by the true madness of Lear . . ."[34] And this is the generally accepted idea even today, as regards this matter.

William Hazlitt is a more eloquent echo of Coleridge but his criticism of *King Lear* is all general. To him the appreciation of the play is beyond words and to attempt its description or its effect upon the mind, "mere impertinence." He calls it "the best of all Shakespeare's plays,"[35] because the passion of which it is the subject "strikes its root deepest into the human heart."[36]

We can readily see from the foregoing, that the most pressing problem that the idolators have had to face, the real thorn in their sides, the Gordian knot, as it were, was the absurdity of Lear's actions in first dividing the kingdom, then asking for his daughters, professions of love, and basing upon their answers his action in casting out from his heart and home his daughter Cordelia, whom he had always loved the most. This is a real problem and critics have had to face it until the present day. Where is the motivation for such unnatural action? Here is a king who has supposedly ruled his kingdom with judgment and equanimity for many years, who has loved a youngest daughter dearly who has had a nobleman, Kent, as a faithful servant and follower, but who divests himself of his kingdom, casts off his beloved daughter and banishes his faithful follower for pointing out his folly. These are absurd, irrational, improbable, motivationless actions.

Now it has been held by many critics that this improbability of the first scene is of no importance to the purpose of the play and must be accepted merely for the postulation of a situation. Thus, Raleigh states that Shakespeare's "opening scenes are often a kind of postulate, which the spectator or reader is asked to grant. At this stage of the play improbability is of no account, the intelligent reader will accept the situation and become alert and critical only when the next step is taken."[37] Schucking is in accord with this, for he remarks, with regard to the improbability of the king's actions, that "what we have to decide is rather *whether the behavior of the King toward his daughter can be brought into agreement, not with the laws of reason but with the rest of his conduct.*"[38]

Granville-Barker agrees with these two. He definitely states:

> "The scene in which Lear divides his kingdom is a magnificent theme . . . Its probabilities are neither here nor there. A dramatist may postulate any situation he has the means to interpret, if he will abide by the logic of it after."[39]

Stoll develops this theme more thoroughly. He holds that Shakespeare was primarily interested in emotional effects arising out of human conflicts and like all great dramatists was eager for a good situation, that is one "in which the contrast of conflict is sharpest and most striking, *the probability or psychological reasonableness of it being a secondary consideration.*"[40] In fact, as Stoll points out, the greatest tragedies in the world are built on improbable and unreasonable situations. "Their improbability is the price of their effectiveness."[41] From this standpoint, of course, the improbabilities of the first scene, must cease to trouble critics. But why, it may be asked, did Shakespeare seem to go out of his way to make this first scene improbable, for most of the old sources of the play do supply better motivation. Thus in Geoffrey of Monmouth's "Chronicles of British Kings," the division of the kingdom is made dependent on the expressions of love from the three daughters. The divisions are not already made when the play starts as in Shakespeare's *Lear*. In Holinshed's *Chronicles* Lear had, in the beginning, intended to give Cordelia the entire kingdom and only her failure at flattery changed this. Only in Spenser's *Faerie Queene*, (Book II. Canto 10) do we find the kingdom already divided at the beginning and the questioning of daughters pictured as merely a means of gratification for Lear, as Shakespeare has it. Why, of all the versions, did Shakespeare pick this most improbable one; for, selection there must have been.

Indeed, the older play *King Lear*, which was Shakespeare's immediate and most important source, gives acceptable motivation for Lear's actions as Allardyce Nicholl points out, for in this play, King Lear after the death of his queen, feeling unable in the task of governing his three daughters, for "fathers best do know to govern sons," decides to divide his kingdom among the three of them. Goneril and Regan have been provided with husbands. But Cordelia objects to any husband chosen for her "unless love allows." Lear decides to ask for public professions of his daughters' love in order that he may trap Cordelia into some extravagant verbal expression of her love for him, upon which he is merely to ask her such a simple request as marrying a king of Brittany, "which she cannot well deny . . ."

"Although, her fences will be mute:"

This is definite motivation for the trial of professions and the explanation by many critics that Lear's action in this respect was but the result of a "silly trick," "a momentary impulse of vain nature,"[42] "or a freak of the imagination"[43] "suddenly and most unexpectedly baffled and disappointed,"[44] is more applicable to this older play than to Shakespeare's *King Lear*. Nor is the explanation that this improbability was allowed by Shakespeare because of popular acceptance entirely valid, for whoever wrote the older *King Lear* apparently did not depend upon this popular acceptance but provided motivation: and we know that this older version of *King Lear* was put on the stage at about the same time as Shakespeare's *King Lear*. So there it is. Can the idolators, who are suspicious... of all criticisms which suppose a want of art in Shakespeare, admit that here was a flaw, "a glaring absurdity"? But come the medical idolators to the rescue. And their case is certainly a strong one, although pushed to extravagant extremes. These medical idolators go into rapturous spasms of praise over Shakespeare's ability at delineating insanity and the psychoneurotic states. To them the character of Lear presents an out and out case of insanity, the so-called senile dementia. The actions of Lear in the first scene are unnatural and hard to explain. All critics agree in this. But only the medical critics have the most logical explanation. However, we shall take this up in a later chapter.

III

The Twentieth Century and Its Interpretations of *King Lear*

Now, thus far, the criticism considered has practically all been of a subjective nature. It represents an emotional reaction in the sentimental romantic vein. And so busy were these idolators in heaping superlative praise upon the characterization and the depiction of passion in *King Lear,* that they were blind to its many faults. What of the dramatic construction of the play? Is it a great drama even from the literary viewpoint? This takes us to a group of critics whose idolatry is tempered with reason and who view *King Lear* with a discerning judgment and a calm eye. To these critics *King Lear* is still Shakespeare's "greatest work." It is still his "most beautiful work of art from the poetic point of view." It still has "epic grandeur." But it is also "imperfectly dramatic." It is also a "careless production," too complicated by the sub-plot with the consequent multiplicity of important characters, to produce a unity of effect. According to Spedding, writing in 1877, "the interest," "in the last two acts" "is not well sustained" . . . "Lear's passion rises to its full height too early and his decay is too long drawn out." "The fate of Edgar or Edmund was not interesting enough; it seemed a separate thing, almost an intrusion upon the proper business of the play."[45] And the battle scene of the last act Spedding considers, poor, from every standpoint.

Professor A. C. Bradley agrees in the main with Spedding. He considers the play "too huge for the stage" and having too vast a material to use with complete dramatic effectiveness.[46] He believes that "The principal structural weakness of King Lear" ... "arises chiefly from the double action"[47] involved in the two plots, which Prof. R. M. Alden (1922) agrees serves "to divide the interest in a rather perplexing way."[48] And the result of it all is that "The number of essential characters is so large, their actions and movements are so complicated, and events toward the close crowd on one another so thickly, that the reader's attention, rapidly transferred from one center of interest to another, is overstrained."[49] As to the battle he considers it "ludicrous" and insignificant. And he devotes a great deal of space to pointing out the many improbabilities and dramatic inconsistencies in *King Lear* which he feels "far surpass those of the other great tragedies in number and in grossness."[50] And although he excuses many of these faults and inconsistencies on the basis of popular acceptance of an old plot, yet the conclusion remains that *King Lear,* though of grandest epic proportions in imaginative poetry, is but a poor play from the standpoint of the drama and the theatre.

Allardyce Nicoll in his book *"Studies in Shakespeare"* (1927) goes into a thorough and painstaking consideration of *King Lear* and comes to a similar conclusion. He contrasts the older play *King Lear* with Shakespeare's *King Lear* noting his changes, his omissions and his additions, and finds that from the standpoint of motivation and dramatic logic, Shakespeare's *King Lear* is inferior to the older *King Lear.* A "mighty," "comprehensive production" it is, of great "tragic universality." But it "must fail to capture our full attention in the playhouse and . . . even in the study does not present that unity of interest which is apparent in the other dramas."[51] The presence of so many major characters tends "to take our minds away from the one dominant person."[52] And so intent was Shakespeare on depicting this dominant person and creating through him the impression of "tragic universality" that it absorbed his imagination to the exclusion of everything else. So that "considered as a play, *Lear,* because of its puppet figures, because of its several artificial scenes, is decidedly the least powerful of the four tragedies . . . Exhaustion or a certain carelessness is evident from first scene to last."[53] And only in its grand epic proportions similar to that of the *Divine Comedy* does it attain its great poetic power.

But shall it be allowed that Shakespeare should be considered anything but perfect without some excuses? Heresy of heresies! There is a school of Shakespearean critics who have a never-failing formula for such a situation. If there are improbabilities and absurdities in a Shakespearean play, why then it is because such were the conventions and usages of the time. This has already been referred to. If there are poor passages or grave dramatic faults, why then by means of ingenious mental gymnastics involving rhyme and meter and endings and what nots, these critics can show that Shakespeare was not responsible for such passages and such faults, but that some other collaborator or collaborators were responsible. Thus The Shakespeare skeptic Hardin Craig makes the sweeping statement that "In most instances of apparent carelessness there are indications that the work was tampered with after it left his hand."[54] Or failing in this, it can always be shown that the play involved was revised by Shakespeare from an imperfect play which he had written in the early days of his apprenticeship. And sure enough, in 1923, we find all the faults and imperfections in *King Lear* explained away by Frank Mathew in just such a manner. All the shocking incidents were written in his youth, such as the gouging out of Glo'ster's eyes, and all the finer elements are but due to later alterations. He links *King Lear* to *Titus and Andronicus* pointing out its similarities which to him "seems one of the signs that the first form of this tragedy (*King Lear*) sprang from the latter play."[55]

But, what of the philosophy, the interpretations of life that numerous critics have found in *King Lear*. They are many and various. And certainly, judging by the many apparent expressions of a philosophic nature which Shakespeare put into the mouths of the characters in *King Lear,* there is indeed room for much reflective speculation. As has been pointed out before, the latter part of the seventeenth century, the whole of the eighteenth and the great part of the nineteenth centuries, rejected the obvious tragedy of life involved in *King Lear* and made it more palatable by substituting the triumph of virtue and the conquest of evil as a final evidence of divine justice in the world. To this, there is nothing more to be said.

Later critics, however, particularly Swinburne, have seen in *King Lear* the expression of a bitter profound pessimism, a 'tragic fatalism' without even that "promise of the morning on which mystery and justice shall be made one." without even that "twilight of atonement" in which there shall be "pledge of reconciliation."[56] . . . "Requital, redemption, amends, equity, explanation, pity and mercy, are words without meaning here" . . . "for here is very Night herself."[57]

> As flies to wanton boys are we to the gods;
> They kill us for their sport.

And to Swinburne, "these words . . . strike the keynote of the whole poem, lay the keystone of the whole arch of thought."[58] So that instead of a "light of revelation," we have here the very "darkness of revelation."

Prof. Bradley differs somewhat from this interpretation. He holds that "man is not represented" in *King Lear,* as "the mere plaything of a blind and capricious power, suffering woes which have no relation to his character and actions . . ."[59] for in reality the tragedy arises out of definite flaws and actions in Lear and Cordelia so that in a sense, they themselves are responsible for their own misfortunes. In the case of Lear, according to Hazlitt and others, "It is his rash haste, his violent impetuosity, his blindness to everything but the dictates of his passions or affections, that produce all his misfortunes."[60] And in the case of Cordelia "it is the faulty admixture of pride and sullenness"[61] and "an unaccommodating vigor."[62] And it is the result equally of both of these that the catastrophe takes place.

Nor, to continue with Bradley, "is the world represented as given over to darkness . . ."[63] Its keynote is surely to be heard neither in the words wrung from Glo'ster in his anguish, nor in Edgar's words 'the gods are just.' Its final and total result is one in which pity and terror, carried perhaps to the extreme limits of art, are so blended with a sense of law and beauty that we feel at last, not depression and much less despair, but a consciousness of greatness in pain, and of solemnity in the mystery we cannot fathom.[64]

Many have seen in *King Lear* a biographical reflection of a particular time of Shakespeare's life, when bitterness and disillusion lay heavily upon his soul. The play has been indirectly linked with the sonnets, as marking a further stage of this disappointed infatuation involving his famous "dark lady." Thus Frank Harris sees in *King Lear* innumerable evidences of erotomania which he attributes to this unrequited infatuation. The play has also been linked up with *Timon of Athens* by Prof. Bradley and others. In both is there violent cursing and bitterness. And what leads to the tragic death of fate in the one, leads to the suicide of misanthropy in the other. Whether such an interpretation, based on the old problem of Shakespeare's biography in his works is valid or not, is still a question, though the new psychoanalytic criticism has indeed, correctly accepted this principle as valid, but of course in the light of the psychoanalytic depth psychology. Let us therefore summarize for a moment before proceeding further. We have seen the seventeenth and eighteenth centuries, because of the general tone of the times, accept *King Lear* as an unrefined production, "wanting in art." These centuries acknowledged the many faults of the work, but they also appreciated its points of greatness. In the nineteenth century we have seen how the tide of Romanticism carried the appreciation of *King Lear* into channels of extreme idolatry, wherein reverence and enthusiasm gave rise to unbridled extravagance in interpretation. And finally we have seen a return to the method of Joseph Warton of the eighteenth century in that group of critics who are just as aware of the shortcomings of *King Lear,* as they are of its fine qualities. And so we are brought down to the skeptics of the twentieth century.

Skepticism in Shakespearean criticism today is an inevitable consequence of two main factors. First, it is a natural reaction to the extreme idolatry of the previous century in which, as has been shown, Shakespeare was deified with the crown and sceptre of all-knowledge and all-wisdom. And secondly, skepticism is but the natural temper of the times. The same forces that are cynically calling into question all our accepted institutions, all our accepted principles, and all our accepted standards are skeptically calling into question all the principles and standards by which we have judged and interpreted Shakespeare.

The age with regard to Shakespeare is merely fulfilling itself. Skepticism, as such, is the order of the day, the fashion in Shakespearean criticism. The voices raised are indeed voices to be reckoned with. However there is grave danger lest these critics become the victim of their own ingenious system and taking skepticism as an end in itself, rationalize around it a body of criticism that is barren and bloodless and cold. Skepticism in its proper proportions and in its proper place is a healthy attitude. But it should be directed towards the so-called facts, and the system based on such facts which Shakespearean critics have been bringing forward. We must recognize that in spite of the most painstaking scholarship, there are limitations, and always will be, to our ability at arriving at a complete understanding of Elizabethan England. The prejudices of the scholar must always be taken into consideration in his interpretation of facts. We can never hope to enter completely into the same spirit with which the Elizabethan groundling viewed Shakespeare. Nor can we ever know definitely what Shakespeare intended when he wrote his plays. So how can we judge Shakespeare as Shakespeare's audience judged him? How can we understand him and interpret him as he meant to be understood and interpreted? And yet this is precisely what Shakespearean skeptics would have us do. They want us to interpret Shakespeare in the light of his own age and yet the most that can be offered to illumine our way are but dim reflections of that light, though it must be granted that in the field of medicine and psychiatry in Shakespeare, we are on brighter and firmer ground.

But to get back to *King Lear* from the standpoint of these skeptics. Can we explain *King Lear* on the basis of the study of Elizabethan conventions and Elizabethan life. No doubt any absurdity or inconsistency or improbability in *King Lear* can be explained away on such a basis. The dictum is: such was the dramatic convention of the Elizabethans, such was the accepted usage of the time, such was the popular faith of the audience. And all difficulties disappear. As mentioned previously, it is a never-failing formula.

On such a basis, "Shakespeare's purpose as a writer of plays," and this includes *King Lear,* "was really very simple; it was to tell a story." [65] And "the characters are but symbols and dramatic puppets employed with the object of narration."[66] But the story of King Lear is not much of a story. It begins, as it were, with a climax, the division of his kingdom and the disinheriting of his youngest daughter. After that, King Lear is essentially actionless, adding very little to the narration but nevertheless dominating the play. Are we then to consider the Glo'ster sub-plot as the main interest of Shakespeare in *King Lear?* For here is a story which is more interwoven with the characters of Goneril and Regan and Albany and Cornwall, than with King Lear. In that case the play should have been called by another name and Lear been made a subordinate character. But the truth of the matter is, that Lear does dominate the play and Shakespeare intended him to dominate the play. He puts into the mouth of Lear fully seven hundred and four lines (704) of speech, almost twice as much as that of any other character in the play; and not for purposes of narration as a dramatic puppet, but rather for exposition of character and emotion. The very fact that Shakespeare took King Lear out of the old Leir and made him what he is, points definitely to the direction of Shakespeare's interest. The very fact also that he added a sub-plot which parallels that of the Lear plot, also points to the direction of Shakespeare's interest. And this was not so much in telling a simple story but in painting "a head distempered by misfortune" and filial ingratitude. The numerous inconsistencies which Shakespeare allowed in the story of the play, also point to Shakespeare's disregard of story. Here in *King Lear* at least, it is character and emotion that count.

The skeptics would consider the gross improbability in Lear's action in the first scene, when without apparent definite motivation he exiles Cordelia and Kent, as acceptable to Elizabethan conventions, and hence proper in itself. Psychology as such cannot be applied they argue to Shakespeare's characters. All that the characters say are to be accepted for their full face value, because this was an accepted dramatic convention. The action of Gloucester then against Edgar would fall in the same category, as that of Lear against Cordelia and Kent. And to Stoll this discrediting of their own children by two fathers without apparent motivation "prove (s) conclusively how unpsychological the device is in Shakespeare." In truth, it proves nothing of the kind. In the case of Lear it may be argued that the action arose out of and was made possible by a mind in a stage of senile decay. And in the case of Gloucester it may be argued with equal plausibility that it is merely evidence of

Shakespeare's growing carelessness and exhaustion in the finer points of motivation. And that in *King Lear* particularly, the dramatist gave place to the poet. One argument is as good as another.

So that because psychology as such did not exist in Shakespeare's time, does not mean that it was not in operation. Human nature was then about the same as it is today. And Shakespeare was a great observer and competent delineator of this human nature. Gravity was not known as such before Newton but its laws were nevertheless operative long before his life. Likewise psychology was operative in Shakespeare's day in the same way that it is operative today, though Shakespeare had different ideas about it than we have today in psychoanalytic psychology.

Now, two main interpretations of *King Lear* have arisen out of the views of the modern Shakespearean skeptics. The one finds its source and inspiration mainly in the Public Record Office in London; and the other finds its source and inspiration mainly in *Wilson's Arte of Rhetorique.*

The first interpretation is based on the general assumption that "Shakespeare sought to people his plays from among the individuals and events of his own immediate neighborhood and time," making "definite historic identities of some of the most interesting of them."[67] According to this interpretation *King Lear* becomes nothing more than a vast allegory of symbolic mythology made up of definite political factors. And the key to this symbolic mythology of political import, Lillian Winstanley believes, can be found readily in the examination of "state papers, Huguenot memoirs, accounts of the Gunpowder plot, and histories, memorials and letters of Mary Queen of Scots," as well as, "accounts of current French politics and the massacre of St. Bartholomew."[68] To Lillian Winstanley King Lear is a "fugitive transcript" of the events surrounding the murder of Darnley, father of James I and the St. Bartholomew massacre. Lear becomes the symbol for both Darnley and Coligny, Huguenot Chief and victim of Catherine de Medici; and no doubt, if there had been another sensational murder, we would have had a third to enter into the makeup of the composite. Goneril and Regan are each, and both together, symbols representing Mary, Queen of Scots, and were there a third evil woman in *King Lear,* she would undoubtedly also have been made to serve as Mary Queen of Scots. Oswald represents none other than Rizzio, and Edmund stands symbol for Bothwell. These are the real subjects of *King Lear* and the nursery tale that Shakespeare used, forms merely the skeleton for symbolism "and their apparent subjects serve as 'symbolic' of 'mystic' disguises."[69]

The difficulty with an interpretation of this kind is, that it is too flexible and too indefinite, and Shakespeare did not compose this way. Miss Winstanley, making "the 'complexes' of emotions and ideas which gathered about . . . the murder of Darnley (and) the massacre of St. Bartholomew's Eve"[70] as her starting point, has fitted the events surrounding these storm-centers to *King Lear.* She might just as well have fitted them to the older play *King Leir,* for in this play Regan does actually plan to murder Lear. Or you might consider any play of Shakespeare's day which has in it a father mistreated by children as symbolic mythology of this kind. And furthermore, why can't we just as plausibly have Darnley represented by Albany for actually, Darnley resembles very little the "Titanic Lear of Shakespeare."

In addition to this can we suppose, that in spite of the fact that the government pounced upon plays that had in them political allusions—and many authors were punished for this—can we suppose that Shakespeare hid his political allusions so thoroughly that they escaped detection by the government that was on the lookout for them? And if so, could his audience of groundlings pierce through the hieroglyphics of his symbolism? Did they come to be entertained by seeing a play or was it to decipher a political crossword puzzle? Or did Shakespeare purposely veil things to such an extent that it might await three centuries, like the 'cipher' of Bacon for its true reading? But then Shakespeare wrote for the theatre with little idea of posterity.

That occasional allusions to political events are present in *King Lear* nobody can deny but that they are the subject matter of the play is highly improbable. The chances are that Miss Winstanley has fallen a "victim to the fascination of (her) own critical system."[71]

Hardin Craig has expounded the second mentioned skeptical interpretation of *King Lear*. And this interpretation concerns itself with the ethics involved in the play. But these ethics are not the ethics of today but the ethics of Shakespeare's day, for how could Shakespeare know anything of our system of thought and our ethics? "Neither the Elizabethan writer nor the Elizabethan audience had a body of ideas like ours, knew what we know or in the way we know it."[72] And, "Since," argues Hardin Craig, "Shakespeare did not and could not talk about such things he should not be made to do so."[73] He should not be made to utter philosophies that he could possibly know nothing of. Shakespeare could "merely give us the best that his age was able to discover about life."[74] Its ethical system was based on medieval and Renaissance thought. And *King Lear* is based on medieval and Renaissance systems of thought and ethics. This does not mean, says Hardin Craig, "that Shakespeare made an intimate study of ethical writers;. . . but one must believe that when he approached an ethical subject, he saw it in the broad inclusive outline which appeared in the thought of his time."[75]

In such a case then *King Lear* becomes a tragedy of the violation of nature as understood in the Renaissance sense. According to this, four principal virtues make up nature. These are: Wisdom, courage, temperance and justice. And *King Lear* presents "a world which suffers wreck through the violation of these virtues . . ."[76] This justice, which is "the highest manifestation of nature" and the foundation of all social and political life is violated by Lear's folly in dividing his kingdom and disinheriting Cordelia. The result is "chaos in family and state."[77] and chaos also in Lear's mind paralleling this "chaos in family and state." "Reason is dethroned in his mind and justice is dethroned in the state."[78] And the Fool, as well as Kent, is used by Shakespeare to constantly point out this situation.

The violation of Renaissance ethics, as outlined in *Wilson's Arte of Rhetorique*[79] is presented point by point in *King Lear* according to Craig. 1. "Religion and acknowledgement of God," are violated in that Edmund denies the influence of the heavens and of the supernatural. 2. "Natural love to our children, and other" is violated in the extreme cruelty and wickedness of

Goneril, Regan and Edmund. 3. "Thankfulnesse to all men" is violated since, in spite of the fact that Lear has given "all" he is met with that "marble-hearted fiend" ingratitude. 4. "Stoutnesse, booth to withstand and revenge" is evidenced in the conduct of Edgar and the kindliness of Lear when he calls upon the gods to touch him "with noble anger." 5. "Reverence to the superior" is violated in that "The royal state of the king, the embodiment of authority and honor, is lost, and the loyal service of Kent is rejected in favor of the base flattery of Oswald." 6. and finally, "Assured and constant treuth in things" is violated since Cordelia and Kent (the very essence of truth) are banished. All in all, to Hardin Craig, "the ultimate of evil" (as held in the philosophy of the Renaissance) prevails in *King Lear,* which "pictures, in the tragedy of a king, who is also kingship, and of a father who is also fatherhood, the return to chaos in a kingdom and a royal family, the ruin of the centers and therefore, of the whole body politic."[80]

The danger with an interpretation of this type is this: that one starts with what is supposedly the general trend of ethical thought of the time and then seeks evidences of such ethical thought in the play. And what one seeks, one is prejudiced generally to find. This is precisely what Hardin Craig has done. He assumes from a study of Elizabethan thought, the acceptance of a particular ethical system by the Elizabethan mind. And from this he assumes that Shakespeare could not possibly mean anything else in *King Lear* than what Hardin Craig has interpreted. Is it not just possible that Hardin Craig steeped in Renaissance ethics, is reading into *King Lear* things that are not there at all? Judging from the interpretation one would think that Shakespeare had *Wilson's Arte of Rhetorique* before him when writing *King Lear* rather than Holinshed and the old *King Leir.* And anyway, did Shakespeare approach *King Lear* as an ethical subject? Or was he interested in merely telling a story or fitting a part to Richard Burbage?

According to Craig the grand crime of Lear was a crime against nature. This crime he committed "when Lear gives over the sovereignty of his kingdom to the wicked."[81] This is the crime that brings about chaos: the abdication of his kingdom. But then this heinous crime is committed before the play opens and Shakespeare evidently does not put much stress upon it. Kent and Glo'ster in the very first words of the play discuss Lear's division of the kingdom not from the standpoint of its folly, but rather from the standpoint of the equality of the divisions.

Kent: I thought, the king had more affected the Duke of Albany, than Cornwall.

Glo.: It did always seem so to us: but now, in the division of the kingdom, it appears not which of the dukes he values most;. . .

Here is a great crime being perpetrated against nature and all the comment it produces is a commonplace regarding Albany and Cornwall. Surely, Kent, the blunt teller of truth should have been given scathing words to say in the face of such a crime that according to Craig was responsible for the chaos involved in the play. But Shakespeare evidently did not consider this the ethical basis of the play. It is only when Lear disinherits Cordelia and banishes Kent that folly is committed. And it is out of this folly that the chaos arises. If Lear had not disinherited Cordelia, the division would have remained just the same. Two thirds of his kingdom, at least, would have passed under the sovereignty of the wicked. But no chaos would have resulted and no play.

The doctrine of the four cardinal virtues, which according to Craig, formed an essential part of Elizabethan ethical thought, also plays an important part in the ethics of *King Lear.* These virtues are prudence, (wisdom) fortitude, (courage) temperance and justice. And it is the violation of these virtues, according to Craig that brings on the tragedy in *King Lear.* Surely these virtues being such an essential part of Elizabethan thought, should have entered into the common language of Shakespeare; and especially so in *King Lear,* for here, according to Craig, he is dealing with these virtues. But what do we actually find? They are not even named as such in *King Lear.* The word justice does appear once or twice, but then only in an insignificant capacity not connected with the cardinal virtue which it represents. If these cardinal virtues had even been an unconscious part of Shakespeare's thought, surely, the least we might have expected is an allusion to them in their Renaissance names. But Shakespeare seems actually to have gone out of his way not to mention them. Even the virtue of justice "the highest manifestation of nature," upon which Craig puts so much importance as to its place in *King Lear,* finds no definite mention in the play. Are we to suppose that Lear violated Renaissance justice when he divided his kingdom in such a way as to disinherit Cordelia? And does this violation of justice bring about the chaos? Craig wishes us to believe so. But then Shakespeare is very careful, throughout the play, not to call Lear's action a violation of justice. Shakespeare calls it 'folly' and he meant it to be folly, the folly of old age perhaps or of pride. And he certainly did not wish to hide his meaning for decipherment.

Furthermore, in connection with his ethical interpretation of *King Lear,* Hardin Craig states, that "Shakespeare held very firmly to this belief in the ultimate punishment of the wicked, in other words in eternal justice, exemplifying it" in all of his tragedies and being "certainly neither skeptical nor bewildered."[82] But where is the eternal justice in *King Lear* even from a Renaissance point of view? Let us say that Lear, Goneril, Regan, Edmund, Cornwall and Oswald all receive their just due for violation of "nature." But why should Cordelia be hanged, why should Gloucester be blinded, why should Edgar suffer as he does? But even if Cordelia be considered justly punished for her 'disobedience' to Lear, even if Gloucester be considered as justly punished for his folly in believing Edmund against Edgar, there is still Kent. Wherein has Kent violated "nature" even in the Renaissance sense? And the agony of Lear! Shakespeare throughout the play intentionally creates sympathy for him, and we are actually unconscious of the violation of "nature" which he has committed at the beginning of the play even though we attempt to place ourselves, as much as possible, in the same state of mind as the Elizabethan audience.

> Alb. Bear them from hence.–Our present business
> Is general woe.– (To Kent and Edgar) Friends of
> my soul, you twain
> Rule in this realm, and the gored state sustain.

Kent. I have a journey, sir, shortly to go:
My master calls me,–I must no say, no

Edgar: The weight of this sad time we must obey;
Speak what we feel, not what we ought to say.
The noblest hath borne most; we, that are young
Shall never see so much, nor live so long.

Surely, there is no 'eternal justice' here to the very last lines of the play, but rather an acceptance of things as they are.

The trouble with the skeptics is this, that with pre-conceived ideas of Elizabethan life and thought, they have examined *King Lear* objectively as a case. They have examined all around it, but have failed to pierce to the center–to the spirit of it. They have not given due credit to the power of genius, holding in fact that "Genius did not project Shakespeare far ahead of his age,"[83] since Genius, according to Stoll, "is nothing mystical and is not uplifted beyond reach of reason and common sense."[84] Be that as it may, here in *King Lear,* Shakespeare did indeed apply genius of the highest degree.

So here we stand. We have carried *King Lear* through the vicissitudes of three centuries of criticism and interpretation ranging from extreme idolatry to extreme skepticism. But *King Lear* stands out greater than any of its criticism. After all is said and done, art is a personal experience to be aesthetically enjoyed. And *King Lear* has art in it of the highest type. And if certain critics focus upon the play with their "aesthetic 'blind spots,'" why then, so much the worse for them. As far as we are concerned our skepticism should be directed against the so-called facts and theories that would explain Shakespeare on a mechanical basis, as well as against criticism based on rhetorical idolatrous extravagances. Let us therefore shake ourselves free of the torpor of logic brought on by the emotional wishy-washy gushings of superlatives of the idolators. Let us also beware of the anemic tendencies of the twentieth century skeptics. And let us look at *King Lear* again with a sane natural eye.

NOTES AND REFERENCES

CHAPTER XII

1. Cited from Shelley's **Defense of Poetry, 1840, Furness's Variorum edition of King Lear, p. 429.**
2. Hudson, H. N., **Lectures on Shakespeare,** Vol. II, **p. 226.**
3. Dowden, E., **Shakespeare, His Mind and Art.** p. 229.
4. Quoted from "The Shakespeare Skeptics" by **Karl Young in the N. A. Review,** Vol. 215: 382-313, 1921.
5. Nicoll, Allardyce, **Studies in Shakespeare, p. 167.**
6. Wilson, Dover, **The Essential Shakespeare.**
7. Quoted from "Shakespeare" by Hardin **Craig in the preface to King Lear,** p. 720.
8. In 1823 Kean restored the tragic ending. In 1835 Macready added the fool and thus Shakespeare's complete text **was** restored again on the stage.
9. These are also the last words of the old **King Lear** which **also** has a happy ending.
10. From **The Works of Charles Lamb,** cited in D. Nichol Smith'**s Shakespeare Criticism,** p. 233.
11. From **Of Dramatic Poesie** by Dryden, 1668; cited in D. Nichol Smith's **Shakespeare Criticism,** p. 17.
12. Ibid., p. 23. From various **Prefaces and Prologues,** in D. N. Smith's **Shakespeare Criticism.**
13. Cited in D. Nichol Smith's **"Shakespeare Criticism"** p. 69, from Joseph Warton's **The Adventurer, 1753-64.**
14. Cited in Nichol Smith's **Shakespeare Criticism, p. 76.**
15. **Ibid., p. 79.**
16. Cited in Nichol Smith's Shakespeare Criticism, p. 78.
17. **Ibid.,** p. **79.**
18. Quoted from Samuel Johnson's Edition of **Shakespeare's Works,** 1765, and cited by Nichol Smith in **Shakespeare Criticism, p. 135.**
19. **Ibid., p. 136.**
20. **Ibid., p. 136.**
21. **Ibid.,** p. **136.**
22. Ibid., Nineteenth century **Shakespearean Criticism** and **King Lear.**
23. Cited in the introduction of D. Nichol Smith's in his Shake**spearean Criticism, p. XXIV.**
24. **Ibid.**

25. Quoted from Charles Lamb's **The Tragedies of Shakespeare,** p. 219.
26. **Ibid.,** p. 232.
27. **Ibid.,** p. 233.
28. **Ibid.,** 232.
29. **Ibid.**
30. Quoted from Coleridge's **Lectures** in Nichol Smith's book, **op. cit.,** p. 286.
31. **Ibid.**
32. **Ibid.**
33. **Ibid.**
34. **Ibid.,** p. 288.
35. Quoted from **Characters of Shakespeare's Plays,** 1817, **op. cit.,** p. 328.
36. **Ibid.**
37. Quoted by L. L. Schucking, in **Character Problems in Shakespeare's Plays,** p. 192.
38. **Character problems in Shakespeare's Plays,** N.Y., Henry Holt & Co., 1922, p. 181.
39. **Prefaces to Shakespeare,** Lond., Sidgwick & Jackson Ltd., 1927, p. 146.
40. **Art and Artifice in Shakespeare,** Lond., Cambridge Univ. Press, 1933. p. 3.
41. **Ibid.**
42. Quoted from **Shakespeare and His Predecessors,** by Frederick S. Boas, p. 422.
43. Quoted from Ulrici and cited in Furness's Variorum Edition of **King Lear,** p. 9.
44. Quoted from Coleridge's Lectures in Nichol Smith's **Shakespeare Criticism,** p. 286.
45. Cited from **New Sh. Soc. Trans.** Part I, p. 15 in Furness' Variorum edition of **King Lear,** p. 312.
46. Quoted from Chapter on **King Lear** in Bradley's **Shakespearean Tragedy,** p. 256.
47. **Ibid.**
48. Quoted from his book **Shakespeare,** (1922), p. 269.
49. From Bradley's book **Shakespearean Tragedy,** p. 255.
50. **Ibid.**
51. Quoted from **Studies in Shakespeare** by A. Nichol, p. 141.
52. **Ibid.**
53. From **Studies in Shakespeare** by **A. Nichol,** p. 167.
54. Quoted from **Shakespeare** by Hardin Craig, p. 51.
55. Quoted from **An Image of Shakespeare** by Mathew, Frank, p. 247.
56. Cited in A. C. Bradley's **Shakespearean Tragedy,** p. 277.
57. **Ibid.**

58. **Ibid.**
59. **Ibid.**, p. 379.
60. Quoted from **Shakespeare's Characters** by William Hazlitt, p. 119.
61. Quoted from Coleridge and cited in Furness' Variorum edition, p. 16.
62. **Ibid.**
63. From A. C. Bradley's **Shakespearean Tragedy**, p. 279.
64. **Ibid.**
65. Quoted from **Shakespeare** by Hardin Craig, p. 53.
66. **Ibid.**
67. Quoted from **Shakespeare and Chapman as Topical Dramatists** by Percy Allen, P. I.
68. Quoted from **Shakespeare** by Hardin Craig, p. 711.
69. Quoted from review by C. Hereford of Lillian Winstanley's **Macbeth, King Lear and Contemporary History** (1922) in **Modern Lang. Rev.**, 18:209.
70. **Ibid.**
71. Cited by R. W. Babcock in **Sewanee Review**, Jan. 1927, 35:15.
72. Quoted from the introduction to **Shakespeare** by Hardin Craig, p. 48.
73. **Ibid.**, p. 49.
74. **Ibid.**, p. 5.
75. **Philol. Quart.** Vol. 4; p. 98, "The Ethics of King Lear" by Hardin Craig.
76. **Ibid.**
77. **Philol. Quart.** Vol. 4, p. 108.
78. **Ibid.**, p. 108.
79. Cited by Craig from **Wilson's Arte of Rhetorique**, edited by G. H. Mair, p. 32.

    "Religion and acknowledging of God
    Naturall love to our children, and other
    Thankfullnesse to all men
    Stoutnesse, both to withstand and revenge
    Reverence to the Superior
    Assured and constaunt trueth in things."
80. **Shakespeare** by Hardin Craig, p. 120.
81. **Shakespeare** by Hardin Craig, p. 719.
82. Quoted from Hardin Craig "The Ethics of King Lear" in **Philol. Quart.** Vol. 4, p. 105.
83. **Ibid.**, Note #82, p. 98.
84. Cited by R. W. Babcock in **Sewanee Review**, Jan. 1927. Vol. 35, p. 15.

CHAPTER XIII

KING LEAR: THE PSYCHIATRIC APPROACH

Let us now return to our psychiatric critics and particularly to the drama. Both Drs. Bucknill and Kellogg, as well as the majority of medical commentators, in their more detailed discussions of the mentally aberrant characters, individually, come to the same conclusions. Because both were physicians to the insane, because their work on the subject appeared about the same time, and because their points of view are similar, we shall discuss this phase of their work together. In their consideration of the character of Lear, both hold that he represents a definite case of senile dementia, not only from the beginning of the play, but also previous to it. "The mind of Lear is, from the first, in a state of actual unsoundness, or to speak more precisely, of disease."[1] Only when the character is approached from such a standpoint, they claim, can all the actions be explained. And this, in fact, is the general opinion of most of the neuropsychiatric idolators. This viewpoint solves the absurdity of motivation in the first scene of the play, over which other critics have pondered and puzzled, and failed of explanation. Thus, Dr. Bucknill says, "The accepted explanation of Lear's mental history, that he is at first a man of sound mind . . . is a gross improbability . . . but if . . . it be accepted that the mind of the old King has, from the first entered upon the actual domain of unsoundness, the gross improbability at once vanishes."[2] "That the trial was a mere trick,"[3] Dr. Bucknill considers unquestionable, but asks he, ". . . Does it not lead us to conclude that from the first the king's mind was off its balance, that the partition of the Kingdom involving untenable feuds and wars, is the first act of his developing insanity, and that the manner of its partition, the mock trial of his daughters' affections and its tragical denouement is the second, and, but the second act of his madness."[4] Referring to Lear's curse in the first scene (11: 107-110) Bucknill says,

(This curse) "is madness, or it is nothing. Not indeed raving, incoherent, formed mania, as it subsequently displays itself, but exaggerated passion, perverted affection, enfeebled judgment, combining to form a state of mental disease—incipient, indeed, but still disease . . ."[5] And again, "Lear's treatment of Kent; his ready threat in reply to Kent's deferential address, his passionate interruptions and reproaches; his attempted violence checked by Albany and Cornwall; and finally the cruel sentence of banishment, cruelly expressed—all of these are the acts of a man in whom passion has become a disease."[6] "All this is exaggerated passion, perverted affection, weakened judgment; all the elements in fact, of madness . . . and as we read the play, the mind of Lear, is, from the first, in a state of actual unsoundness, or, to speak more precisely, of disease."[7]

Dr. Kellogg also, is not in sympathy with those who regard "the ingratitude and unkindness of his daughters,"[8] as the cause of Lear's insanity. This, he states, is the view entertained by those critics who are "far more ignorant of psychology than the poet who wrote two hundred years before them . . ."[9] Dr. Kellogg further affirms that "In none of Shakespeare's plays, is the psychological knowledge of the dramatist more admirably exhibited than in Lear."[10] And he holds that the case of Lear is a genuine case of insanity, from beginning to end, such as we often find in aged persons.[11] Both Amariah Brigham and Isaac Ray, previous to Bucknill and Kellogg, consider Lear "a real case of insanity, correctly reported . . . instructive, not as an interesting story merely, but as a faithful history of a case of senile insanity . . ."[12]

In fact, all critics today, who have any special knowledge of pathological psychology, consider Lear as a case of genuine senile dementia. Thus Dr. Herman Pomeranz (1934) writes that "The case of Lear is one of senile dementia, with attacks of acute mania, shown by his faulty judgment, waywardness, disorientation . . ."[13] Dr. G. E. Price (1928) affirms, "It is in *King Lear* . . . that Shakespeare gives his finest description of senile dementia."[14] Practically all critics, indeed, are unstinted in their praise of Shakespeare's marvelous ability at portraying this condition from the very beginning to the very end. They wonder at the little touches here and there and the little psychological details which only specialists can recognize as significant. "At every step through this wonderful play (*King Lear*) we find evidence . . . of Shakespeare's wonderful medico-psychological knowledge—a knowledge scarcely possessed by any in our day, except those few who devote themselves to this special department of medical science."[15] Thus, Dr. Isaac Ray states, "that the development of the early stage of Lear's insanity, or its incubation, as it is technically called is managed with masterly skill, . . ."[16] Referring to the scene on the heath between Lear, Edgar and the fool, he exclaims "... who can finish this scene without feeling that he has read a new chapter in the history of mental disease of most solemn and startling import?"[17] Referring to Edgar's feigned insanity in the same scene, he remarks that, "The management of Edgar's simulation strikingly evinces the accuracy and extent of Shakespeare's knowledge of mental pathology."[18]

Dr. Kellogg, along the same lines, points out that "with great psychological exactness, Shakespeare has from the first endowed Lear with those mental peculiarities and eccentricities which experienced medical psychologists recognize at once as the forerunners of confirmed mental disease, but which are usually overlooked by ordinary observers."[19] And it is only for this reason as Bucknill agrees, that ". . . the literary critics of Shakespeare (being ordinary observers) have overlooked the early symptoms of Lear's insanity,"[20] and failed thereby to recognize, that from the first, the king's mind is off its balance.[21]

As a matter of fact, the medical idolators were not the only ones to hold Lear insane from the very beginning. Thus, "Mrs. Lennox was the earliest . . . to assert that Lear was really insane from the first."[22] She says, "Lear acts like a madman, and from his first appearance to his last seems to be wholly deprived of his reason."[23] Hudson also suggests the same thing when he says, "The opening thus forecasts Lear's madness by indicating that dotage has already got the better of his reason and judgment."[24] And Rumelind[25] and Kreysig[26] agree with these in considering Lear as having a "screw loose" from the very beginning.[27] But as mentioned before, it is the medical idolators who carry this point as a major premise in the understanding of the play. To them the character of King Lear is a remarkable delineation of a case of insanity from beginning to end.

Speaking of Lear's consciousness of oncoming madness, Dr. Kellogg refers to the truth of this observation, saying that, "It is one of the most common things in the world to find a man decidedly insane and yet conscious of his infirmity."[28] Dr. Bucknill agrees with Dr. Kellogg, in this respect, saying that "This self consciousness of gathering madness is common in various forms of this disease."[29] Referring to the cruel treatment accorded Lear by his daughters,[30] Dr. Kellogg says,

> If a modern psychological writer, with all the knowledge of modern times at his command, were laboring to convey to the minds of his readers the manner in which insanity is induced in those predisposed by nature to the disease, . . . he could not do better than point out the conduct of Goneril and Regan towards Lear, as set forth in Act II, Scene 4 of the play.[31]

The psychology involved in the scenes of Lear on the heath[32] calls forth the following from Dr. Kellogg: "Nothing in the whole range of dramatic literature can excel this . . . in psychological interest."[33] Thus, the apparent failure of Lear to suffer physically from the storm is a piece having remarkable psychological import. Lear says,

> When the mind's free—
> The body's delicate, the tempest in my mind
> Doth from the senses take all feeling else,
> Save what beats there.[34]

To this Dr. Kellogg says, "It is a well known fact, that, when the mind is swayed by intense emotions, the sensibility even to intense bodily pain is often completely suspended. The physical endurance manifested by the insane . . . is truly astonishing."[35] Dr. Bucknill, of the same opinion remarks, "In the excitement of insanity physical injury is not felt in the heat of battle."[36]

The ingratitude of Lear's daughters worming its way into his mind with the persistency of an auger, also gives rise to points of interest. The scene in the hovel (Act III, Scene 4) is considered by Coleridge, Schlegel, Hazlitt and others, as marking the true beginning of Lear's madness, Coleridge actually remarking, "This scene ends with the first symptoms of positive derangement."[37] To which Dr. Bucknill says, in strong disagreement: "Hardly so; it is but the climax of the disease . . . the malady, which has existed from the first, has increased and developed, until it is now completed."[38]

In this scene too, Lear suffers from delusion, a sure evidence of insanity. He says to Edgar, "Hast thou too, given all to thy daughters?" To which Dr. Kellogg says, "How beautifully true all this is to nature those who are at all acquainted with insanity can furnish ample testimony; as also how admirably the genuine disease contrasts with the counterfeit, with which it is here brought in contact."[39] Edgar's assumed madness presents a fine contrast to the reality of Lear's[40] for "it has the fault, which to this day feigning maniacs almost invariably commit, of extreme exaggeration."[41] To the incident of the trial of Regan and Goneril in the form of stools, Dr. Kellogg has this to say: "Scenes quite as ludicrous as the one set forth above are of daily occurrence in the wards of all extensive establishments for the insane . . ."[42] What a compliment to that man Shakespeare!

Dr. Bucknill cites many more points of psychological interest in this play. Thus he mentions the apparent physical vigor of Lear and adds, "it is worthy of remark that Lear's age is physically strong and vigorous,"[43] holding that "this state of hale bodily strength in senile mania is true to nature."[44] He mentions the presence of all the factors of insanity in Lear—exaggerated passion, perverted affection, weakened judgment, incoherence and delusion. He points out the tranquility of Lear when among the insane as an evidence of Shakespeare's remarkable knowledge of pathological psychology. This is contrary to the opinion of Ulrici and other literary critics. Dr. Bucknill says, "The singular and undoubted fact was probably unknown to Ulrici that few things tranquilize the insane more than the companionship of the insane."[45] Dr. Bucknill concludes that "There is little, indeed, which in the features of madness, Shakespeare allowed to escape his observation."[46]

A later commentator in this field of Shakespearean criticism is J.S.H. Bransom (1934).[47] He also contends that the improbability of the first scene of *King Lear* can be understood "by our medical knowledge that the King's behavior was an ominous symptom of impending insanity."[48] though he feels that "he is not insane when the play opens but his actions are."[49] He further goes on to state that Shakespeare's Lear went mad, the Lear of the Chronicles did not.[50] Bransom likens Lear's speeches on the heath to flashes of lightning illuminating the mind of Lear and the progress of his madness; in the scene where he confronts Edgar, Bransom terms Lear's reaction, monomania, in which he attributed his plight to the unkindness of children.[51] Bransom goes on to point out, in the various scenes in the play, Shakespeare's skill in using the symptoms of insanity.[52] Thus in mentioning Lear's fear of insanity he states, "the fear of insanity is a common symptom of patients suffering from mental disease from whatever cause and . . . Shakespeare had obviously observed it."[53] Again when Lear assumed that Edgar was brought to his condition by unkind daughters and Kent answers that Edgar has no daughters, Lear flies into a passion, to which Bransom says, "This is another island of Shakespeare's skill in using the symptoms of insanity. The king is calm enough till the subject of his monomania is touched; then he flies into a passion."[54] Referring to the many literary critics' "oft-mentioned obtrusive parallelism of the main and sub-plots of this play," he remarks that it "is not at all obtrusive . . . I should say that what Shakespeare wanted to do was to give us a further exposition of his mental life, another page of his insanity . . . to illustrate the development of the king's insanity."[55] Did Shakespeare then create the tragedy, *King Lear* to illustrate a case of insanity. Bransom hastens to deny this for he states "I repeat, we must not regard the play as Shakespeare's report on a case of insanity to the Royal College of Physicians. Nevertheless I often wonder what opportunities of observing insanity Shakespeare had had."[58] However, in spite of this denial, he remarks later that the real "theme of *King Lear* is the rise and course of the king's madness."[57]

Bransom delves deeper into the psychology of the character of Lear than the previous commentators considered, for, he brings the new insights of the psychoanalytic approach to bear on the dynamics of Lear's development. He states that the "causes of Lear's insanity were very deep seated" and that "Repression of certain experiences and emotions" seemed to have been one of them,[58] "an old repressed incestuous passion for one of his daughters."[59] This is a valid psychoanalytic explanation of Lear's love test and the tremendous strength of the feelings aroused by the resistance of Cordelia and Goneril, and practically all psychoanalysts accept this in their understanding of the play. As Bransom puts it, "It is possible that the greatness of *King Lear,* so difficult to define, is in part due to its subtle acceptance of this world old truth as a dynamic force in life. . ."[60]

Bransom comes to the conclusion that when Lear ". . . divided his kingdom, proposed his love test and came into conflict with his daughters, a group of emotions, separated from consciousness, was to a large extent in control of his conduct,"[61] in the form of a dissociation of consciousness. "Lear's insanity therefore must be regarded as originating . . . in this group of emotions . . . long before Lear actually became insane his conduct was affected by factors which were eventually responsible for his insanity,"[62] and "the conception and exposition of Lear's character is not open to the charge of inconsistency or improbability (as so many critics have held), but must rank among the greatest things in Shakespearean tragedy, perhaps the greatest of them all."[63]

Dr. John Donnelly (1953)[64] agrees with Bransom in this psychoanalytic interpretation of the character and actions of Lear. He considers his illness, from a diagnostic standpoint, as an acute schizophrenic-like episode. Like Bransom also, he feels that Lear was not actually insane, in a psychiatric sense, at the beginning of the play, as some commentators have contended. He considers the division of his kingdom and the violence of his reactions, not as a proof of his insanity as some would have it, but rather as a character trait reaction; since Lear, it must be kept in mind, was vain, proud, stubborn, subject to flattery, impulsive, so that when frustrated or thwarted he tended to react with excessive anger, especially when the satisfaction of some basic need was involved, such as his dependence on his daughters, which was an evidence of immaturity in Lear's character requiring constant reassurances of affection from his daughters. Psychoanalysts are well aware of such manifestations in many of their patients. When Cordelia, in the beginning of the play refuses to give her father complete assurances of her love, Lear's over-reaction indicates that what he is demanding is *total* and hence incestuous love from his daughter. He himself of course does not realize the incestuous nature of his feelings, but from a psychoanalytic standpoint, the massive violence of his curse gives evidence of the depth and intensity of his feelings, the feelings of a lover rejected by a loved one for another. Later, as Donnelly points out, when he is reunited with Cordelia, his speech might well be made by a lover to his sweetheart.

Donnelly goes on to point out the extent of Lear's unconscious sexual phantasies in the scene in which he is psychotic and in delirium, importuning the gods to seek out incestuous sinners for punishment, "He becomes preoccupied with the ingratitude of his daughters and as the disturbance becomes more obvious the emphasis on ingratitude is accompanied by references in the sexual field. The two subjects are finally linked in one passage. The content of the delirium surely illustrates the nature of Lear's unconscious drives. All of his affection is centered on his daughters and this appears to be linked with a latent incestuous orientation. He is dependent on all three, and when he is rejected by all three, the foundations of his emotional stability are threatened. He endeavors to retain control, but later, exposure to the elements is too much, and unable to cope with both the emotional and physical stress, Lear, becomes insane." There are many other psychiatric commentators dealing with *King Lear,* but in general, they all reach the same conclusion.

This does not mean that Shakespeare intended to paint Lear primarily as a case of insanity, but it is indeed a monument to his genius that in the depiction of the ruin of a great nature, he painted so true to life as to evoke the admiration of experts, centuries later. That Lear is a case of senile dementia is merely incidental to the fact that the bent of life often flows in such characters as Lear's, and the great Shakespeare created him as true to human nature, regardless of the centuries. This certainly neither detracts from the greatness of the play nor from the huge tragedy of the character. As far as we are concerned, the play *King Lear,* pictures the tragedy of life, through the misery, impulsiveness, irrascibility of old age, implicit in a type of *senility,* the ingratitude and cruelty of children, the irreverence for fatherhood and the fall from kingship. Can greater tragedy be made to arise out of a lesser combination of factors to which universal emotions are attached? And the hair splitting consideration of the improbabilities in the play sink to minute insignificance in the light of this understanding of the character of Lear.

It can readily be seen now, that after several centuries of criticism and interpretation, we have finally come to a more complete understanding of the character of Lear through the deep insights afforded by psychoanalytic psychology; and the acceptance of such an interpretation does not necessarily exclude the other interpretations put forward through the years since Shakespeare lived. It has rather added a new dimension to Shakespearean criticism.

NOTES AND REFERENCES

CHAPTER XIII

1. Bucknill, **The Mad Folk of Shakespeare, op. cit., p. 117.** The psychoanalyst Karl Abenheimer (1945) says precisely the same thing: "He is insane and has lost all sense of reality from the very beginning of the play." "On Narcissism—Including an Analysis of Shakespeare's **King Lear," Brit. J. Med. Psychol.,** 20: 322-329.
2. **Ibid.,** p. 162.
3. **Ibid.,** p. 208.
4. **Ibid., p. 174.**
5. **Ibid.,** p. 176.
6. Cited from Bucknill, p. 193.
7. **Bucknill, The Mad Folk of Shakespeare, op. cit., p. 177.**
8. **Ibid.,** 143.
9. **Shakespeare's Delineations, etc., N.Y., 1866, p. 17.**
10. "Shakespeare as a Physiologist and Psychologist," **Amer. Journ. of Insanity, XVI (1859), p. 140. Shakespeare's Delineations, etc., p. 16.**
11. **Shakespeare's Delineations, etc., op. cit., p. 16.**
12. Brigham, A., "Shakespeare's Illustrations of Insanity," **Amer. Journ. of Insanity, I (1844), p. 31.**
13. "Medicine in the Shakespearean Plays and Era," **Med. Life,** XXXXI (Oct. 1934), p. 522.
14. "William Shakespeare as a Neuropsychiatrist," **Ann. Med. Hist., X (1928), p. 161.**
15. Kellogg, A. O., **"Shakespeare as a physician and psychologist," Amer. Journ. Insanity, XVI (1859), p. 143. Also Shakespeare's Delineations, etc., op. cit., p. 21.**
16. "Shakespeare's Delineations of Insanity," **in his Contributions to Mental Pathology, p. 486.**
17. **Ibid.,** p. 494.
18. **Ibid.,** p. 500.
19. **Shakespeare's Delineations, etc., op. cit., p. 21.**
20. **The Mad Folk of Shakespeare, op. cit., p. 169.**
21. **Ibid.,** p. 174.
22. See Furness, **King Lear.** The **Variorum Shakespeare, p. 412.**
23. **Shakespeare Illustrated, III, p. 287.**
24. **Furness, King Lear. The Variorum Shakespeare, p. 5.**

25. Ibid., p. 60.
26. Ibid., II, p. 13.
27. See L. L. Schucking, Character Problems in Shakespeare. 1922, pp. 178-9.
28. Ibid., p. 193.
29. Ibid., p. 183.
30. Act II, Scene 2.
31. "Shakespeare as a Physician and Psychologist," op. cit., p. 143. Also, Shakespeare's Delineations, etc., op. cit., p. 21.
32. Act III, Scene 2.
33. Op. cit., p. 22.
34. Act III, Scene 4, 11-14.
35. Shakespeare's Delineations, etc., op. cit., p. 23.
36. The Mad Folk of Shakespeare, op. cit., p. 174.
37. Quoted in Bucknill, op. cit., p. 193.
38. Ibid., p. 193.
39. "Shakespeare as a Physician and Psychologist," op cit., p. 146. Shakespeare's Delineations, etc., p. 25.
40. Bucknill, The Mad Folk of Shakespeare, op. cit., p. 208.
41. Ibid., p. 208.
42. Shakespeare's Delineations, op. cit., p. 26.
43. The Mad Folk of Shakespeare, op. cit., p. 173.
44. Ibid., p. 174.
45. The Mad Folk of Shakespeare, op. cit., p. 207.
46. Ibid., p. 205.
47. Bransom, J. S. H. The Tragedy of King Lear, B. Blackwell, Oxford, 1934.
48. Ibid., p. 20.
49. Ibid., p. 25.
50. Ibid., p. 25.
51. Ibid., p. 98.
52. Ibid., p. 101.
53. Ibid., p. 98.
54. Ibid., p. 101.
55. Ibid., p. 117.
56. Ibid., p. 135.
57. Ibid., p. 203.
58. Ibid., p. 65.
59. Ibid., p. 221.
60. Ibid., p. 223.
61. Ibid., p. 224.
62. Ibid., p. 225.
63. Ibid., p. 227.
64. "Incest, Ingratitude and Insanity Aspects of The Psychopathology of King Lear," Psychoanal. Rev., 40: 149-155, April, 1953.

CHAPTER XIV

HAMLET

I

Interpretations of The Character of Hamlet

Hamlet too, offers us a wealth of evidence of Shakespeare's astounding ability to delineate the abnormal states of mind. Here again critics disagree only in interpretation. After reading the mass of commentary and criticism and controversy, one is tempted to ponder the questions: Was the Elizabethan audience also puzzled in understanding the play?

Briefly stated, there are four main interpretations of the character of Hamlet: 1. that the character represents a true feigned psychosis in a weak and indecisive soul; 2. that it represents a combination of feigned psychosis and actual psychosis, a remarkable illustration of Shakespeare's ability to portray a real form of insanity; 3. the historical interpretation which holds that Hamlet portrays the melancholy type common in Elizabethan literature and Elizabethan psychology; and 4. that the character represents a true example of an unresolved Oedipus complex.

The first interpretation is held by practically all literary critics not special students of psychological pathology. To this group belong Johnson, Schlegel, Goethe, Hallam, Robertson and many others.

Most recently however (1950), we have Dr. Max Huhner propounding this view of the character of Hamlet. He specifically states "that Hamlet was neither insane, a fool, nor a villain. . . . and his insanity was feigned."[1] He correctly points out "that in the first three scenes of the play which precede the Ghost scene, none of the principal characters considers Hamlet insane,"[2] and that only after this scene when Hamlet actually decides to put "an antic disposition on," do most of the characters in the drama consider him insane. Indeed all critics readily agree that there is an element of feigned insanity in the play for there is no gainsaying the direct evidence involved. However, this alone does not explain the full character of Hamlet nor all of his actions. Why the labored and prolonged hesitancy in the carrying out of the revenge for his father's murder, which has been the chief center of active controversy for nearly two centuries? Why the brutal attitude toward Ophelia? Why the devastating skepticism, the self-contempt, the self-torturing, the depression, the contemplations of suicide? Dr. Huhner would explain Hamlet's procrastination on his natural temperament, for he speaks of the "sluggishness—and inactivity in Hamlet's makeup,"[3] of "his sluggish disposition,"[4] "of the enormous amount of inertia in his makeup"[5]—calls him a mere "student, inexperienced in the ways of the world, very conscientious, very loath to shed blood."[6] This explanation is essentially the same one expressed more fully by numerous critics previously.

Thus Henry Mackenzie (1780) writes of Hamlet's disposition as one of "extreme sensibility of mind, apt to be too strongly impressed by its situation, and overpowered by the feelings which that situation excites."[7] Goethe explains Hamlet's vacillation in the following words: "A pure, noble, highly moral disposition, but without that energy of soul which constitutes the hero, sinks under a load, which it can neither support nor resolve to abandon."[8] Schlegel writes of his temperament as one of "reflective deliberation—often a pretext to cover cowardice and lack of decision."[9] Frank Harris writes that Hamlet "became a type for ever of the philosopher or man of letters who, by thinking, has lost the capacity for action."[10] While Sir E. K. Chambers implies the same thing when he speaks of the tragedy as "the tragedy of the intellectual, of the impotence of the over-cultivated imagination and the over-subtilized reasoning powers, to meet the call of everday life for practical efficiency."[11] There are others of like mind. This view, however, can readily be proved untenable from even a superficial perusal of the drama itself. What of the resoluteness indicated in the words of

Hamlet (I, 2) when he imparts to Horatio his decision to meet the ghost:

> I'll speak to it, though hell itself should gape
> And bid me hold my peace

Does this indicate 'sluggishness,' 'inactivity,' 'inertia'? What of his resoluteness and action when Horatio and Marcellus try to hold him back from following the ghost? He cries (I, 4):

> Unhand me gentlemen;
> By heaven! I'll make a ghost of him that lets me:
> I say away!

breaks away, and follows the ghost courageously to the summit of the cliff. Is this the action of a sluggish disposition?

What of the decisiveness of action in the stabbing of Polonius and the complete lack of conscience indicated after his death? What of the deliberate decisiveness in the planning of the deaths of Rosencrantz and Guildenstern? Of the resoluteness in planning of the play to be acted before the King and Queen? What again of Hamlet's courageous attack upon the pirates, his leaping into the grave with the revengeful Laertes, his accepting of the challenge to a duel? What of his aggressiveness implied in the incisive mocking scorn and denunciation of his mother and of Ophelia? Are these the actions of a timid, kind, gentle "student, inexperienced in the ways of the world, very conscientious, very loath to shed blood" as Dr. Huhner and others would have us believe? No, indeed. Hamlet can spur to activity readily enough in the play in all situations except in this most important one of avenging his father's death, the reason for which he is certainly unaware of, for it represents that something "within (him) which passeth show," (I, 2), that "something in his soul, O'er which his melancholy sits on brood" (III, 1) and which we shall later take up as the probable cause of Hamlet's inhibition in carrying out the ghost's repeated command.

Dr. Huhner would partly explain the cause of Hamlet's gloom, dejection and tendency to suicide on the premise that he was "disappointed in not succeeding to the throne"[12] and on the uncertainty of "not knowing whether his love was reciprocated or whether he would be able to marry the object of his affections."[13] As to the first of these, it can truthfully be said that there is not a single line that Hamlet utters that indicates any disappointment of this nature. On the contrary he uses this reason in grand ironic mockery, to confuse Rosencrantz who, at the King's request, is trying to find out the cause "of Hamlet's transformation." Rosencrantz asks Hamlet (III, 2):

> Good my lord, what is your cause of distemper?
> You do surely bar the door upon your own liberty,
> If you deny your griefs to your friend.

To which Hamlet facetiously and mockingly replies,

> Sir, I lack advancement

To which Rosencrantz validly answers,

> How can that be when you have the voice of the
> king himself for your succession in Denmark?

Finally, after scornfully baiting both Rosencrantz and Guildenstern Hamlet bursts out in irritated anger,

> Why, look you now, how unworthy a thing you make of me. You would play upon me; . . . you would pluck out the heart of my mystery; You would sound me from my lowest note to the top of my compass; and there is much music, excellent voice, in this little organ, yet cannot you make it speak. S'blood, do you think I am easier to be played on than a pipe? Call me what instrument you will, though you can fret, you cannot play upon me.

The "heart of the mystery" is certainly not "lack of advancement" with resulting "disappointment in not succeeding to the throne."

Similarly, we cannot accept the premise that the uncertainty of Ophelia's love is a cause of Hamlet's actions, for here too, we are unable to find any utterance of the prince to indicate that it played a direct part in his transformation. Actually, up to the time that Hamlet decides to feign madness we have no reason to state that Hamlet was at all deeply involved in any conflict as to Ophelia's love. His depression and suicidal thoughts are very early expressed fully in the first soliloquy even before the ghost scene and certainly before Laertes' and Polonius' advice to Ophelia against Hamlet's love-making. On the contrary, it must be remembered that when Polonius tries to prove the cause of Hamlet's lunacy, as unrequited love—the common so-called lover's melancholy of Elizabethan England—he fails completely, for the planned meeting with Ophelia does not turn out successfully according to the regularly prescribed method of treatment of this malady at this period which is the obtaining of the love object. Hamlet cruelly rejects his supposed love object which is, indeed, a true factor in the causation of Ophelia's real insanity.

We are down then to the last factor which Dr. Huhner points out as a cause and explanation of Hamlet's conduct—"that his sensibilities had been shocked, not only at the indecent haste of his mother's marriage but by its illegality and its adulterous nature according to the canons of his Church."[14] But he is vociferous in his denial that the result is true madness but rather than the depression, skepticism, suicidal ideas particularly expressed in the soliloquies "is the anguish of a broken heart and not the utterance of a melancholiac."[15] Nevertheless he does write of "Hamlet's *peculiar* character"[16] and he takes cognizance of the fact that even before he was considered "crazy" by the characters in the play he was considered "only peculiar." And herein is the clue perhaps to the best explanation of the character problems in *Hamlet.* It is mainly Hamlet's reaction to his mother's marriage that produces his depression and his hesitance, but not in the sense that Dr. Huhner and others of like mind would have us believe, but rather in a much deeper way as the psychoanalysts, which we will take up later, indicate.

The second interpretation—that Hamlet both feigned insanity and was also truly insane—is held by most of the older neuropsychiatrists. Thus Dr. J. C. Bucknill says this of Shakespeare's ability to portray such a character: "The feint is so close to nature, and there is underlying it withal so undeniable a substratum of morbid feelings, that in spite of ourselves, in opposition to our full knowledge that in his antic disposition Hamlet is putting on a part, we cannot dispossess ourselves of the idea, . . . that a mind fallen is presented to us,"[17] and again: "How exquisitely is here portrayed the state of the reasoning melancholiac."[18] Dr. John Connolly says, "It certainly appears to me that the intention to feign was soon forgotten, or could not be steadily maintained in consequence of a real mental infirmity."[19]

Dr. Kellogg believes that "most critics have failed of a true estimate of Hamlet, because of a want of medico-psychological knowledge on their part. It is only when Hamlet is considered insane that the character becomes consistent."[20] In line with this, the case of Hamlet is held up as a genuine case of melancholic madness. Thus Dr. Brigham says, "In the life of Hamlet . . . we have a full history of a case of insanity . . . a case of melancholy madness,"[21] "exquisitely drawn," and "finely portrayed." Dr. Kellogg states, "such a case he has given us in the character of Hamlet, with a fidelity to nature which continues more and more to excite our wonder . . . the delineation (being) . . . so true to nature that those who are at all acquainted with this intricate disease are full convinced that Hamlet represents faithfully a phase of genuine melancholic madness."[22] Dr. Kellogg further waxes so enthusiastic on Shakespeare's abilities in this direction that he no doubt allows his idolatry to run away with his reason for he says, "such are the varied phases of madness (portrayed), and how wonderful is that power of observation in our great dramatist, which has enabled him to draw them so minutely and accurately. His knowledge of the human heart and mind, under all circumstances and in all forms, whether of health or disease, is so accurate that he never makes a mistake."[23] There are many more points of psychiatric interest in *Hamlet* as showing the amazing knowledge of Shakespeare in his delineations of madness, as brought out by the neuropsychiatrists.

II

Other Interpretations of The Character of Hamlet

From the foregoing, it must be readily apparent that the approach of most of the neuropsychiatrists to the character problems in the mentally aberrant of Shakespeare's plays, is anything but an historical one. They view these characters as cases in their own asylums and make diagnoses by the tests and standards of their own time, too often supplying out of their own enthusiasm and imagination what is lacking in the characters, as Shakespeare intended them. But after all, these critics were specialists in their field and hence are entitled to the greatest respect regarding their opinions. Indeed, their interpretations of the mad folk in Shakespeare are masterpieces of logic and plausibility, entirely satisfactory from the modern psychiatrist's standpoint. Nevertheless, Shakespeare wrote almost three hundred years before these critics were even born; and it is questionable whether he deliberately intended his characters to be psychiatric studies. In fact, as Ruth L. Anderson says, in her most extensive study of *Elizabethan Psychology and Shakespeare's Plays* (1927), "he did not seek consciously to embody psychological principles anywhere in his work, for he was preeminently an artist."[24] Scholarship has ingeniously uncovered "from the psychological treatises contemporary or nearly contemporary with Shakespeare and, for the most part, available to him in English,"[25] a complete system of Elizabethan psychology, with such characteristics and peculiarities as to readily allow for the satisfactory explanation of the numerous character problems without necessity of recourse to modern neuropsychiatric principles. That such character problems easily lend themselves to neuropsychiatric interpretations, is only the greater tribute to Shakespeare, the artist, and not Shakespeare, the psychopathologist. And so we come to the third interpretation—the historical interpretation . . . that Hamlet represents the melancholy type of Elizabethan psychology.

Shakespeare was primarily an Elizabethan. His characters are Elizabethan. The psychology he adhered to was Elizabethan. It seems that the chief difficulty of the commentators in the last century and a half, in regard to the Shakespeare characters, has been this: that in accordance with modern conceptions of personality, they have sought for unity and consistency in these characters. Thus Dr. Kellogg, after considering Shakespeare's delineation of King Lear, which we have already discussed, says,

> Thus far the whole character is psychologically consistent, and the wonderful skill and sagacity manifested by the great dramatist in seizing upon those premonitory signs, which are usually overlooked by all . . . and weaving them into the character of his hero as a necessary element, without which it would be incomplete, like those of inferior artists, is a matter of wonder to all modern psychologists.[26]

Of Hamlet too, he speaks as "furnishing . . . evidence of the wonderful sagacity of the poet, and the truthfulness to nature, and consistency with which he works out whatever he undertakes."[27] But there is no consistency and there is no unity; the actions of the characters and their motivation are often grossly improbable, and to say the least, highly perplexing.[28] Hence, these characters must be mad folk; and they are,—when measured by modern rules of behaviour. But the fact is, that "The Elizabethan did not search for unity in human behaviour. His theory of the soul and of its relation to the macrocosm," as Miss Anderson has so aptly pointed out, "accounts for inconsistencies."[29] In truth, continues Miss Anderson, ". . . Elizabethan thinking emphasizes variability and even inconsistency in conduct. . . Usually, moreover, he (Shakespeare) was handling old material sometimes even old plays. His characters do the things previously set down for them to do, and this fact may account in part for their inconsistencies."[30] In the case of Lear as already shown, Allordyce Nicol explained away the inconsistencies and improbabilities on the ground that Shakespeare was simply following the older play *King Leir* which does give acceptable motivation for Lear's actions.

In the case of *Hamlet,* Professor E. E. Stoll has shown that Hamlet's madness is a feigned madness taken over by Shakespeare from the *Fratricide Punished* and the *Spanish Tragedy* of Kyd as a device to make Hamlet's access to the king easier.[31] In line with this, the neuropsychiatrist, Dr. Laehr (*Die Darstellung Krankhafter Geistezustande in Shakespeare's Dramen,* 1898, p. 179) presented the hypothesis that Shakespeare took over the Ghost episode from the old saga and had to depict Hamlet as a melancholic, because this was theatrically the most presentable form of insanity in which hallucinations occur.[32]

Furthermore, the works of Anderson, Bundy, O'Sullivan, Stoll, G. B. Harrison, Schucking and others have proved that the character of Hamlet can very well be considered as a representation of the melancholy type as understood in the Elizabethan period, and not as a type of psychosis or psychoneurosis, as the neuropsychiatrists we have considered, would have us believe. We shall take this up further in a later chapter.

This historical interpretation certainly can be made to account for the character problems in *Hamlet,* but as we shall see later it does not go deep enough and is not too far removed from the viewpoint of the neuropsychiatrists that there actually is an element of true insanity in Hamlet, for it is quite possible to prove that the melancholy man in question may be within the boundary of "disease" even according to the Elizabethan treatises.

NOTES AND REFERENCES

CHAPTER XIV

1. Shakespeare's Hamlet, Farrar, Straus and Co., N.Y., p. 1.
2. Ibid., p. 10.
3. Ibid., p. 68.
4. Ibid., p. 71.
5. Ibid., p. 71.
6. Ibid., p. 68.
7. The Mirror, April 18, 1780.
8. Wilhelm Meister's Lehrjahre, 1795, Bd. IV, Kap. XIII.
9. Vorlesungen uber dramatisch Kunst und Litteratur, III, 1809, Quoted By Ernest Jones in Essays in Applied Psychoanalysis, The International Psychoanalytic Press, London, 1923, p. 10.
10. The Man Shakespeare and his Tragic Life Story, 1909, p. 267.
11. Hamlet in Shakespeare: A Survey, p. 182.
12. Op. cit., p. 1.
13. Op. cit., p. 2.
14. Op. cit., p. 1.
15. Op. cit., p. 12.
16. Op. cit., p. 31.
17. The Mad Folk of Shakespeare, op. cit., p. 71.
18. Ibid., p. 71.
19. A Study of Hamlet, London, 1863, p. 54.
20. "William Shakespeare as a Physiologist and Psychologist," op. cit., XVI (1859), p. 409.
21. "Shakespeare's Illustrations of Insanity." Amer. Journ. Insanity, I (1844), p. 27.
22. "Shakespeare's Delineations," op. cit., p. 37.
23. "Shakespeare as a Physiologist and Psychologist," op. cit., p. 429.
24. University of Iowa Studies, III, No. 4 (Iowa City, Iowa, 1927), p. 4.
25. Ibid., p. 4.
26. Shakespeare's Delineations, op. cit., p. 20.
27. Ibid., p. 67.
28. It is interesting to note in this regard, as Professor Stoll has pointed out (Hamlet: an Historical and Comparative Study, of Minnesota Studies in Language and Literature, No. 7, 1919, pp. 85 ff.) that previous to 1780, Hamlet was not considered a perplexing character. The probable explanation of this is, that

up to this time men continued along the same avenues of thought as did Shakespeare.

29. Op. cit., p. 174.

30. Op. cit., p. 175. See also Professor Stoll's articles on Hamlet and Othello listed in the bibliography; also Professor L. L. Schucking, Character Problems in Shakespeare's Plays (1922), pp. 19 ff.

31. "Hamlet: an Historical and Comparative Study." University of Minnesota Studies in Language and Literature, No. 7 (1919), p. 14.

32. See Essays in Applied Psychoanalysis, by Ernest Jones, op. cit,. p. 41.

CHAPTER XV

SHAKESPEARE'S HAMLET AND THE 'MELANCHOLY' OF THE SIXTEENTH CENTURY

The Elizabethans as reflected in their total literature, both scientific and creative, were much concerned with the melancholy humour, the melancholy man and with melancholy in general.[1] The character of Shakespeare's Hamlet has been explained on this basis by Shakespearean historical criticism. Indeed, the works of Stoll, Bundy, Anderson, O'Sullivan, G.B. Harrison, Schucking and others, as previously pointed out have tended to prove that Hamlet is actually a representation of the melancholy type as understood in the Elizabethan period, and not as a type of mental illness or insanity as some critics, and more particularly the medical critics, would have us believe. Thus, Professor Levin L. Schucking[2] takes the characteristics of Hamlet and shows how they comply with the characteristics of the general melancholy type as described in the character books so common at this time. According to Anderson, the psychological treatises of this period consider these very characteristics, and "since we have found that Shakespeare was conversant with their theories, it is possible that he drew from them here."[3] In fact, as Miss Mary I. O'Sullivan has shown, Shakespeare actually made use of Timothy Bright's *Treatise of Melancholy* in the writing of *Hamlet*.[4] She refers to Bright's characterization of the melancholy man in various ways as "doubtfulle before and long in deliberation: suspicious, painful in studie, and circumspect: his resolution riseth of long deliberation because of doubt and distrust," that their "sorrowful humour breedeth in them . . . a negligence in their affaires and dissolutenesse, where there should be diligence," that "contemplations are more familiar with melancholike persons, than with others by reason they be not so apt for action," and that "while their passions be not yet vehement, the vehemencie of their affection once raysed . . . carrieth them . . . into the deapth of that they take pleasure to intermeddle in."[5] G. B. Harrison going over the same material also comes to the conclusion that "Hamlet . . . is the fullest embodiment of the melancholic humour in all Elizabethan literature and the picture is painted with such close attention to detail that it gives the impression that Shakespeare had made a text book study of the disease."[6] All in all then, the problem of Hamlet ceases to become perplexing and enigmatical from this standpoint, and is readily and rationally explained on the basis of a feigned madness in an individual of the melancholy type of the period in whom the faculties of the soul (in the Elizabethan sense) are at war, wherein the heart and the imagination conspire to blind the reason.[7]

The historical interpretation certainly can be made to account for the character problems in Hamlet, but it does not go deep enough and is not too far removed from the viewpoint of those critics who hold that there actually is an element of true insanity in Hamlet, for we shall soon prove, as already mentioned, that the melancholy man in question may be within the boundary of "disease" even according to the Elizabethan treatises. One can indeed accept the principle that Hamlet fits the melancholy type as described in Bright and Burton and others, yet this does not exclude the probability of the presence of true mental disease. The question arises, where does melancholy end and melancholy madness begin even in the Elizabethan sense? The scientific writers of the period were much aware of this problem and they are careful to make distinctions between the melancholy constitution, temperament, disposition, complexion and true melancholy madness.

Andreas Laurentius (1558-1609), Professor of Medicine at Montpellier, one of the most prominent physicians of the period, whose treatise "Of Melancholike Diseases" went through many editions, and who is quoted by Burton over sixty times, takes this matter up quite thoroughly. He writes,

> All such as we call melancholike men, are not infected with this miserable passion which we call melancholie;

there are melancholike constitutions which keep within the bounds and limits of health.[8]

To which category does Hamlet fit into? Laurentius carefully describes the four psychological types of men or complexions common to this period as determined by an excess of one of the four humours:

> . . . it is not possible to see any perfect living creature in which the foure humours are equally mixed, there is alwaies someone which doth over rule the rest, and of it is the parties complexion named: if blood doe abound, we call such a complexion sanguine; if phlegme, phlegmatike; if choler, cholerike; and if melancholie, melancholike. . .[9]
>
> The melancholike are accounted as most fit to undertake matters of weighty charge and high attempt . . . most wittie and ingenious. . .[10]

He concludes:

> See here the effects of the foure complexions and how *they may all foure be within the bounds of health.* It is not . . . of these sound melancholike persons that we speake in this treatise. We intreate only for the sick, and such as are pained with griefe men call melancholie.[11]

Surely, we cannot by any stretch of the imagination, place Hamlet as merely representing a man of melancholy complexion "within the bounds of health." It is most likely that both Bright and Burton, on whom the critics lean for this interpretation actually were describing the disease melancholie; and from this historical standpoint Hamlet may rather be considered mentally ill in addition to the feigned insanity. In fact "Hamlet is in every way the greatest of the pretenders 'to insanity,' and, indeed, of the madmen."[12] Hamlet may well have been of melancholy complexion in the Elizabethan sense but certainly when the play opens he is already surfeited with "unnatural melancholy" which in the words of Bright "destroyeth the braine with all his faculties and disposition of action."[13] Indeed, if we continue with Laurentius in his symptomatology of the disease, we become more and more convinced that Hamlet is suffering from disease. Laurentius says:

> The melancholike man... (I mean him which hath the *disease in the braine*) is . . . out of heart . . . fearfull and trembling . . . he is afraid of everything . . . a terror unto himselfe... he would runne away and cannot goe, he goeth always fighting, troubled with . . . an unseparable sadnesse which turneth into dispayre . . . disquieted in both bodie and spirit . . . subject to watchfulness, which doth consume him . . . and unto sleepe which tormenteth him . . . dreadful dreams . . . he is become as a savadge creature haunting the shadowed places, suspicious, solitarie, enemie to the sunne, and one whom nothing can please, but only discontentment, which forgeth unto itselfe a thousand false and vaine imaginations.[14]

He further defines "melancholie,"

> . . . it springeth of a melancholike humour . . . a kind of dotage without any fever having for his ordinarie companions, fear and sadness, without any apparent occasion . . . We call that dotage when some one of the principall faculties of the minde as imagination or reason is corrupted. All melancholike persons have their imagination troubled. . .[15]

Both Robert Burton and Timothy Bright, as already indicated, agree with Laurentius and summarize the symptoms of melancholy to include fear, sorrow, grief, restlessness, suspicion, fearful dreams, "solitariness, avoiding of light, that they are weary of their lives, hate the world . . . avoid company . . ."[16] etc.

If we examine the play itself now we can readily see that Hamlet truly falls into the category of this historical symptomatology of the "melancholike man . . . (him which hath the disease in the braine)." He certainly is sorrowful and full of sadness with "nighted colour," "inky cloak" and clouds still hang (ing) on him, and though he protests that he is *"too much i' the sun,"* these very words that he uses belie his state for "avoiding of the sunne," "enemie to the sunne" were common phrases of the period in the description of the tendency to withdrawal, solitariness, in those with the disease Melancholie. That Hamlet's depression is deep unto his very soul "beyond the bound of health" is further evidenced by his answer to the queen (I, 2, 78-86):

'Tis not alone my inky cloak, good mother
Nor customary suits of solemn black,
Nor windy suspiration of forc'd breath,
No, nor the fruitful river in the eye
Nor the dejected behaviour of the visage,
Together with all forms, modes, shows of grief
For they are actions which a man might play
But I have that within which passeth show

Indeed, this "unseparable sadnesse which turneth into dis-dispayre" leads Hamlet even to ideas of suicide. He wishes that, (I, 2)

. . . this too too solid flesh would melt
Thaw and resolve itself into a dew:
Or that the Everlasting had not fix'd
His canon 'gainst self-slaughter

He asserts,

I do not set my life at a pin's fee;

and that (III, 1)

To die. . .
. . . 'tis a consummation
Devoutly to be wished. . .

He is one of those that "are weary of their lives, hate the world," "one whom nothing can please, but only discontentment." He cries out in great emotion (I, 2),

O God! O God!
How weary stale, flat and unprofitable
Seem to me all the uses of this world
Fie on't O fie! 'tis an unweeded garden,
That grows to seed;

He calls the earth "a sterile promontory;" the "o'erhanging firmament . . . a foul and pestilent congregation of vapours;" and "man . . . this quintessence of dust." He is restless "disquieted in bodie and spirit," irritable. He is sharp, biting to his friends and "goeth always fighting." Thus, at the very beginning of the play when his good friend Horatio says to Hamlet that he came to see his father's funeral Hamlet antagonistically replies (I, 2):

> I pray thee, do not mock me fellow student,
> I think it was to see my mother's wedding.

Again when Horatio and Marcellus try to prevent Hamlet from following the ghost he threatens to kill them. He is overly suspicious, sensitive to the point of ideas of reference. Thus when he tells Rosencrantz and Guildenstern (II, 2), that he has lost all his mirth and that nothing delights him neither man nor woman, he suspects a meaningful smile on Rosencrantz's face indicating to him significant disbelief. Rosencrantz answers,

> My lord, there was no such stuff in my thoughts

to which Hamlet queries,

> Why did you laugh then when I said,
> 'Man delights me not'?

Later Guildenstern says of Hamlet (III, 1):

> Nor do we find him forward to be sounded
> But with a crafty madness, keep aloof.

Furthermore, there is indication that Hamlet's faculty of imagination is troubled in the Elizabethan sense that "All melancholike persons have their imagination troubled." Thus, at the very beginning of the play (I, 2) when Horatio tries to persuade Hamlet not to follow the ghost to the edge of the cliff Hamlet threatens him and Horatio remarks, "He waxes desperate with imagination." Later (I, 5), Horatio also tells Hamlet that he is using "wild and whirling words." In addition, we have reason to consider the appearance of the ghost in the queen's apartment (III, 4) after Hamlet stabs Polonius, as an hallucination, evidence of his "corrupted" "imagination," for the queen does not see the ghost at all, in contradistinction to earlier scenes when both Horatio and Marcellus do see the ghost. It is at this point that the queen calls him "mad" (III, 4) to "bend (his) eye on vacancy"

> And with the incorporal air to hold discourse?

> This is the very coinage of your brain:
> This bodiless creation ecstasy
> Is very cunning in

And "ecstasy" in the Elizabethan sense, it must be remembered, was one of the classifications of insanity. This then is the "dotage" of the "corrupted" "imagination" in the definition of the disease "melancholie" we are considering.

Moreover, there is evidence that Hamlet has "dreadful dreames" for in speaking to his friends Rosencrantz and Guildenstern calling Denmark "a prison" to him, he cries out (II, 2):

> O God! I could be bounded in a nutshell, and
> count myself a king of infinite space, were it
> not that I have bad dreams

This is also directly related "to watchfulness, which doth consume him (the melancholike man) . . . and unto sleepe which tormenteth him . . ." There are implications throughout the play that Hamlet could not sleep. A more direct evidence of this is in Hamlet's own words (V, 2):

> Sir, in my heart there was a kind of fighting
> That would not let me sleep.

This "kind of fighting," in Hamlet's heart is present throughout the play. Hamlet has a deep conflict in himself. He is full of self-contempt for not speeding to his revenge as he has promised his father's ghost. He procrastinates. He does not understand himself. Actually we might say with Laurentius that he is ". . . a terror unto himselfe . . . he would runne away and cannot goe." —he cannot make up his mind—calls himself "coward," "lily-livered" rants at the world and himself, is tense and cynical, cruel and particularly misogynous. Whether this could also cover the symptom of "fearfulness" is problematical unless we attribute his hesitancy and procrastination to some inner fear, although in the Elizabethan pattern of thinking this would probably not be valid. On the other hand it must be remembered that a text book picture of a disease must necessarily cover the whole field and it is rare that all the possible symptoms of a disease appear in one person with that disease.

On this basis we can definitely say that Hamlet was truly mentally ill with the disease Melancholie as Laurentius, Burton and Bright understood it, especially if we add that Hamlet had no fever and that his "pulse temperately" kept "time;" and that further, his "sadness" was "without any apparent occasion," as evidenced by his own feelings that there was something "within (him) which passeth show," "the heart of his mystery" the loss of his mirth and the going "heavily" with his "disposition," *"Wherefore I know not."* Certainly no other character in the play knew the cause of Hamlet's disease, melancholie, for, as previously pointed out, it was not love melancholy and it was not a simple feigned madness.

The medical critics, particularly the neuropsychiatrists can validly claim that the character of Hamlet does represent a form of mental illness, not only in the Elizabethan sense, with feigned madness as an added factor, but also in the modern sense. Whether he can be classified under a particular heading, such as manic-depressive psychosis or melancholia is questionable. It is certain, however, that Shakespeare did not intend consciously to depict a madman in his greatest tragedy and nothing else. Rather he depicted the flow of human life out of his own soul and projected it into his greatest tragedy through such characters. All the characters in *Hamlet* are puzzled by the causation of Hamlet's actions and feelings. Hamlet himself does not understand his conflicts. The audiences of this great tragedy have always been puzzled and shaken emotionally by it. And the reason why this is so has been supplied to us by the psycho-analysts in their doctrine of human dynamics, which interprets *Hamlet,* as the tragedy of an unresolved Oedipus complex.

NOTES AND REFERENCES

CHAPTER XV

1. See Harrison, G. B. "An Essay on Melancholy" in Nicholas Breton's **Melancholike Humours, London: The Scholartis Press, 1929.**
2. **Character Problems in Shakespeare's Plays. Henry Holt and Company, 1922, pp. 157 ff.**
3. **Op. cit., p. 163.**
4. "Hamlet and Dr. Timothy Bright." **PMLA, XLI, 1926, pp.** 667-679.
5. "Hamlet and Dr. Timothy Bright," **op. cit., p. 677.**
6. "An Essay on Melancholy" in Nicholas Breton's **Melancholike Humours,** London: The Scholartis Press, 1929, **p. 36.**
7. Bundy, Murray W., "Shakespeare and Elizabethan Psychology." **Journ. of Eng. & German Philos., XXIII (1924), pp. 530 ff.**
8. **A Discourse of the Preservation of the Sight: of Melancholike Diseases: of Rheumes and of Old Age (1599), Shakespeare** Association Facsimiles **No. 15 (1935), p. 84.**
9. **Ibid.**
10. **Ibid., p. 85.**
11. **Ibid., p. 85.**
12. Peers, E. A., **Elizabethan Drama and Its Mad Folk, W. Heffer and Sons Ltd., Cambridge, 1914, p. 175.**
13. Quoted by Mary I. O'Sullivan "Hamlet and Dr. Timothy Bright," **PMLA, XLI, 1926, p. 677.**
14. **Op. cit., p. 82.**
15. **Op. cit., p. 86.**
16. **Burton, op. cit., p. 359.**

CHAPTER XVI

THE PSYCHOANALYTIC APPROACH TO SHAKESPEARE'S *HAMLET*

The interpretation of the character of Shakespeare's *Hamlet,* and of the play itself, as that of an Oepidus situation, is a logical result of the fundamental principles of psychoanalytic psychology. It is necessarily dependent on the acceptance of the presence of primitive forces and motivations in the Unconscious and of their transformation into sublimatory channels of socially-accepted activity. On this basis, all creative art, and in this case, poetic creative expression in particular, finds its psychogenesis in the original conflicts which every individual is supposed to have experienced in early infancy and childhood. To go one step further than this, the psychoanalysts have shown the close relationship existing between myth, dream, day-dream and creative expression. Since myth and dream are considered wish fulfillments of the race and of the individual, respectively, then poetic creative expression also represents the expression of deep conflicts, the solution of deep wish fulfillments. This has opened up the whole field of creative art to the psychoanalytic interpretation. By their works shall you know them for the man is in his creative work. Thus a whole new body of Shakespearean criticism has arisen since Freud, and all of his plays have come under scrutiny of the psychoanalytic microscope. In the case of *Hamlet,* which is generally considered Shakespeare's greatest drama and one of the greatest pieces of literature of all time, Dr. Ernest Jones considers it as expressing "the core of Shakespeare's philosophy and outlook on life . . ."[1] and that the conflict involved in Hamlet "is an echo of a similar one in Shakespeare himself, to a greater or lesser extent with all men."[2] "The intrinsic evidence from the play," he states, "decisively shows that Shakespeare projected into it his inmost soul."[3] Freud himself, declared it to be "the poet's own psychology with which we are confronted in *Hamlet*."[4] But even before the advent of psychoanalytic Shakespearean criticism, some of the most important literary critics expressed themselves of similar opinion. Thus Bradley writes that Shakespeare "put his own soul straight into this creation . . . wrote down his own heart."[5] F. S. Boas similarly speaks of Shakespeare as choosing a theme in *Hamlet* "as the vehicle of thoughts surging in his own breast" and surmising "that only out of overwhelming subjective impulse could *Hamlet* have arisen."[5a] Taine says, "Hamlet is Shakespeare . . ."[6] Figgis speaks of Hamlet as "Shakespeare's completest declaration of himself,"[7] while Dr. Bucknill states that "the sceptical doubts of Hamlet probably indicate a phase in the poet's own mind . . ."[8] Indeed, in the creative works of all poets must come out the eternal patterns of conflict of the race and of the individual.

From this standpoint, Freud himself set the tenor of interpretation. He considers Hamlet as "rooted in the same soil as Oedipus Rex"—and he points out that while in "Oedipus Rex—the basic wish phantasy of the child is brought to light and realized as it is in dreams; in Hamlet it remains repressed, and we learn of its existence as we discover the relevant facts in a neurosis—only through the inhibitory effects which proceed from it."[9] And he goes on to show that the chief inhibitory effect is Hamlet's hesitation. In fact, he considers that "The play is based upon Hamlet's hesitation in accomplishing the task of revenge assigned to him;"[10] and that this hesitation is based upon Hamlet's own guilt surrounding infantile incestuous wishes and consequent identification with his own father and with his uncle-step-father, Claudius.

Ives Hendricks is in agreement with Freud. He holds that ". . . Hamlet portrays the universal tragedy of the race cast by the genius of Shakespeare in a form which lulls the conscience of his audience, while yet it arouses their inmost passions,"[11] and that "the drama tells the story of incest and patricide with more disguise"[12] than Sophocles' *Oedipus Rex*. This, he proceeds to emphasize in the following statement:[13]

The morality of his audience is appeased by the device of emphasizing the guilt of Claudius' behaviour and concealing the unconscious guilt of Hamlet's phantasy, by Hamlet's tragic failure to achieve his murder; by the theme of Hamlet's sexual failure with Ophelia and his flight to England. The motive of patricide is disguised by replacing the real father as object of Hamlet's infantile hatred by the uncle, though the mother is openly accused of "incest".

Fritz Wittels also considers that "Hamlet is the great Oedipus tragedy of the late Renaissance"[14] and points out that "Hamlet cannot love Ophelia because he has a mother fixation," cannot revenge his father, cannot fulfill the ghost's command to kill his step-father, because the murder of his father was a deed which Hamlet, himself, has long harbored as a design in his unconscious,[15] all leading to his irresolution, his hesitancy.

Dr. Arthur Wormhoudt more recently (1949) not only agrees with the previously quoted psychoanalysts "that Hamlet's unconscious attachment to his mother accounts plausibly for the delay and a good many other puzzling factors in the play"[16] but he carries the interpretation deeper along the psychoanalytic road to the oral level and comes to the conclusion that "*Hamlet* may be considered a very nearly perfect oedipal defence for the more deeply repressed oral conflict"[17] which Dr. Wormhoudt considers a general basic source of creative literary expression. While Ella F. Sharpe (1950) implies the same thing, for in considering the fundamental problem of the play as "the unresolved Oedipus conflict" she states that, "Shakespeare dramatized in *Hamlet* his own regression after his father's death. In externalizing the introjected objects in dramatic form he delivered himself from 'the something in his soul'. He freed himself through sublimation . . ."[18]

In like manner, Dr. Robert Fliess (1961) referring to *Hamlet,* as ". . . a masterpiece in both analytic psychology and dramatic art"[19] and to ". . . the special position occupied by Shakespeare's *Hamlet* amongst the great documents of western civilization"[20] states that "The play is . . . the modern equivalent of Sophocles' Oedipus Rex"[21] and that "Hamlet's active oedipus complex requires . . . that he identify with a father figure, the uncle. It is the identification, i.e., the ensuing guilt feelings over wanting the mother himself, that paralyzes him for almost five acts."[22]

Numerous other psychoanalysts echo these views, but it remained for Dr. Ernest Jones, founder of the psychoanalytic movement in Great Britain to explore the whole subject of Shakespeare's *Hamlet* in all its meanings and psychoanalytic manifestations. His essay, "A Psychoanalytic Study of Hamlet"[23] is indeed a masterly piece of scholarship that deals elaborately and at great length with the whole problem of the psychogenesis of poetic creative expression as well as with the particular problem and interpretation of *Hamlet* as an Oedipus tragedy. He painstakingly takes up the thesis that Hamlet is merely an unusually elaborated form of a vast group of legends[24] *"the main theme* (*of which*) *. . . is the highly elaborated and disguised account of a boy's love of his mother and consequent jealousy and hatred towards his father."*[25] Step by step he takes us through the play in proving the thesis and concludes as follows:

> There is thus a reason to believe that the new life which Shakespeare poured into the old story was the outcome of inspirations that took their origins in the deepest and darkest regions of his mind. He responded to the peculiar appeal of the story by projecting into it his profoundest thoughts and emotions in a way that has ever since wrung wonder from all who have heard or read the tragedy. It is only fitting that the greatest work of the world-poet should have had to do with the deepest problem and the intensest conflict that have occupied the mind of man since the beginning of time—the revolt of youth and of the impulse to love against the restraint imposed by the jealous old.[26]

This then can be considered as adequate dynamics for Hamlet's emotional status and his actions according to the analysts.

From the standpoint of diagnosis, most neuropsychiatrists label him as having a type of psychoneurosis. Freud calls it a form of hysteria and admits that "this is the deduction to be drawn from my interpretation."[27] Jones specifically feels that there is "no question of insanity" but that "Hamlet's behaviour is that of a psychoneurotic."[28] Rosner,[29] describes him as a hystero-neurasthenic. Kellogg,[30] de Boisman,[31] Hense,[32] Nicholson,[33] and Laehr,[34] diagnose Hamlet as suffering from melancholia, while Thierish[35] and Sigismund[36] consider Hamlet as actually insane without specifying the type. We shall take this up in greater detail in the following chapter.

NOTES AND REFERENCES

CHAPTER XVI

1. **Essays In Applied Psychoanalysis,** The International Psychoanalytical Press, London, 1932, p. 6.
2. **Iibd., p. 59.**
3. **Ibid., p. 65.**
4. **The Basic Writings of Sigmund Freud.** New York, Random House, 1938, p. 310.
5. **Oxford Lectures on Poetry,** 1909, p. 357.
6. **Histoire de la Litterature Anglaise,** 1886 t. II, p. 254.
7. Figgis, D. **Shakespeare: A Study,** 1911, p. 320.
8. **The Medical Knowledge of Shakespeare,** op. cit., p. 5.
9. **The Basic Writings of Sigmund Freud,** op. cit., p. 309.
10. **Ibid.**
11. **Facts and Theories of Psychoanalysis,** N. Y. Alfred Knopf. 1939, p. 299.
12. **Ibid.,** p. 298.
13. **Ibid.,** p. 298.
14. **Psychoanalysis Today.** Chap. on "Psychoanalysis and Literature." Sander Lorand. The International Univ. Press. 1944, p. 377.
15. **Ibid.**
16. **The Demon Lover.** Exposition Press. New York. p. 2.
17. Ibid., p. 14.
18. "The Impatience of Hamlet" in **Collected Papers on Psychoanalysis.** The Hogarth Press Ltd., p. 205.
19. Fliess, Robert Dr. **Ego and Body Ego,** Schutle Publishing Co., New York, 1961, p. 297.
20. **Ibid., p. 285.**
21. **Ibid.**
22. Ibid. p. 4.
23. This essay first appeared in Jan. 1910 **Amer. Journ. Psychology.** An enlarged version appeared in German in 1911 under **Das Problem des Hamlet, und der Oedipus-Komplex** in the **Schriften zur Angewandten Seelkunde,** Reft. 10.
24. "A Psychoanalytic Study of Hamlet," op. cit., p. 310.
25. **Ibid.,** p. 86. The italics are Dr. Jones'.
26. **Ibid.,** p. 98.
27. **Basic Writings of Sigmund Freud,** op. cit., p. 310.
28. **Essays in applied Psycho-analysis,** op. cit., p. 87.
29. **Shakespeare's Hamlet im Lichte der Neuropathologie,** 1895.

30. Shakespeare's Delineations of Insanity, 1866, op. cit.
31. Annales Medico-psychologigues. 1866, 4e. sir., 12e fasc.
32. Jahrbuch der deutschen Shakespeare-Gesselschaft, 1876, Jahrg. XIII.
33. Trans. New Shakespeare Society, 1880-85, Part II.
34. Die Darstellung Krankhafter Geisteszustande in Shakespeare's Dramen. 1898.
35. Nord und Sud, 1878, Bd. VI.
36. Jahrbuch der deutschen Shakespeare-Gesselschaft, 1879 Jahrg. XVI.

CHAPTER XVII

THE PSYCHOGENESIS OF CREATIVE LITERARY EXPRESSION AND SHAKESPEARE'S *HAMLET*

Behind all creative expression there stands the creator. To understand fully the highly artistic product of the creative mind we must enter into the very workings of that mind as it shapes the varied forms of creative expression, for you cannot separate the creative product from the source of its creation in the emotional chemistry of the soul of man. Ultimately, the whole problem of creative expression, whether it be in painting or poetry, or drama, or sculpture or music, resolves itself into a problem of psychology. What is the source of poetic and dramatic energy? How is it transformed into creative expression? How is it particularly exemplified in Shakespeare's dramas and especially in *Hamlet?*

From the very beginning, and to an extent, even unto this very day, the inexplicability of the poetic utterance led to a consideration of poetry and drama as the product of divine inspiration. The poet was regarded much as the prophet, the priest, the oracle, the dreamer, the seer. He was the chosen human instrument through whom the divine spoke in awesome beauties of language stirring man to the very depths of his being. Apollo, the Muses, God—these were held responsible for all poetic expressions. Hence the invocation of prayer to the Muse, with which we are all familiar, so often offered up by poets of the past as a preliminary to their more ambitious poetic flights. That titanic Greek mind, Plato, voicing his belief in the divine causation of poetic utterance calls it a form of madness not in the sense of insanity as we know it today but rather in the sense of a suspension of the Conscious mind and the welling forth of overflowing springs of ecstatic creative expression from out of the unfathomable depths of the Unconscious. He says that

> ". . . not by art does the poet sing but by divine power. God takes away the minds of poets and uses them as his ministers . . . in order that we who hear them may know them to be speaking . . . these priceless words in a state of unconsciousness."[1]

He is even more explicit than this when he writes of

> "the madness of those who are possessed by the Muses, which taking hold of a delicate and virgin soul, and there inspiring frenzy, awakens Lyrical and all other numbers. . . ."[2]

No matter how much art a poet may possess if he be without that "touch of the Muses' madness in his soul" he cannot enter the temple of true poetry. Practically all writers who have given thought to this matter since Plato, from Cicero through Plutarch, through Dante, Bacon, Shakespeare. Dryden, Wordsworth, Shelley, Byron, Emerson and a host of others—all these echo in one form or another the divine inspiring factor involved in poetic creative expression working in a form of "frenzy" or "madness" in the sense that Plato used the terms.

That other titanic Greek mind, Aristotle, in his consideration of tragedy as a means of catharsis or purgation for painful emotions, went a step further than Plato for, although he refers to the audience of tragedy as being healed of the emotions of pity and fear, indirectly we may apply this to the poets and consider poetic creative expression as a catharsis and healing for them also. Thus it may be inferred from Aristotle that Poetry is both a release and relief for the poet of painful emotions as well as for his audience. It is not by coincidence indeed that Apollo was designated both the God of Poetry and the God of Healing. Here in Aristotle we already get a glimpse of the germ of the Freudian conception of creative expression.

Bacon, too, that great English intellect, seems to have had a glimmering of the true function of poetry for he considers that its main use "hath been to give some shadow of satisfaction to the mind of man in those points wherein the nature of things doth deny it."[3] This definitely implies that poetic creative expression serves as a means of satisfaction for denied desires in the "nature of things."

Friedrich Schiller states that

> "the poet . . . begins with the Unconscious"

and that poetry

> ". . . consists . . . in being able to utter and impart that unconscious. The Unconscious combined with reflection, makes the poetic artist,"[4]

while Edward von Hartmann likewise writes that

> "the creation of the beautiful may proceed from unconscious processes."[5]

Nietzsche carried the point even closer to the Freudian conception for he considers the basis of creative expression in the arts as an indirect longing for sexual ecstasy. He puts the matter distinctly in these words,

> "The desire for art and beauty is an indirect longing for the ecstasy of sexual desire which gets communicated to the brain."[6]

John E. Keble, too, became a forerunner of Freud in this matter. He develops the thesis that the poet writes to gain relief from pent up emotions that stir within him uncomfortably. His definition of poetry is worthy of repetition. He considers poetry as

> "a kind of medicine divinely bestowed upon man which gives healing relief to secret mental emotions . . ."[7]

So, then, we are down to Freud. And it is in Freud that we get a complete and satisfactory basis for the causation and meaning of creative expression. It is he that cast the light of his genius into the remote recesses of the human mind and developed conceptions that have had as great and far-reaching an influence on human thought and human behavior as the conceptions of Copernicus, Newton and Darwin.

Briefly stated the basic psychoanalytic doctrine may be developed as follows: From childhood on, and this applies also to the childhood of the race, it is the tendency of the human being to immediately gratify all the desires that arise into his consciousness. Hunger, thirst, sexual desire—these are the most primordial of the emotions clamoring for gratification. This is termed the Pleasure-Principle in life. The child's desires arising in the emotions involved in the Pleasure-Principle are immediately gratified. All his wants of hunger, thirst, love, bodily elimination, etc., are well-attended to almost automatically. Primitive man also tended to eat and drink when hungry and thirsty; he sought a mate when love moved him; he killed when hate arose in him; he fled when fear impelled him and so on. The energies engendered by his emotions all spent themselves and he was but an animal—nothing much more than a thing of reflexes. However, as man became a member of a horde—a social animal, with certain taboos, he had to deflect his desires or be destroyed. The growing complexity in civilization made it increasingly necessary for continual adjustments to reality. More desires had to be thwarted. Freud calls this the Reality-Principle. It continuously opposes and modifies the Pleasure-Principle. However energy is indestructible; when desires arise out of the *emotions* in the human being that cannot be gratified, these desires do not disappear. The emotional energy is not destroyed. The desires are repressed deep, deep down into awareness into that portion of the mind Freud terms the Unconscious. The Unconscious forms by far the greatest portion of the human mind for here all the memories of our developing race from the dawn of time are kept. Here all the memories of individual man are kept from conception through infancy and onward. Here are all the repressed desires of the race and of the individual. It is a vast domain of accumulated energy that this Unconscious represents, guarded ever from breaking forth into awareness by a mighty censorship. The Unconscious is a huge reservoir of latent potential energy made up of repressed desires. Latent in this submerged cauldron of repressed energy are the powers that can raise man to the very heights of godhood and sink him to the very depths of grovelling swine.

Energy is indestructible. The emotional energy generated by man's desires and dammed up into the Unconscious does break forth. It breaks forth in dreams wherein the repressed desires are gratified. It breaks forth in reveries. It breaks forth into psychoneuroses and insanities destroying the individual, or into the psychoneuroses of mass hate bringing on wars and persecutions and massacres—for the destruction of the race.

But by far the most important channel for this repressed emotional energy in man is the channel of creative expression It is man's saving feature raising him out of the hulk of beasthood. All the arts, and particularly poetry, are transformations of repressed desires of energy flowing from the Unconscious into untold beauties of form, sound poetic utterance. Poetry arises out of the Unconscious and is uttered to relieve an ache, a longing within the poet he cannot fathom. It is a lyric cry from the depths. It is a touching of the heart to things. Sara Teasdale expresses this aptly when she says:

> "Poems are written because of a state of emotional irritation. It may be present for some time before the poet is conscious of what is tormenting him. The emotional irritation springs, probably from subconscious combinations of partly forgotten thoughts and feelings. Coming together like electric currents in a storm, they produce a poem. Any poem not written to free the poet from an emotional burden is only a piece of craftsmanship."[8]

Thus, in a sense, may poetic creative expression be truly considered as Aristotle considered it—a form of catharsis for pent-up emotions, the emotions arising from repressed desires sunk into the Unconscious as Freud conceived it. This is the genesis and meaning of all creative expression. And it is no complex task to master the true creative literature of the world and show through psychological analysis, that it is a compensatory channel flowing from its creator's Unconscious, under pressure of repressed desires in sublimation. How this manifests itself in the character of Hamlet we shall soon see.

NOTES AND REFERENCES

CHAPTER XVII

1. Quoted in G. E. Woodberry, The Inspiration of Poetry. The Macmillan Company, New York, 1910, p. 1.
2. Quoted in G. C. Prescott, The Poetic Mind, p. 264.
3. Advancement of Learning, Book II.
4. Letters on the Aesthetical Education of Man, 8:33-126 in Complete Works of Friedrich Schiller, New York, P. F. Collier and Sons, 1902.
5. Philosophy of the Unconscious, New York, Harcourt, Brace and Company, 1931, I, p. 291.
6. Quoted in A. Mordell, The Literature of Ecstasy, p. 28.
7. Ibid.
8. Quoted in W. W. Ellsworth, Creative Writing, Funk & Wagnalls Company, New York, 1929.

CHAPTER XVIII

SHAKESPEARE'S HAMLET: THE GREAT MODERN OEDIPUS TRAGEDY

I

In the psychoanalytic world outlook, the Oedipus constellation with all of its implications is not only a cornerstone of personality structure and development, but it is also a basic recurring theme in mythology, folklore, dream and creative art. Creative literature at its best is the deepest expression of the creative artist. It is a manifestation of his soul, his mind, his unconscious. Hence the creative artist is in his creation. It is valid then to apply psychoanalytic principles to the product of the literary artist.

Indeed, the last half century has witnessed not only a remarkable influence of psychoanalysis upon contemporary literary creation, but also the development of a psychoanalytic criticism and interpretation of the great masterpieces of the literature of the past. He who bares humanity bares the self and he who bares the self bares humanity.

From this standpoint, let us consider Shakespeare's *Hamlet,* probably the greatest dramatic tragedy of all time. It is also the greatest Oedipal drama ever written.

Numerous psychoanalysts have dealt with *Hamlet* within this frame of reference including Freud, Ives Hendricks, Fritz Wittels, Arthur Wormhoudt, Ella F. Sharpe, Robert Fliess and, most important of all, Ernest Jones, who treated the subject extensively as a great Oedipus drama. Nevertheless, there is still much need for a more thorough elaboration of the great tragedy.

If now one examines the play itself, more directly and more completely than has heretofore been done, act by act, and action by action, one can readily see the tenability of the psychoanalytic interpretation. Here in the drama, on the very face of it, is the typical son-mother-father triangle of the Oedipus situation, around which, in early childhood, there are so many repressions which are sunk into the subconscious to be transformed, in various ways by psychological mechanisms, into varying degrees of socially acceptable human behavior. In the character of Hamlet the repressions surrounding this Oedipus constellation break through into a psychoneurosis manifesting itself by depression, suicidal ideas, misanthropy, profound misogyny, loss of interests, self-depreciation, irritability, indecisiveness, and the final homicide with its full denouement.

Certainly the story is not much of a story. Except for the last scene, there is very little action. The play deals mainly with the character of Hamlet. It is called the tragedy of Hamlet. Hamlet speaks many more lines than any other character. He dominates the play. That Shakespeare consciously or unconsciously meant it to be so is further evidenced by the fact that none of the earlier versions of the play based on *The Amlethus* of Saxo Grammaticus contain the many monologues of Hamlet which form such an important and decisive part of the play. In addition, we must ever be impressed by the fact that it is not Elizabethan ethics here or the Elizabethan man, or regicide which "dominates both the plot and the characters of the play," as some of the historical critics would have us believe, but rather it is incest, and the inconstancy of woman and disgust at sexuality. These are the elements that are Shakespeare's own unconscious elaborations, for they are not present in the mentioned sources of the drama. He seems to be obsessed by them and they flow out from the tongue of Hamlet and even of the ghost as though in unconscious compulsion. Indeed, most of the substance of the monologues is directed in one form or another against his mother or against woman in general, or against himself in conflict and self-contempt, and not against the murderer of his father or against regicide.

At the very beginning of the play, before there is knowledge that Hamlet's father was murdered, Hamlet is already in a deep depression and it is obvious that this is not so because of his father's death or because of his "lack of advancement" to the throne, for very little is said by Hamlet to indicate this. On the other hand from the very first few lines spoken by Hamlet

(I, 2), we note the antagonism toward his mother because of her "o'erhasty marriage" to Claudius. In fact, we have a positive right to assume, from the very evidence in the play, that Hamlet's deep depression and abnormal attitude toward the world was directly precipitated by his mother's marriage and not by his father's death. We are led to this conclusion by the fact that before the marriage of his mother at least two months had elapsed following the funeral and that during these two months Hamlet found enough interest in the world and in womankind to have "made many tenders of his affection" toward Ophelia "of late" and to have "importun'd" her "with love in honourable fashion." And a man loving a woman as much as Hamlet "lov'd Ophelia" that "forty thousand brothers/Could not, with all their quantity of love,/Make up [the] sum," could not possibly be as melancholic and so bitterly misogynous. Furthermore, he tells Guildenstern (II, 2) that it is *"of late"* that he has lost all interest in life, never mentioning by a single word the death of his father as a possible cause thereof. Indeed, the very fact that Hamlet could supposedly, love a substitute mother love object in Ophelia, is, from a psychoanalytic sense, evidence that his Oedipus complex might have satisfactorily solved itself. But then occurs the hasty marriage of the Queen to his uncle. It is this which shocks Hamlet to his foundations. For here a revivification of one of the important elements in the Oedipus situation takes place. The mother has rejected the son for the uncle-father, and there is jealousy turned to rage against the mother, against incest, against woman, and only secondarily, with psychologically determined procrastination, against the uncle-father.

When the king asks Hamlet why the "clouds still hang on" him, he merely parries the question in courtesy by saying "Not so, my lord; I am to much i' the sun." A number of lines later when the king chastises him at length for persevering in his "obstinate condolement," his "impious stubbornness," his "unmanly grief" as "A fault against the dead, a fault to nature" and further openly announces him as "most immediate to our throne," Hamlet shows very little emotion and says nothing in reply. But when his mother asks him much more simply to "cast thy nighted colour off" and questions why this supposed grief over the death of his father "seems so particular" with him, he answers in apparent antipathy, irritability and emotion, "Seems, madam! Nay it is; I know not seems," and he continues to enumerate the outward "shows of grief," "the trappings and the suits of woe," as though pointing the accusing finger at her, "For they are actions that a man might play." As for him, he "has that within which passeth show." Here Shakespeare gives us a hint of the turmoil and conflict possessing him; and it is this which forms the main subject of the drama. Now what is that something "within" him,

> More than his father's death that thus hath put him
> So much for the understanding of himself

> This is something-settled matter in his heart,
> Whereon his brains still beating put him thus
> From fashion of himself

that

> . . . something in his soul
> O'er which his melancholy sits on brood

that has caused "Hamlet's transformation" and made him the "too much changed son" "wherefore [he] know[s] not"? This is soon made manifest in Hamlet's first soliloquy (I, 2). It strikes the note and contains the core of the drama. It is charged with deepest passion and intensest emotion. It is as though all the suppressed rage and emotional conflict within him breaks through and he cries out from the depths of his soul against life, against the world,

> O! . . . that the Everlasting had not fix'd
> His canon 'gainst self-slaughter: O God! O God!
> this world
> Fie on't! O fie! 'tis an unweeded garden
> That grows to seed;

Following upon these lines, as though in direct association, we get at the true "heart of [his] mystery,"—the rage at the marriage of his mother, which is certainly way beyond the limits of accepted normality even in the Elizabethan culture; and this is so, because the emotion is powerfully reinforced from deep sources in the Unconscious revolving about his own unsolved childhood jealousy of his father and his feeling of rejection by his mother with its then oft repeated drama of hate and love. His heart cries out,

> That it should come to this!
> But two months dead: nay, not so much, not two:
> So excellent a king; . . . so loving to my mother.
>
> Heaven and earth!
>
> Must I remember?

He tries to throw it out of his mind but it has become a fixed obsession. He recalls how his father would not let "the winds of heaven visit her face too roughly," and how "she would hang on him,/As if increase of appetite had grown/By what it fed on;" which obviously points to Hamlet's early observations of the love-making of his parents even to the sexual elements hinted at here, but more openly emphasized as the drama progresses. He is actually ranting against his mother because she gave her love to his own father in the Oedipus triangle. Hamlet returns to the theme again and again:

> Within a month,
> Let me not think on't: Frailty, thy name is woman!
> A little month;
>
> O God! a beast, that wants discourse of reason,
> Would have mourn'd longer,—married with mine uncle,
>
> Within a month,
>
> She married. O! most wicked speed, to post
> With such dexterity to incestuous sheets.

The creeping in of the incest element here has great significance. It occurs numerous times in the drama, as we shall see. The incest taboo is the corner stone of the Oedipus complex. It is the child's early wish, but repressed out of consciousness, Hamlet projects his own guilt for the incest wish, upon the father surrogate—his actual uncle-father-king. He thus purges his own self. This psychological mechanism of projection is common enough. There is no evil we hate so much in others than that which we ourselves possess. Apropos of this factor, it must be emphasized that in a biological sense there really was no incest involved in the marriage of Claudius to the Queen. Yet Shakespeare has Hamlet and the Ghost dwell upon it. It arises from his own soul as a projection. But even if we accept it, that in the Elizabethan period such a union was considered incest by the Church, yet Shakespeare could have availed himself of the device used in the earlier sources of the Hamlet tragedy, wherein the incest element is merely handled by a dispensation from the Pope and dismissed by a few words. But Shakespeare goes out of his way in this regard and seems to be driven to this incest motif. When Horatio says to Hamlet that he came to see his father's funeral, Hamlet replies,

> I pray thee, do not mock me, fellow-student;
> I think it was to see my mother's wedding

Then, in tragic, mocking irony he remarks

> Thrift, thrift Horatio! the funeral bak'd meats
> Did coldly furnish forth the marriage tables.

And, just as in the first soliloquy, he thinks of suicide, so here, too, in this association, he says,

> Would I had met my dearest foe in heaven
> Ere I had even seen that day, Horatio!

This obsession with incest, with its disgust at sexuality is carried on further in the Ghost scene (I, 5). The Ghost in his longest speech calls Claudius "that incestuous, that adulterate beast" who with "wicked wit and gifts" seduced and "won to his shameful lust" the "seeming virtuous queen," such

> lust, though to a radiant angel link'd
> Will sate itself in a celestial bed
> And prey on garbage

The speech reaches its highest point of emotion when the Ghost cries out to Hamlet

> O, horrible! O, horrible! most horrible!
> If thou hast nature in thee, bear it not;

But here again Shakespeare cannot keep away from the incest motif. Not so much to avenge his murder, not so much to avenge the taking of the crown, but

> Let not the royal bed of Denmark be
> A couch for luxury and damned incest

this is the exhortation of the Ghost to Hamlet, at the same time cautioning him against tainting his mind to contrive against his mother. Nevertheless when Hamlet answers that he will "wipe away all trivial fond records" from his memory to carry out his commandment, his first remarks are against his mother, not against Claudius, for the words escape out of the depths of his soul, "O most pernicious woman!" and then, only then, is it followed by calling his uncle "O villain, villain, smiling damned villain!" It becomes more and more evident that his rage is more against his mother for having rejected him in childhood in favor of the father in the psychoanalytic sense—and now having symbolically rejected him again in her marriage to his uncle, another father figure, than against the murderer, the uncle-father-king.

So at the end of the first act we have all the elements present of the Oedipus situation: a father has been murdered and his wife has married the murderer in an incest relationship. This is the wish fantasy of the child—to kill the father and thus possess exclusively the mother's love. In the case of Hamlet, however, the mother has hastily married another father-figure resulting in a reactivation of the early Oedipal conflict, and the consequent development of psychological defenses and reaction formations against the rise of the incest wish to consciousness. The defense is his psychoneurosis with depression and suicidal ideas, and, further than this, his bitterly expressed rancor against his mother, against Ophelia, against all women, against sexuality. This, as we shall see, continues with even greater intensity to the end of the drama. As for the avenging of his father's murder, he cannot get himself to do it, he hesitates, he procrastinates throughout the play. Claudius has done what Hamlet in the Oedipal conflict has fantasied doing over and over again. He identifies himself with his uncle as the murderer. To kill his uncle is to kill himself, especially since the uncle becomes an actual father symbol—uncle-father-king. A good deal of the play involves the conflict surrounding this factor. Of course in the end the tragedy involves the murder of all the principals, the only fitting tragic end to all activated Oedipus conflicts. Already, in the last few lines of this first act, we get a glimpse of Hamlet's unconscious resistance and distaste against killing his uncle-father-king resulting in his irresolution, for Shakespeare has Hamlet cry out,

> The time is out of joint; O cursed spite,
> That ever I was born to set it right!

We shall return to this psychological defense mechanism of indecisiveness unconsciously used by Hamlet against carrying out his revenge. But now let us pursue further the unfolding of Shakespeare-Hamlet's misogyny, his bitterness against his mother and the sexual content coloring his attitude and his thinking in this regard—all being reaction formations in handling his Oedipal conflict.

When Hamlet encounters Ophelia (III, 1) and she chides him for his unkindness, he questions tauntingly of her honesty and of her beauty, aiming his belittling words at all women, in that their

> power of beauty will sooner transform honesty from what it is to a bawd than the force of honesty can translate beauty into his likeness;

He tells her,

> God hath given you one face, and you make yourselves another: You jig, you amble and you lisp, and nickname God's creatures, and make your wantonness your ignorance . . . I say we will have no more marriages

He calls down a plague upon her that if she does marry, though she be as "chaste as ice, as pure as snow" she shall "not escape calumny;" that she should marry a fool; "for wise men know well enough what monsters you make of them." He rants at her to go to a nunnery and not be "a breeder of sinners" such as himself that "could accuse me of such things that it were better my mother had not borne me." He calls such as he, "arrant knaves" "crawling between heaven and earth" and exhorts her not to believe "any of us." This is reminiscent of Laertes' and Polonius' admonitions to Ophelia in a previous scene (I, 3), although under much different circumstances, and emphasizes again Shakespeare's almost compulsive preoccupation with the theme of sexuality and his revulsion thereat. They advise her to be "wary" of Hamlet, not to "believe his tenders," not "believe his vows," not give "too credent ear" to "his songs," for these are "springes to catch woodcocks." They tell her not to lose her heart or her "chaste treasure open." They warn her to keep

> Out of the shot and danger of desire.
> The chariest maid is prodigal enough
> If she unmask her beauty to the moon;
> Virtue herself 'scapes not calumnious strokes;

Now why should Hamlet be so devastatingly bitter against Ophelia? Some critics would attribute this to his rejection by her to cause the so-called Lover's Melancholy of Elizabethan psychology. Thus, G. B. Harrison, in agreement with Polonius, considers, as one of the main causes of Hamlet's melancholy "a love melancholy of his own; he is himself the forlorn lover rejected by his mistress." But Hamlet utters not one word to indicate this. Furthermore, the experiment of Polonius to prove this is a failure, as previously pointed out, and the king is forced to the conclusion that "Love! his affections do not that way tend," while the Queen similarly concludes as to "the very cause of Hamlet's lunacy" that "it is no other, but the main;/His father's death, and our o'erhasty marriage."

Moreover, let it not be forgotten that long before Ophelia took her father's advice to repulse Hamlet he was already in the throes of his melancholy raging at his mother's hasty marriage and imputing to all womankind: "Frailty, thy name is woman!"

Indeed, we might, with better logic, consider Hamlet's changed attitude toward Ophelia as part of his "antic disposition" or part of his determination to "wipe away all trivial fond records" "from the table of [his] memory" so better to carry out the commandment of his father's Ghost to avenge his murder.

None of these reasons fundamentally answer our question. From a psychological standpoint it is readily obvious that Hamlet, in striking at Ophelia, is really striking at his mother and at all womankind. His mother once loved him and would "hang on his very looks." She rejected him in her "O'erhasty marriage" to his uncle, this acting to arouse out of the Unconscious the emotionally highly charged Oedipus elements. He cannot strike as yet from internal inhibitions, directly at the true object of his rage, for though his heart break, "[he] must hold [his] tongue." So he strikes at substitute love objects—Ophelia-woman. How often in every day life the rejection of a man by a beloved woman results in misogyny! And how often, from a psychoanalytic sense, does early rejection by the mother in all its various ways result in flight from woman in all its forms!

As the drama of Hamlet proceeds onward and Hamlet's psychological defenses and inhibitions break down, there is an ever increasing crescendo towards the bursting open from the confines of the Unconscious of the bare and forbidding face of the Oedipus triangle that can only result in the final littering of the stage with the dead.

When his mother asks Hamlet to sit beside her to watch the play that he has arranged for the court (III, 2) he answers stingingly with purposive aim "No, good mother, here's metal more attractive" and proceeds to carry through a vulgar sexual joke about lying in Ophelia's lap, and "country matters" and "That's a fair thought to lie between maid's legs," although it is very evident that he is anything but "merry." He soon gives his real feelings away however revealing again what is eating at his soul—his mother's inconstancy to his father and more deeply to himself. He cries out in sarcastic ironic mockery,

> O God . . . What should a man do but be merry? For, look

you, how cheerfully my mother looks, and my father died within two hours.

And again, when Ophelia remarks that it is "twice two months" he says, in similar vein

O heavens! die two months ago, and not forgotten yet?
Then there's hope a great man's memory may outlive his life half a year Providing he build churches

Still later when Ophelia notes that the prologue of their play is brief, Hamlet cannot refrain from retorting, "as woman's love" is brief. In like manner, when Rosencrantz imparts to Hamlet that his "behaviour hath struck her (his mother) into amazement and admiration," he replies "O wonderful son, that can so astonish a mother!" Hamlet cannot veer away from the theme that represents the canker corroding his soul. He cannot hold his tongue longer; and he "speak(s) daggers at her" in spite of the fact that the Ghost has admonished Hamlet (I, 5):

Taint not thy mind, nor let thy soul contrive
Against thy mother aught

and again (III, 4):

But look! Amazement on thy mother sits;
O! step between her and her fighting soul;

Indeed Hamlet cries out (III, 2) as he goes to see his mother,

O heart, lose not thy nature; let not even
the soul of Nero enter this firm bosom
Let me be cruel, not unnatural;
I will speak daggers to her, but use none.

Is it not of marked significance here in relation to the Oedipus situation that Nero committed incest with his mother and also murdered her? Has incest and matricide then in the symbol of Nero, reached awareness enough in Shakespeare's Hamlet, that he must call upon himself to guard against it so that he be merely "cruel" not "unnatural"? He cannot fulfill his father's wish to be kind to his mother, for here is evidence of the hated rival's love for his own love-object, adding injury upon injury. How transform the deep unending jealous rage of a child into kindness toward the guilty love object? Hamlet cannot do it, no more than he can get himself immediately to avenge his father's death.

He strikes more directly at his mother in the closest scene (III, 4) telling her "would it were not so" that she is his mother. He wants to "wring" her heart "If it be made of penetrable stuff." He calls her marriage to his uncle

Such an act
That blurs the grace and blush of modesty,
Calls virtue hypocrite, takes off the rose
From the fair forehead of an innocent love
And sets a blister there, makes marriage vows
As false as dicers' oaths; O! such a deed
As from the body of contraction plucks
The very soul, and sweet religion makes
A rhapsody of words; heavens face doth glow,
Yea, this solidity and compound mass,
With tristful visage, as against the doom,
Is thought-sick at the act.

And what is this act? The marrying with his father's brother! He compares the qualities of the two brothers and lashes out at her, for her *choice*

Have you eyes?
Could you on this fair mountain leave to feed
And batten on this moor? Ha! Have you eyes?
You cannot call it love, for at your age
The hey-day in the blood is tame, its humble,
And waits upon the judgment; and what judgment
Would step from this to this?
What devil was't
That thus hath cozen'd you at hoodman-blind?
O shame! Where is thy blush? Rebellious hell,
If thou cans't mutine in a matron's bones,
To flaming youth let virtue be as wax,
And melt in her own fire; proclaim no shame
When the compulsive ardour gives the charge.

Yet it is perfectly obvious that Hamlet's mother could not really have made any choice, for Shakespeare is careful to make it plain, that there was no adulterous affair between the two before his father's death, and that it was after his death that Claudius seduced the Queen "With witchcraft of his wit, with traitrous gifts;" with the king dead, there were no two to choose from. Moreover, Hamlet does not emphasize here any further, the hastiness of the marriage as a decisive factor. It is the *fact* of the marriage itself that is responsible for initiating Hamlet's "weakness and [his] melancholy," and his neurotic *actions.* The real choice in the immediate situation was between Claudius and Hamlet. She chose Claudius and rejected Hamlet just as in the earlier Oedipus situation, she chose his father and rejected him, the son. These two reinforce each other strongly. It is this which rankles so keenly in his bosom. Added to this is the knowledge of the actual murder of the father, thus completing the important revivification of the full Oedipus complex. The early wish fulfillment for the murder of the father has taken place, but the mother has married another father figure and again rejected the son.

Hamlet now openly accuses his mother that it was her "trespass" that is the cause of his feelings. He cries out at her

> Mother, for love of grace
> Lay not that flattering unction to your soul,
> That not *your trespass* but my madness speaks

He calls upon her to

> confess yourself to heaven;
> Repent what's past; avoid what is to come;
> And do not spread the compost on the weeds
> To make them ranker.

He dwells more and more upon the sexual factors as though obsessed by them, speaking of his mother as "a mother stain'd" and referring to his uncle-father, as having "whor'd my mother."

He tells her not

> to live
> In the rank sweat of an enseamed bed

Stew'd in corruption, honeying and making love
Over the nasty sty,—

More directly he exhorts her:

go not to mine uncle's bed
Assume a virtue if you have it not

Refrain to-night;
And that shall lend a kind of easiness
To the next abstinence: the next more easy;

And again, he orders her not to

Let the bloat king tempt you again to bed;
Pinch wanton on your cheek; call you his mouse;
And let him, for a pair of reechy kisses,
Or paddling in your neck with his damn'd fingers,
Make you ravel all this matter out.

It is as though the son in the Oedipus triangle is alternately raging at the mother and begging her not to sleep with father, but to stay with him; for the which, he promises her

And when you are desirous to be bless'd
I'll blessing beg of you.

Only thus can a reconciliation take place with his mother and this part of the wish-fulfillment of the Oedipus constellation of pregenital childhood assert itself. In fact, from this point forward, no more does he rant against his mother for he has, as it were, made his peace with her and become reconciled.

But Hamlet is an adult and the reactivation of his unsolved mother complex must inevitably lead to tragedy. Nor can Hamlet directly carry out the other important action inherent in the Oedipus situation—the killing of the uncle-father. And, just as the reactivated incest wish, as has been shown, was neurotically handled by reaction formations and defense mechanisms leading to cruel vituperation against the mother, against the previously substituted love object, Ophelia, against womankind, disgust at sexuality with emphasis on the incestuous relationship, so, by similar psychological means, does hesitancy, irresolution, procrastination, determine Hamlet's gyrations in the carrying out of the Ghost's commandment to revenge.

II

Hamlet's Irresolution

From the very first, we can recognize the antagonism of Hamlet for his uncle-father. When the king addresses Hamlet (I, 2), calling him "my cousin Hamlet, and my son,"—he says, in an aside, "A little more than kin and less than kind," thus setting the stage for what is to follow, also hinting as to the identity of the protagonists in the drama. A little later in the same scene when Horatio has apprised him of the Ghost's appearance, Hamlet says,

> My father's spirit in arms! All is not well;
> I doubt some foul play

Here unconsciously, Shakespeare is expressing the thought that is father to the wish. Hamlet in the psychoanalytic sense has fantasied the killing of his father. Since this is completely unacceptable to the Ego, it is easy to project this wish upon someone else. This someone else here is the uncle who in fact has become the father with whom he identifies himself now, as he has identified himself with his own father in childhood. Thus, in this sense, to kill the uncle is to displace the father over again. We get a hint of this when Hamlet, hearing from his father's Ghost that Claudius has murdered him, cries out (I, 5): "O my *prophetic* soul!/My uncle!" and though Hamlet is many times sworn to sweep to his revenge

> with wings as swift
> As meditation or thoughts of love

he certainly does anything but this; and a good deal of the drama is taken up with his inner conflict and the hesitation in carrying out the Ghost's command. For, as noted before, to kill the king is to kill the father and possess exclusively the mother in the Oedipus triangle, and there are too many inhibitory forces preventing Hamlet from doing this, though again and again he raises himself to emotional heights to spur himself on to his accepted duty.

When the Ghost in his lengthy speech admonishes Hamlet to remember him (I, 5), Hamlet in monologue emotionally answers,

O all you hosts of heaven! O earth! what else?
And shall I couple hell? O fie! Hold, hold, my heart!
And you, my sinews, grow not instant old,
But bear me stiffly up! Remember thee!
Ay, thou poor ghost, while memory holds a seat
In this distracted globe. Remember thee!
Yea, from the table of my memory
I'll drive away all trivial fond records,
All saws of books, forms, all pressures past,
That youth and observation copied there;
And thy commandment all alone shall live
Within the book and volume of my brain,
Unmix'd with baser matter: Yes, by heaven!

He tells Horatio that the ghost "is an honest ghost," yet immediately thereafter as if the inhibitory forces were already holding him back from his accepted duty he states, (I,5),

The time is out of joint; O cursed spite,
That ever I was born to set it right!

and proceeds with his plan "To put an antic disposition on," although it serves very little purpose in furthering his father's Ghost's commandment. In fact, the feigned madness of Hamlet, though important to the plot of the early sources in the *Amlethus* of Saxo Grammaticus, is entirely extraneous to Shakespeare's *Hamlet,* and furthers neither the plot nor the theme. And those critics who claim that Hamlet's feigned madness was necessary in order to make it possible for him to get at the king to fulfill his vengeance are grossly mistaken. Not one word does Hamlet utter to indicate this and the progressive movement of the play completely denies it. Shakespeare may have kept the feigned madness in his drama merely because Elizabethan audiences loved it. More likely, Shakespeare unconsciously allowed Hamlet to carry on his "antic disposition" as a rationalization to maintain his irresolution in sweeping on to his revenge. Actually something in the Unconscious within him will not let him kill the king. He finds many excuses to foster his hesitancy. He pays a price for this, however, in torturing conflict and in depression. Indeed, all through the drama Hamlet knows full well how sick he really is for he speaks in various ways (V, 2) of

> how ill
> All's here about my heart.

He finds that "Denmark's a prison," and tells Guildenstern (II, 2),

> I have of late,— but wherefore I know not,—lost all my mirth, forgone all custom of exercises; and indeed it goes so heavily with my disposition that this goodly frame, the earth, seems to me a sterile promontory; this most excellent canopy, the air, look you, this brave o'erhanging firmament, this majestical roof fretted with golden fire, why, it appears no other thing to me but a foul and pestilent congregation of vapours. What a piece of work is a man! How noble is reason! how infinite in faculty! in form, in moving, how express and admirable! in action how like an angel! in apprehension how like a god! the beauty of world! the paragon of animals! And yet, to me, what is this quintessence of dust? Man delights not me; no, nor woman neither . . .

When, after hearing the Players declaim, he is left alone, he lashes out at himself for his hesitancy, He calls himself "a rogue and peasant slave," and other contemptuous terms. He cries out in great passion,

> What's Hecuba to him or he to Hecuba
> That he should weep for her? What would he do
> Had he the motive and the cue for passion
> That I have? He would drown the stage with tears,
> And cleave the general ear with horrid speech,
> Make mad the guilty and appall the free,
> Confound the ignorant, and amaze indeed

The very faculties of eyes and ears.
Yet I,
A dull and muddy-mettled rascal, peak
Like John-a-dreams, unpregnant of my cause,
And can say nothing; no, not for a king,
Upon whose property and most dear life
A damn'd defeat was made. Am I coward?
Who calls me villain? breaks my pate across?
Plucks off my beard and blows it in my face?
Tweaks me by the nose? gives me the lie i' the throat
As deep as to the lungs? Who does me this?
Ha!
Swounds, I should take it, for it cannot be
But I am pigeon-liver'd, and lack gall
To make oppression bitter, or ere this
I should have fatted all the region kites
With this slaves offal. Bloody bawdy villain!
Remorseless, treacherous, lecherous, kindless villain!
O! vengeance!
Why, what an ass am I! This is most brave
That I, the son of a dear father murder'd
Prompted to my revenge by heaven and hell,
Must like a whore, unpack my heart with words,
And fall a cursing, like a very drab,
A scullion!

There is not one word in this monologue to indicate the reason for Hamlet's procrastination (as being in the nature of the task itself), except his own inner indecision. He is a coward "unpregnant of [his] cause" who cannot sweep to his revenge. He produces another rationalization. Though previously he has considered the Ghost "an honest ghost," he now is not quite sure but that

The spirit that I have seen
May be the devil

and he decides,

I'll have grounds
More relative than this: the play's the thing

> Wherein I'll catch the conscience of the king

But this does not quiet the turmoil in his soul. He is beset by doubts. He is self-contemptuous. He utters his famous "To be, or not to be" soliloquy wherein he contemplates

> The heart-ache and the thousand natural shocks
> The flesh is heir to

and that to die is "a consummation devoutly to be wished." Then, as though recognizing his own inhibitions to action and his reaching out for all straws of rationalization as mere intellectual exercises to justify his tardiness, he says,

> Thus conscience does make cowards of us all;
> And thus the native hue of resolution
> Is sicklied o'er with the pale cast of thought,
> And enterprises of great pitch and moment
> With this regard their currents turn awry,
> And lose the name of action.

The play does catch the conscience of the king (III, 2) and Hamlet again is convinced that he can "take the ghost's word for a thousand pound." Yet when he comes upon the king alone, praying, and he draws his sword to pierce him through and thus be "reveng'd," he again holds back with still another rationalization. He sicklies "o'er with the pale cast of thought" his "enterprise [s] of great pitch and moment," and does nothing. For to kill the king while he is "in the purging of his soul," Hamlet argues to himself, is no true revenge. He decides that he must wreak his revenge on the king at the gaming, swearing, when he is drunk asleep, or in his rage, not forgetting particularly, when he is "in the incestuous pleasure of his bed." And so we have another postponement.

A little later (III, 4) when the ghost appears again to "whet [his] almost blunted purpose," Hamlet anticipates with self-accusation, the purpose of his father's ghost's visitation, for he says,

> Do you not come your tardy son to chide
> That, laps'd in time and passion, lets go by

> The important acting of your dread command?

Hamlet is well aware of his lapse "in time and passion," but here again, nothing is said about any external difficulties as barring the fulfillment of his task, as some critics hold. Nor is anything said by Hamlet to indicate any defect in his disposition or temperament that is preventing him from carrying out the "dread command." For the real reason is repressed from his consciousness. He cannot kill the uncle-father-king because of inhibitory forces loosed dynamically from within the Unconscious and rooted deeply in Shakespeare-Hamlet's reactivated unsolved Oedipus complex.

However, an assassination of a father-surrogate does take place by Hamlet. He stabs Polonius (III, 4). But let it be noted here that it is done on the impulse of the moment; that though Hamlet might naturally expect only the king to be in his mother's bedroom, yet he is hidden by the arras and Hamlet pierces an unknown figure and merely asks: "is it the king?" When he finds that it is Polonius he shows little remorse or conscience and says to the dead Polonius:

> Thou wretched, rash, intruding fool, farewell!
> I took thee for thy better;

Not one word is spoken by Hamlet to indicate his disappointment that he has failed in his only real try to kill the king. Perhaps Hamlet unconsciously is really glad that it wasn't the king? Furthermore, is it not more than of accidental significance, that Shakespeare has Hamlet murder Polonius, whom he thought was the uncle-father-king, in the setting of the primal scene, and this in the process of symbolic eavesdropping Voyeurism? From a psychoanalytic standpoint, how often does the son in the Oedipal phase fantasy the primal scene in its complete Oedipus implications including the destruction of the father? At any rate the king still lives, and Hamlet still procrastinates and suffers in his conflict.

Shakespeare proceeds soon to give us another soliloquy (IV, 4) almost precisely paralleling in meaning, the "Hecuba" soliloquy at the end of Act II,—again indicating his preoccupation with his conflict and his irresolution. He beholds the army of Fortinbras ready to "fight for a plot" and die "for a fantasy and trick of fame," and he ponders his own lack of action with pessimism and misanthropy calling man "a beast, no more," "but to sleep and feed." He is reminded

> How all occasions do inform against me
>
> And spur my dull revenge!

He again hints of his cowardice and his tendency to intellectualize. He specifically states that he has "cause and will and strength and means" to carry out his revenge but yet does not accomplish it. He says in rationalization again,

> Now, whe'r it be
> Bestial oblivion, or some craven scruple
> Of thinking too precisely on the event,
> A thought, which, quarter'd hath but one part wisdom,
> And ever three parts coward, I do not know
> Why yet I live to say 'This thing's to do';
> Sith I have cause and will and strength and means
> To do't. Examples gross as earth exhort me:
>
> Rightly to be great
> Is not to stir without great argument
> But greatly to find quarrel in a straw
> When honour's at the stake.

Hamlet's honour, especially by Elizabethan standards, is certainly at stake. He asks in self-beratement

> How stand I then
> That have a father kill'd, a mother stain'd,
> Excitements of my reason and my blood,
> And let all sleep, . . . to my shame . . .

He resolves again for the fourth or fifth time,

> O, from this time forth
> My thoughts be bloody, or be nothing worth!

Yet he does not sweep to his revenge and allows himself to be shipped off to England without the least protest. Indeed, when the king apprises him of their plan to send him to England for his own "special safety" Hamlet actually answers, "Good." What happens then to his numerous resolves to kill the king? Is it not reasonable to suppose that unconsciously Hamlet is even glad to leave Denmark by virtue of the very inhibitory forces that will not let him kill the king? Here is a perfect rationalization to prevent him forever from carrying out the task that he has previously cursed, for ever having been "born to set it right."

When Hamlet returns from England, having yet added another reason to kill the king by virtue of his uncle's plan to assassinate him, he seems still to need reassurance that he is justified. He says to Horatio in enumeration of reasons,

> Does it not, thinks't thee, stand me now upon—
> He that hath kill'd my king and whor'd my mother,
> Popp'd in between the election and my hopes,
> Thrown out of his angle for my proper life,
> And with such cozenage—is't not perfect conscience
> To quit him with this arm? end is't not to be damn'd
> To let this canker of our nature come
> In further evil?

But Hamlet does nothing. He has stewed in his own ironic misanthropy philosophizing about "the noble dust of Alexander" as "stopping a bung-hole," and "Imperious Caesar, dead and turn'd to clay," as stopping "a hole to keep the wind away." He contemplates poor Yorick's skull in his hands and says to Horatio rhetorically;

> Now get you to my lady's chamber and tell her, let her paint an inch thick, to this favour she must come; make her laugh at that

thus reiterating his deep misogyny rooted in his rejection by his own mother and the consequent ambivalent conflict of hate and love toward her.

In point of fact, let it be noted here that Hamlet never really carries out the ghost's command to avenge his father's murder. Rather he actually kills the uncle-father-king *in impulsive re-*

venge for the murder of his mother, knowing that he himself is about to die. Laertes, dying (V, 2), cries out to Hamlet

Thy mother's poison'd
Never to rise again. The king, the king's to blame

It is then, and only then, that he stabs the king and also forces the poisoned cup upon him crying out,

Here, thou incestuous, murderous damned Dane,
Drink off this potion; is thy union here?
Follow my mother.

and to his dead mother,

Wretched queen, adieu!

Thus to the very tragic end, incest, murder, "damned Dane," "wretched queen" dominate Hamlet's soul. The Oedipus triangle has inexorably reached its denouement in death and both Shakespeare and the audience are purged of their own Oedipal emotions.

By way of summary and clarification let us reconstruct now, the full Oedipus tragedy of Prince Hamlet. (1) We can safely state that Hamlet was an only child loved perhaps excessively and indulgently by his mother, for we are given to understand that she "lives almost by his looks." (2) There is no direct evidence in the drama that Hamlet loved his father particularly, the duty to revenge being one of honour and respect, rather than of love. It is not the death of his father that causes Hamlet's melancholy, for Hamlet says little to indicate this. On the other hand, he carries on a love relationship with Ophelia during the two or three months following the father's death. (3) There is evidence to indicate that his mother was always demonstratively affectionate to his father. (4) Early in his childhood development then the natural jealousy of a son toward the father for the exclusive love and attention of the mother must have been exaggerated in the case of Hamlet, and his feelings of rejection and frustration must have been profound indeed, causing an incomplete solution of the Oedipus complex with its wish-fulfillment aspects for the death of the father and the exclusive possession of the love of the mother. Nevertheless, sufficient repression and adjustment has taken place so that Hamlet is able to normally fall in love with a substitute love object in Ophelia. (5) However, at this point, Hamlet's mother hastily marries his uncle. This acts as a trigger mechanism that opens up the old wounds of his childhood Oedipal frustrations that were inadequately transformed in the progress of his psychosexual development. It is as though he has been rejected again by his mother for another father figure,—the uncle-father-king. This results in the neurotic manifestations we have noted and dynamically explained in connection with his actions towards his mother and Ophelia. (6) Then comes the revelation to Hamlet that his father was murdered by the now uncle-father-king. He is sworn to vengeance. Thus the second factor in the Oedipus situation maintains, and Hamlet is actually saddled with the task of the much fantasied wish-fulfillment to kill his now father symbol—the uncle-father-king. (7) He cannot get himself to do this, for there are too many unconscious Oedipal inhibitions aroused. Hence the irresolution and indecisiveness in carrying out his task using dynamically determined rationalizations. He never really does fulfill this task.

CHAPTER XIX

THE CRITICS AND THE PSYCHOANALYTIC INTERPRETATION OF *HAMLET*

The critics cannot satisfactorily explain away the psychoanalytic interpretation of *Hamlet.* But here we must pause and reiterate that to accept even the possibility of the validity of the psychoanalytic approach to Shakespeare's dramas, is to accept the basic tenets upon which applied psychoanalysis stands. We must not forget that in its broadest sense psychoanalysis represents a new world outlook, a new philosophy, a new approach to man and society. As such, its influence on the various departments of knowledge has been tremendous and far-reaching not unlike the impact of Darwinian evolution. In this matter of psychoanalytic Shakespearean criticism we must accept (1) the existence of the Unconscious as a vast reservoir of repressed wishes of the individual as well as of the race; (2) the dynamic power arising out of this Unconscious, as the motivating driving forces governing the individual; (3) the premise that creative, poetic expression is part of this dynamic power transformed by sublimation; (4) that these transformed sublimatory products can be dissected and analyzed in the same way as the dream, the myth, the fantasy, the neurotic symptom—all leading in turn to a revolution of the creative artist himself, and of man in general.

From this standpoint, the generally accepted standards of Shakespearean criticism cannot be made to apply to the ever-growing body of psychoanalytic Shakespearean interpretation, for we are here dealing with an entirely new frame of reference. Indeed, psychoanalytic criticism can admit most of the approaches and hypotheses of the older criticism and yet not be shaken. Dr. Ernest Jones, after noting the numerous interpretations of *Hamlet,* implies this when he states that such interpretations "overlook a characteristic of all Shakespeare's works, and indeed of those of any great artist—namely, the subordination of either current or tendentious interest to the inspiration of the work as an artistic whole."[1]

It makes very little difference, from the psychoanalytic viewpoint, whether Shakespeare was topical or allegorical, or wrote according to Elizabethan ethics, or borrowed his plots, or consciously intended his dramas to mean one thing or another. All these are acceptable, yet the psychoanalysts can validly reserve the right to go beyond the direct evidence of the plays themselves and deduce the unconscious meanings therein without the mutual exclusion of the various viewpoints, for as Dr. Ernest Jones again and again points out, "Hamlet is suffering from an internal conflict the essential nature of which is inaccessible to his introspection . . ."[2] Hamlet's hesitance lies in some unconscious source of repugnance to his task, . . .[3] which source, we hope, we have adequately indicated.

This accounts for the failure of those who attack the psychoanalytic approach to adequately hit their mark. Thus Emil Ludwig in his most vituperative attack upon Freud and psychoanalysis fails utterly to make his point. Discussing Freud's interpretation he states: "Freud . . . imputes to Hamlet the sexual impulses toward his mother plus the obligatory 'death-wish' toward his father. Shakespeare denies the whole thing. Hamlet's specific purpose was to avenge the murder of his noble father."[4] And again, "We state that during the five acts of the play no word or no gesture on the part of Hamlet point in the direction of Freud's conclusion."[5] Even if this were literally true, and Dr. Ernest Jones and others have shown that it *is not,* Ludwig is miserably unsuccessful in proving it, because he does not attack the viewpoint on its own ground.

He particularly fails to attack the premise that unconscious motivations show themselves in a poet's creative work in various ways not apparent to him, and, in fact, especially hidden from him because of the very repugnant nature of these motivations. Ludwig ends his frustrated attack upon the psychoanalytic interpretation by ridicule and derision calling it "lunacy" and "delirious fancy." But then however, Emil Ludwig never claimed to be a literary critic.

A much more tenable criticism of the psychoanalytic interpretation of *Hamlet* comes from the student of Shakespeare, John Ashworth.[6] But here also the point is missed. Ashworth attacks the premise of the psychoanalysts, that Hamlet's 'hesitancy, vacillation,' 'procrastination is caused by an Oedipus conflict, by denying that such hesitation exists at all. He states that "Because he, Freud couldn't perceive Hamlet's motives, he swallowed the nonsense that a workmanlike dramatist like Shakespeare had written a play without showing the motives of the central character."[7] Thus, "Literature is perverted to serve contemporary myth."[8] Yet in almost the same breath he goes on to point out that the hesitation was due to the fact that Hamlet was not sure of the king's guilt till the play is half over, and he did not want to kill an innocent man, that the king was constantly guarded and he could not get at him, and that to the Elizabethan audience such a motivation was well understood and accepted and not a puzzle at all. Now Dr. Ernest Jones has gone to great lengths to show that Hamlet was a man of action in the drama but that only in the matter of carrying out his revenge to murder his uncle-stepfather did he falter and hesitate and offer up excuses, such excuses being actually in the nature of evasions and rationalizations as we have repeatedly proved. No one can question that there is conflict going on in Hamlet's soul. Throughout the play there is deep melancholy and self-beratement expressed by Hamlet, especially in his monologues, leading him to misanthropy, misogyny and to suicidal ideas. And again, it must be emphasized here that it is 'blunted purpose', 'lapsed . . . passion', 'tardy son' that permeates his self-reproaches, and not as Ashworth would have us believe, fear of public opinion, doubt that the Ghost is what it appears to be but rather the masquerade of a demon.

Ashworth concludes by saying ". . . let's not lay that flattering unction to our souls that 'hesitation,' even if allegedly caused by an Oedipus complex, is the act of Shakespeare's here."[9] But even if 'hesitation' did not exist as a factor, yet this would not eliminate the validity of the psychoanalytic approach, there would still remain the fundamental psychoanalytic premises mentioned before, untouched and unshaken. The fact remains that you cannot dissociate a creative literary product from its creator; and just as the archaeologist can often recreate a knowledge of a past civilization by the results of a digging, according to the principles developed by archaeology and its related sciences, so can the psychoanalyst, even more precisely, take the creative literary expressions of writers past and present, and, by means of the psychoanalytic principles developed in our century, better understand and interpret and appreciate the product of the literary mind, as well as of that mind itself. As long as we accept the presence of an unconscious area in the mind, with the various laws related to it, as developed by dynamic psychoanalysis, so then must we accept as legitimate, the various approaches of psychoanalytic criticism to literary artistic creations, and more especially to the great creative expressions of the greatest literary artists, such as Shakespeare.

In the early years of the development, of psychoanalysis and of its application in the various fields of human endeavor, including the area of creative literary expression, understandable rejection of the basic psychoanalytic doctrines was the rule, for psychoanalysis "disturbed the sleep of the world."

This has certainly been true in the field of Shakespearean criticism until more recently. In truth, orthodox Shakespearean criticism generally resisted all psychoanalytic approaches to his dramas in the first half of the twentieth century. As the Shakespearean scholar Norman N. Holland points out, the interpretation of *Hamlet* as an Oedipal tragedy was termed, Freud's "brainstorm"[10] by one critic; and this attitude reflected the general opinion of literary critics of this period.

However, gradually as the psychoanalytic principles began to be understood, and as their influence began to permeate the various areas of our culture psychoanalytic literary criticism has been accepted as a meaningful approach to creative literary expression, and certainly to the works of Shakespeare. Indeed, psychoanalytic criticism has now come of age.[11]

This does not mean that present psychoanalytic criticism has accepted all the original approaches that the earlier analysts used in considering the creative literary material they were handling. The fact is that many changes have taken place in psychoanalytic theory which have made it more palatable to literary criticism in the past twenty years.

Back in 1940 Lionel Trilling though accepting basically the psychoanalytic approaches to literary criticism nevertheless points out some of the fallacies to which he takes exception. He writes of "the inadequacies of the Freudian Method."[12] He especially objects to viewing any literary product as having but one meaning. Trilling writes,

> There is . . . nothing to be quarreled with in the statement that there is an Oedipus situation in *Hamlet* . . . and there is no reason to quarrel with Freud's conclusion when he undertakes to give us the meaning of *King Lear* . . . to be found in the tragic refusal of an old man to "renounce love, choose death and make friends with the necessity of dying" . . . but it is not *the* meaning of *King Lear* anymore than the Oedipus motive is *the* meaning of *Hamlet*.
>
> There is no single meaning to any works of art; . . . historical and personal experience show it (this) to be true.[13]

"Besides, " he continues, ". . . the audience partly determines the meaning of the work."[14]

Trilling also criticizes validly the attempt at exact biographical knowledge of Shakespeare through the study of a drama such as *Hamlet* as though it were a dream. Dr. Wertham[15] calls this, "psychoanalysis without psychoanalysis" since free association of a dead creative literary artist is impossible. Trilling states that "one research into the mind of the artist is simply not practicable . . . the investigation of his unconsicous intention as it exists apart from the work itself."[16]

Trilling goes on to point out in criticising Dr. Jones' ideas on *Hamlet,* that he has focussed on this one drama as expressing "the core of Shakespeare's philosophy and outlook as no other work of his does," and that ". . . all the contradictory or modifying testimony of the other plays is dismissed on the basis of

Dr. Jones's acceptance of the peculiar position which he believes Hamlet occupies in Shakespeare's canon"[17] and that *"therefore* . . . anything which will give us the key to the inner meaning of the play (*Hamlet*) will necessarily give us the clue to much of the deeper workings of Shakespeare's mind" (the italics are Lionel Trilling's). Trilling considers this as an inadmissible judgment[18] of Dr. Jones; and he affirms that Shakespeare did not *intend* the Oedipus motive"[19] in *Hamlet,* and further "that it is *Hamlet* which affects us, not the Oedipus motive."[20] Trilling hastens to point out:

"Of late years, the more perceptive psychoanalysts have surrendered the early pretensions of their teachers to deal 'scientifically with literature"[21] and he mentions approvingly Dr. Franz Alexander's essay on *Henry IV* on the basis that it does not pretend to "solve" but only to illuminate the subject," that "it has the tact to *accept* the play, and not like Dr. Jones's study of *Hamlet,* search for a "hidden motive" and a "deeper working."

Trilling concludes his essay on "Freud and Literature' 'with an implied acceptance of the basic tenets of psychoanalysis:

> If then, we can accept neither Freud's conception of the place of art in life, nor his application of the analytical method, what is it that he contributes to our understanding of art or to its practice? In my opinion what he contributes outweighs his errors; it is of the greatest importance and it lies in no specific statement that he makes about art but is rather implicit in his whole conception of the mind.[22]

Professor Holland, already mentioned, is even more specific in his conclusion that "psychoanalysis offers a rich dynamic approach to all aspects of literature from the minutiae or particular words to the grand hermetic mysteries of literary value . . ."[23]

We cannot help but feel that the psychoanalysts are correct in viewing Shakespeare's dramas from their standpoint. Only future history will determine the final acceptability of their doctrines. And upon this will depend the truth of their interpretations of Shakespeare, and of *Hamlet* particularly. In the meantime, let us point out that the psychoanalysts do not hold up Shakespeare as a 'neuropsychiatrist' or as having any special knowledge in this field, as so many other idolatrous medical men have done. They more rightly look at him as a great creative artist, through the fire of whose soul, universal racial experience was wrought into great drama. On this he stands above all interpretation.

NOTES AND REFERENCES

CHAPTER XIX

1. "A Psycho-analytic Study of **Hamlet,**" **op. cit.,** p. 8.
2. **Op. cit.,** p. 29.
3. **Op. cit.,** p. 73.
4. **Ludwig, Emil, Doctor Freud,** New York; **Hellman-Williams & Co., 1947, p. 237.**
5. **Ibid., p. 238.**
6. **"Oliver, Freud and Hamlet." Atlantic Monthly. 183: No. 5. May 1949, pp. 30-33.**
7. **Op. cit., p. 30.**
8. **Ibid.**
9. **Op. cit., p. 33.**
10. **Holland, Norman N., "Shakespearean Tragedy and The Three** Ways" of **Psychoanalysis and Literature.** An anthology edited **by Henrik M. Ruitenbeek, E. P. Dutton & Co., Inc., New York,** 1964, pp. 207-217, p. 209. Reprinted from the **Hudson Review,** Summer, 1962. Vol. XV, No. 2.
11. Manheim, Leonard, "Psychoanalytic Criticism Comes of Age" A review of Norman N. Holland's **The Dynamics of Literary Response,** Oxford Univ., 1968, in **Psychiatry and Social Science Review.** Vol. 2. No. 11 pp. 9-11. Professor Manheim considers Norman Holland's book "the definitive work in Pyschoanalytic Criticism."
12. Trilling, Lionel, "Freud and Literature" in **The Liberal Imagination,** New York. The Viking Press, 1940. Reprinted in **Psychoanalysis and Literature, op. cit.,** p. 264.
13. **Op. cit.,** p. 263.
14. Ibid., p. 264.
15. Wertham, Fredric, "An Unconscious Determinant In Native Son, in **Psychoanalysis and Literature, op. cit.,** p. 321.
16. **Op. cit.,** p. 264.
17. **Ibid., p. 265.**
18. **Ibid.**
19. **Ibid. (italics are mine)**
20. **Ibid., p. 266.**
21. **Ibid., p. 265.**
22. **Ibid., p. 266.**
23. Holland, Norman N., "Shakespearean Tragedy," in **Psychoanalysis and Literature, op. cit., p. 217.**

CHAPTER XX

CONCLUSION

Shakespearean criticism in the medical and psychiatric aspects has long needed review and revision. We have waded through a vast field of medical-psychological comment. We have focused the searchlight of the historical method upon Shakespeare's dramas and related him organically to the age in which he lived. We have seen how the currents and thought patterns of Elizabethan England flowed through the channels of Shakespeare's mind and became woven into his dramas. Shakespeare had his roots in this Elizabethan England and was only a child of his age; and the medical and psychiatric commentators who have raised him out of this age have merely projected their own idolatry into an appropriate figure. The status of sixteenth-century medicine and psychiatry are well exemplified in Shakespeare's dramas and may be studied in relation to medical and psychiatric history.

The most important new approach to Shakespeare within the last half century is the psychoanalytic interpretation. Unfortunately, for a long time, most Shakespearean scholars had either been violently opposed to this approach or had completely ignored it. The dominant historical criticism, by its very nature, would tend in this directon. Nevertheless, it is a valid approach to Shakespeare's dramas, within a new frame of reference. As a matter of fact, Shakespearean Psychoanalytic Criticism is now coming of age and is contributing greatly to the understanding of Shakespeare and his works. As to the previously dominant historical criticism, it may be in danger of becoming a prisoner of its own system, and like the Romantic Criticism of the previous century project historical meanings into our poet's dramas that are not there at all.

At any rate, once and for all, let us shake ourselves free from the anaesthesia of reason often brought on by fanatic Shakespearean commentators. From a logical standpoint, is it necessary to make of Shakespeare a great physician, a great scientist, a great psychiatrist? The sane attitude is this: that in the works of the great poet we have a keen brain, an observing mind, a general education, a universality of feeling, and above all, a mighty genius especially for using language; that out of these attributes, and these alone, he fashioned unconcernedly the great works we know by the name of Shakespeare.

BIBLIOGRAPHY

An attempt has been made here to gather together the most nearly comprehensive bibliography on the subject. It is obvious, however that such a task must necessarily fall far short of its aim. A complete bibliography on the psychopathology in Hamlet alone would require a whole volume. Nevertheless, this bibliography is presented as an ambitious attempt along these lines. For our purpose, we have made free use of the British Museum **Catalogue,** Detroit Public Library **Catalogue, Catalogue** of the Carnegie Library of Pittsburgh, Peabody Institute Library Index, **Catalogue of the Surgeon-General's Library, Poole's Index, International Index, Reader's Guide, Dramatic Index, Magazine Subject Index, Catholic Periodical Index, Index Medicus, Cumulative Book Index, Subject Index to Periodicals of the American Library Association, Digest Shakespeareana,** to 1866 of the N.Y. Shakespeare Society, **Shakespeare—Jahrbuch der Deutschen Shakespeare Gesellschaft, Jaggard's Shakespeare Bibliography, Magg's Shakespeare and** Shakespeareana, H.B. Meyer's **A Brief Guide to the Literature of Shakespeare,** comprising books in the Library of Congress, The Wellcome Historical Medical Library's quarterly, **Current Work in The History of Medicine,** etc., etc.

GENERAL WORKS

Adams, James Q., **William Shakespeare,** Boston: Houghton, 1923.—**Pre-Shakespearean Dramas,** N.Y., 1924.

Alden, Raymond, M., **Shakespeare,** Duffield and Co., New York, 1922.

Allen, Percy, **Shakespeare and Chapman as Topical Dramatists,** Cecil Palmer, 1929.

Babcock, R. W., **The Genesis of Shakespeare Idolatry,** Chapel Hill, University of North Carolina, 1931.

Barley, John, **Shakespeare,** Longmans, Green & Co., New York 1929.

Boas, Frederick, S., **Shakespeare and His Predecessors,** Charles Scribner's Sons.

Brady, G. E., **Problems of Hamlet,** Oxford Univ. Press, 1928.

Bradley, A. C., **Shakespearean Tragedy,** N.Y.: The Macmillan Co., 1928.

Brandes, George, **William Shakespeare, A Critical Study,** The MacMillan Co., 1898.

Bridges, H. J., **Our Fellow Shakespeare,** A.C. McClurg & Co., Chicago, 1918.

Buchner, A., **Hamlet Le Doncis,** Paris: Librarie Hachette and Cis., N.D.

Campbell, Lilly B., **Shakespeare's Tragic Heroes, Slaves of Passion,** Cambridge Univ. Press, 1930.
Chambers, E. K., **William Shakespeare,** London: Sidgwick & Jackson, Ltd. 1925.
— **William Shakespeare, A Study of Facts and Problems,** Oxford Univ. Press, 1931.
— **Shakespeare: A Survey,** Oxford Univ. Press., N.Y., 1926.
Craig, Hardin, **Shakespeare,** Scott Foreman & Co., New York, 1931.
Dowden, Edward. **Essays Modern and Elizabethan,** J. M. Dent Sons, 1910.
— **Shakespeare, His Mind and Art,** Harper & Bros., New York, 1878.
Ebisch, Walttner and Schucking, Levin L., **A Shakespeare Bibliography,** Oxford: Clarendon Press, 1931.
Figgis, D., **Shakespeare: A Study,** 1911.
Gervinus, George G., **Shakespeare Commentaries,** trans., F.E. Burnett, New York., Scriber, Welford & Armstrong, 1875.
Grey, Zachary, **Critical Historical and Explanatory Notes on Shakespeare,** London, Richard Manby, 1754, Vol. 1.
Harris, F., **The Man Shakespeare,** Mitchell Kemerley, N. Y., 1919.
Hazlitt, W., **Characters of Shakespeare's Plays,** Everyman's Library, E. P. Dutton & Co., 1926.
Hirschfield, I., **Koenig Lear,** Danzig, 1882.
Hudson, H. N., **Lectures of Shakespeare,** Baker & Scribner, 1848.
Ingleby, C. N., **Shakespeare's Centurie of Prayes** (1591-1693), London: Scribner, 1879.
Kittredge, George L., **Shakespeare,** Harvard Univ. Press, Cambridge, 1916.
Knight, Charles, **A History of Opinion on the Writings of Shakespeare,** (Introductory vol. in **Studies of Shakespeare** and cabinet edition.) London, 1847.
Lamb, C., **Essays on the Tragedies of Shakespeare,** 1812.
Lanier, Sidney, **Shakespeare and His Forerunners,** N. Y., Doubleday Page & Co., 1902.
Mathew, Frank, **An Image of Shakespeare,** Moffat Yard & Co., N. Y., 1923.
Matthews, Brander, **Shakespeare As a Playwright,** Scribner & Sons, N.Y., 1916.
Neilson, W. A., **Facts About Shakespeare,** N.Y., Macmillan & Co., 1913.
Nicol, Allardyce, **Studies in Shakespeare,** Harcourt Brace & Co., N.Y., 1928.
Pollard, W., **The Works of Chaucer,** London, Macmillan Co., 1925.
Raleigh, Sir Walter, **Shakespeare,** London, Macmillan Co., 1928.
Ralli, Augustus, **A History of Shakespearean Criticism,** Oxford Univ. Press, 1932.

Richardson, W., Essays on Shakespeare's Dramatic Characters of Richard III, King Lear and Timon With Observations On Hamlet, J. Murray, 1784.

— A Philosophical Analysis of Some of Shakespeare's Remarkable Characters, London: J. Murray, 1780.

Schucking, Levin L., Character Problems of Shakespeare's Plays, Henry Holt & Co., New York, 1922.

Sherman, L.A., What is Shakespeare?, Macmillan Co., N.Y., 1902.

Smith, D. Nichol, Shakespeare Criticism, Oxford Univ. Press, 1916.

Stoll, Edgar E., Shakespeare Studies, Macmillan Co., N.Y., 1927.

— "Certain Fallacies and Irrelevancies in the Literary Scholarship of the day", (pp. 216-218), in his Poets and Playwrights, Minneapolis, 1930.

Swinburne, Algernon, A Study of Shakespeare, Chatto & Windus, Piccadilly, London, 1895.

Ulrici, Herman, Shakespeare's Dramatic Art, trans. by L.D. Schmitz, London, George Bell & Sons, 1876.

Wales, Julia G., "Character and Action in Shakespeare," Univ. of Wisconsin Studies, No. 18.

Wilson, J.D., The Essential Shakespeare, 1932.

WORKS DEALING WITH SHAKESPEARE'S MEDICAL AND OTHER KNOWLEDGE

Books and Pamphlets

Aubert, H., Shakespeare als Mediciner. London: Williams and Norgate, 1875.

Beisly, S., Shakespeare's Garden. London: Longmans, Green, Roberts and Green, 1864.

Bloom, J. H., Shakespeare's Garden. London: Mathuen & Co., 1903.

Bucknill, J. C., The Medical Knowledge of Shakespeare. London: Longmans & Co., 1860.

Cantaz, A., La Toxicologie dans les drames de Shakespeare. Paris: 1911.

Cartwright, Robert, The Footsteps of Shakespeare. London: John Russel Smith, 1888.

Chesney, J.P., Shakespeare as a Physician. Chicago: J.H. Chambers & Co., 1884.

Clark, C., Shakespeare and Science. Birmingham: Cornish Brod., Ltd., 1929.

Clesco, S. G., Medizinische Blumenless aus Shakespeare. Stuttgart: J. F. Blumhardt, 1865.

Ellacomb, A. N., The plant lore and Gardencraft of Shakespeare.

Epstein, Dr. Harry., William Shakespeare, M.D. Newark: Lasky Co., Inc., 1932.

Field, B. R., **Medical Thoughts of Shakespeare.** Eaton, P.: Andrews and Clifton, 1885.

Gill, D.C., **Certain Aspects of the Treatment of Death in Shakespeare's Later Plays.** (Master's thesis in M.A. 1931). N.Y.: Columbia U. Library.

Grindon, L.H., **The Shakespeare Flora.** Manchester: Palmer & Howe, 1883.

Morgan, N., Shakespeare: **Law and Medicine in his Plays.** N.Y.: W. E. Benjamin, 1888.

Moyes, Dr. J., **Medicine and Kindred Arts in the Plays of Shakespeare.** Glasgow: MacLehose, 1896.

Owen, O.W., **Sir Francis Bacon's Cipher Story.** Detroit: Howard Publishing Co., 1893.

Savage, F. G., **The Flora and Folklore of Shakespeare.** Cheltenham, 1923.

Schelenz, H., **Shakespeare und sein Wissen auf den Gibieten der Arznei.** Leipzig: Leopold Voss, 1914.

Simpson, R.R. **Shakespeare and Medicine,** E. & S. Livingston, Ltd., Edinburgh and London, 1959.

Thomson, W., **Bacon and Shakespeare on Vivisection.** Melburne: Sands and McDougal, 1881.

Wainright, J. W., **The Medical and Surgical Knowledge of William Shakespeare.** New York: the author, 1915.

Yearsley, Macleod, **Doctors in Elizabethan Drama,** London: John Bale, Sons and Danielsson, Ltd., 1933.

Zuno, G., **Shakespeare e la scienza modernia Studio medicopsicologico e giuridico.** Messina: 1897.

Periodicals

(Anon.) "Shakespeare as a physician and metaphysician," **DeBow's Commercial Rev.,** (New Orleans XXVII, 705.)

(Anon.) "The Ars Medendi of Shakespeare," **Practiconer,** LXXXV (1910), 251.

(Anon.) "Shakespeare's Insane Root," (Editorial), **Brit. Med. Journ.,** (1907), 29.

(Anon.) "Shakespeare on Death" (Editorial), **Spec.,** LV (Oct. 7, 1882), 1282.

Blake, E. V., "The Impediment of Adipose: a celebrated case," **Pop. Sc. Month.,** XVII (1886), 60.

Bradnack, F., "Shakespeare on the Practice of Medicine," **Med. Record,** XI (1879), 116.

Bristow, W.J. "Shakespeare as a Physiologist as Evidenced by His Allusions to the Circulation of the Blood," **South Med. & Surg.,** LXLIV (May, 1932) 274-6.

Bock, G., "Shakespeare and Medicine," **Ticlsckr. f.d. norske Laegefor, Kristiania, XXXVI** (1916), 442-6.

Cantaz, A., "La toxicologie dans les drames de Shakespeare," **R. Scient.** (Paris), XI (1909), 203-09.

Cerna, D., "Shakespeare and the Circulation of the Blood," **Med. Rec. & Ann., XXIV** (J1., 1927), 443.

Chesterton, F., "Pathology in Shakespeare," **Sat. R., CXXII** (1916), 179, 199, 200.

Chesterton, F., "Hamlet and the Psychoanalyst," in **Fancies and Fads** (1923), 24, 41.

Clarke, W. B., "Shakespearean Medicine," **Am. Homoeop. (N. Y.),** XXIV (L898), 377.

Clarke-Williams, M. J., "Shakespeare and Medicine," **Sf. Barth. Hosp. J., LII** (Apr. 1948), 45-48.

Clippingdale, S. D., "Shakespeare and Medicine," **Lancet, I** (1916), 923.

Cooke, J., "The Astrology of Shakespeare," **MacMillan's Mag.,** (1895), p. 5.

Dodek, S. M., "Shakespeare's Knowledge of Medicine," **Med. Ann. Dist. Columbia,** I (Dec. 1932), 317-321.

Donnellan, P. S., "Medical Allusions in Shakespeare's Plays," **Amer. Med. Phila.,** III (1902), 278.

Dowden, E. "Shakespeare as a Man of Science," **Liv. Age, CCXXXIV** (1902), 513; CCXXV (1902), 121. Also in **Essays, Modern and Elizabethan.** J. M. Dent and Sons, 1910, pp. 282-307.

Early, P. V., "Birth of Macduff," **China Med. J.,** XLV (Mr., 1931), 253-56.

Earp, S. E., "Some Medical References in Shakespeare," **Med. Pickwick,** (Saranac Lake, N. Y.) I (1915), 243.

Edgar, I. I., "Shakespeare's Medical Knowledge," **Ann. Med. Hist.,** VI (1934), 150-158.

— "Medical Practice and the Physician in Elizabethan England and in Shakespeare's Dramas," **Med. Life, XLI** (1934), 331.

— "Shakespeare's Medical Knowledge with Particular Reference to his Delineations of Madness," VI (March, 1934), 150-158.

— "Shakespeare's Psychopathological Knowledge," **The Journ of Abn. and Soc. Psych., XXX** (1935), 70-83.

— "The Acquisition of Shakespeare's Medical and Psychopathological Knowledge," **Canad. Med. Assoc. Journ., XXXIII** (1935), 319-326.

— "Shakespeare's Medical Knowledge: A Study in Criticism," **Ann. Med. Hist.,** VII (1935), 519-531.

— "Elizabethan Conceptions of the Physiology of the Circulation," **Ann. Med. Hist.,** VIII (1936) 355-370, 456-457.

— "Shakespeare, Harvey and the Circulation of the Blood," **Med. Record, CXXXXIV** (July, 1936), 37-39.

Emery, D. W., "Shakespeare and Nature," **Sat. N.,** LI (April, 1924), 644.

Engeln, O. D. Van, "Shakespeare, the Observer of Nature," **Sci. Month.,** II (Je., 1916), 573.

Field, B. R., "Medico-Shakespearean Fanaticism," **N. Y. Shakespeariana,** VI (Jan., 1889), 1-19.

Foville, A., "Les Medicine dans les drames de Shakespeare," **Gaz. hebd. de med.** (Paris), S2. XXII (1885), 561, 577, 609.

Fraser-Harris, D. F., "Biology in Shakespeare," **Scient. Month.,** XXXIV (Jan., 1932), 54-68.

Gettchell, A. C., "The Medical Knowledge of Shakespeare," **Boston Med. & S.J.,** CLVI (1907), 65, 109.

Gillespie, J. C., "Medical Notes about Shakespeare and his times," **Edinburgh Med. J.,** XX (1875), 1061.

Goldbloom, A., "Shakespeare and Pediatrics," **Am. J. Dis. of Child.,** LI (March, 1936), 653-665.

Green-Armytage, V. B., "Gynecology and Obstetrics in Shakespeare," **J. Obst. & Gynec. Brit. Emp.** XXXVI (1930), 272.

Green-Armytage, V., "Gynecology and Tropical Diseases in Shakespeare," **Indian Med. Gaz.,** LXV (1930), 333.

Greenwood, G. G., "Bacon, Shakespeare, Harvey and Dr. Knott," **Westm.,** CLIX (May, 1903), 573; CLXIV (Nov., 1905), 552.

Griffiths, L.M., "Shakespeare and the Practice of Medicine," **Ann. Med. Hist.,** III (1921), 50.

Griffiths, L.M., "Shakespeare and Medical Sciences," **Bristol Med. Chir. J.,** V (1887), 225-256.

Gwynn, E., "Shakespeare and Sanitation," **Pub. Health** (London), XI (1898), 695.

Hackman, L.K.K., "Shakespeare and Harvey," **Lancet,** II (1888), 789.

Hagemann, J., "Shakespeare's Conception of Medical Topics," **Med. Rec.,** LXXXIX (Apr., 1916), 780.

Hall, J., "Shakespeare's Family as Patients," **Bristol Med. Chir. J.,** IX (1891), 238.

Harris, D. F., "Shakespeare: His Knowledge of Biological Science as revealed in his plays," **Univ. of Mich. Publ.** XV (Dec., 1916), 552.

Harris, D. F., "Biology in Shakespeare," **Discovery** III (May-Je., 1922), 132, 160; also in **Stratford on Avon Herald** (Oct. 21, 1927), "Shakespeare's Medical Knowledge defined."

Harrison, W.A., "Hamlet's Juice of Cursed Hebona," **Tr. New Shakespeare Soc.** (1880-6), 21.

Hawley, R.N., "The Medical Lore of Shakespeare," **Med. Age,** X (1892), 740, 753.

Hexheimer, K., "Shakespeare und die Hautkrankeiten," **Dermatolog-Wochenschrift**, XLI, 1599.

Hirschberg, J., "Shakespeare — Anmerkung eines Augenarztes," **Shakespeare Jahrbuch**, LVI (1920), 95-105.

Howath, W. J., "Shakespeare's References to Public Health and Kindred Subjects," **Pub. Health** (London), XXVIII (1914), 33.

Kahn, Max, "Shakespeare's Knowledge of Medicine," **N. Y. Med. Journ.**, XCII (Oct. 29, 1910), 863.

Knott, J., "The Medical Knowledge of Shakespeare," **Med. Press and Circular**, CIV (1892), 78, 101; also in **Westm. R.**, CLIX (Apr., 1903), 436.

Knott, J., "The Scientific Aspect of the Bacon-Shakespeare Controversy," **Med. Press & Circ.**, N. S. LXXIV (1902), 392.

Leftwich, R. W., "John Hall, physician," in **Shakespeare's Handwriting and Other Papers** (pp. 61-81), Worthing: 1910.

Lilly, M. P., "Good Drink Makes Good Blood," **Mod. Lang. Notes**, XXXIX (1924), 153-55.

Lindley, Walter, "Shakespeare's Son-in-law," **Med. Rec.**, LXXXIX (1916), 910.

Line, W. H., "Shakespeare's Doctors," **Midland Med. J.** (Birmingham), V (1906), 86.

Lippman, E. O. Von, "Medizinisches aus Shakespeare," **N. Med. Presse Berl.**, II (1902), 235.

Lippman, E. O. Von, "Medizinisches aus Othello," **N. Med. Presse Berl.**, II (1902), 88.

Lockhart, F.A., "Medicine on Shakespeare," **Vermont Med. Month.**, XII (1906), 257.

Luce, M., "Botany in Shakespeare," **19th Cent.**, XCVIII (Oct., 1925), 591.

Macht, D.I., "Pharmacological Appreciation of Shakespeare's Hamlet," **Bull. John Hopk. Hosp.**, XXIX (1918), 165.

Manzano, F. Escobar, "Medicine in Shakespeare's Works," **Gac. med. espan.**, XIX (May, 1945) 137-42.

Melvin, G. S., "The Medicine of Shakespeare," **Maritime Med. News** (Halifax) XXII (1909), 51.

Meyer, A.W., "The Physician and Surgeon in Shakespeare," **Bull. John Hopk. Hosp.**, XVIII (1907), No. 200, p. 430.

Meyer, A.W., "Some Characteristics of the Medicine in Shakespeare," **Bull. John Hopk. Hosp.**, XVIII (1097), No. 190, p. 1.

Minges, G., "Medicine in Shakespeare," **St. Louis Clinique**, XVII (1904), 263.

Montgomery, M., "Cursed Hebona," as Guaicuin offician or Lignum Vital in Shakespeare's Hamlet, I, V, 62, Bale, 1921.

Morgan, W.G., "Shakespeare's Knowledge of Medicine," **Gen. Mag. and Hist. Chronicle Phila.**, XXXII (1930), 307-323.

Morton, M.D., "Shakespeare on Death," **Amer. Sur. M.** (Dec., 1897), 372-5.
Nicholson, B., "Hamlet's 'Cursed Hebenon,'" **Tr. New Shakespeare Soc.** (1879), pp. 21, 218.
Owen, O.W., "The Medicine in Shakespeare," **Physician and Surgeon** (Detroit), XV (1893), 289; also in **Trans. Detroit Medical and Library Assn.** (1893), Det., Mich.
Packard, F. J., "References to Syphilis in the Plays of Shakespeare," **Ann. Med. Hist.**, VI (1924), 194 (No. 2).
Pomeranz, H., "Medicine in Shakespearean Plays and Era," **Med. Life**, XXXXI, 351, 479.
Richardson, B. W., "Shakespeare and the Pia Mater, with a note on the originality of Harvey," **Lancet**, II (1888), 757; also in **Asclepiad** (Lond., 1886), pp. 386, 388.
Rogers, J.F., "Shakespeare as Health Teacher," **Scient. Month.**, II (Jel, 1916), 589.
Rorke, J., "Medical quotations of Shakespeare," **West Lancet** (San Francisco), VIII (1879), 481, 541.
Scarlett, E.P., "Shakespeare's Son-in-Law: Doctor John Hall," **Canad. Med. Assoc. J.**, XXXXIII (Nov., 1940), 482-8.
Schelenz, H., "Shakespeare und die von ihm genanten alkoholischen Getranke," **Berl. d. deutsch. pharm. Gesellsch. Berl.**, XXI (1911), 373-408.
Schelenz, H., "Shakespeare's Kenntnisse auf dem Gebiete der chemi," **Ber. d. deutsch. pharm. Gesellsch. Berl.**, XXII (1912), 268, 359; XXIII (1913), 441.
Stearns, C.W., "The Medical Knowledge of Shakespeare," in **The Shakespeare Treasury** (N.Y.: G. P. Putnam Sons, 1869, 1878).
Sigismund, R., "Die Medizinische Kenntniss Shakespeares," **Cor. Bl. d. allg. arztl Ver. V. Thuringen**, X (1882), 357-67; XI (1882), 1-17.
Sigismund, R., "Die Medizinische Kenntniss Shakespeares," **Shakespeare Jahrbuch**, XVI (1881), 39-143; XVII (1882), 6-66; XVIII (1883), 36-80.
Stender, J.L. "Master Doctor Caius," **Bull. Hist. Med.**, VIII (Jan. 1940), 133-8.
Stronach, G., "The Scientific Aspects of the Bacon-Shakespeare Controversy," **Med. Press and Cir.**, N. S. LXXIV (1902), 341.
Tannenbaum, S.A., "A medical Absurdity in King Lear," **Sat. R. Lit.**, VIII (Aug. 8, 1931), 46.
Thiersch, S.A., "Medizinische Glossen zum Hamlet," **Nord U. Sud. Berl.**, VI (1878), 231.
Thomas, C.E., "Shakespeare and Teeth," **Brit. Dent. Journ.** (Lond.), XC (1919), 845; XCI (1920), 14.
Thomson, St. C., "Shakespeare as a Guide in the Art and Practice of

Medicine," **Canadian Med. Assn. J.,** IX (1919,) 901.

Thomson, St. C., "Shakespeare and Medicine," **Annual Oration, Med. Soc. Lond.,** 1916, **Trans. Med. Soc. Lond.,** 1916.

Thomson, St. C., "Shakespeare and Medicine," abridged from **Annual Oration, Med. Soc. Lond.,** 1916, **Lancet,** CXC (May 6, 1916), 961-2.

Thomson, St. C., "Shakespeare's References to Consumption," **Brit. Med. J. Tuberc.,** XI (July, 1917), 95.

Turner, L. J., "The Signs of Approaching Death Illustrated by Shakespeare," **Shakespeariana,** I (1884), 274-76.

Venables, G., "Ophelia's Madness," **Library Mag.** (Apr., 1885), 293.

Vest, W. E., "William Shakespeare, Syphilographer," **West Virginia Med. J.** XXXIV (March, 1938), 130-7.

Vest, W. E., "William Shakespeare, Therapeutist," **South. M. J.,** XXXVII (Aug., 1944), 457-64.

Vest, W. E., "William Shakespeare, Therapeutist," **The Canadian Doctor,** Dec., 1946, pp. 36-41.

Vigorous, A., "La Pathologie Mentale dans les drames de Shakespeare," **Ann. Med. Psychol.** (Paris), SX: X (1818), 153, 225.

Wadd, W., "Commentary on Shakespeare's Medical Knowledge," **Med. Times and Gaz.,** II (1885), 230.

Wadd, W., "Medico-Chirurgical Commentary on Shakespeare," **Quart. J. of Science of the Royal Institute,** No. 234 (1824), (1829).

Wachholz, L., "Medicolegal Problems in Shakespeare," **Bertrage Z. Gerichtlichen Medizin.,** VIII (1928), 338.

Wainwright, J.W., "A Few Quotations from Shakespeare," **Med. Rec.,** LXVI (1904), 135.

Wainwright, J., "The Medical and Surgical Knowledge of Shakespeare," **Dietetics & Hygiene Gaz. N.Y.,** XXII (1906), 463, 527, 591, 661, 725; XXIII (1907) 21, 85, 149, 213, 279.

Wellstood, F.C., "Dr. John Hall: Shakespeare's Son-in-law," **Lancet,** (Dec. 7, 1935), 1332-3.

West, J.F., "William Shakespeare from a Surgeon's point of view," **Birmingham M. Rev.,** N.S., IV (1881), 265-86.

White, R.G., "Anatomizing of Shakespeare," **Atlantic Mo.,** LIII (1882-7), 595, 815; LIV (1882-7), 25, 313.

Wilson, H.S., "Three desperate deaths in Shakespeare," **Theatre,** I (1885), 159.

Winckel, F., "Shakespeare's Gynakologie," **Samml. klin. Vortr. Leipzig,** (1906) N.F. (No. 441), X Gynak, CLXVI (1906) 151-173.

Witt, W.H., "Medical References in Shakespeare," **J. Tenn. M.A.J.,** XXXI (Jan., 1938), 1-10.

Wolff, L., "Medical Conceptions in Shakespeare's Works," **Hygiea,** XCIX (March 31, 1937), 177-204.

Yearsley, M., "Death of Shakespeare," **Lancet, II** (Sept. 5, 1931), 562-63.

WORKS DEALING WITH SHAKESPEARE'S PSYCHO-PATHOLOGICAL KNOWLEDGE

Books

(Anon.) **Shakespeare e la Scienza Moderna, Studio Medico psicologica e giuridico.** Messina, 1897.

(Anon.) **Was Hamlet Mad?** Melbourne, 1867, Lond.: 1871.

(Anon.) **A Treatise on Mental derangement.** (Lear, Ophelia & Edgar) London: Longman's, 1823.

Anderson, A.G., **Hamlet: A Study,** Lond: R. W. Simpson, N. D.

Barnard, F., **Science and the Soul, The Psychology of Shakespeare as Revealed in the Sonnets.** Stratford-on Avon: Selwyn and Blount, 1918.

Beller, H., **Zur Hamlet frage.** Dresden: C. Bierfon, 1882.

Benedict, R.R., **The Mystery of Hamlet.** Philadelphia: J.B. Lippincott and Co., 1910.

Blackmore, S. A., **A Great Soul in Conflict: A critical Study of Shakespeare's Masterwork (Macbeth).** Chicago: Scott, Foresman & Co., 1914.

Blunden, E., **Shakespeare's Significances.** Oxford University Press, 1929.

Bucknill, J.C., **The Mad Folk of Shakespeare.** London: Macmillan & Co., 1867.

Bucknill, J.C., **The Psychology of Shakespeare.** London: Exeter, 1859.

Connolly, J., **A Study of Hamlet.** London: Moxan, 1863.

Cooke, M.W., **The Theme of Hamlet.** Privately printed, 1887.

Cooke, M.W., **The Human Mystery in Hamlet.** New York: Ford, Howards and Hulbert, 1888.

Coriat, I.H., **The Hysteria of Lady Macbeth.** Boston: The Four Seas Co., 1920.

Cox, E.W., **The Psychology of Hamlet.** London: The Psychology Society of Gt. Britain, 1879.

Cox, W.H., **Analyses of Othello, Hamlet, Macbeth and King Lear.** Baltimore: Cushings & Bailey, 1886.

D'Alfonso, N.R., **La Personalita di Amlets** (note psicologiche). Torino: Fratelli Bocca, 1894.

D'Alfonso, N.R., **Note Psicologiche al Macbeth di Shakespeare.** Torino: Roma, 1892.

D'Alfonzo, N.R., **La Follia di Ofelia.** Torino: Fratelli Bocca, 1896.

Davis, W.J., **Philosophical Explanation of Shakespeare's Hamlet.** Amsterdam: J. D. Brouwer, 1867.

Delbruck, A., **Ueber Hamlet's Wahnsinn.** Hamburg: 1893.

Dorynne, J., **The True Ophelia.** New York: G.P. Putnam's Sons, 1914.

Farren, G.O., **Essays on the Varieties of Mania, exhibited by the Characters of Hamlet, Ophelia, Lear and Edgar.** London: Dean & Munday, 1833.

Frank, H., **The Tragedy of Hamlet, a Psychological Study.** Boston: Sherman, French & Co., 1910.

Freud, Sigmund. **The Basic Writings of Sigmund Freud.** New York: The Modern Library, 1938.

Freud, Sigmund, **Collected Papers,** Vol. IV. London: The Hogarth Press, 1948.

Friedrich, G., **Hamlet und seine Gemutskrankeit.** Heidelberg: Georg. Weiss, 1899.

Gallenkamp, W., **Hamlet ein Sexuelles Problem.** Frankfort Am Main: Die Umschau, 1910.

Gelkes, A.H., **Electra and Macbeth.** Lond: Longmans, Green & Co., 1880.

Goll, B.A., **Verbrecher bei Shakespeare.** Stuttgart: 1908.

Gelkes, A.H., **Electra and Macbeth.** Lond.: Longmans, Green & Co., 1909.

Hendricks, Ives., **Facts and Theories of Psychoanalysis.** New York: Alfred A. Knopf, 1939.

Hernon, J., **The Query "Was Hamlet Mad"? fully answered** (etc.) Exeter: 1864.

Hoche, A.E., "Shakespeare und die psychiatrie." In his **Aus der Werkstatt.** Muenchen, 1935, pp. 25-37.

Hoffman, F., **Freudianism and the Literary Mind.** Louisiana State Univ. Press, 1945.

Horne, R.H., **Madness as Treated by Shakespeare.** Lond.: 1849.

Horne, R.H., **Was Hamlet Mad?** Lond.: T.H. Lacy, 1867.

Jones, E., **Das Problem des Hamlet und der odipus-Komplex.** Leipzig: F. Deuticke, 1911.

Kellogg, A. O., **Shakespeare's Delineations of Insanity, Imbecility and Suicide.** N.Y.: Hurd & Houghton, 1868.

Knight, G.W., **The Wheel of Fire.** Oxford University Press, 1930.

Kohler, J., **Verbrechertypen in Shakespeare's Dramen.** Berlin: Otto Elsner, 1903.

Kolbe, F.G., **Shakespeare's Way: A Psychological Study.** London: Sheed and Ward, 1930.

Kuhne, W., **Venus, Amor und Bacchus in Shakespeare's Dramen.** Braunschweig: E. Applhaus & Co., 1902.

Laehr, H., **Die Darstellung Krankhafter Geisteszustande in Shakespeare's Dramen.** Stuttgart: Paul Neff, 1898.

Leighton, W., **The Subjection of Hamlet.** Philadelphia: J. B. Lippincott & Co., 1882.

Ludwig, Emil, **Doctor Freud.** N.Y.: Hellman, Williams & Co., 1947.

Meyer, H., **Hamlet und Die Blutrache.** Leipzig: A. Deichert, 1892.

Miller, W., **Shakespeare's Macbeth and the Ruin of Souls. Madras:** G. A. Wateson, 1901.

Parker, S.W., **Effects of Certain Mental and Bodily States Upon the Imagination, especially as Illustrated by Shakespeare. Birming-**ham: 1876.

Peers, Edgar A., **Elizabethan Drama and Its Mad Folk. Cambridge:** W. Heffer & Sons, Ltd., 1914.

Pleiderer, W., **Das Seelische Verhaltnis Zwichen Hamlet und Ophelia.** Berlin: H. Paetel, 1908.

Rahner, R., **"Ophelia" Eine Psychologische Psychiatrische Studie.** Leipzig: Xemen Verlag, 1910.

Ray, I., **Contributions to Mental Pathology, Shakespeare's Delineation of Insanity.** N.Y.: Little, Brown & Company, 1873.

Rees, George, **Studies Biographical and Literary.** Chapter on the Mad Characters in Shakespeare, pp. 6-62. London: Simpkin, Marshall & Co., 1867.

Rosner, K., **Shakespeare's Hamlet un Lichte der Neuropathologie.** Berlin: H. Kornfield, 1895.

Rubinstein, F., **Hamlet als Neuroastheniker.** Leipzig: H. Haache, 1896.

Sachs, Hans, **The Creative Unconscious.** Cambridge: Sci-Art, 1942.

Schroder, C. Von, **Willn und Nervösitat in Shakespeare's Hamlet.** Riga: R. Ruetz, 1893.

Sharpe, E.F., **Collected Papers on Psycho-Analysis,** The Hogarth Press, Ltd., 1950.

Sommerville, H., **Madness in Shakespearean Tragedy.** London: Richards Press, 1929.

Stark, C., **König Lear, Eine Psychiatrische Shakespeare Studie.** Stuttgart: 1871.

Stearns, C.W., **Shakespeare's Medical Knowledge.** N.Y.: Appleton, 1865.

Storffrich, D.B., **Psychologische Aufschlusse Uber Shakespeare's Hamlet.** Bremen: 1859.

Tannenbaum, S.A., **Slips of the Tongue.** Shakespeare Studies No. 1. N.Y.: Tenny Press, 1930.

Trerck, H., **Das Psychologische Problem in der Hamlet Tragedie.** Leipzig: 1890.

Turck, H., **Hamlet, ein Genie.** Leipzig: Max Hoffman 1886.

Vehese, E., **Shakespeare als Protestant, Psycholog und Dichter.** Hamburg: 1851.

Venable, E., **The Hamlet Problem and its Solution.** Cincinnati: Stewart and Kidd Co., 1912.

Warde, F. B., **The Fools in Shakespeare.** N.Y.: McBride, Mast & Co., 1913.
Wainwright, J.W., **Hamlet's Sanity.** N.Y.: William Wood & Co., 1914.
Watts, N., **Was Hamlet Mad?** London: 1880.
Wittels, Fritz, **Freud and His Time.** New York: The Liveright Publishing Corp., 1931.
Wittels, Fritz, "Psychoanalysis and Literature" in **Psychoanalysis Today** (Lorand). New York: International University Press, 1944.
Woods, W.D., **Hamlet from a Psychological Point of View.** London: Wakefield, 1870.
Wulffen, E., **Shakespeare's Hamlet ein Sexual Problem.** Berlin: 1913.
Wulffen, E., **Kriminal psychologie.** Berlin: 1907.
Wulffen, E., **Shakespeare's Grosse Verbrecher.** Berlin: P. Langenscheidt, 1911.

Periodicals

[Anon.] "Shakespeare and Sanity," (Editorial) **Independent,** LXXVIII (Apr. 20, 1914), 117.
[Anon.] "True Ophelia and Other Studies of Shakespeare's Women," (Editorial) **Nation,** LXLVIII (Apr. 23, 1914), 476.
[Anon.] "Hamlet as a Type of Human Degeneracy," **Cur. Lit.,** XXXXI (Jl., 1906), 66.
[Anon.] "Madness of Ophelia," **Dennie's Portfolio,** XXXI I, 187.
[Anon.] "On the Feigned Madness of Hamlet," **Blackwood's Magazine,** XXXXVI (Oct., 1839), 449.
[Anon.] "Hamlet's Madness," **Athenaeum,** Part II (1863), 104.
[Anon.] "On the Madness of Ophelia," **Philadelphia Portfolio** (1824), pp. 187-193.
[Anon.] "Hamlet's Insanity," **Chicago Med. Journ.** (Sept., 1872), 7.
[Anon.] "Hamlet, the Hysterical," **London Society** (Dec., 1874).
[Anon.] "Hamlet, the Hysterical," **Athenaeum, Part II,** (1874), 761.
[Anon.] "Criterion of Hamlet's Madness," **Quarterly Rev.** XXXXIX, 184, 185.
[Anon.] "The Very Cause of Hamlet's Lunacy," **Scribner's Mag.** (July, 1908), 122.
[Anon.] "Die Charakterzuge Hamlet's," **Shakespeare Jahrbuch** (Berlin, 1867), Vol. II.
[Anon.] "Ob Hamlet Wahnsinning War," **Shakespeare Museum,** I (1875), 32.
[Anon.] "Clue to personality in Shakespeare's Plays," **Science N. L.,** LV (Ja. 20, 1949), 60.

Abenheimer, K.M., "Narcissism—Including an Analysis of King Lear." **Brit. J. Med. Psychol., XX (1945), 322-29.**

Abenheimer, K.M., "Shakespeare's Tempest: A Psychological Analysis," **Psychoanal. Rev., XXXIII (Oct. 1946), 399-415.**

Alexander, F., "Note on Falstaff," **Psychoanalytic Quart., II (July-Oct., 1933), 592-606.**

Alexander, R., "Hamlet-Classical Malingerer," **Med. Journ. & Record, CXXX (1929), 287.**

Alexander, W.J., "The Mystery of Hamlet," **University M., VI (Dec. 1907), 454.**

Allen, J.C., "Was Hamlet Insane?" **The Open Court (July, 1904), 434.**

Allen, L.H., "Repression in Hamlet," **Australasian J. of Psychology and Philosophy (Sydney), III (1925), 52-6.**

Allen, L., "The Hypnosis Scene in the Tempest," **Australasian Journ. of Psych. and Phil., IV (1926), 110-18.**

Allen, L. "Aversion in Timon of Athens," **Australasian Journ. of Psych. and Phil., III (1925), 207-10.**

Ashworth, John, "Oliver, Freud and Hamlet," **Atlant. Monthly, CXXCIII (May, 1949), No. 5.**

B. M. O., "Hamlet, a Lunatic," **Solicitors J. and Weekly, LVI (Jan. 14, 1922), 192.**

B---r (V.M.), Hamlet, Shakespeare s Urachebno-psikologichiskof tachki Z rienya (Shakespeare's **Hamlet** from a medico-psychological point of view—history of his mental condition) **Arch. Psychiat. St. Perb., XXX (No. 2) (1897), pp. 39-107.**

Barret, W., "On the Sanity and Age of Hamlet," **Lippincott's Mag., XXXXV (1890), 580.**

Beaute, "Etude medico-psychologique sur Shakespeare et ses Oeuvres sur l'Hamlet en particulier," **Echo Med. Toulouse, 2.S. III (1889), 52-65, 76, 87, 99.**

Benttencourt-Ferreira, J., "La folie au theatre; quelques considerations sur l'état morbid represent dans Hamlet," **Rev. de psychol- clin. et therap. (Paris) IV (1900), 108.**

Bigelow, H.R., "Hamlet's Insanity," **Chicago Med. Journ., XXX (1873), 513.**

Brierre, B., "Etudes psychologiques; Shakespeare ses connaissances en alientation mentale Lear," **Cincin. Med. Psychol., S4 XII (1868), 329; S5 VII (1869), 493.**

Brigham, "Shakespeare's Illustrations of Insanity," **Am. J. Insan., I. (July, 1844), 27.**

Bucknill, J.C., **"King Lear: a psychological Study," J. Ment. So., London, V (1858), 301.**

Bucknill, J., "Macbeth, a psychological Study," **Journ. Ment. Sciences, July, 1858.**

Bucknill, J.C., "**Hamlet, a psychological Study,**" **J. Ment. Sciences., Lond., V (1858), 1.**

Blunden, E., "**Madness of Lear,**" **Nation (Lond.), XLIII (Je. 7, 1928), 458.**

Clark, F., **As You Like It (and Adlerian Psychology) Purpose (Lond.), I (1929), 159-66.**

Cohn, E., "Ueber Hamlet's Wahnsinn," **Morgenblatt. 1811.**

Cohn, I., "Shakespeare als Kenner des Wahnsinns," **Das Neue Reich, No. 29, 1871.**

Conrad, B.R., "The Problem of Hamlet's Delay," **Pub. Mod. Lang. Assoc. XLI (1926), 680-87.**

Corbin, J., "Cherish the Fools, Idiots, Madmen," **Sat. R. Lit., XXVI (Je. 19, 1943), 34.**

Coriat, I.H., "Die Psychoanalyse de Lady Macbeth," **Zentralblatt fur psychoanalyse und psychotherapie, IV (1914), 384-400.**

Cox, S., "The Psychology of Hamlet," **Proc. Psychol. Soc. Gr. Brit., 1875-9; 1880, 263.**

Craighton, C., "Falstaff's Death-bed," **Blackwell's Mag., CXLV (Mr., 1889), 325-36.**

D'Alfonso, R., "Filosofi et psicog, nell 'amletto," **Nuova Anolagia, CCXXXIX (Jne, 1925), 183-94.**

Dana, C., "The Handwriting in Nervous Diseases with special reference to William Shakespeare," in **Problems of Personality, a Festschriff to Morton Prince.**

Davie, T.M., "Hamlet's Madness," **J. Ment. Sc., XXCVIII (Jl., 1942), 449.**

Davis, T.L., "The Sanity of Hamlet," **J. of Philosophy, XIX (1931), 629-34.**

Draper, E.J., "The Choleric Cassio," **Bull. Hist. Med., VII (June, 1939), 583-94.**

Draper, E.J., "Kate the Curst," **J. Nerv. and Ment. Dis., XXCIX, (June, 1939), 757-764.**

Draper, E.J., "The Melancholy Duke Orsino," **Bull. Hist. Med., VI (Nov., 1939), 1020-29.**

Draper, J.W., "Psychology of Shylock," **Bull. Hist. Med., VIII (Apr., 1937), 142-147.**

Draper, J.W., "Psychology of Shylock," **Bull. Mist. Med., VIII (Apr., 1940), 643-50.**

Draper, J.W., "Psychology of Shylock," **Bull. Hist. Med., VIII (Apr., (June, 1941), 16-26.**

Draper, J.W., "Lady Macbeth," **Psychoanalyt. Rev., XXVIII (Oct., 1941), 479-86.**

Draper, J.W., "Shakespeare's Attitude Towards Old Age," **J. Gerontol., I (Jan., 1946), 118-125.**

Draper, J.W., "Patterns of Humor and Tempo in **King Lear," Bull. Hist. of Med.,** XXI (May-June, 1947), 390-401.

Dees, "Timon von Athens: Drama Von Shakespeare, noch psychopathologischen Gesicht punkten, erklart," **Ztschr. f. d. ges. neurol. u. psychiat.** Berlin, XXVIII (1915), 50-64.

Del Greco, F., "Follia nell donne dello Shakespeare e psicologia femminille," **Manicomio, Nocera,** XXXI (1914), 1-16.

Del Greco, F., "Exozioni e follia in alcuni erci de Guglieelnio Shakespeare," **Manicomio, Nocera,** XXXI (1916), 203-14.

Dennet, J.R., "Shakespeare's Delineations of Insanity," **Nation,** II (Je. 14, 1866), 758.

Ellis, A.N., "Some few Observations on Hamlet; Was he sane or Insane? If Insane was he responsible?" **Cincin. Lancet-Clinic,** N.S. LII (1904), 391.

Farren, W., "Madness of King Lear," London Mag., X (Jl. 1824), 79.

Farren, W., "On the Madness of Ophelia," **Port-folio Phila.,** XVIII (1824).

Feinstein, G.W., "How Shakespeare prescribes for Worry," **Ind. Woman,** XXIX (Ja., 1950), 9.

Flint, A., "Cases of Insanity in Shakespeare," **The Open Court,** (May, 1904), 257.

Fraser-Harris, D., "Thought and Brain, (a guess by Shakespeare)" **Cornhill Mag.,** LIV (1928), 671-77.

Freud, S., "Das Motiv der Kastchenwahl," **Imago** (Leipzig & Wein), II (1913), 257-66.

Goldblat, H., "Shakespeare als physiognomiker," **Psychologie und Medizin** (Stuttgart), IV (1930), 83-110.

Griffiths, L.M., "Hamlet's Mental Condition," **N.Y. Shakespeariana,** VI (Nov. 1889), 467-77.

Halford, Sir H., "Shakespeare's Test of Insanity," in **Essays and Orations** (London: J. Murray, 1832).

Hendrickson, O., "Comprehensible yet Misunderstood Characters of Shakespeare's Hamlet: Psychological Study," **Schweiz. Arch. f. Neurve. u. Psychiat.,** XXXI (1933), 261; XXXII (1933), 33.

Hendrickson, O., "Is Problem of Hamlet's Insanity Solved," **Psychiat-Neurve. Wchnschr.,** XXXIX (Jan. 16, 1937), 36-40.

Hinkle, B.M., "Shakespeare," in the **Recreating of the Individual: A Study of Psychological Types and their Relation to Psychoanalysis,** N.Y., 1923, pp. 358-60.

Hoche, E., "Shakespeare und die psychiatrie," **Arch. f. psychiat. Ber.,** XXXIII (1900), 666.

Holmes, G., "Shakespeare: Master Reader of Humanity," **Munsey,** X (Nov. 1893), 117.

Hopkin, A., "Hamlet and Olivier," **Theatre Arts, XXIII (Aug., 1948),** 30-31.

Horne, R.H., "Madness as Treated by Shakespeare: **a psychological** Essay," **J. Psych. Med. London,** II (1849), 589.

Jekels, J., "Shakespeare's **Macbeth," Imago** (Leipzig & Wien, 1917-18), 170-195.

Jekels, L., "Riddle of Shakespeare's 'Macbeth,'" **Psychoanalyt. Rev.,** XXX (Oct., 1943), 361-385.

Jones, E., "Oedipus Complex as an Explanation of Hamlet's Mystery," **Am. J. Psychol.,** XXI (Je., 1910), 72.

Kellogg, A.O., "William Shakespeare as a Physician and Psychologist," **Am. J. Insanity,** XVI (1859), 129, 409.

Kellogg, A.O., "Shakespeare's Psychological Delineations," Am. J. **Insanity,** XX (1863), 1, 257; XXI (1863), 1.

Kellogg, A.O., "Shakespeare's Delineations of Mental Imbecility **as** Exhibited in his Fools and Clowns," **Am. J. Insanity,** XVIII (1861-63), 97, 224; XIX (1861-63), 176, 322.

Kellogg, A.O., "Shakespeare's Psychological Delineations," **Am. J. Quart. J. Psychol. Med.,** VI (1872), 209.

Kennedy, "Hamlet's Melancholy," **Notes and Queries,** 5S IV, p. 305.

Klein, L.A., "Another Slant on Hamlet — A Study in Hysteria," **Phi Delta Epsilon News** (N.Y.), Dec., 1932.

Lambroso, C., "Insane Characters in drama," **Pop. Sci. Month.** (May, 1899), 52.

Landmann, S., "Zur Diagnose Psychischer Vorgange mit besonderer bezungnahme auf Hamlet's Geisteszustand," **Ztchr. f. Psychol. d. sinnersorg.** (Hamb. u. Leipzig), XI (1896), 134, 152.

Latham, S., "O Poor Ophelia," **New Shakespeare Soc. Trans.** (Lond.), IX (1874-1904), 401.

Libby, M.F., "Shakespeare and Psychognosis," **Univ. Colorado Studies,** III (1906-07), 63, 229.

Libby, M.F., "Shakespeare **and** Adolescence," **Pedagog. Sem.,** VIII (Je., 1901), 163, 205.

Libby, W., "Shakespeare **as** a Psychologist," **Archeion,** XII (July-Dec., 1930), 282-295.

Lipscomb, A.A., "Psychological Study of Hamlet," **Meth. Quart. Rev.,** XLIV (Oct., 1884), 665.

Lloyd, J.H., "The So-called Oedipus Complex in Hamlet," **Journ. Amer. Med. Assoc.,** LVI (1911), 1377.

Mackenzie, H., "On the feigned Madness of Hamlet," **Blackwood's Mag.,** XLVI (1839), 449.

Mairet, P., "Hamlet as Neurotic," **Internat. Ztschr. f. Individual-psychol.,** IX (Dec., 1931), 424-37.

Mallinckrodt. F., "Zur Psychoanalyse der Lady Macbeth," **Zentral-**

blatt psychoanalyse und psychotherapie, IV (1914), 612-13.

Maudsley, H., "Hamlet" in **Body and Mind,** N.Y.: Appleton & Co., 1874, p. 123.

McDermot, G., "Hamlet's Madness and German Criticism," **Cath. World,** LXVIII (1898), 243.

Meninger, C.F., "Insanity of Hamlet," **J. Kansas M. Soc.,** XXXV (Sept., 1934), 334-38.

Mercier, A., "Hamlet: his mental state," in **Ancient Essays on English Poets,** New Orleans, 1887.

Milligan, A., "Study of Lady Macbeth," **African Month.,** II (Je., 1907), 27.

Nicholson, B., "Was Hamlet Mad?" **Tr. New Shakespeare Soc.,** (1880), 212.

Ominus, Fl., "La Psychologie Medicale dans les drames de Shakespeare," **Rev. d. deux Mondes,** p. S3, XIV (1876), 635.

O'Sullivan, M.I., "Hamlet and Dr. Timothy Bright," **Modern Lang. Assn. Publ.,** XXXXI (Sept., 1926), 667.

Palmer, J.F., "Macbeth—A Study in Monomania," **Med. Mag.** (Lond.) XIX (1910), 577.

Palmer, J., "Hamlet: A Study in Melancholia," **Med. Mag.** (Lond.) XX (1911), 396.

Palmer, J., "Ophelia: a Short Study in Acute Delirious Mania," **Med. Mag.** (Lond.) XXI (1912), 448.

Paulson, F., "Hamlet: de tragedie des pessimismus," **Deutsch Rundschau,** LIX (1889), 237.

Plewa, F., "Shakespeare and his Attitude Toward Power; individual psychologic Study," **Internat. Ztschr. f. Individualpsychol.,** XIV (Jan.-March, 1936), 26-36.

Price, G.E., "William Shakespeare as a Neuropsychiatrist," **Ann. Med. Hist.,** X (1928), 159.

Racker, E., "Jealousy of Othello," **Rev. Psicoanal.,** III (July, 1945), 1-18.

Ray, I., "Shakespeare's Delineations of Insanity," **Am. J. Insanity,** III (184), 289.

Rose, E., "Sudden Emotion; its effect upon different Characters," **Tr. New Shakespeare Soc.** (1880-82), pp. 1-20.

Sachs, H., "The Tempest," **Internat. J. Psycho-analysis,** IV (1923), 43.

Sadger, J., "Macbeth," in **Ueber Nachtwandeln und Mondsucht; Eine Medizinisch,** (pp. 143-169), Leipzig: F. Deuticke, 1914 (Tr. L. Brink) Monograph Series No. 31 N.Y. 1920.

Schelenz, H., "Shakespeare und sein Heilfakter Musik," **Berl. Klin Wchnschr.** (1912), 99, 1352-55.

Schell, E.A., "Hamlet, The Tragedy of Inaction," **Meth. Rev.,** No. 190, 877.

Scherer, B., "Polonius, der typus des senilen; eine psychiatrische Shakespearstudie," **Anglia, LIV** (1930), 149.
Sharp, E., "Hamlet's Impatience," **Internat. J. Psychoanalysis X** (1929), 270.
Sharp, E., "Hamlet's Ungeduld," **Internat. Zeits f. psychoanalyse,** XV (1929), 329-39.
Sharpe, E.F., "From 'King Lear' to the 'Tempest.'" **Internat. J. Psychoanal.,** XXVII (1946), 19-30.
Sharpe, E.F., "The Impatience of Hamlet," **Int. J. Psycho-Anal., X,** 270.
Somerville, H., "Review of his **Madness in Shakespearean Tragedy," Nation** (Lond.), Aug., 10, 1929; also in **Sat. R.,** CXLVIII (Aug. 31, 1929), 247.
Stearns, C.W., "Hamlet's Insanity," in **The Shakespeare Treasury,** N.Y.: G. P. Putnam Sons, 1878.
Stenger, E., "Der Hamlet-charakter Eine psychiatrische Studie," Berlin: 1883, p. 39.
St. John, S., (ed.) "Sleep and Dreams," in **Essays on Shakespeare and his Works,** Lond.: Smith Elder & Co., 1908.
Stern, E.S., "Three Ganser States and Hamlet," **J. Ment. Sc.,** XXCVIII (Jan. 1942), 134-41.
Stoll, E.E., "Criminals in Shakespeare and in Science," **Mod. Phil.,** X (Je., 1912), 55.
Stoll, E. E., "Shakespeare's Criminals" (**Shakespeare Studies**), **Shakespeare Assn. Bull.** Apr., 1928, p. 337.
Symons, N.J., "The Graveyard Scene in Hamlet," **Internat. J. Psycho-Analysis,** IX (1928), 96.
Sypher, W., "Hamlet: the Existential Madness," **Nation,** CLXII (Je. 22, 1946), 750.
Tannenbaum, S.A., "Shakespeare and the New Psychology," **Dial,** LIX (Dec. 23, 1915), 601.
Tannenbaum, S.A., "Slips of the Tongue in Shakespeare," **Bull. Shakespeare Ass'n. of Amer.,** V (1930), No. 2.
Thorpe, E.B., "The Case of Lady Macbeth, Medically Considered," **Harper's New Monthly Mag.** (Feb. 1854), p. 391.
Tolman, J. E., "A View of the Views About Hamlet," **P.M.L.A.** (June, 1898), p. 155.
Towne, J.E., "A Psychoanalytic Study of Shakespeare's **Coriolanus," The Psychoanalytic Rev.** (Nervous and Mental Disease Pub. Co. Jan. 1921), p. 84.
Vessie, P.R., "Psychiatry Catches up with Shakespeare," **Med. Rec.,** CXLIV (Aug. 5, 1936), 141-45.
Vessie, P.R., "Interpretation of Shakespeare's Sex Play, 'All's Well that Ends Well,'" **Med. Rec.,** CXLVI (Jl. 7, 1937), 14-16.

Wainwright, J.W., "A Psychological Study of Hamlet," **Med. Rec. LXXXIII (1908), 172.**

Waugh, Martin, "Othello: The Tragedy of Iago," **Psychiat. Quart., Vol. XIX, No. 2, 1950.**

Whitmire, C.L., "Psychoses of Shakespeare's Characters," **Illinois Med. J., LIII (1928), 64.**

Wickham, H., "Did Shakespeare Murder his father? Freud-Shakespeare hypothesis," **Cath. World, CXXXIX (Feb. 1932), 538.**

Wile, I.S., "Personality of King Lear as a Young Man," **Am. J. Orthopsychiat, V (Jl., 1935), 325-36.**

Wile, I.S., "Shakespearean Characters in the Light of Present-day Psychologies," **Psychiat. Quart., XVI (Jan. 1942), 62-90.**

Wood, F.T., "Hamlet's Madness," **Notes & Queries, CLX (Jan. 3, 1931), 7.**

Woods, A.H., "Syphilis in Shakespeare's 'Tragedy of Timon of Athens,'" **Amer. J. of Psychiat., XCI (July, 1934), 95-107.**

Winslow, F., "Madness as Portrayed by Shakespeare," **The Arena, XV (Feb. 1896), 415.**

Winslow, F., "Madness as Portrayed by Shakespeare," **The Arena, XV (Feb. 1896), 123.**

Züno, G., "Fu W. Shakespeare un psicopata susuale?" **Arc. d. psicopat. Sess Roma, I (1896), 307.**

WORKS DEALING WITH MEDICAL AND PSYCHO-PATHOLOGICAL KNOWLEDGE IN ELIZABETHAN ENGLAND IN RELATION TO SHAKESPEARE'S PLAYS

Books

Anderson, R.L., **Elizabethan Psychology and Shakespeare's Plays.** Iowa City, University of Iowa, 1927.

Aristotle's Psychology (De Anima and Porva Naturalis). William A. Hammond, translator, New York: Macmillan Co., 1902.

Bacon, Francis, **Works.** New edition, 7 vols., edited by Spedding, Ellis and Heath, London, 1889.

Barckley, Sir Richard, **The Felicitie of Man or His Summum Bonum.** London, 1631. The work appeared first in 1582.

Bartholomaeus, Anglicus, **De Proprietatibus Rerum** translated and enlarged by Stephen Batman under title, **Batman upon Bartholome, his Booke De Proprietatibus Rerum.** London, 1582.

Bieber, G.A., **Der Melancholiker typus Shakespeare's und sein Usoprung. Anglistiche Arbeiten,** 1913.

Berdoe, Edward, **The Healing Art.** London: Swan, Sonnenschein & Co., 1893.

Boaistnan, Pierre, **Theatrum Mundi, the Theatre or Rule of the World.** John Alday, translator, London, 1581.

Boorde, Andrew, **A Compendyous Regyment or a Dyetary of Health.** 1542? Reprinted in Early English Text Society (Ex. Ser) No. 10.

Boorde, Andrew, **The Book of the Introduction to Knowledge,** edited by J.F. Furnivall, for the early English Text Society.

Bright, Timothy, **A Treatise of Melancholy, containing the Causes thereof.** Newly corrected and amended. London, 1613.

Bullein's Dialogue of the Fever Pestilence, 1564. Early English Text Society. (Ex. Ser) 1888.

Burton, Robert, **The Anatomy of Melancholy.** 3 vols., A. R. Shillete, editor, George Bell and Sons, London: 1896.

Castiglione, Baldassare, **The Courtier.** Translated into English by Thomas Hoby, 1561. Reprinted in the **Literature of Italy 1265-1907.**

Charron, Pierre, **of Wisdom,** 3 bks. George Stanhope, translator, London, 1697, The original **De La Sagesse** was printed at Bordeaux in 1601. There is a translation by Samson Lennord contemporary with Shakespeare.

Coeffeteau, Nicholas, **A Tale of Humane Passions.** Edw. Grimeston, translator, London, 1621.

Davies, Sir John, "Nosse Terpisce," 1599, **Works in Verse and Prose.** 3 vols. A. B. Grosort, editor. Fuller Worthies Library, 1869, Vol. I, pp. 39-162.

Davies, John of Hereford, **Complete Works,** 2 vols. A.B. Grosort, editor, Chertsey Worthies Library, Edinburgh, 1878.

Elyot, Sir Thomas, **Of the Knowledge which Maketh a Wise Man; a Disputacion Platonike;** London, 1533; Reprinted in **Palaestra,** LXXXIII, 1920.

Essays of Michael Lord of Montaigne, done into English by John Florio, 3 vols., London, Grant Richards, 1908.

Ferrand, James. **A Treatise Discoursing of Essence, causes, symptoms, Prognosticks and cure of Love or Erotique Melancholy:** 2nd ed., Oxford, 1645. The earlier edition appeared in 1640.

Fletcher, Phineas, "The Purple Island, or the Isle of Man," 1633. **Poetical Works of Giles and Phineas Fletcher.** 2 vols., Frederick S. Boas, editor, Cambridge University Press, 1909, Vol. II, 1-89.

Huarte, Navarre, Juan de Dios, **Examen de Ingenios, the Examination of Men's Wits,** translated out of the Spanish tongue by M. Camilli. Inglished out of his Italian by R. C. (arew)? London, 1596. The first edition was printed in 1594.

La Primaudaye, Pierre de, **The French Academie; Fully discoursed**

and Finished in Faure Bookes, London, 1618.
Nemesius, The Nature of Man. Geo. Wither, translator, London, 1636.
Vives, Joannes Ludovicus, Introduction to Wysedome, bound with Sir Thomas Elyot's Banket of Sapience and the Preceptes of Agapetus, London, 1550.
Wright, Thomas. The Passions of the Minde in Generall; corrected enlarged, and with sundry new discourses augmented, London, 1630.
Andres, S., The Doctor in History, Literature and Folklore. Ind.: Hull Press, 1896.
Peers, E.A., Elizabethan Dramas and it's Mad Folk. Cambridge: Heffer and Sons Ltd., 1914.
Liebe, C., Der Arzt in Elizabethanischen Drama. Halle A.S., R. Espenhahn, 1907.
Hoehana, H., Der Physiologus in der Elisabethani'schen Literatur. Erlanger, 1930.
Osler, Sir W., The Growth of Truth as Illustrated in the Discovery of the Circulation of the Blood. London: Henry Frowde, 1907.
Chapman, H.C., History of the Discovery of the Circulation of the Blood. Phila.: P. Blakiston, Son & Co., 1884.
Spencer, H.R., Medicine in the Days of Shakespeare. London: J. Bale & Co., 1929.
Malloch, A., William Harvey, N.Y.: Paul B. Hoeber, 1929.
Shakespeare's England, Oxford University Press, 1918.
Cotta, John, A Short Discoverie of the Unobserved dangers of severall sorts of ignorant and unconsiderate Practisers of Physicke in England. London, 1612.
Merret, Christopher, The Accomplisht Phy'sician, the honest Apothecary, and the skilful Chyrurgeon. London, 1670.
Godfrey, Robert. Various injuries and abuses in Chymical and Galenical Physick, committed both by Physicians and Apothecaries, detected. London, 1674.
Griffith, Richard, A la mode Phlebotomy, no good fashion. London, 1681.
Nedham, Marchmont, Medela Medicine; a plea for the free profes'sion and renovation of the Art of Physick. London, 1665.
Walker, Richard, Memoirs of Medicine. London, 1799.
Good, John Mason, History of Medicine. London, 1799.
Ferris, Samuel, General View of Physic. London. 1795.
[Anon.] Medicina flagellata; or the Doctor scarify'd. London, 1721.
Richards, J.M., A Chronology of Medicine, Ancient, Mediaeval and Modern. London, 1880.
Astruc: A treatise of the venereal disease. London, 1737.

Banester, J., **A needful, new, and necessary treatise of Chyrurgerie briefly comprehending the general and particular curation of ulcers drawn forth of sundry worthy masters.** John Banester, Gentleman practiser in Physicke and Chyrurgery. London, 1575.

Banester, John, Compendious Chyrurgerie. 1585.

Hall, John, **Select observations on English bodies; or cures both** empiricall and historicall performed upon very eminent persons in desperate diseases. First written in Latine By John Hall, living at Stratford-on-Avon in Warwickshire, where he was very famous, as also in the countries adjacent, as appears by these observations, drawn out of several hundreds of his as choysest. Now put into English for the common benefit by James Cook. London, 1657.

Halle, John, **An historical expostulation against the beastyle abusers, both of chyrurgerie and physyke,** in our time with goodly doctrine and instruction necessary to be marked and followed of all true chirurgiens. All these faithfully gathered and diligently set forth by the said John Halle, 1565 (appended to Halle's translation of Lafranc's surgery).

Halle, John, **A most excellent and learned work of Chirurgerie called Chirurgerie parva Lanfranci, Lanfranke of Mylayne, his briefe;** reduced from dyvers translations to our vulgar or usual frase, and now first put into English prynte by John Halle, Chirurgien, etc., London, 1565.

Harris, Walter, (1651-1725): **Pharmacologia anti-empirica; or a rational discourse of remedies both chyrurgical and Galenical** together with some remarks on the cause and cures of the gout the universal use of the cortex, or jesuits powder, and the most notorious impostures of divers empiricks and mountebanks. London, R. Chiswell, 1683.

Wigon, John, **The most excellent workes of chirurgery made and set forth by maister John Wigon, head Chirurgien of oure tyme in Italy,** translated into English. Whereunto is added an exposition of strange terms and unknown simples belongynge unto the arte. Imprinted by Edward Whytchurch, with the Kynges most gracious privilege for seven yeres. London, 1550.

Stubbs, Phillip, "The Anatomie of Abuses Contayning a Discoverie ... of such Notable Vices, etc.," 1583, edited by Furnivall, New Shakespeare Publications, Series VI, No. 4.

Woodall, John, **The surgeon's mate, or military and domestic surgery.** Discovering faithfully and plainly ye method and ye order of ye surgeons chest, ye uses of ye instruments, ye vertues and operations of ye medicine, with ye exact cures of wounds, etc. London, 1639.

McKay, **History of Ancient Gynaecology.** London, 1901.

Meryon, **History of Medicine.** London, 1861.

Harvey, Gideon. **The conclave of physicians, in two parts, detecting their intrigues, frauds, and plots against their patients, and their destroying the faculty of physick, also a peculiar discourse of the Jesuits bark: the history thereof with its true use and abuse.** London, 1683.

Munk, W., **The roll of the Royal College of Physicians of London.** Completed from the annals of the college and from the other authentic sources. London, 1861.

Munk, W., **Comprising biographical sketches of all the eminent physicians whose names are recorded in the annals from the foundation of the college in 1518 to its removal in 1825 from Warwick Lane to Pall Mall East.** London, 1878.

Merrit, C., **A Collection of acts of Parliament, charters, trials at law, and judges' opinions concerning those grants to the College of Physicians, London, taken from originals, law books, and annals.** London, 1660.

Pepys, Samuel, **The Diary of Samuel Pepys.**

Pringle, **Professional Anecdotes or Ana of Medical Literature.** London, 1825.

Ward, John, **Diary of the Rev. John Ward of Stratford-on-Avon.** extending from 1648-1679; from the original MSS, preserved in the library of the Medical Society of London, arr. by Charles Severn. 1839.

Royal College of Physicians, London: Authentic memoirs, biographical critical, and literary, of the most eminent physicians and surgeons of Great Britain, with a choice collection of their prescriptions, on account of the medical charities of the metropolis, etc. London, 1818.

Stow's **Memoranda** (Lambeth M.S.) Camden Soc. 1880.

Machyn's Diary, ed. J. Gough Nichols Camden Soc. No. 42.

Fyshe, Symon, **The Supplication of Beggars,** London, 1546.

Certain Works of Chirurgerie Newly Compiled and published by T. Gale. London, 1563.

Lowe, Peter, **An easie, certaine and perfect method to cure and prevent the Spanish sickness,** London, 1596. For an account of the book see The Life and Works of Marstes Peter Lowe. By James Finlayson, M.D. Glasgow, 1889.

South's **Memorials of the Craft of Surgery.**

Garrison, F.H., **History of Medicine.** W.B. Saunders Co. Philadelphia. 1924.

Armstrong, John, **A Synopsis of the History and Cure of Venereal Diseases.** London: Miller, 1737.

Clawes, William, **Short and Profitable Treatise Touching the Disease called Morbus Gallicus by Unctions.** London, Daye, 1579.
Jaffreson, J.C., **A Book About Doctors.** Budd & Carleton, N.Y., 1861.
Creighton, Charles, **A History of Epidemics in Great Britain.** Cambridge University Press, 1891.
[Anon.] **The Marriage of Wit and Wisdom.** J. O. Halliwell, London, 1846. Printed by the Shakespeare Soc.
Bandello, Matteo, **The Tragicall History of Romeus and Juliet** written first in Italian by Bandello and nowe in Englishe by Arthur Brooke, London, 1875. (New Shakes, Soc. 3S., No. 1) Also, the goodly **History of the true and constant love betweene Romeo and Juliette.** Transl. by Wliliam Painter from the French paraphrase, by Pierre Boaistnan of Bandello's version of "Romeo e Gulietta." Reprinted from the second edition (N.D.) of the second volume of Painter's "Palace of Pleasure," collated with the first edition, 1567, and with the reprints of Haslewood, Collier and Halliwell, London, 1875 (New Shakes. Soc. 3S. No. 1).
Beaumont and Fletcher, **The Works of.** Vols. I and II, Edw. Moxon, London, 1839.
Chapman, George, **The Works of George Chapman, Play's.** R.H. Shepherd, London: Chatto and Windres, Piccadilly, 1874.
Fletcher, Robert, Johns Hopkins Hospital Bulletin. May and June, Nos. 50 and 51, Vol. VI, 1895.
Jonson, Ben, **The Works of.** Vols. I, II and III. William Gifford, London. John Camden Holten 74-75, Piccadilly.
Harsnet, Samuel, **Declaration of Egregious Popish Imposters,** etc. London, 1603.
Heywood, John, **The Foure PP. Specimens of Pre-Shakespearean Drama.** Manley, Ginn & Co., 1903.
Holinshed's Chronicles. . . London, J. Johnson. . . , 1808, V.
Marlowe, Christopher, **The Works of,** Bullen, Houghton, Mifflin & Co., New York, 1885.
Marston, John, **The Works of,** Bullen, London, 1887, John C. Nimmo.
Massinger and Ford, **The Dramatic Works of.** Edward Moxon, Dover Street, London, 1840.
Middleton, **The Works of.** Bullen, London, 1885, John C. Nimmo.
O'Connor, E., "Possible Sources for Shakespeare's Culture," **Poet Lore** (Boston), XXIII (1912), 114-24.
Pollard, A.W., **The Works of Chaucer,** London: Macmillan Co., 1925.

ADDITIONAL BIBLIOGRAPHY DEALING WITH SHAKESPEARE'S MEDICAL AND PSYCHOPATHOLOGICAL KNOWLEDGE

WORKS DEALING WITH SHAKESPEARE'S MEDICAL AND OTHER SCIENTIFIC KNOWLEDGE

[Anon.] Medicine in Shakespeare, William Shakespeare and John Hall, **Conn. Med.** 1964, 28:797.

[Anon.] "The Doctor in Shakespeare" **Canad. Med. Assoc. J.,** 90: 792-3, March 28, 1964.

[Anon.] "William Shakespeare and John Hall" **Conn. Med.,** 1964, 28:797.

Bradley, H., "Cursed Hebenon" (or "Hebona") **Modern Lang. Review,** XV, 1920.

Brown, I. "The Bard and the Body" **Med. World.** (London) 91: 60-4, July, 1959.

Bryant, R.D. "Unusual Obstetric Case History derived from the pen of William Shakespeare by version of meaning and extraction from context" **J. Obst. & Gynec.,** 2: 187-200 Aug. 1953.

Casey, R.L., "Shakespeare and Elizabethan Surgery" **Surg. Gynec. Obstet.,** 1967, 124:1324-8.

Cawthorne, T. "How Hamlet's father died" **Proc. roy. Soc. Med. (Sect. Hist. Med.),** 1964, 57, 905-6.

Chandler, S.B., "Shakespeare and Sleep." **Bull. Hist. Med.,** 29: 255-260, May-June 1955.

Cooper, P., "Cursed Hebona" **Pharmacolog. Journ.,** 1965, 195, 633.

Crosfill, J.W.L., "Classified Medical References in the Works of Shakespeare" **Journ. Roy. Navy Med. Service,** 34: 22-28; 38:113-130, 1952; 38: 193-209, 1953; 39: 15-36, 1953; 39: 96-112, 1953; 39: 240-251, 1953; 40: 2-29, 1954; 40: 139-149, 1954; 41: 35-53; 149-167, 1956; 42: 23-56; 166-175, 1956.

Crosfil, J.W.L. "Plague in Shakespeare and Pepys," **J. Roy. Nav. M. Serv.,** XXXIV (Jan., 1948), 22-28.

Davison, M.H.A. "Shakespeare: Some Medical Problems." **Scott. Soc. Hist. Med. Proc.,** 1963-64, 14-26.

Dodek, S.M., "William Shakespeare's Knowledge of Medicine." **Med. Ann., D.C.,** 1965, 34: 326-9.

Doran, A., "Shakespeare and the Medical Society," **Brit. Med. Journ.,** I (1889), 1201.

Ehrlich, G.E., "Shakespeare's Rheumatology" **Ann. Rheum. Diseases.** 26: 562-3. Nov. 1967.

Gandevia, B., "Shakespeare and Chaucer: Their Use of Medical Allusions in the story of **Troilus and Cressida" Roy. Melbourne Hosp. Clinic Reports**, 28: 8-12, Dec. 1953.

Giani, E., Shakespeare and His Knowledge of Pathology. (Italian) Osped. Ital. Chir., 1965, 13: 453-69.

Hoffman, B., "Shakespeare, the Physicist" **Il. Sci., Am.**, 184: 52.

Kaltreider, F.D. "Was the Bard an Obstetrician?" **Obstet. and Gynec.**, 1964, 24: 491-96.

King, T.J., "Botany in Shakespeare," ('Darnel' in **King Lear**) IV, 4, 5. **Not. and Queries**, 1968, N. Ser. 15: 141.

Lueth, P. "Der Arzt und Shakespeare Ratsel." Otoch. Arztbl., 1964, 61: 1825-30.

— "Shakespeare und die Medizin, Zum 400 Geburtstag des Dichters." **Munch. Med. Wschr.**, 1964, 106: 1151-6, illus.

Macht, D.I., "Calendula or Marigold in Medical History and in Shakespeare." **Bull. Hist. of Med.**, 29: 491-502. Nov.-Dec., 1955.

MacAlpine, I. (Letter Concerning the Whereabouts of the lost casebook of John Hall). **Brit. Med. Journ.**, 1965, i, 926.

Martin, W.S., "Shakespeare, Medicine and the Law." Canad. Med. Assoc. J., 1965, 93: 255-260.

Matthews, F.S., "Tobacco and Shakespeare" **Proc. Charake Club.** 9: 31-88, 1938.

Meek, Walter A., "Medicine in Shakespeare" **Texas Reports, Biology and Medicine**, 10: 372-398, Summer, 1952.

Mikulowski, W., "Paramedical Reading of Shakespeare." (Polish) **Przegl. lek.**, 1965, 21: 527-30.

Miller, A. H., "Medical Science in Shakespeare's Day," **Med. Press and Circular**, CI (1916), 376.

Plichett, A. P. "Shakespeare and His knowledge of Medicine." **Press Medicale**, 62: 1845-1849, Dec. 25, 1954.

Poynter, F.N.L., "Medicine and Public Health" **Shakespeare Survey** 17, ed. by A. Nicoll., Cambridge Univ. Press, 1964, pp. 152-166, **illus.**

Rolhe, H., "Physick and Physicians in Shakespeare's Plays" Ciba Symposia, 1964, 12: 184-9, **Illus.**

Rosenburg, L.M., "Sixteenth Century German Medicine," **California and Western Medicine**, XXX (1930, July, Aug., Sept.).

Rubin, E.L., "Shakespeare & Radiography" **Radiography**, 16: 67-72. Apr. 1950.

Schmutzer, R. "Animal Diseases in the Works of Shakespeare" **Arch. f. Gesh. d. Med.**, 35: 325-338. 1943.

Schneider, W. "Pharmazeutisches bei Shakespeare." **Pharmaber Bayer**, 1964, Heft 7, 21-3, illus.

Simpson, J. "A note on Epidemic Disease in Shakespeare's Plays."

Med. Offr., 1964, **112**, 359-361.

Simpson, P.R., "Shakespeare on Ear, Nose and Throat." **J. Laryng. & Otol.**, 64: 342-352. June, 1950.

Summershill, W.H.J. "Aquecheek's Disease" in Shakespearean Plays. **Lancet**, 2: 288, Aug. 1955.

Vest, W. E., "(Shakespeare) Gerontologist." **Geriatrics**, 9: 80-82, Feb. 1954.

Vest, W.E., "Shakespeare's Knowledge of Chest Diseases." **Journ.** A.M.A. 144: 1232-1234, Dec. 9, 1950.

Wall, A.H., "The Doctors Shakespeare Knew," in **The Doctor in History, Literature and Folklore**, edited by W. Andrews, London: Hull Press, 1896.

Walsh, James, "Clinical Medicine in the Middle Ages—Bartholomew's Proprietatibus Rerum," **Med. Life**, 39: 365-382. July 1932.

Watson, E.M., "Medical Lore in Shakespeare" **Ann. Med. Hist.**, 8: 249-265, May 1936.

Whitteridge, G. "Growth of Harvey's ideas on the circulation of the blood." (Harveian Lecture, Harv. Soc. Lond., March, 1966.) (And subsequent correspondence on circulation of the blood in Shakespeare.) **Brit. Med. J.**, 1966, ii, 7-12, refs.; 300; 590.

Whittet, T.D. Shakespeare and his apothecaries. **Proc. roy. Soc. Med. (Sect. Hist. Med.)**, 1964, 57, 899-905, **port.**, **refs.**

Wile, I.S. "Dentistry and Dentists Portrayed by Shakespeare." **Mouth and Health Quart.**, 4: 5-17, Jan.-March, 1953.

— "Teeth and Personality as portrayed by Shakespeare." **Mouth and Health Quart.**: 4: 8-11, Apr.-June 1935.

Wilkinson, B.W. "A Doctor Looks at Shakespeare." **W. Va. Med. J.**, 1964, 60: 182-186.

Wilson, J.D., "New Ideas and Discoveries About Shakespeare." **Va. R.**, 23, No. 4: 537.

Woods, A.H. "Syphilis in Shakespeare's Tragedy of **Timon of Athens**." **Am. Journ. Psychiat.** 91: 95-107, July, 1934.

Zannoni, T., "William Shakespeare and Augusto Murri, two giants of thought on drunkenness." Policino, 60: 361-363, March 9, 1953.

WORKS DEALING WITH SHAKESPEARE'S PSYCHOPATHOLOGICAL KNOWLEDGE

Alexander, N. "Hamlet and the Art of Memory." **Not. and Quer.**, 1968, N.S., 15: 136-9.

Amrine, M. "Scientist as Hamlet." Sat. R., 35: 9.

Anthonisen, N.L. "The Ghost in Hamlet" **Amer. Imago.** 22: 233-249, Winter 1965.

Aring, C. D. "Perception as a Moral Test" **J. Nerv. Ment. Dis., 1967,** 144: 539-45.

Armakjlan, H. "Psychoanalysis and the Future of Literary Criticisms." **Psychoanalysis.** 49: 3-28, Spring 1962.

Ashton, J.W. "The Wrath of King Lear" **J.E.G.P.,** 31: 530-6.

Askew, M. "Psychoanalysis and Literary Criticism." **Psychoanal. Rev.,** 51: 211, Summer 1964.

Babcock, R.W. "Modern Skeptical Critics of Shakespeare: Elmer E. Stoll" **Sewanee Rev.,** 35: 15. Jan. 1927.

Bergler, Edmund. "A Clinical Approach to the Psychoanalysis of Writers," **PSa. Review,** 31 (1944), p. 74.

Bodenstedt, Friedrich. **Shakespeare's Frauencharacter,** Berlin, A. Hoffman & Co., 1874.

Bransome, J.S.H. **The Tragedy of King Lear,** B. Blackwell, Oxford, 1934.

Bundy, Murray W., "Shakespeare and Elizabethan Psychology," **Journ. Eng. and Germ. Philol.,** XXII (1924), 516, 549.

Butler, P. "Stage Mad Folk." **Amer. J. Insan.,** 73: 19-42. Jl. 1918.

Cady, L. W. "Lear as an Old Man." **Univ. Cal. Chron.,** 31: 19-30.

Campbell, Lilly B., **"Shakespeare's Tragic Heroes,"** etc. Review in N. & O. 159: 431.

Campbell, O.J. "What is the Matter with Hamlet." **Yale R., Ns.** 32, No. 2, 309-22.

Cawthorne, T. "How Hamlet's Father Died." **Proc. Roy. Soc. Med. (Sect. Hist. Med.)** 1964, 57: 905-6.

Chandler, S.B. "Shakespeare and Sleep." **Bull. Hist. of Med.,** 29: 255-260. May-June, 1955.

Craig Hardin, "The Ethics of King Lear," **Philol, Quart.,** IV (1925), 97-109.

Craig, Hardin, "The Ethics of King Lear," **Philol. Quart.,** IV (1925), IV (1925), 289-301.

Crawford, A.W. **Hamlet, an Ideal Prince.** Boston, R. G. Badger, 1916.

Davidson, H. "King Lear, Scapegoat." **Vassar Journ. Undergrad Studies.** V, May 1941, pp. 117-136.

Dowden, E., "Elizabethan Psychology," in **Shakespeare's England.** (pp. 308-333), Oxford University Press, 1918.

Draper, J.W. "Speech Tempo and Humor in Shakespeare's **Antony."** 20: 426-432. Oct.. 1946.

— "Signor Brabantio's Humor (Choler)" **Bull. Hist. Med.,** 18: 539-543. Dec., 1945.

Draper, J. "The Humors. Some Psychologic Aspects of Shakespeare's Tragedies." **J.A.M.A.,** 188: No. 3. Apr. 20, 1964, pp. 259-262.

Draper, J.W. "A Nedvek — Shakespeare **tragedial pzichologial**

megvilagitasban." **Orv. Hetil.**, 1964, 105: 1803-7, **port.**
Draper, J.W. "Scattered Personality in Shakespeare's **Antony.**" **Psychiat. Quart.**, 39: 448-56. July 1965.
Ellsworth, W.W. **Creative Writing.** Funk & Wagnalls Co., N.Y., 1929.
Elton, O., "Hamlet the Elizabethan," in **A Sheaf of Papers.** Boston, 1923 (pp. 17-35).
Faber, M.D., "Oedipal Patterns in Henry IV." **Psychoanal. Quart.**, 1967, 36: 426-34.
Feinstein, H.M. "Hamlet's Horatio and the Therapeutic Mode." **Am. J. Psychiat.**, 123: 803-9. Jan. 1967.
Fliess, R., M.D. **Erogeneity and Libido.** Internat. Univ. Press, New York, 1956.
— **Ego and Body Ego.** Schulte Publishing Co., New York, 1961.
Frankel, P.E. "Parapsychologic Phenomena in Shakespeare's **Hamlet.**" **Rev. Brasil. Hist. Med.**, I: 275-279, 1950 p.
Fuzier, J. "Shakespeare et la medecine mentale, de-son temps. **D'apres La Comedie Des erreurs, Etudes Anglaises**, 1964, 17: 421-33.
Goll, A. "Criminal Types in Shakespeare." **J. Crim. Law & Criminology.** 29: 492, Nov.-Dec., 1939.
Guido, A. "Humor of Juliet's Nurse." **Bull. Hist. Med.**, 17: 297-303. March 1945.
Harrison, G.B. "Bard at Mid-Century" **Sat R.**, 40: 17.
— "Hamlet, Enigma at Elsinore" Il. Life, 37: 81.
— "Bard Book Shelf." **Illus. Sat. R.**, 37:22.
Hartmann, Edward von, **Philosophy of the Unconscious,** Harcourt, Brace & Co., 1931, N. Y.
Hartwell, L.H., **The Critical Appreciation of Shakespeare's King Lear in the First Half of the 19th Century.** (Master's Thesis in M.S., 1931), N.Y., Columbia U. Library.
Hoffman, Frederick S. **Freudianism and the Literary Mind,** 1945, Louisiana State Univ. Press.
Holland, Norman N. "Shakespearean Tragedy and the Three Ways of Psychoanalytic Criticism." **The Hudson Rev.** Summer, 1962, Vol. XV. No. 2.
Holland, N.N., "Caliban's Dream." **Psychoanal. Quart.**, 37: 114-25. 1968.
Holland, Norman N. **The Dynamics of Literary Response,** Oxford Univ. Press, 1968.
Huhner, Max, **Shakespeare's Hamlet,** Farrar, Straus & Co., N.Y., 1950.
James, T., "Madness in Shakespeare." **South Af. Med. J.**, 35:154-7, Feb. 25, 1961.
Jekels, Ludwig, "The Riddle of Shakespeare's **Macbeth,**" in **Psycho-**

analysis and Literature. E.P. Dutton & Co., Inc., New York, 1964. Also in **Selected Papers by Ludwig Jekels**, London, Imago Publishing Co., Ltd., 1952.

Jennens, C. **The Tragedy of King Lear Vindicated from the Critical Reviewers.** 1772.

Jones, E., **Hamlet and Oedipus,** W.W. Norton & Co., Inc., N.Y., 1949.

— **Essays in Applied Psychoanalysis.** The International Psychoanalytical Press. London, 1923.

— "A Psychoanalytic Study of Hamlet," in **Essays in Applied Psychoanalysis.**

— "The Death of Hamlet's Father." **Internat. J. Psychoanal.,** Vol.

Jorgensen, P.A., "Hamlet's Therapy." **Huntington Library Quart.,** 1964, 27: 239-258.

Kanzer, M. "Imagery in King Lear" **Amer. Imago,** 22:3-131, Spring, 1965.

Kelcy, A., "Notes on **King Lear." P.L.** 11:359-73.

Knight, Charles. **A History of Opinion on the Writings of Shakespeare,** (Introductory Vol. in **Studies of Shakespeare** and cabinet edition), London, 1847.

Kris, Ernst. **Psychoanalytic Exploration in Art. Internat. Univ. Press.** New York, 1952.

Lacgnet-Lavostine, "Shakespeare, Psychiatrist." **Semaine d. hop. Paris.** 25: 1007-1014. March, 30, 1949.

Lewin, K.I. "The Value of Psychoanalytic literary Criticism." **Psychiat. Commun.** 5:103-6, 1962.

Mack, M. "World of Hamlet." 41: No. 4. 502-

Monheim, Leonard. "Psychoanalytic Criticism Comes of Age." **Psychiatry & Social Science Rev.,** Vol. 2 No. 11. Nov. 1968, pp. 9-11.

Margoshes, A. "Projective Imagery in Shakespeare." **J. Projective Techn.,** 30: 290-2. June, 1966.

Mirek, R. "Characters in Shakespeare's Tragedies and their Personalities." (Polish) Przegl. lek., 1967. 23:415.

— Personalities of Characters in Shakespeare's Tragedies **Troilus and Cressida, Coriolanus, Timon of Athens, Pericles, Titus Andronicus, Cymbeline, Romeo and Juliet.** (Polish) Przegl. lek., 1967, 23: 477-80.

Mirek, R. Sketches of the Personality of figures in Shakespeare's Tragedies, I: **King Lear** and **Othello** (Polish) **Przegl. lek.,** 1966, 22:557-61.

Mirek, R. "Dramatic Chronicles of Shakespeare in Psychiatric Evaluation." II: **Tragedy of Richard III, Life and Death of King John, Famous History of the Life of Henry the 8th.** (Polish) **Przegl. lek.,** 1967, 23:861-4.

Moore, E.A. "Moral Proportions and Fatalism in King Lear." PL., 11:102-16, Jan. 1899.

Norwood, G. "A Twisted Masterpiece." **Contemp. Rev.,** 27:590.

Noyes, E.S. "On the Dismissal of Lear's Knights and Goneril's Letter to Regan." **Philol. Quart.,** 9:297-305.

Oberndorf, Clarence P. "Psychoanalysis in Literature and its Therapeutic Value," in **Psychoanalysis and the Social Sciences,** New York, International Universities Press, Inc., 1947.
Also in **Psychoanalysis and Literature,** edited by Henrick M. Ruitenbeek, E.P. Dutton & Co., Inc., New York, 1964.

O'Sullivan, Mary I., "Hamlet and Dr. Timothy Bright," **Pub. Mod. Lang. Ass'n.,** XLI (1926), 667-679.

Pearson, P.H. **Study in Literature,** 1903. ("How the Action Starts in **King Lear**") pp. 195-210.

Polonyi, K. "Hamlet." **Yale R.,** 43, No. 3: 336-50.

Ponitz, K. "Shakespeare and Psychiatry" (German) **Ther. d. Gegenw.,** 1964, 103:1463-78.

Putney, R. "Coriolanus and his Mother," **Psychoanal. Quart.,** 31:364-81, July 1962.

Rank, O., **Das Inzestmotiv in Dichtung und Sage,** Deuticke, Leipzig, 1912.

Ravich, A.A. "A Psychoanalytic Study of Shakespeare's Early Plays." **Psychoanal. Quart., 33: 386-410.**

Richmond-Green, K., **Interpretation of . . . King Lear.** Chicago, 1890.

Roheim, Geza (Editor, **Psychoanalysis and The Social Sciences**), 1947, New York. International Univ. Press.

Ross, T.A. "Note on **Merchant of Venice.**" **Brit. J. Med. Psychology.** 14:303-311, 1934.

Ruitenbeek, Henrick M. **Psychoanalysis and Literature,** edited, and with an introduction by Henrick M. Ruitenbeek, E.P. Dutton & Co., Inc., New York, 1964.

Saul, Leon J. Othello: Projection in Art. **J. Amer. Med. Ass'n.,** 1967, 200:39-40.

Sharpe, Freeman E. "An Unfinished Paper on Hamlet," In **Collected Papers on Psychoanalysis,** Hogarth Press, London, 1950, pp. 242-265.
— "From King Lear to The Tempest," in **Collected Papers,** pp. 214-241.

Sheldon, W.L. **Does Justice Triumph in the End? A Study of King Lear.** Phila., 1887.

Sims, R.E. "Green Old Age of Falstaff." **Bull. Hist. of Med.,** 13:144-157, Feb., 1943.

Stockert, F.G. von, "Shakespeare und die Moderne Psychiatrie." **Jb. Psychol. Psychother.,** 1964, 11:42-50.

Stoll, E.E. "Hamlet: An Historical and Comparative Study," **University of Minnesota Studies in Language and Literature.** No. 7, 1919.

Stoll, E.E., "Hamlet and Iago," **Anniversary Papers by Colleagues and Pupils of George Lyman Kittredge.** Ginn & Co., 1913. pp. 261-272.

Stoll, E.E., "Othello: an Historical and Comparative Study" **University of Minnesota Studies in Languages and Literature.** No. 2, 1915.

Stoll, E.E., "Shakespeare, Marston and the Malcontent Type," **Mod. Phil,** III (1906), 281-332.

Stoller, R.J., "Shakespearean Tragedy (Coriolanus)" **Psychoanal. Quart.,** 35:263-74. Apr., 1966.

Sypher, W. "Hamlet, the Existential Madness." **Nation,** 162:750.

Trilling, Lionel: "Freud and Literature," in **The Liberal Imagination** by Lionel Trilling, New York, The Viking Press, Inc., 1950.

Trosman, H. "Freud and the Controversy over Shakespearean Authorship." **J. Amer. Psychoanal. Assn.,** 1965, 13: 475-98.

Varga, L. et al "Ghost & Antic Disposition." **Psychiat.** Quart., 40: 607-27.

Vigourous, A., "La Pathologie Mentale dans les drames de Shakespeare," **Ann. Med. Psychol.,** (Paris), SX:X (1818), 153, 225.

Walsh, G. & Pool, R. M. "Laterality Dominance in Shakespeare's Plays." **South Med. and Surg.,** 104: 51-58, Feb. 1942.

— "Antithetical Views on Twinning Found in the Bible and Shakespeare." **South Med. & Surg.** 103:111-112, 1941.

Walsh, G. and Pool, R.M., "Shakespeare's Knowledge of Twins and Twinning." **South. Med. & Surg.,** 102: 173-176. Apr. 1940.

Waugh, M. "A Psychoanal. Commentary on Shakespeare's **The Tragedie of King Richard II.**" **Psychoanal. Quart.,** 37:212-38. 1968.

Wertham, Fredric "The Matricidal Impulse. Critique of Freud's Interpretation of Hamlet." Journ. of Criminal Psychopath., II (4), 1941, 455.

— **Dark Legend,** Duell, Sloan & Pearce, New York, 1941.

Wertham, Frederic, "An Unconscious Determinant in Native Son" **Journal of Clin. Pathology.,** Vol. VI, 1944-45, pp. 111-115.

Wilhan, Dr. Josef, "Die Hamlet frage, ein Beitrag Zup Geschichte der Renaissance in England," **Leipziger Beitrage zur Englischen** Philologie, Heft, III Leipzig, 1921.

Wilson, J.S. "Shakespeare in the Interpretation of the Times." **Vd. 2R.,** 19, No. 3 476.

Wilson, R.W. King Lear. **Calcutta R.,** 35:2918, 356-69.

Winstanley, Lillian. **King Lear as Symbolic Mythology. Cambridge, 1922.**

Winstanley, Lillian "King Lear as Symbolic Mythology" (Review) M.L.R. 18: 209, 1923.

Wohlfarth, Paul, "Melancholie und Kurzschrift," (Kurzschrift). Ein Englischer Arzt der Shakespeare Beeinflusst Hat (Timothy Bright), Dtsch. Arztebl. Mitt., 1957, 64: 603-7.

Woodberry, G.E., The Inspiration of Poetry. The Macmillan Co., New York, 1910.

Wormhoudt, Arthur, Ph.D. The Demon Lover, a psychoanalytical ap-

Young, Karl, "Shakespeare Skeptics." No. Am. Rev., 215:382.

proach to Literature, Exposition Press, New York, 1949.

INDEX

LIBRARY
OF
MOUNT ST. MARY'S
COLLEGE
EMMITSBURG, MARYLAND